Volume 12

MOUNTAIN OF FIRE AND MIRACLES MINISTRIES

Fire in the WORD

Ye Shall know the Truth, and the Truth Shall Make You Free (John 8:32)

Dr. D. K. Olukoya

FOREWORD
UNCOMMON FAVOUR AND OPEN HEAVEN BREAKTHROUGHS FOR YOU

This book is actually a compendium of the divine message delivered at the altar of God at the Mountain of Fire and Miracles Ministries. God has used each of these messages to do the miraculous, to make the impossible possible, to exalt valleys and to bring low, problem mountains.

The God that answers by fire has variously used the messages as sword of deliverance in situations where all human efforts have failed.

This book is spiced with live testimonies of people that have trod the valley of the shadow of death but were delivered by the mighty hand of God.

It is the same messages that are presented to you as a pack. As you read the messages and pray the prayers in faith, the living God shall fulfill His promise of uncommon favour and open heaven breakthroughs in your life.

It is recommended for those who desire to live in the miraculous.

God bless you, in Jesus' name. Amen.

Dr. D.K. Olukoya
General Overseer,
Mountain of Fire and Miracles Ministries Worldwide

CONTENTS

FIRE IN THE WORD

Ye Shall Know the Truth, and the Truth Shall Make You Free (John 8:32)

ISSN 978-2947-10-5   Vol. 12 No. 1   Sun. 11th - Sat. 17th Nov., 2007   ₦10

Glory be to God
FIRE IN THE WORD IS ELEVEN

BURIED BUT NOT DEAD

My Year of Uncommon favour & Open Heaven Breakthroughs
Genesis 28

Beloved, you will do yourself a world of good by reading this message very carefully. It is titled, "Buried but not dead."

John 11:1-3 says, *"Now a certain man was sick, named Lazarus, of Bethany, the town of Mary and her sister Martha. (It was that Mary which anointed the Lord with ointment, and wiped his feet with her hair, whose brother Lazarus was sick). Therefore his sisters sent unto him, saying, Lord, behold he whom thou lovest is sick."* Lazarus was described as somebody whom the Lord loved. He was a friend of Jesus. But despite the fact that he was a friend of Jesus he was sick. Why should he be sick if he was a friend of Jesus? Can he whom Jesus loves be sick? The whole of his family were friends of Jesus, yet something bad was happening there. In spite of the fact that they sent for Jesus, Lazarus was still sick. The first lesson we pick from this passage is this: The presence of the Lord does not mean you will be excused from the storms of life. The fact that you are a Christian does not mean you have automatic discharge certificate from the battles of life

because the storms of life are very strange. They have no respect for your academic level, family background, beauty or handsomeness. They have no respect for most things that you do and they bombard people anyhow. It means that you could love the Lord with all your heart and yet be facing a battle, it has happened to somebody before. Here was the person whom Jesus loved and yet the storm of sickness bombarded him.

When problems arise, some people break down completely but there are others who will use the problems to break record. Problems may make you better or bitter. The Bible says in Proverbs 24:16: "*For a just man falleth seven times, and riseth up again...*" Falling down is not defeat but staying down.

John 11:4: *"When Jesus heard that, he said, This sickness is not unto death, but for the glory of God, that the Son of God might be*

ONLY A FEW WORDS FROM THE MASTER WILL WIPE AWAY TEARS AND RESTORE JOY.

glorified thereby." It means that there are some sicknesses that can lead to death. This is why both physical and spiritual sicknesses should not be ignored. Pride, bad tongue, unforgiveness, bitterness, and anger could be sicknesses, and you could excuse them the way people excuse mild headache or mild stomach disorder until they become something serious.

One little physical or spiritual sickness that is ignored can lead to death. Jesus said the sickness was not unto death and immediately He made that pronouncement, His words melted away the power of the sickness. At this juncture I would like you to raise your right hand and take the following prayer point aggressively: "Lord Jesus, speak death unto all my sicknesses, in the name of Jesus."

When Jesus speaks unto your ugly circumstances, they may still be pretending as if they are alive but they have lost their power. Perhaps, as you are reading this magazine, the enemy has cast you into a furnace of fire, there shall be a Fourth Man in your fire, in the name of Jesus. When all things are against you, that is when faith prospers and the worse can become your best.

John11:5-7: *"Now Jesus loved Martha, and her sister, and Lazarus. When he had heard therefore that he was sick, he abode two days still in the same place where he was. Then after that saith he to his disciples, Let us go into Judea again."*

Jesus did not panic, He gave death and satan extra four days to perform their worst. Jesus is the Master and could in one moment destroy what satan has been building for years. Jesus arrived when all hope was lost. One moment is enough for Jesus to destroy what satan has been building for years. Jesus arrived when all hope was completely lost. People may look at your case as hopeless but you must stand and prove that your God is never late. They should find out that no condition is hopeless before God.

In one day, and with a few words, Jesus undid what satan through sickness, death and the grave had taken so long to accomplish. Lazarus was already secured with the padlock and bolt of the grave. It does not matter how ancient the gate or the problems that make you cry, the Lord can still make a way for

DELIVERANCE CASE

IS THE DEVIL MANIPULATING YOUR HEART? CONSIDER THIS: PHILIPPIANS 4:8

you. Many people are struggling against ancient gates. Many years ago, we prayed for a certain brother who had a strange name. He came from a place where a strange voice tell the people which name to give to their babies when they are born. The brother got the name and was carrying it about, and as the name was, so was his life. The name meant light feather. So any where he worked, he was sacked. The maximum time he worked in any place was one month before he was sacked. In some places, they would ask him to go home and would send the termination letter to him

because they did not even want to see him around at all. He was struggling against an ancient gate. One day, he prayed some prayers and with a few words in those prayers, the ancient gate was broken. It does not matter for how many years or generations, sickness and death have enveloped you, it will take the Master only one moment to rectify the ancient damage. Only a few words from the Master will wipe away tears and restore joy.

John 11:7-8: *"Then after that saith he to his disciples, Let us go into Judea again. His disciples say unto him, Master, the Jews of late sought to stone thee; and goest thou thither again?"* Verses 18-23:

"Now Bethany was nigh unto Jerusalem, about fifteen furlongs off; And many of the Jews came to Martha and Mary, to comfort them concerning their brother. Then Martha, as soon as she heard that Jesus was coming, went and met him: but Mary sat still in the house. Then said Martha unto Jesus, Lord, if thou hadst been here, my brother had not died. But I know, that even now, whatsoever thou wilt ask of God, God will give it thee. Jesus saith unto her, Thy brother shall rise again." The statement of Martha: "But I know that even now..." showed that she was a woman of faith. After she had made that pronouncement, Jesus said, "Thy brother shall raise again."

Verse 28: *"And when she had so said, she went her way, and called Mary her sister secretly, saying, The master is come, and calleth for thee."* When Jesus was called to the scene of the storm at the sea, He turned the great storm into a great calm. When Jesus arises in a storm, He turns the storm into a cool breeze, He turns tears into a smile. He turns sorrow into joy, He turns weeping into laughter,

and adversity to triumph. He turns night to day, and every frustration to fulfillment. He turns ashes to beauty, and failure to success. When Jesus is invited into the scene, He would turn poverty to prosperity. He turns destruction to construction, disgrace to grace and weakness to strength. When Jesus comes into the scene, darkness will turn into light and all the losses will become gain. Martha said to her sister, "The Master is come." And as soon as the Master came things began to happen.

Please raise your right hand and declare the following prayer points loud and clear:

- My problems, hear the word of the Lord; the Master is come, in the name of Jesus.
- My tears, hear the word of the Lord, the Master is come, in the name of Jesus.
- My trouble, you are in trouble today because the Master is come, in the name of Jesus.

When Jesus got to the tomb of Lazarus, He cried with a loud

THERE IS NO PROMISE TOO HARD FOR GOD TO FULFILL.

voice, "Lazarus, come forth." And the Bible says that he that was dead came forth. Only God could do that. Only God can release a spirit from the grave and send it back to the body. Then a second miracle was needed: The grave cloth that was still on him had to be taken off. The tokens and tools of death still surrounded him so Jesus made another pronouncement: "Loose him, and let him go." Many people today are being revived by the Master, but the grave clothes still remain. Many have received the baptism of the Holy Spirit, they have been sanctified and filled with power but the grave clothes still remain. That is why Jesus said, "Loose him and let him go," because although Lazarus had received freedom, he was not free, he was still bound. Likewise there are many Christians today, who are born again, sanctified and Spirit filled but are still bound by sins, evil covenants, bondage of darkness, and powers of the night. Anytime they want a release from these powers, they meet strong opposition. These powers may allow them to practise Christianity but will ensure that they wallow in poverty or sickness.

Jesus said, "Loose him and let him go." It is a language of heaven. God was the first person to issue that cry; He issued it against Pharaoh when He said, "Let my people go."

The Bible is a book that is supposed to answer questions but sometimes, we find questions being asked and the answers are not supplied. For example, you find the following question: "If the foundations be destroyed what can the righteous do?" (Psalm 11:3). And no answer is given. "When the Son of Man comes will he really find faith on earth?" (Luke 18:8) No answer was given. Genesis 18:14 says, *"Is anything too hard for the Lord?"* Thank God in Jeremiah chapter 32 verse 17, the Bible answers the question: *"Ah Lord God behold, thou hast made the heaven and the earth by thy great power and stretched out arm, and there is nothing too hard for thee."* So the question asked in Genesis has an answer in the book of Jeremiah. There is no promise too hard for God to fulfill, there is no prayer too hard for God to answer, there is no problem too hard for God to solve, there is no stubborn situation too hard for God to resolve, there is no enemy too hard for God to dismantle, there is no mountain too hard for God to climb, and there is no reproach too hard for God to remove.

God is a Spirit, He is the Holy One of Israel, and He is the God of Abraham, Isaac and Jacob. He is the God of vision, dream and angelic visitation. If He needs to send an angel to resolve your situation, He will do so. God was the One that covered the dry land with sea in His anger in Noah's days. He was the same person who removed the sea and created dry land for the deliverance of the children of Israel. God has sent rain, fire, whirlwind and bread from heaven. God has brought water from the rock, He has made snakes from wood: Moses threw his stick down, and it became a snake. God made man from the dust, He was the One that broke the long leg of Jacob and He buried Korah, Dathan, Abiram and their company alive.

He was excited looking at Elijah on Mount Carmel and when Elijah called for a contest, He said, "Yes that is my boy, call them for a contest." And when Elijah said, "Let fire fall, He was the One that poured fire on Elijah's altar. God was the same person that withered Jeroboam's hand. It was our God that turned the River Nile to

THE PROPHET

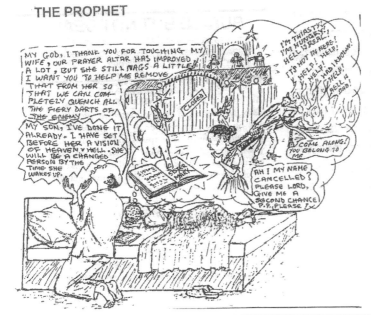

blood. It was our God that sank the Jericho wall; our God was the first person to provide an aeroplane to carry somebody from the earth, the aeroplane was called the chariot of fire. Our God walked three men through a fiery furnace. There was a man that came to the world without his eyeballs, He created fresh ones with sand and put them back to the man's eyes. It was His angel that dealt with Pharaoh; His angels did all kinds of terrible warfare against His enemies in the Bible. His resurrection was announced by the angels, and because He is the resurrection and the life, when He speaks life unto death, there is revival. The grave could not hold Him back on the day of His resurrection, the voice of resurrection and the spirit of resurrection that brought Lazarus to life was in Jesus and so the grave could not hold Him too back on His resurrection day. Therefore, any grave cloth that is limiting you now shall limit you no more once the Master comes in to your situation. And until you have met the Master Jesus, you will be limited.

Beloved, you need to pray against grave clothes. If you are born again and Spirit filled, the enemy cannot put grave clothes on you. You must call on the Lord today to destroy every limitation. If God has to promote, or demote, or transfer, or kill, let Him do so but the grave clothes must be removed, because the Master is come. You must be aggressive with your prayers against the power of the grave. You must let the enemy know that he does not have the final say. Call the Master to your situation now.

PRAYER POINTS

1. Every grave cloth of my father's house limiting my life, die, in Jesus' name.

2. Every power of limitation and disgrace, what are you waiting for? Die, in Jesus' name.

3. Every power that wants to bury me while I am still alive, die, in the name of Jesus.

4. O God arise, and manifest your power as a Man of war in my situation, in the name of Jesus.

5. Inherited bad luck, die, in the name of Jesus.

6. Every power that says I will not be congratulated, be wasted, in the mighty name of Jesus.

7. My enemies shall die in my place, in the name of Jesus.

8. I shall not give up, my problems shall give up, in the name of Jesus.

9. I am ripe for a miracle by the power in the blood of Jesus, in Jesus' name.

10. O God, arise and speak words of breakthroughs into my life now, in the name of Jesus.

BURIED BUT NOT DEAD

is a message delivered at the Mountain of Fire and Miracles Ministries by the General Overseer, Dr. D.K. Olukoya.

A CALL TO SERVE

Are you a member of MFM with a burden to help the needy, are you interested in alleviating the plight of the poor or in the spread of the gospel through the sponsorship of the publication of tracts? Your resources, time and talent can be extended to several groups that are in charge of these areas. These groups include:

o   We care Ministry,
o   Mission Outreach
o   Tracts and Publications
o   Ministry to Drug addicts
o   Campus fellowship
o   Ministry to School
o   Ministry to Glorious Children, etc.

Thus says the Lord, "Verily I say unto you, in as much as ye have done it unto one of the least of these my brethren, ye have done it unto me" Matthew 25 : 40.

WONDERFUL JESUS!

SAVED FROM A RITUALIST

Recently, I travelled to Benin and couldn't get a taxi to my final destination so I boarded a motorbike. Suddenly the cyclist took a different direction and headed towards the bush. He parked his bike, dragged me to the bush and asked me to take off my clothes that he was going to assault me. When I refused, he brought out his gun and knife and threatened to kill me if I did not coorperate with him. I started shouting and crying to God. God overpowered him and I escaped. When I came out of the bush, I met a sister to whom I narrated my ordeal, and she gave me transport fare to Benin and told me to give her the address of my church because what God did for me was awesome. Praise the Lord!

Sis. Tina
MFM Headquarters

DELIVERED FROM HARDSHIP

I lost my job for quite a long time and was searching for another one. But even before I lost my job, I was not doing well. However, each time I was invited for an interview, some animals would be pressing me down in my dreams and I would not do well at the interviews. This ugly situation continued until I came here for a service. During the service, there was a word of knowledge from the GO that there was an Ishekiri man who was being pounded in a mortar by some powers but the powers had taken his place in the mortar and he was pounding them. The message of that Sunday was "Overcoming the spirit of hardship." After the message and prayers, two people died in my compound mysteriously. After that I secured a job. I am doing well now. Praise the Lord!

Bro. Samuel
MFM Headquarters

LONG TERM STOMACH ACHE GONE

I was afflicted with a terrible stomach ache for six months. All efforts to get a cure proved futile. I was invited to this church for a monthly programme called "Total recovery." During the programme, God stepped into my situation and healed me completely. I am grateful to God Almighty for His mercies. Praise the Lord!

Bro. Akinyele
MFM Shibiri

GOD CANCELS DEATH SENTENCE

In the church where I used to worship before I joined this ministry, there was an evil prophecy, which said I would die in 1999. I came to this ministry and passed through deliverance. Thank God I am still alive till today. Praise the Lord!

Bro. Seun
MFM Benin City

GOD PROMOTES ME

I worked in the bank and never got promoted in my place of work. My wife brought me to this church and I was advised by the pastor to undergo deliverance. Three months after the deliverance, I was promoted to the rank of bank manager. Praise the Lord!

Bro. Emma
MFM Uselu Benin city

CHRONIC ULCER GONE

I was suffering from stomach ulcer for many years without solution. I was counseled to go for deliverance, during which I vomited blood and black substance on the third day. Since then I have been perfectly healed Praise the Lord!

Sis. Josephine
MFM Ogudu/Ojota

TRAGEDY AVERTED

Recently, I boarded a bus which developed a fault suddenly and consequently, the driver lost control. Just as the bus was about to have a head-on collision with an on-coming vehicle, God intervened and it fell into a gutter and then stopped. Praise the Lord!

Bro. Ajibola
MFM Abaranje

DELIVERED FROM WITCHCRAFT ATTACK

Before I got born again, I visited a herbalist for consultation. My regular visits to the herbalist could not stop the attack and oppression on my life by witchcraft powers. Thereafter, I joined this ministry and immediately gave my life to Christ. Then I went for deliverance and was completely delivered from the attacks of witchcraft oppression. Praise the Lord!

Bro. Kola
MFM Abule-Anu

DELIEVERED FROM EVIL EMBARGO

For two years after I left school I could not get a job. Anytime, I was supposed to attend an interview, my phone would be dead and would only get the message after the interview. This happened many times. I put this to God in prayer and by His power, I have got a good job now as God Himself has lifted the embargo. Praise the Lord!

Bro. Adeniyi
MFM Ogudu

POWER MUST CHANGE HANDS MAGAZINE
IS OUT AGAIN!

YOUR LONG AWAITED QUARTERLY MAGAZINE POWER MUST CHANGE HANDS IS OUT AGAIN WITH A BANG.
WITH A COPY OF THIS EDITION IN YOUR HAND, THE ENEMY IS IN TROUBLE.
IT IS TITLED, "THE ENEMY MUST EXPIRE."
HURRY NOW FOR YOUR OWN. COPIES ARE LIMITED. PRICE IS N100 ONLY.

Hello Children!
Your popular
Spiritual tonic
"Junior Fire in the
Word"
Is on the stand again.
It is still as refreshing
as ever.
Now you have more
opportunities to win
Fanstastic prizes every
month as you send in
your entries
Hurry grab your
copy from the
vendors.
The price is still
N20.

FIRE IN THE WORD, is a weekly Spiritual Bulletin of the Mountain of Fire and Miracles Ministries, published by Tracts and Publications Group. All Enquiries should be addressed to The Editor, Mountain of Fire Magazine, 13, Olasimbo Street, off Olumo Road, Onike, P.O. Box 2990, Sabo Yaba, Lagos, Nigeria. Telephone 01- 867439, 864631, 868766, 08023180236.E-mail: mfmtractsandpublications@yahoo.com Copyright reserved.

FIRE IN THE WORD

Ye Shall Know the Truth, and the Truth Shall Make You Free (John 8:32)

ISSN 1595 - 7314 Vol. 12 No. 2 Sun. 18th - Sat. 24th Nov., 2007

₦10

12 FACTS YOU NEED TO KNOW ABOUT SPIRITUAL FREEDOM

My year of unprecedented greatness and unmatchable increase
Deuteronomy 28:13, Psalm 71:21, Ephesians 3:20, Psalm 92:10.

2 Timothy 2:26 says, *"And that they may recover themselves out of the snare of the devil who are taken captive by him at his will."* This verse means that many people are already in the snare of the devil. Hebrews 2:15 says, *"And deliver them who through fear of death were their entire lifetime subject to bondage."*

The Bible says in James 4:7: *"Resist the devil and he will flee from you."* It means that if you do not resist him, he will stay. If the enemy is not fleeing from you what you should check is your resistance – your manner of resistance. The Bible says, "And give no place to the devil" meaning, if you give place to him, he will cause trouble. It also says, *"Lest satan should get an advantage of us: for we are not ignorant of his devices"* (2 Corinthians 2:11). This means that if you remain ignorant of his devices he will take advantage of that and cause trouble. If you are born again but you are not resisting the enemy or you are ignorant of his devices, the enemy will move in, your freedom will be curtailed and you will get under bondage.

KINDS OF CAPTIVITY

The Bible divides captivity into two:

1. **Lawful captivity:** This takes place when you have done something that qualifies you to come under bondage. So the enemy has the legal right to keep you there.

2. **Unlawful captivity:** This is when you have not done anything wrong and the enemy is harassing you at his own will. It is therefore necessary to know how to remain free all the time.

Bondage means limitation. To be in bondage is to be confined. To be in bondage is to be caged. It also means to be bound. A good illustration of bondage is a beautiful bird singing in a cage. The bird is beautiful and has a beautiful voice but it is in a cage. This means that one could be handsome or beautiful but

THE DAY YOU DECIDE THAT YOU MUST FULFILL YOUR DIVINE DESTINY, THE WHOLE OF HELL FIRE WILL RISE AGAINST YOU.

caged. You could be a talented person in a cage and everything you are doing is inside that cage.

To be in bondage is to be a slave. To be in bondage is to be in subjection to a force of power. To be in bondage is to be powerless in the face of your aggressor. To be powerless in the face of an aggressor is bondage because the enemy will do whatever he wants. To be in bondage is to be unable to stop when you want. To be in bondage is to be restricted. It is to be under the control of another power. On the wedding day of a certain sister, at the reception table, her mother in law said to her, "Let me announce to you that I am wife number one, while you are wife number two. As far as you keep to this arrangement, there will be no problem but the day you decide to be wife number one, you will be in trouble." The sister thought it was a joke. Shortly after, problem started. Her husband ran to his mother for everything. The man was under the control of another power, he was in bondage.

To be in bondage is to be demoted. To be in bondage is

to be in captivity. Some people are in bondage to the demon of slumber. To be in bondage is to become sport for the enemy like Samson. To be in bondage is to have the prison warder as your regulator. He decides for you when to go out and when you should sit down. To be in bondage is to have closed progress. To be in bondage is to be under embargo. It is to resist profitable changes, and to operate under strange commands. Some people who are in bondage obey strange commands from the enemy. The enemy command them to lose their temper, or to go out and display their beauty, and they obey. To be in bondage is for your captors to decide your life. It is therefore a tragedy for you to be in bondage and be ignorant about it.

Many people are educated but in bondage. Many people are befriending their enemies. Many are in the school of bondage everyday. Many are labouring under bondage every day and night. Anyone that bites the finger that fed him will remain in bondage.

DELIVERANCE CASE

TYPES OF BONDAGE

- Conscious bondage.
- Unconscious bondage.
- Bondage by choice.
- Bondage by inheritance.
- Bondage by force.
  Bondage by accident.
  Self-inflicted bondage.

Bondage by force is the most painful. There are many people who are witches against their will. They want to be free but cannot. At this juncture, I would like you take these prayer points aggressively:

- Every bondage by force, what you are waiting for? Die, in the name of Jesus.

- Every witchcraft bondage manipulated by force, die, in the name of Jesus.

FREEDOM

Freedom is a very important thing. Physical freedom enables people to move around but unfortunately, some people do not appreciate the ability to move around until it is taken away. People do not know the value of what they have until they lose it. Spiritual freedom is a must for all who want to fulfill their destiny. The day you decide that you must fulfill your divine destiny, the whole of hell fire will rise against you. But if you are not interested in fulfilling your divine destiny, they will leave you alone.

STATEMENTS ABOUT FREEDOM

1. Freedom is never free. You must fight for it.
2. Freeing yourself may be easy but remaining free is harder. You could fight to get to the Promised Land and when you get there, you must continue to fight so that the enemy will not remove you.
3. All of life is crossing the Red Sea. Once you are unable to cross it, the enemy will destroy you. Many people are walking goldmines. God has deposited gold in people's lives but the spirit of bondage does not allow them to tap it. Many people are supposed to be employing those they are working under but the spirit of bondage put them there. Many people are supposed to be flying like the eagle

but the enemy has cut off their wings and they have become ground birds.
4. Freedom is to know what enslaves you.
5. It is better to be hungry and be free than to be a fat slave.
6. Every chain you manufacture with your hand, you will wear. It is the rule of life.
7. Every man makes his own prison.
8. Liberation is not deliverance. A slave is still a slave if he cannot think independently. There are many Nigerians in bondage. For example. Nigerians who speak like Americans are not free yet. They got independence but are still not free inside.
9. The best definition of insanity is the inability to learn from your mistakes.
10. Defending your weakness is a foundation of slavery. Compulsive lying,

THE FACT THAT ALL IS WELL NOW MEANS NOTHING IF YOU SPEND YOUR LIFE PURSUING VANITY

talkativeness, careless eating, alcoholism, and inordinate love for money are forms of bondage.

TWELVE FACTS YOU MUST KNOW ABOUT SPIRITUAL FREEDOM

1. There can be no true freedom when the internal is in bondage. Internal instability of many people is what they transfer outside which results into confusion in the society. Most people are struggling to get earthly possessions, power, and wealth yet they are not satisfied. Therefore, we have nations of slaves to sin, demons, fear, lust, money, poverty etc. There is no programme any government can organize to deal with the heart of man, and until the heart of man is delivered from the bondage of the kingdom of darkness, it is useless to God. Internal bondage cannot be changed by political, social or educational programmes. As far as the inside is in bondage, there can be no true freedom. The first deliverance that anybody needs is deliverance of the mind.

2. The enemy is using witchcraft to cage man and until those powers are defeated the bondage remains in place. Modern-day witchcraft has entered the church, school and entertainment industry. It has entered into advertisement, medicine etc. You must know how to destroy them.

3. The devil has no free gift. He operates a primitive trade by barter. If he has given you money, you will vomit it. If he has given you children, you will regret it. He has no free gift. You cannot obtain something from the camp of the enemy and expect God to prosper it. When some people get born again,

they first become poorer because what they had was from the evil camp so God has to dismantle it and then give them His own which is genuine.

4. Business is one of the hottest areas of spiritual warfare. If you are going into business, you have to be prayerful because the enemy wants to control wealth. The enemy contests against prosperous businesses. If you are into business you must be ready to fight. Immediately you are determined to be clean and prosperous, the battle against you will be hard. But at the end of the day, every crooked business will swallow itself.

THE PROPHET

5. Your dream life is your spiritual monitor. It tells you what goes on in your life. Certainly, eating in the dream, swimming, seeing dead relatives, sex, flying, taking examination, being pursued, seeing masquerades, and returning to old places in the dream are indications of bondage.

6. Life problems are like trees; they have root. Many people attack the leaves, branches and trunk instead of the root. By the time they start fighting, they discover that the enemy has taken a grip on them. Find out the root of what you are fighting. If you do not know the root, you will fight aimlessly.

7. One hundred years of worry will not pay one kobo of debt. Worry will not remove any problem. It will only empty the strength of today. It will increase high blood pressure, depression and insanity. If you always worry, then you are in a cage and you should get out of it. Worry is interest paid before the trouble is due. Unfortunately, the modern man is always afraid that something bad is going to happen. He is afraid of most things that do not happen. When

you add tomorrow's weight to the burden of today, it becomes too heavy for you to carry. Many people just crack and sit down inside their trouble licking their wounds.

8. Problems cannot be solved at the same level of awareness that caused them. You must call a higher power to solve a problem. Darkness does not fight darkness. If your enemy is operating on earth, you have to contact the heavenly. If your enemy is using witchcraft powers against you, you should obtain power from above.

9. Any growth that is not towards God is growth into decay. This means that living your life outside God is a disaster. Unfortunately, many people are like Christmas goats; the enemy is feeding them fat to deal with them later. The fact that all is well now means nothing if you spend your life pursuing vanity. Grow towards God.

10. You cannot be permanently caged unless you made the prison. Many people build personal cages for themselves. They decorate their personal prison. They co-operate with their enemies. Paul was in bondage physically in the prison, a prison warder locked him up but later, the warder got to understand that he was the one in bondage and that Paul was a free man. He said. "Men and brethren, what must I do to be saved."

11. Your life here determines your life hereafter. It means that you are on probation here; you are living a borrowed life. You brought nothing here and it is certain you will take nothing out.

12. There is power in the blood of Jesus to deliver to the uttermost. The blood of Jesus has redeeming power. It has cleansing power, melting power and life-giving power. If you tap into it now, you will be free from all bondage.

PRAYER POINTS

1. I shall not cooperate with any bondage, therefore, any bondage in my life, die, in the name of Jesus.

2. I receive power to divide my Red sea, in the name of Jesus.

3. After the order of Daniel, Oh God, deliver me from satanic lions, in Jesus' name.

4. Every altar of affliction in my compound, what are you waiting for? Die, in the name of Jesus.

5. Woe unto the wolves coming to me in sheep clothing, in the name of Jesus.

6. Every enemy of my promotion, be arrested, in the name of Jesus.

7. Every tree of persistent problem, I cut you down, in the name of Jesus.

12 FACTS YOU NEED TO KNOW ABOUT SPIRITUAL FREEDOM

is a message delivered at the Mountain of Fire and Miracles Ministries by the General Overseer, Dr. D.K. Olukoya.

A CALL TO SERVE

Are you a member of MFM with a burden to help the needy, are you interested in alleviating the plight of the poor or in the spread of the gospel through the sponsorshing of the publication of tracts? Your resources, time and talent can be extended to several groups that are in charge of these areas. These groups include:

o   We care Ministry,
o   Mission Outreach
o   Tracts and Publications
o   Ministry to Drug addicts
o   Campus fellowship
o   Ministry to School
o   Ministry to Glorious Children, etc.

Thus says the Lord, "Verily I say unto you, in as much as ye have done it unto one of the least of these my brethren, ye have done it unto me" Matthew 25 : 40.

WONDERFUL JESUS!

DIVINE INTERVENTION/

When I became pregnant, I started seeing my dead relatives in the dream. When I went for ultra scan, it showed the baby lying transverse, so I decided to come for deliverance and on the fourth day of the programme, I went for another scan and my baby was in the right position. Also, the dream stopped. Praise the Lord!

Sis. Kemi
MFM Headquarters

DIVINE HEALING

My son was sick to the point of death and I took him to a programme organized by this church. I called on one of the ministers to pray for him and immediately after the prayer, he received his healing. The younger one too was sick. I laid my hand on her, and prayed fervently and God healed her. Both of them are hale and hearty now. Praise the Lord!

Sis. Chinyere
MFM Oworonshoki 2

COVENANT OF DEATH BREAKS

I bless the Lord for breaking the covenant of death over my daughter. At the age of 5, a covenant was formed with the kingdom of darkness that she would die at the age of 9. But after the deliverance programme at the Prayer City, the Lord broke the covenant and delivered her totally. Praise God!

Sis. Rhoda
MFM Abule- Egba

MULTIPLE VICTORY

Seven years ago, my daughter who was an undergraduate fell from a high place and hit her head on the ground. She lost her memory as a result of the fall. I took her to many hospitals and prayer houses but she could not read or recognize anybody. Four years ago, I brought her to this church and today things have changed, she can now recognize many things and even read. Secondly, I was given a consultancy job to do. I called my son who had graduated, but had no job, and we did it together. We were paid handsomely for the job. Thereafter, my son secured a job after a deliverance programme. Praise the Lord!

Bro. Peter
MFM Abaranje

DIVINE HEALING

Sometime ago after the service, on getting home, I met my wife seriously sick. I told God to heal her and He did. God healed me too of persistent pain. Praise the Lord!

Bro. Samuel
MFM Ijaiye Ojokoro

LORD OF INCREASE

I give glory to the name of the Lord of increase. The pastor, during one of the ministrations talked on the need to honour the Lord in tithe, offering and our first fruits. To the glory of the Lord, when schools resumed I sowed the first fruit of the school fees of our school, and the Lord indeed surprised us. There is no debtor to the business this term. Praise the Lord!

Sis. Salami
MFM Apata

GOD RESTORES MY JOB

I lost my job and was jobless for almost two years. At a monthly prayer programme in this branch, a word of knowledge came from the man of God concerning my situation with the Lord promising to restore me that week. I claimed it. I was to attend a job interview but I could not find my credential. I decided to go to my former office to get the photocopies of my credentials in my file. The Managing Director saw me and asked me to return to work. I was restored, promoted and given a good accommodation. Praise the Lord!

Sis. Joy
MFM Ojo

DELIVERANCE BY FIRE

I had fibroid for a long time. I went to the hospital and was billed N50,000 for surgery. I came to the pastor and he advised me to undergo deliverance. On the last day of the deliverance programme, a prayer point was raised which touched my body like fire. Surprisingly, I felt something like rope drawing the fibroid in my stomach. Suddenly, I started bleeding. I rushed to the toilet and on getting there, a very thick and big bloody lump dropped from my body and that was the end. Praise the Lord!

Sis Patience
MFM Benin city

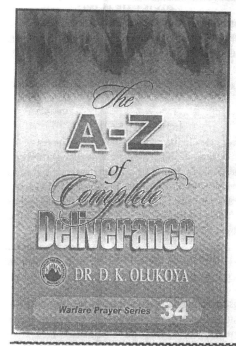

FIRE IN THE WORD

Ye Shall Know the Truth, and the Truth Shall Make You Free (John 8:32)

ISSN 978-2947-10-5   Vol. 12 No. 3 Sun. 25th Nov. - Sat. 1st Dec., 2007   ₦10

Glory be to God
FIRE IN THE WORD IS ELEVEN

BUILDING ON A
SINKING GROUND

My Year of Uncommon favour & Open Heaven Breakthroughs
Genesis 28

Hebrews 11:10 says, *"For he looked for a city which hath foundations, whose builder and maker is God."* The fact that the Bible says there is a city which has foundations, it means that there is another city that has no foundations.

In Hebrews 13:14, the Bible makes another astounding statement: *"For here have we no continuing city, but we seek one to come."* As much as people would like to live on earth forever, they have discovered that it cannot be because we have no continuing city here, but seeking a city that is to come.

Beloved, you and I are living in a city without foundations. We are accumulating things into a deep pit. Many have spent a major part of their lives looking for money, and they found to their amazement that they never found money and the money seemed to be pursuing those who did not look for it.

If your place of abode has no foundation it will soon collapse. We are putting too much trust on the vanity of the earth here. The world is a city without foundation that is why it is sinking fast — it is not a continuing city, it is a temporary city without foundations. Look at these eternal words of Jesus in Matthew 6:19-21: *"Lay not up for your selves treasures upon earth, where moth and rust doth corrupt, and where thieves break through and steal: But lay up for yourselves treasures in heaven, where neither moth nor rust doth corrupt, and where thieves do not break through nor steal. For where your treasure is, there will your heart be also."* Everything you accumulate in this sinking world shall sink with it, because the city has no foundation. A lot of people are so aggressive when it comes to material things, but they are not going to take anything away from the world; it is a sinking world.

ANY LIFE WHOSE FOUNDATION IS NOT ON CHRIST WILL BECOME THE SERPENT'S FOOD

A certain man had a revelation, where he saw himself in heaven and an angel of God was taking him round. He got to a beautiful building and asked the angel, who owned it and the angel told him it belonged to his houseboy, David and he was happy. He asked the angel to take him to his house. He had concluded that since his houseboy's mansion was so big and nice, definitely, his own who was the master must be better. He thought that the master-slave relationship applied to heaven too. He was taken to his own house, and was surprised to see a small boys quarters with no roof, and he protested. The angel looked at him straight in the eye and told him the houses were built based on the materials that people sent up. He continued to protest that he was David's master and paid his salary. But the angel explained further that God does not measure what you give by how much you give but by how much you have left after you have given. When he woke up from that revelation he became a new person and began to realize that this is an old sinking world, and if you cling to it, you will sink with it.

If you stick to this world, you will sink with it. If you have a good friend in the world, that friend will fail you. All of a sudden you will wake up and find out that the money you accumulated is worthless. In this world, metals can rust, garments can wax old, flowers can fade, and beauty can vanish. Many students in the university do not listen to the gospel because they are more interested in their beauty and clothes that will show their shapes. They do not know that all these things will fade away. In this world, stones crumble, gold and petroleum fade, treasures are stolen, good men get corrupted with time, people meet with disappointment, people's health fail, wealth disappears, etc.

Many years ago, I used to have a friend, who was very rich. Every other day he was at a party somewhere. He hosted parties with musicians who sung his praise in attendance. Recently, I had to give him N100. But he was the fellow who used to block the street and dance with assorted

DELIVERANCE CASE

women. Indeed wealth disappears, nothing lasts, because we are living in a city without foundations.

Beloved, do you want to hold on to this world where the money of today may not carry you tomorrow; where the most sure is absolutely unsure? Do you want to cling on to this world where sadness and gladness lie on the same bed; strife and peace stay inside the same boat and war and peace drink from the same cup? Do you want to stick to the world where parents hinder

and kill their own children through witchcraft powers? Do you want to cling to the world where evil and good look alike and you cannot differentiate anymore, the world where the line between hatred and love is sometimes very thin?

Do you want to cling unto the world where the man at the top is not too far from the ground, a world where anything can happen at any time? Sometime ago, I was in a queue to buy fuel, and by the time I bought mine, the people said they were no longer selling to anyone. I looked behind me and there stood a former commissioner. He demanded for fuel but was rebuffed. When he was a commissioner, he did not even need to come to the gas station, meaning that the man at the top is not far from the ground. In this world, the man that is hailed today could be stoned tomorrow. It is a world where people fail to learn from history. This is a world where men sow seeds to bring fruits, and they will not want to eat them, yet they planted them. It is a world where people shout your praise loudly, but their hearts are far from you. They could not be bothered whether you fell down and died, although in your presence they shout your praises.

Why is this world like this? you may ask. It is because we are living in a city without foundations. Man came from the dust, and as a matter of necessity, he must return to the dust. The Bible says the food of the serpent shall be the dust. All the beautiful things of this world, including human flesh is all dust and back to the dust they must go. And anyone who does not allow the Lord Jesus

to be in his life, the serpent will feed on his body because that body is dust. Look at what the Bible says in Job 4:19: *"How much less in them that dwell in houses of clay, whose foundation is in the dust, which are crushed before the moth?"* Eventually, dust will go back to dust. Any life whose foundation is not on Christ will become the serpent's food because God has decreed: "Dust shall thou eat all the days of thy life." The dust referred to there is the fallen nature of man. The Bible says other foundation can no man lay, except that which is laid in Christ Jesus. And let them that name the name of the Lord depart from iniquity.

Why should a person want to sink with this whole world where things are changing everyday? There was a time in Nigeria when there was an oil boom, it was so serious that it was said that money was no longer the problem but

NO POSITION IS PERMANENT IN THIS SINKING WORLD.

how to spend it; but today the situation is different. There was also a time when Nigeria had an epidemic of finance houses. The finance houses eventually succeeded in killing more people before their time. Where are they now? In the world there is political convulsion everywhere, and also a gradual community break down.

I want you to understand that these are the last days, and nothing is permanent. That is why you should not follow the fashion of the world, very soon the fashion will change, and where will you be? In the 1960s to 1970s, a university degree gave one access to all the good things of life. That time before students left the university, employers would come their campuses to recruit people, and within six months, they got a car. If a graduate went abroad and got an additional degree and came back, he would be treated with respect, but now all that is gone.

When I was a student in the university, all the money that each student required for three square meals a day for three months was N45. Now it is no longer so. Things of yesterday no longer apply now. Things have changed. You may think you have friends, but friends can go overnight. The thing you hold tight to, and do not want to release so that God can use you will leave you one day.

Marriages are breaking down at an alarming rate. In those days, Christians did not beat up their wives and still came for counselling. But now marriages conducted in Pentecostal churches are breaking down.

Beloved, the truth is that all other ground presented in this world is sinking sand. The only person you can cling unto

and be safe is Jesus Christ. No position is permanent in this sinking world. Give up what you can never gain for what you can never lose. What is that thing you can never lose? It is the Lord Jesus Christ and the city with foundations. Jesus Himself knew all these things, and so He warned us seriously never to lay our treasures here, because you will lose anything you deposit here. Anything you do in the house of the Lord energized by the flesh will fail. The Bible says the flesh profiteth nothing; it is the spirit that quickeneth. Are you building your eternity on this city without foundation?

THE PROPHET

Are you running after what people of the world are running after? Is it not better to invest on things that will last? Revelation 21:1-2 says, *"And I saw a new heaven and a new earth for the first heaven and the first earth were passed away: and there was no more sea. And I John saw the holy city, new Jerusalem, coming down from God out of heaven, prepared as a bride adorned for her husband."* Verses 14-19: *"And the wall of the city had twelve foundations, and in them the names of the twelve apostles of the Lamb. And he that talked with me had a golden reed to measure the city, and the gates thereof, and the wall thereof. And the city lieth foursquare, and the length is as the breadth: and he measured the city with the reed, twelve thousand furlongs. The length and the breadth and the height of it are equal. And he measured the wall thereof, an hundred and forty and four cubits, according to the measures of a man, that is,*

of the angel. And the building of the wall of it was of jasper: and the city was pure gold, like unto clear glass. And the foundation of the wall of the city was garnished with all manner of precious stones. The first foundation was jasper; the second sapphire; the third, a chalcedony; the fourth, an emerald." Verse 27: *"And there shall in nowise enter into it any thing that defileth, neither whatsoever worketh abomination, nor maketh a lie; but they which are written in the Lamb's book of life."* Is your name written there? If not, you will sink with the world.

I read a story many years ago about a certain place. Suddenly in that place, somebody discovered that there was gold everywhere in that city. People rushed there with madness. They picked gold and became instant millionaires and billionaires. There was technological explosion, and the city was very prosperous. But after some time the gold finished. And because the foundation of that city was based on gold, immediately gold finished, the city got finished. Now, the place is like a ghost town. Industries and houses are still there, but no one lives there anymore. The people in that place were trying to build a permanent structure on a city without foundation.

The Lord is drilling and training so many people, and they are asking God why they are passing through the experience. Many have a wrong idea of how God operates. If God has use of you, and finds out that you are not doing what He wants you to do, He will run you through the university of adversity, where you will learn your lesson. If you refuse to learn, you will be cut down and replaced. That will not be your portion, in Jesus' name. Build on the Lord Jesus Christ, and enjoy eternal bliss and glory.

PRAYER POINTS

1. Strangers of darkness in my life, die, in the name of Jesus.
2. O Lord my God, have mercy on me; do not cut me off, in the name of Jesus.
3. Every desire of darkness on my destiny, die, in the name of Jesus.
4. O Lord, uphold and keep me standing, in Jesus' name.
5. Any power writing my name in the book of darkness, die, in the name of Jesus.
6. (Raise your two hands to the Lord) In my dream tonight, O Lord my Father, appear, in the name of Jesus.

BUILDING ON A SINKING GROUND

is a message delivered at the Mountain of Fire and Miracles Ministries by the General Overseer, Dr. D.K. Olukoya.

A CALL TO SERVE

Are you a member of MFM with a burden to help the needy, are you interested in alleviating the plight of the poor or in the spread of the gospel through the sponsorshing of the publication of tracts? Your resources, time and talent can be extended to several groups that are in charge of these areas. These groups include:

o   We care Ministry,
o   Mission Outreach
o   Tracts and Publications
o   Ministry to Drug addicts
o   Campus fellowship
o   Ministry to School
o   Ministry to Glorious Children, etc.

Thus says the Lord, "Verily I say unto you, in as much as ye have done it unto one of the least of these my brethren, ye have done it unto me" Matthew 25 : 40.

WONDERFUL JESUS!

EVIL AVERTED IN MY HOME

One of my sons developed a severe stomachache. The whole family prayed fervently and violently for him and he was given the anointing oil. He got healed but the attack affected my heart. I managed to attend the Power Must Change Hands programme the following month at the Prayer City and through the word of knowledge from the G.O, I was healed. Praise the Lord!

Sis Olayemi
MFM Alagbole

MY MOUNTAIN BECOMES PLAIN

Before the last Power Must Change Hands Programme at the Prayer City, anytime I opened my door, I always saw a mountain. But since after the programme, I have stopped seeing the mountain. Praise the Lord!

Sis. Folayan
MFM Igando

DIVINE INTERVENTION

Recently, my brother-in-law boarded a vehicle, and before he knew it he found himself in a bush near Ijegun village with some other people. One of the passengers was slapped by the ritualist and he fell down dead. my brother in law started praying out loud saying that he would not die but live. The ritualists asked if he was a pastor and he said yes. Then they left him alone and he escaped. Praise the Lord!

Sis. Okafor
MFM Abaranje

SAVED AND DELIVERED

I took the last SSS examination, but had no result because my number could not be traced on the computer. Later, I became sick and went for deliverance. As I was doing my prayer assignment, bullets started coming out of my body. There were 583 bullets in all. I am now completely free . Praise the Lord!

Bro. Omoyemi
MFM Abule-Egba

Since I accepted Christ into my life my life has not been the same. Also, the doctor said my wife would be delivered through ceasarian session but she gave birth safely and normally. Secondly, I was given a sack letter in my department and many other people as well. But to God be the glory when we are to be paid off, the angels of God rubbed off my name and I was asked to go back to work. Praise the Lord!

Bro. Ezewegnus,
MFM Ijebu Ode

DIVINE HEALING

I thank God for healing me of serious stomach problem. Also, I had a serious itching on my entire body and anytime I scratched my body, worms would be coming out. During a 21 day vigil here, the itching stopped and the worms have disappeared. Also during the vigil, there was a word of knowledge which said that we would recover our lost items. So, I prayed for my brother who lost a purse with N4,000 as he was returning from Onitsha and the money was brought to him by a man from Imo State. Lastly, after a Power Must Change Hands programme, I received the gift of tongues. Praise the Lord!

Sis. Ezimoanne
MFM Amichi

FRUIT OF THE WOMB

Last year, during the women deliverance programme, I interceded for one family that was believing the Lord for the fruit of the womb and God has blessed them with a bouncing baby boy. Praise the Lord!

Sis. Omotosho
MFM Ijaiye Ojokoro

Tracts and Publications Group
MOUNTAIN OF FIRE AND MIRACLES MINISTRIES

Cordially invites you to

Its six-day 9th Annual Book Fair & Conference

Theme: *Power in the* WORD

Hebrews 4:12

Date: 10th - 15th December, 2007
Venue: Mountain of Fire and Miracles Ministries International Headquarters,
13, Olasimbo Street,
Onike, Yaba, Lagos.
Time: 9am Daily.

Jesus is Lord!

MFM BAMIDELE: 9, Bamidele Street, Idiaraba, off Odo Era, Ekore Bus Stop, Oworonshoki, Lagos.
MFM OMOLEYE: De-Home Guest House Street, Omoleye Bus Stop, Ogijo, Ikorodu.

FIRE IN THE WORD is a weekly Spiritual Bulletin of the Mountain of Fire and Miracles Ministries, published by Tracts and Publications Group. All Enquiries should be addressed to The Editor, Mountain of Fire Magazine, 13, Olasimbo Street, off Olumo Road, Onike, P.O. Box 2990, Sabo Yaba, Lagos, Nigeria. Telephone 01- 867439, 864631, 868766, 08023180236. E-mail: mfmtractsandpublications@yahoo.com Copyright reserved.

FIRE IN THE WORD

Ye Shall Know the Truth, and the Truth Shall Make You Free (John 8:32)

ISSN 978-2947-10-5   Vol. 12 No. 4   Sun. 2nd - Sat. 8th Dec., 2007   ₦10

Glory be to God

FIRE IN THE WORD IS ELEVEN

THE PEACE OF GOD

My Year of Uncommon favour & Open Heaven Breakthroughs

Genesis 28

n our message this week, we are looking at "The Peace of God." Philippians 4 verses 4-8 says, *"Rejoice in the Lord always and again I say, Rejoice. Let your moderation be known unto all men. The Lord is at hand. Be careful for nothing but in every thing by prayer and supplication with thanksgiving let your requests be made known unto God. And the Peace of God, which passeth all understanding shall keep your hearts and minds through Christ Jesus. Finally, brethren whatsoever things are true, whatsoever things are honest, whatsoever things are just, whatsoever things are pure, whatsoever things are lovely, whatsoever things are of good report, if there be any virtue, and if there be any praise, think on these things."*

Isaiah chapter 26 verse 3 says, *"Thou will keep him in perfect peace whose mind is stayed on thee; because he trusted in thee."*

Beloved, as your pray and wait on the Lord concerning any issue, I want to encourage you to keep the peace of God in your heart and do not

MANY PEOPLE NEED TO RECEIVE DELIVERANCE FROM THE GRASSHOPPER MENTALITY

allow any form of discouragement to enter into your spirit because discouragement is a disease and a destroyer.

One way to completely swallow discouragement is to allow the peace of God to reign in your heart. When you get discouraged, you give the enemy the chance to fight back and to win. To be discouraged means that you have taken a decision for defeat. When you proclaim that you are tired of everything then you are giving room to discouragement. Unfortunately, many people do not know that it takes a personal decision to be discouraged. You need to make a conscious decision not to be discouraged.

Contrary to popular belief, discouragement is a decision that a person takes consciously. Therefore, you must make a conscious decision to be encouraged. You have to make a conscious decision not to be discouraged. Make a decision to encourage yourself in the Lord everyday, then you will hear clearly from the Lord. Do not wait for somebody to encourage you, encourage yourself in the Lord.

Unfortunately, it is difficult to come by people who want to encourage anybody. As you begin to render thanksgiving unto God

DELIVERANCE CASE

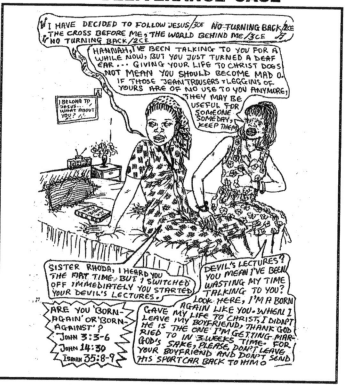

and to tell Him how you appreciate His blessings and faithfulness and you make a decision that your circumstances will not swallow you, and you refuse to watch the serpents of the magicians, the Lord will see you through. If you watch the serpents of

the magicians, they will bite you but if you command your own serpent to swallow their serpents, things will begin to happen.

Many people need to receive deliverance from the grasshopper mentality. The Israelites said they were like grasshoppers and as

The Peace of God

such would not be able to overcome the giants, whereas the Lord had said they should go and deal with them.

God knows what He wants to do and He will do what He wants to do. The truth is that once God is ready to do what He wants to do, there is nothing that can stand in His way. Sometimes, even when a person does not believe and God is ready to do His work, He will go ahead not minding the person.

WHAT IS THE PEACE OF GOD?

The peace of God can be defined as the divine calm and happiness from God. When you have the peace of God, you find this calm within, which you cannot explain. There may be a lot of storms surrounding you but within, you will be calm.

The peace of God is the quiet and lasting joy that you feel internally. The peace of God is ability to rest on the Lord because you believe that He will not let you down and you know that crying will not solve any problem. If crying could solve problems, the whole world would be one crying arena and a very noisy place.

The peace of God is when you are able to look unto the Lord and

DISCOURAGEMENT IS A KILLER. DO NOT ALLOW IT TO GET INTO YOU

praise Him in the face of all kinds of adversity surrounding you.

The peace of God is the tranquility of the mind; that is when the mind is at rest even in the face of unfavourable situations. That is the peace of God which passes all understanding.

The peace of God is having a perpetual calm disposition. The peace of God is when you allow the Prince of peace to reign in your heart; you are confident of His power. You know that your God will arise no matter what the enemy says and you will be an overcomer. That is why the Bible encourages us to rejoice in the Lord always. It endeared

David to God's heart and he was a winner all the time. The habitual praise worship of David is called prophetic warfare. Paul and Silas did the same thing in the prison and God elevated them. When you doubt God, you will keep seeing more obstacles but when you have faith in Him, you will see the way out of any situation in which you find yourself. If after prayer you still say; "I can't," what you are saying is that God can't.

Every good reader of the Bible would discover that anytime God got angry with the children of Israel, the major offence was unbelief. So, if you spend time and effort feeding your doubt, your faith will die.

THE PROPHET

Discouragement is a killer. Do not allow it to get into you. The Bible tells us that knowing Christ means deliverance in trouble and not deliverance from trouble. God waited for Shadrach, Meshach, and Abednego to get into the fire then He brought them out. We need to pray that the peace of God would always reign in our heart. Also, we should refuse to be discouraged, no matter the situation.

Learn to praise and thank God at all times. Thank Him from the bottom of your heart. Thank Him for what He has done, for what He will do and for what He will continue to do. Thank God for the blood of Jesus. He is worthy to be praised. He is worthy to be glorified. He is the King of kings and the Lord of lords. There is none like Him, what a mighty God we serve. Thank Him for the blood of Jesus which is powerful to avail for you in every situation. Thank God for His mighty power. Thank God for His mighty strength. He is the one who has all powers in His hands. Before you go to the prayer section below, pick a song of praise and sing it to the King of kings and Lord of lords.

PRAYER POINTS

1. I bear in my body the marks of the Lord Jesus Christ; therefore the God of Elijah will trouble any power that wants to trouble me, in the name of Jesus.

2. Blood of Jesus, Holy Ghost fire, envelope my life, in the name of Jesus.

3. Power to pursue, power to overtake and power to recover what the enemy has stolen from me, come upon me now, in Jesus' name.

4. Any witch that flies against me shall fly no more, in the name of Jesus.

5. O God arise and make me an example of what your power can do, in the name of Jesus.

6. I ride the horse of fire into the camp of the oppressor and I possess my possession, in the name of Jesus.

7. Every power planning disgrace for me, die, in the name of Jesus.

THE PEACE OF GOD
is a message delivered at the Mountain of Fire and Miracles Ministries by the General Overseer, Dr. D.K. Olukoya.

A CALL TO SERVE

Are you a member of MFM with a burden to help the needy, are you interested in alleviating the plight of the poor or in the spread of the gospel through the sponsorship of the publication of tracts? Your resources, time and talent can be extended to several groups that are in charge of these areas. These groups include:

o　　We care Ministry,
o　　Mission Outreach
o　　Tracts and Publications
o　　Ministry to Drug addicts
o　　Campus fellowship
o　　Ministry to School
o　　Ministry to Glorious Children, etc.

Thus says the Lord, "Verily I say unto you, in as much as ye have done it unto one of the least of these my brethren, ye have done it unto me" Matthew 25 : 40.

WONDERFUL JESUS!

DIVINE HEALING

Few weeks ago, I had a dream where I saw my daughter at a crossroad with some strange people and I told her to come out by force. When I woke up, I narrated the dream to her and we prayed together. Few days later, she fell sick and started vomiting. We prayed for her and took her to the hospital. God intervened and now she is totally healed. Praise the Lord!

Sis. Babalola
MFM Oyo

TOTAL DELIVERANCE

Before I came for a deliverance progamme here, I was on drugs on daily basis and I was really discouraged due to my condition. I decided to participate in the deliverance programme and to my surprise, I have not used the drugs again since after the programme. To the glory of God, I became healed and all I have lost in my life have been restored. Praise the Lord!

Sis. Pat
MFM Igando

AFFLICTIONS GONE

I noticed that I used to be afflicted in the month of April every year. This year April, I was afflicted again but God took control. I complained to the men of God and they prayed against the evil oppression and I became free. Also, I forgot my bag containing N45,000 and some vital documents in a bus I boarded. I rushed back to the motor park but could not get it. God used a good Samaritan who monitored the driver of the bus, and ensured that the bag was returned to me. All the money and documents were untouched. Praise the Lord!

Sis. Olawuyi
MFM Aboru

SAVED FROM ARMED BANDITS

Recently, on my way to the church for a service, I did not know that the bus I boarded was full of bandits. Suddenly, they faced me and said I should cooperate with them and bring everything I had on me. I shouted that the blood of Jesus should deliver me using my offering and tithes to fight for me at that moment. They became angry and pushed me out of the bus. I thank God for saving my life. Praise the Lord!

Sis. Mfon
MFM Headquarters

UNCOMMON FAVOURS

I worship in another church. My son sat for G.C.E and JAMB and made all his papers. He also made all his A level papers and was supposed to be given scholarship. But problems set in and he was not given the scholarship. Also, he could not gain admission to his first choice of university because he did not do well in the entrance examination. However, in a dream somebody directed me to MFM. I told my husband and he accepted that I should come here. I came to MFM and asked the pastor to pray for us. We were told to go for deliverance and we did. The day we completed the deliverance programme, we got a call that the VC had cancelled the entrance examination into the university and decided that G.C.E and JAMB results only should be used for admission. So my son was given admission to his first choice course. Also, after the deliverance, two doors of unexpected favour opened unto us. My brother who live in London has started making preparation to relocate us to London with all expenses paid. Praise the Lord!

Sis. Ngozi
MFM Adaloko

VISA BREAKTHROUGH

I had been nursing the idea of travelling abroad and was believing God for visa breakthrough for a long time. I mentioned this to my pastor who introduced me to the prophetic group. They prepared for me and when I went for the visa interview, I was given a visa. Praise the Lord!

Bro. Ojo
MFM Alagbole

DEMONIC POWER DESTROYED

We were experiencing physical and spiritual problems in the family. So I decided to come to the pastor for counselling, after which he placed us on 12 days prayers. Within the 12 days, different things happened. Each day, we woke up to find dead birds around the compound on daily basis. During the period, we saw a dead scorpion under the bed. At the end of the 12 days, we were advised to continue and we did. One day, we woke up and saw a live tortoise being escorted by five birds going round my house. I rushed to the pastor and he came, caught and burnt them. Since then my life and family have been peaceful. Praise the Lord!

Bro. Lucky
MFM Agodo

DEVOURER REBUKED

The enemy suddenly turned my car to a devourer to me. The car developed series of problems and it got to a stage that I got fed up and decided to park it. I went into series of prayers concerning the situation and the good Lord intervened and the power of the devourer was rebuked. Praise the Lord!

Bro. Michael
MFM Egan

GOD UPLIFTS ME

Before I joined MFM in 2001, I was a cleaner and a pauper. Nobody reckoned with me in my family. Suddenly, things began to change in my life due to fervent prayers. To the glory of God, I am now an educated person with a good job. Just few weeks ago, God blessed me with a Mercedeze Benz car. Praise the Lord!

Sis. Christy
MFM Ewutuntun

TRACTS & PUBLICATIONS GROUP

Presents

Six-Day

9th ANNUAL **Book Fair** AND CONFERENCE

POWER IN THE *word*

(Heb 4:12, Jer 23:29)

Date: ▶ **10th – 15th December, 2007**

Venue: ▶ **MOUNTAIN OF FIRE & MIRACLES MINISTRIES**
13, Olasimbo Street, by Unilag 2nd Gate, Onike, Iwaya, Lagos.

Time: ▶ 9.00am Daily

JESUS IS LORD!

OTHER HIGHLIGHTS

● Groups and individuals involved in evangelism should register for free evangelism materials at the Tracts and Publications office. Registration ends on December 13, 2007.

● Individuals who wish to represent the Headquarters at the MFM Bible Quiz competition on the 15th December, 2007 should gather at the auditorium near the MFM Press on Sunday 9th December, 2007 at 12.30pm. There are lots of fantastic prizes to be won.

● Members should seize the opportunity of the Bookfair to purchase their Christian Literature and other materials at reduced prices.

FIRE IN THE WORD is a weekly Spiritual Bulletin of the Mountain of Fire and Miracles Ministries, published by Tracts and Publications Group. All Enquiries should be addressed to The Editor, Mountain of Fire Magazine, 13, Olasimbo Street, off Olumo Road, Onike, P.O. Box 2990, Sabo Yaba, Lagos, Nigeria. Telephone 01- 867439, 864631, 868766, 08023180236. E-mail: mfmtractsandpublications@yahoo.com Copyright reserved.

FIRE IN THE WORD

Ye Shall Know the Truth, and the Truth Shall Make You Free (John 8:32)

ISSN 978-2947-10-5   Vol. 12 No. 5   Sun. 9th - Sat. 15th Dec., 2007

₦10

 Glory be to God

FIRE IN THE WORD IS ELEVEN

LIVES ON SALES

My Year of Uncommon favour & Open Heaven Breakthroughs

Genesis 28

This week, we are looking at the message titled, "Lives on Sale."

There are men and women in our world who have been sold off consciously or unconsciously. It does not matter what name they call themselves, or how prosperous or big or popular they become. If the sale that took place is a spiritual transaction, a time will come when the owner of the property will lay claim to it. And if the situation is not arrested before then, even prayers will not be able to help the affected persons.

We would consider six scriptures methodically in this message. These scriptures would speak to you and make you do some very deep thinking. There are many people who commit heinous crimes that result in death sentences. When you ask them why they committed those crimes, they say they do not know. The reason is that they have been sold off and they do not know who bought them. Sometimes on deliverance ground, you hear screams of "leave me alone," or "leave her alone, she is mine, she is mine" from deliverance candidates. It is because the spirits in charge of their lives are laying claim over their lives. Incisions, concoctions and birth marks given to a person are powerful enough to sell the person off. Many people have been sold off through one demonic activity or another which they got involved in or their parents got involved on their behalf. A certain woman said that a pig was slaughtered and the blood was poured on her new born baby. Now the child has grown into a lady roaming about the street at night.

Joel 3:3 says, *"And they have cast lots for my people; and have given a boy for a harlot, and sold a girl for wine, that they might drink."* There you see the sale of certain commodities going on, the sale of human lives. There is a

THERE IS A SATANIC SUPERMARKET, WHERE THE SOULS OF MEN ARE ON DISPLAY

terrible spiritual slave trade going on now. Men and women are being sold off. Ezekiel 27:13 says, *"Javan, Tubal, and Meshech, they were thy merchants: they traded the persons of men and vessels of brass in thy market."* They were trading in men.

Isaiah 50:1 says, *"Thus saith the Lord, Where is the bill of your mother's divorcement; whom I have put away? Or which of my creditors is it to whom I have sold you? Behold, for your iniquities have ye sold yourselves and for your transgressions is your mother put away."* It means that it is possible for you to sell yourself to some strange powers. Isaiah 52:2-3 says, *"Shake thyself from the dust; arise, and sit down, O Jerusalem: loose thyself from the bands of thy neck, O captive daughter of Zion. For thus saith the Lord, Ye have sold yourselves for nought: and ye shall be redeemed without money."* Again, people can be on sale. But the most fearful scriptures of them all are what you find in the book of Revelation 18:10-11 which says, *"Standing afar off for the fear of her torment, saying, Alas, alas, that great city Babylon, that mighty city! For in one hour is thy judgment come. And the merchants of the earth shall weep and mourn over her; for no man buyeth their merchandise any more."* And in verses 12-13, the Bible makes a list of the merchandise of Babylon: *"The merchandise of gold and silver, and precious stones, and of pearls, and fine linen, and purple, and silk, and scarlet, and all thyine wood, and all manner vessels of ivory, and all manner vessels of most precious wood, and of brass, and iron, and marble. And cinnamon, and odours, and ointments, and frankincense, and wine, and oil, and fine flour and wheat, and beasts, and sheep, and horses, and chariots, and slaves, and souls of men."* The souls of men is the last item on the list of merchandise that the enemy sells.

There is a satanic supermarket, where the souls of men are on display. The Bible

DELIVERANCE CASE

says, "What shall it profit a man, if he gains the whole world and loses his soul. With what can a man make an exchange for his soul." There are people who have consciously sold their souls to satan. There are also those who have been sold off unconsciously. They just do not know they have been sold off. There was the case of an Ibo man, who had two Ph.D degrees and was living in Germany. All of a sudden one morning, something began to tell him to resign and go back home. That day, he submitted his resignation letter to the amazement of his boss. He did not know what he was doing until he arrived at the airport in Nigeria, then he became conscious of his folly. He tried for many years to move forward but nothing worked. He had to go back to the village with two PhDs to start farming. One day, as he was digging the ground at the backyard in his father's compound, he dug up his own placenta. He saw it packed in something and there was a padlock by the side of it. God helped him that day, he ran to a deliverance ministry close by, where the padlock was broken and he was prayed for. It was then he could move forward in life.

There is a satanic market where flesh, bones, and blood are on sale. The blood would be taken and transferred to the blood bank of satan. Why are they interested in blood? It is because the Bible says that life is in the blood. The Psalmist says, "When my foes and the wicked came upon me to eat my flesh, they stumbled and fell." Isaiah 49:26 also says that all they that oppress you will be fed with their own flesh, and they shall be drunken with their own blood. There is a satanic business center where they trade in destiny. They could grab a person's destiny and transfer it to somebody else. This may sound very strange but it is true. Even God Himself makes us to understand that life can be used to exchange life. He has a law called the law of substitution. He could pick one to replace another. So, there is an exchange that goes on. Proverbs 11:8 says, *"The righteous is delivered out of*

trouble and the wicked cometh in his stead."

Sometime ago, armed robbers accosted a brother and as they were about to shoot him, somebody at that moment drove to the place with a better car than his own. Quickly they lost interest in the brother and pursued this new fellow and shot him dead. Somebody had been programmed to die by the enemy and God said His own would not go, somebody else moved in as a replacement. The reverse can also be the case. Somebody can be used by the enemy to settle an account.

Isaiah 43:1-2 says, *"But now thus saith the Lord that created thee O Jacob, and he that formed thee, O Israel, fear not: for I have redeemed thee, I have called thee by thy name; thou art mine. When thou passest through the waters, I will be with thee and through the rivers, they shall not overflow thee; when thou walkest through the fire, thou*

WHEN YOU FAIL TO DISCOVER YOURSELF IN THE MARKET SQUARE OF LIFE, YOU DIE A FAILURE.

shall not be burned, neither shall the flame kindle upon thee." Isaiah 43:4 says, *"Since thou wast precious in my sight, thou hast been honourable, and I have loved thee: therefore will I give men for thee, and people for thy life."* That is God. There is a divine law of substitution and there is also a satanic law of substitution.

Many people need to pray seriously to recover themselves from the market of darkness. Many sisters are being controlled by familiar spirit but they do not know. That is why anytime they want to move forward, that spirit will say, "No! You cannot go any where!" Many times after some serious prayers, a lot of people see strange things; some almost run mad. Sometimes, immediately somebody starts deliverance, he or she falls ill. It is evidence that such lives are on sale. Many lives have been sold. That is why the prayer point, "My life is not for sale," is a very important one.

When the soul of a person is on sale, there is a great problem. When a life has been sold off, there would be destiny disorder. You have to pray that every satanic claim over your destiny must die.

SIGNS OF A LIFE ON SALE

1. The affected person will fail to discover himself. When you fail to discover yourself in the market square of life, you die a failure.

2. The person's benefit will be transferred to another. Those he taught before an examination would pass while he would fail. At work, those he trained would be promoted while he would not be promoted.

3. Receiving the baptism of the Holy Ghost will be a problem. The person will not be able to flow in the things of the Spirit and will not be able to see the vision of heaven because he needs to be bought back from where he has been sold.

4. He will experience what is called deliverance failure. He could undergo deliverance twenty-one times without any change if the satanic claim over his life is not addressed.

5. He will exhibit what is known as animal behaviour, for example, he would do senseless things and behave abnormally.

6. He will be a candidate of unconscious initiation.

7. He will experience constant failure.

8. He will struggle hard before achieving anything. If it is a woman, going to school will be a problem and when she finishes, marriage too will become a problem. Victims need to buy themselves back. The person will also experience stubborn poverty.

9. The person will experience what is called vagabond anointing. He will be going from place to place, trying many things and achieving nothing.

This is not a situation to joke with because many people have failed in life due to the fact that they were sold off and they failed to address it. If does not matter how high a man who has been sold goes, very soon something will bring him down because he has been sold off. There was the case of a certain sister, anytime, she was alone, an old man would move into her room and be addressing her as his wife. The more she rebuffed the

THE PROPHET

strange man, the more he appeared to her. And the occurrence started when she was around eight years old but she could not tell anybody and the thing continued. Her first husband died and she married the second one who died too and the third one as well. The pastor of the orthodox church that buried the third husband, who attends our Wednesday meetings, advised her to go to MFM. It was then for the first time she opened up and told me about the old man that used to come to her. He was the one killing her husbands because he had a satanic claim over her life. We prayed that claim off and she became free. Complications do set in when there are multiple claims on a single person.

WHAT DO WE DO AGAINST
THE ENEMY'S CLAIMS?

1. Confess all known sins in your life. You need to confess every sin that you know can hinder those claims from being broken.
2. You need to break every foundational stronghold.
3. Aggressively break the claim of the enemy over your destiny. You cannot pacify the powers of darkness, the only language they understand is violence.

If as you are reading this magazine you have not yet surrendered your life to Christ, that is, you are not born again, there is no way you can break any claim of the enemy over your life. If you want to give your life to Christ, make the following confessions: Lord Jesus, I come before you today. I surrender my life to you. I know that I am a sinner.

Forgive my sins and wash me with your precious blood. Take absolute control of my life. Thank you Lord Jesus, in Jesus' name. Amen.

PRAYER POINTS

1. Every witchcraft claim over my life, die, in the name of Jesus.
2. Any material taken away from my body on the day I was born, I recover you by fire, in the name of Jesus.
3. Every power that does not want to let my destiny go, your time is up, die, in the name of Jesus.
4. Every power sitting on my career, calling, marriage etc. die, in the name of Jesus.
5. Every claim over my life from the waters, die, in the name of Jesus.
6. I cover myself with the blood of Jesus, in the name of Jesus.

LIVES ON SALE
is a message delivered at the Mountain of Fire and Miracles Ministries by the General Overseer, Dr. D.K. Olukoya.

A CALL TO SERVE
Are you a member of MFM with a burden to help the needy, are you interested in alleviating the plight of the poor or in the spread of the gospel through the sponsorshing of the publication of tracts? Your resources, time and talent can be extended to several groups that are in charge of these areas. These groups include:
o   We care Ministry,
o   Mission Outreach
o   Tracts and Publications
o   Ministry to Drug addicts
o   Campus fellowship
o   Ministry to School
o   Ministry to Glorious Children, etc.
Thus says the Lord, "Verily I say unto you, in as much as ye have done it unto one of the least of these my brethren, ye have done it unto me" Matthew 25 : 40.

WONDERFUL JESUS!

OUR GOD ANSWERS PRAYERS

I have been praying for my son overseas to successfully secure his resident permit. To the glory of God, recently he came safely to Nigeria and told us that he has successfully secured the resident permit. Praise the Lord!

Sis. Kehinde
MFM Idimu

GOD IS WONDERFUL

I woke up one morning to discover that I had a boil on my face, which gave me severe pain. But after prayers it disappeared. Secondly, I dreamt that my baby died and people were crying but when I poured the anointing oil on her and prayed, she came back to life. In the afternoon, the baby started convulsing and I quickly rushed her to the church. She was prayed for and God healed her. Praise the Lord!

Sis. Uchena
MFM Ojodu

DELIVERED FROM AFFLICTION

I was badly afflicted and when I came here, I received my healing. Secondly, my 7 years old son was suffering from bronchitis and was unbalanced for five years. But when we came to MFM, the power of God touched him mightily and he became normal. Now he can do all the things he couldn't do before. Indeed the Lord is awesome. Praise the Lord!

Sis. Robson
MFM Headquarters

DELIVERANCE FROM
THE SPIRIT OF GLUTTONY

I was under the bondage of the spirit of gluttony. I felt like eating anything I saw at anytime even when I was in for a deliverance programme, and needed to fast. But during a recent deliverance programme, after taking the anointing oil, the power of God fell upon me and I am perfectly alright now. God also healed me of a very terrible cough. Praise the Lord!

Bro. Lamidi

MFM Abuja

DIVINE FAVOUR OF GOD

I came to this church with a particular request to God for the fruit of the womb. God heard my prayers and gave me a child. All along I was coming to church alone without my husband. I prayed to God to touch the heart of my husband. God did and now my husband comes to church with me. We are now worshipping together at MFM Ado Ekiti. The Lord also provided a Mercedes Benz car for us. Praise the Lord!

Sis. Ogunsanya
MFM Ado Ekiti

HYPERTENSION GONE

I was suffering from hypertension and God healed me. However, I failed to testify and the sickness came back. I prayed again to God to heal me and made a vow to testify to His goodness, and the merciful God answered me. Now I am healed. Secondly, a fake pastor came to me and told me that my son was going to die therefore I should buy a white cloth and a banana stem and wrap the banana stem with the white cloth. But I told him that we shall not die but live to proclaim the works of the Lord. I thank God that my son is alive. Praise the Lord!

Sis Busari
MFM Ijebu-Ode

DIVINE VISITATIOIN AFTER 19 YEARS

I thank God for the wonderful gift He has given to my family. For nineteen years, we were looking unto God for the fruit of the womb. Within this period, we visited many places for solution but to no avail. When we joined this ministry and started fellowshipping with other brethren, God answered our prayer by giving us a bouncing baby girl. Praise the Lord

Bro. Andrew
MFM Abule-anu

TRACTS & PUBLICATIONS GROUP

Presents

Six-Day

9th ANNUAL Book Fair AND CONFERENCE

POWER IN THE word

(Heb 4:12, Jer 23:29)

Date: ▶ **10th - 15th December, 2007**

Venue: ▶ **MOUNTAIN OF FIRE & MIRACLES MINISTRIES**
13, Olasimbo Street, by Unilag 2nd Gate, Onike, Iwaya, Lagos.

Time: ▶ **9.00am Daily**

JESUS IS LORD!

OTHER HIGHLIGHTS

● Groups and individuals involved in evangelism should register for free evangelism materials at the Tracts and Publications office. Registration ends on December 13, 2007.

● Individuals who wish to represent the Headquarters at the MFM Bible Quiz competition on the 15th December, 2007 should gather at the auditorium near the MFM Press on Sunday 9th December, 2007 at 12.30pm. There are lots of fantastic prizes to be won.

● Members should seize the opportunity of the Bookfair to purchase their Christian Literature and other materials at reduced prices.

FIRE IN THE WORD is a weekly Spiritual Bulletin of the Mountain of Fire and Miracles Ministries, published by Tracts and Publications Group. All Enquiries should be addressed to The Editor, Mountain of Fire Magazine, 13, Olasimbo Street, off Olumo Road, Onike, P.O. Box 2990, Sabo Yaba, Lagos, Nigeria. Telephone 01- 867439, 864631, 868766, 08023180236.E-mail: mfmtractsandpublications@yahoo.com Copyright reserved.

FIRE IN THE WORD

Ye Shall Know the Truth, and the Truth Shall Make You Free (John 8:32)

ISSN 978-2947-10-5   Vol. 12 No. 6   Sun. 16th - Sat. 22nd Dec., 2007   ₦10

WHEN LIGHT BECOMES DARKNESS

My Year of Uncommon favour & Open Heaven Breakthroughs

Genesis 28

atthew 5:14-16 says, *"Ye are the light of the world. A city that is set on a hill cannot be hid. Neither do men light a candle, and put it under a bushel, but on a candle stick; and it giveth light unto all that are in the house. Let your light so shine before men, that they may see your good works, and glorify your Father which is in heaven."*

One of the names by which Christians are known is "Light." Christians are supposed to be the light in this dark world. Christians are supposed to show the way to people who do not know the way. They are supposed to direct those who are in darkness. Matthew 6:22-23 says, *"The light of the body is the eye: if therefore thine eye be*

single, thy whole body shall be full of light. But if thine eye be evil, thy whole body shall be full of darkness. If therefore the light that is in thee be darkness, how great is that darkness!" Luke 11:33-34: *"No man, when he hath lighted a candle, putteth it in a secret place, neither under a bushel, but on a candlestick, that they which come in may see the light. The light of the body is the eye: therefore when thine eye is single, thy whole body is full of light; but when thine eye is evil, thy body is full of darkness."*

It is a very evil thing for light to become darkness.

IF YOU ARE IN THE LIGHT, YOU WILL BE ABLE TO TAKE CHARGE OF YOUR DESTINY.

When light becomes darkness, many things go wrong. So, in the scriptures above, Jesus was making very deep statements. He was not talking about physical eyes because a person may be able to see physically but be spiritually blind.

When light becomes darkness, many things go wrong. There will be lack instead of plenty because the affected people cannot see where they can get the plenty from. There will be hatred instead of love, where people are meant to show love, they will exhibit hatred. There will be frustration and rejection instead of fulfillment and acceptance. Things certainly go wrong when the light in a person's life becomes darkness.

There will be failure instead of success, and bondage instead of freedom. There will be hardship instead of ease and discomfort instead of comfort. It is therefore a great prayer to decree that the light in you does not become darkness.

The prayers recorded in the Bible are very powerful. For instance, the book of Ezekiel 11:11 says, *"This city shall not be your caldron."* Many people do not understand what it means but it is a powerful prayer. It is also good to pray that every power of spiritual blindness should scatter. It is good to pray that the reign of darkness in your spiritual life should be terminated. It is also good to pray that your dreams and visions should receive divine clarity. It is also good to pray that the veil of darkness

DELIVERANCE CASE

Sincerely, I need protection and self-defence against dream attackers. A pastor without anointing must be very smart and aggressive.

But what if they come against you with 1,000 modern demonic sophisticated weapons?

The weapon of our warfare... (2 Cor. 10:4)

covering your face should be torn off completely.

THE IMPORTANCE OF LIGHT

You need to pray all these anti-darkness prayers regularly because when you have light, you will be advertised. Light gives you visibility. It provides vision, and brightens the most remote areas. Light makes things very clear. It chases away evil, and also prevents evil. Somebody who you know very well may be harming you in the dark because you cannot see the person but when the light comes, the enemy will be revealed.

Light makes things clear. Light displays and confirms the truth. Light illuminates. It is like a disinfectant in the spirit world. It reveals things. Light defeats darkness no matter how thick the darkness is. A little bit of light in a situation will reveal any darkness around it.

Light provides a pathway for people. Light facilitates progress, while darkness slows things down. Light warms you sometimes when it is cold. Light also warns us of danger. It prevents catastrophe and reveals what is missing. It is therefore a terrible thing when the light of a person becomes darkness.

WHEN DOES THE LIGHT OF A PERSON BECOME DARKNESS?

1. When the person's physical eyes are evil, that is, the eyes are carrying out the instructions of darkness.

2. When the eyes register unholy things.

3. When the eyes accept evil things. The eye is like the lens of a camera, it takes pictures, and there is a developer in the heart, where the pictures are produced.

4. When the eyes are giving evil messages. That is when the eyes are used to pass across evil messages.

5. When the spiritual vision is lost.

6. When dreams turn to nightmares instead of vision.

THE DIFFERENCE BETWEEN THE RICH MAN AND THE POOR MAN IS JUST INFORMATION

7. When the eyes photograph iniquity; that is, looking at a person. While imagining evil. Such eyes will put a person's spirit man in trouble.

8. When you are suffering from spiritual ignorance. That is, you really do not know your left from your right spiritually.

9. When your spiritual eyes are blind.

10. When your eyes keep causing spiritual pollution in your spiritual life. That is, such eyes have made a covenant with darkness. It is a terrible thing.

People need to pray that the spiritual cataract in their

eyes should be removed. We need to pray the prayer of the Psalmist who said, "Open my eyes, that I may see" (Psalm 119:18). What does the Psalmist want to see? He wants to see spiritual things.

When your spiritual eyes are open and it is all light, you will discover that where others are failing, you will not fail. You will find that where people are making mistakes you will not make mistake.

And if your prayer is being resisted, you will know why it is so.

If you discover that evil spirits are overcoming you, it means there is something wrong. However, if you are in the light, you will be able to take charge of your destiny. When your light becomes what it should be, you will become someone the enemy cannot put down.

You must pray the accompanying cataract-

destroying prayers in this message so that your spiritual eyes will be opened. If your spiritual eyes are opened, it will not only help you spiritually, but also physically and will bring faith into your heart.

The enemy does not want the spiritual eyes of people to be open. The enemy prefers people to be in darkness, he prefers people to be ignorant. That is why Jesus said, "You shall know the truth and the truth shall set you free."

People need information because information is power. The difference between the rich man and the poor man is just information. The difference between somebody who scored 'A' in class and the person who failed is information. If you need

THE PROPHET

specific information from the Lord and want that informing-spirit to begin to operate in your life, then you must pray the following prayer points aggressively.

PRAYER POINTS

1. Witchcraft blindness caging my eyes, die, in the name of Jesus.

2. In my dreams tonight, angels of light appear, in the name of Jesus.

3. Every veil of darkness, be roasted by the fire of the God of Elijah, in the name of Jesus.

4. Tell the Lord to throw light on the areas where you need information.

5. Father Lord, remove from my life anything that scares you away, in the name of Jesus.

6. Every strange fire burning in my life, quench now, in the name of Jesus.

7. Father Lord, establish me in every good work, in the name of Jesus.

8. Spirit of God, help me and increase me in the knowledge of God, in the name of Jesus.

9. Father Lord, let your word have free course and be glorified in me, in the name of Jesus.

10. Let the Spirit of the Living God reveal my innermost being to me, in the name of Jesus.

11. Father Lord, give me understanding and enlighten me about your ways, in the name of Jesus.

12. O Lord, make perfect what is lacking in my faith, in the name of Jesus.

13. O Lord, do not be a spectator in my life, in Jesus' name.

14. Every seed of spiritual blindness and deafness, fall down and die, in the name of Jesus.

15. O Lord, do not be silent to me, in Jesus' name.

WHEN LIGHT BECOMES DARKNESS

is a message delivered at the Mountain of Fire and Miracles Ministries by the General Overseer, Dr. D.K. Olukoya.

A CALL TO SERVE

Are you a member of MFM with a burden to help the needy, are you interested in alleviating the plight of the poor or in the spread of the gospel through the sponsorshing of the publication of tracts? Your resources, time and talent can be extended to several groups that are in charge of these areas. These groups include:

o We care Ministry,
o Mission Outreach
o Tracts and Publications
o Ministry to Drug addicts
o Campus fellowship
o Ministry to School
o Ministry to Glorious Children, etc.

Thus says the Lord, "Verily I say unto you, in as much as ye have done it unto one of the least of these my brethren, ye have done it unto me" Matthew 25 : 40.

WONDERFUL JESUS!

GOD'S OPENS MY UNDERSTANDING

After reading the book of our father in the Lord titled, "Smite the enemy and he shall flee," my life changed completely and my understanding was opened. I decided to come for deliverance after which God did great and mighty things in my life. Praise God!

Sis. Loura
MFM Headquarters

EVIL ARROWS BACKFIRE

Glory be to God for His healing power. For over two months my right arm was rendered useless as a result of an attack in my dream. I also suffered constant severe pains. However, during the Sunday worship service, the Lord healed me totally. Praise the Lord!

Sis. Morenike
MFM Abule Egba

EVIL LOAD DISAPPEARS

I thank God Almighty for taking care of me and my family. I went for deliverance and while I was praying at night, God showed me some evil loads in my house. I cried unto God and the owners of the evil loads carried their loads. All the evil plantations have disappeared from my life. Praise the Lord!

Sis. Amaka
MFM Ojo

SPIRIT OF DEATH DISAPPEARS

I was terribly sick and was at the point of death when I was brought to the deliverance ground. But after series of deliverance prayers I was revived. I was advised to repeat the deliverance programme the following week and after the programme, God perfected my healing and I am hale and hearty now. Praise the Lord!

Bro. Olutoye
MFM Agodo

I POSSESS MY CAR BY FIRE

I thank God Almighty for His uncommon favour upon my life. In the church programme tagged, "Possess your possession by fire," I prayed seriously for a breakthrough and before the next edition, my brother in-law bought me a car of my choice. Praise the Lord!

Sis. Gbatade
MFM Odogunyan

ANOINTING MAKES THE DIFFERENCE

Recently, I started the foundation for a building in my village and called pastors from MFM Aba to pray on it. But in the night, the enemy excreted on the foundation. The excreta was discovered by construction workers who ran away because a similar charm was seen somewhere before and the owners of the building died. But I prayed seriously and anointed everywhere and the job was completed without any problem, even my mother that suddenly became sick at that time was healed. I thank God I am back in Lagos without problem. Praise the Lord!

Bro. Mike
MFM Egan

GOD RELEASES HIS BLESSINGS UPON ME

I was about to travel when my wife who went to see the pastor for counseling said we should go for deliverance. This we did and I saw the blessings of God descending from above and falling upon me. Also during the deliverance, when we were told to stone our enemies with the stone of fire, I saw my household enemy being defeated. Praise the Lord!

Bro. Nwafor
MFM Adaloko

THE ALMIGHTY GOD

I had severe bleeding for months which refused to cease. This made me to undergo deliverance. The Lord opened my eyes and I saw a mighty personality and a snail with six antennae coming out of my body. Since then the bleeding has ceased. Praise the Lord!

Sis. Prosper
MFM Iba

TOTAL DELIVERANCE AND HEALING

I thank God for the grace to go through deliverance exercise because as an ulcer patient I was afraid the ailment would be aggravated by the dry fasting involved. But to the glory of God, not only did I successfully complete the exercise, I was healed of the ulcer. Praise the Lord!

Sis. Biose
MFM Ogwashi-uku

ARK OF THE LORD IS IN MY HOUSE

I made my house available for house fellowship about the same time the breakthrough programme started in the church, when the minister of God said we should mention our needs. I did and at the end of the programme, the Lord gave me a car. Praise the Lord!

Sis. Esther
MFM Warri

**THIS PAMPHLET CONTAINS HOLY GHOST VOMITED PRAYER POINTS
TO ENSURE THAT YOU CAPTURE ALL YOUR REMAINS BLESSINGS
FOR 2007 AND ENTER INTO 2008 ON A SUCCESSFUL NOTE.
DON'T MISS IT.**

MOUNTAIN OF FIRE AND MIRACLES MINISTRIES
13, Olasimbo Street, Off Olumo Road, Onike,
P.O.BOX 2990, Sabo, Yaba Lagos.

COME TO THE CROSS-OVER NIGHT PRAYER MEETING
WITH THIS PAMPHLET

MOUNTAIN OF FIRE AND MIRACLES MINISTRIES
Invites you to
2007 A.D end of the year prayer vigil

PRAY YOUR WAY Into 2008

Don't drink, dance or waste your time at any ungodly place, rather, end the year 2007 on a prayerful note
and enter into the New Year with the touch of God that answers by fire.

Date: Monday 31st December, 2007
Time: 10.00pm till dawn
Venue: MFM Prayer City, KM 12, Lagos/Ibadan Expressway, Ibafo.

FIRE IN THE WORD

Ye Shall Know the Truth, and the Truth Shall Make You Free (John 8:32)

ISSN 1595 - 7314 Vol. 12 No. 7 Sun. 23rd - Sat. 29th Dec., 2007

₦10

THE MYSTERY OF OUR WARFARE

My year of unprecedented greatness and unmatchable increase
Deuteronomy 28:13, Psalm 71:21, Ephesians 3:20, Psalm 92:10

Ephesians 6:12 says, *"For we wrestle not against flesh and blood, but against principalities, against powers, against the rulers of the darkness of this world, against spiritual wickedness in high places."*

Apostle Paul used the word, "wrestle" to describe our warfare to show how serious it is. In the olden days, during boxing and wrestling matches, the contenders did not fight in rounds. The fights ended when one party surrendered or died. This is the kind of language that Paul used to describe our warfare. It is aggressive and violent.

An ancient hymn says, "Christian, seek not yet repose, hear thy guardian angel say, thou art in the midst of foes, watch and pray" The writer mentioned the watching first before prayer. It says, "Principalities and powers, mustering their unseen array, wait for thy unguarded hours: watch and pray. Gird your heavenly armour on, wear it both night and day because ambush lies the evil one. Watch and pray." It means that you cannot afford to put down your amour whether it is in the night or in the day because the evil one is lying in ambush, waiting. It says, "Watch as if on that alone hangs all the issues of the day. Pray that help may be sent down."

We are in a war that has no rules. The enemy is knowledgeable, obstinate and unfair. It amazes me when I see some people declaring that life is unfair to them. I wonder what makes them think that life will be fair. Is it fair to take the Son of God and nail Him on the cross? Is it fair to beat Him for doing nothing? Life itself is a battle. Many people are going through their battles now. Some people start their battle from the womb like Jacob. Some start theirs at middle age while some start theirs at old age.

Beloved, the world is not a playground. It is a hot battlefield, and in the battle, nobody can be neutral. It is a matter of life or death, heaven or hell! And our enemy, satan has a highly organized kingdom with its headquarters in the second heaven. You either fight or perish, there is no middle camp. The two most effective weapons of our enemy, which he is using to get devastating results now are ignorance and discouragement. Ignorance is a disaster, and discouragement is a killer. All serious Christians, whether they like it or not will attract satanic attention. Once you are serious, you

IF YOU HAVE THE CALL OF GOD UPON YOUR LIFE, AND YOU GO INTO WOOD BUSINESS, BE SURE THAT YOU WOULD BE DRIVEN OUT OF THE FOREST WITH A CUTLASS.

will attract attention. The enemy does not grant freedom, it must be demanded. The enemy will only yield what he must yield, if you are ready to let him have it, he will have it. That is why the Bible makes it clear that the Lord our God is a Man of war, and the Lord is His name. Therefore, Christians too are not civilians, they are soldiers. That is why we must apply the only language the enemy understands: Violence and total defeat. An enemy defeated partially may have the power to resurrect and fight back. Just as the magicians in Egypt imitated God's power in the days of Moses, the devil still counterfeits the power of God today. Just as those magicians used certain powers to perform their magic, the devil still uses powers to work against people today.

Wars do not just arise. They have a source. We shall consider the sources.

WHAT ARE THE SOURCES OF OUR WARFARE?

1. Sin: The first source of our warfare is sin. Sin is horrible and terrible. Sin kept that man by the pool of Bethesda for 38 years. So, one source of warfare is sin. As far as you are living in any known sin, the enemy will not let you go. There is no use in saying, "I know that my only problem is anger," or "I know that my only problem is pride." No! Sin is sin no matter how you polish it.

2. Accidental war: The second origin of warfare is what I call accidental war. Sometime ago, a certain woman was arrested by some brethren. She was going round dustbins placed at the front of people's houses to scavenge for used menstrual pads. The owners had barricaded themselves inside their houses with high walls and iron gates but right there by their gates, a war was going which they did not know anything about.

3. Evil inheritance: The third origin of war is inheritance. Sometime ago, a certain man who was forty years old and a new member in our church suddenly disappeared. We prayed and searched for him, but could not find him. After about three weeks of prayers, the wife who was a muslim got converted. Amazingly, about a year later, somebody found him in Kano wandering about. When the person asked him what he was doing there, and that people had been looking for him in Lagos, he said he came to buy ram for his baby's naming ceremony. That naming ceremony was almost one year earlier. Later, when he started deliverance prayers, it was discovered that in his family, men always walked away at the age of forty. They just walk into thin air. So, war could be inherited. Some people also call it, generational trouble.

DELIVERANCE CASE **Faithless sister**

Enough of faith-faith I'm tired of waiting for God's Will in marriage. I'll be 37-Yrs old this week, and no brother ever takes a second look at me. I need A MAN...

Short or tall, thin or fat, good, bad, nice or not. Ugly or handsome, rich or poor, born again or not, This week, I must get a man to marry. I'm DESPERATE.

WHAAAT

4. Environment: The fourth origin of war could be the environment in which you were born or the environment in which you find yourself. That is why some people from particular areas always experience poverty. There is something known as geographical poverty. In such places, you hardly find storey buildings or beautiful and modern structures.

5. Bad influence: The fifth origin of war is bad influence or what people call evil company, which the Bible says corrupt good manners. Bad influence can be the origin of war. A certain sister noticed that her friend just got wealthy overnight and she began

to harass her friend to show her the way. One day, her friend got tired of the harassment and took her somewhere, where they met an old man sitting on a mat. The old man gave her some instructions and as soon as she started the procedure, her first son started rolling on the floor and was about to die, when it occurred to her that it was as a result of what she was doing. Then she remembered that before her friend became rich the first born died. She ran back to the herbalist to say that she was no longer interested. You could get war from bad company.

6. Curses and evil covenants: The sixth origin of war is curses and evil covenants. Once an evil covenant is running, victims would go from trouble to trouble.

7. **Household wickedness:** The seventh origin of warfare is household wickedness. This evil started right from the book of Genesis.

Sometime ago, a certain sister got married and at the reception, the mother-in-law told her without shame that the marriage would not last more than three months. The sister thought it was a joke, and instead of cancelling the evil pronouncement by saying that it will not come to pass, in Jesus' name, she just smiled and kept quiet. Right from the first day of the marriage, anytime she and her husband sat together, an invisible hand would slap the man and give him a serious beating until they separated. After three months of slapping and beating, the man said he was tired. That was household wickedness.

8. **Spiritual carelessness:** The eight origin of war is what is known as spiritual carelessness. The neglect of prayers, Bible reading, and meditation only introduce war.

9. **Spiritual attacks:** The ninth origin of warfare is spiritual attacks. Many people experience spiritual attack without offending anybody.

10. **Self-imposed war:** The tenth origin of warfare is self-inflicted. That is, when a person is harming himself. For example, it is common knowledge that cigarette smoking is dangerous to health. Therefore, anyone who indulges in it is consciously exposing himself to danger, and whatever problem comes from it is self-inflicted.

11. **Uncrucified flesh:** The eleventh origin of warfare is the uncrucified flesh which attracts the vultures of death to the body. Lack of humility can introduce warfare into a person's life.

12. **God:** War can come from God Himself. If He loves you and you are disobedient to Him, He will make things difficult for you. If you run, He will pursue you. He will scatter what you are doing until you do what He wants you to do. If you have the call of God upon your life, and you go into wood business, be sure that you would be driven out of the forest with a cutlass. If you have the call of God upon your life and you reject it and enter into transportation business, the vehicles will be flying into the Lagoon on a daily basis. If you have the call of God upon your life, and you go into buying and selling, you will be in debt always because He is the one fighting you. Deliverance will not save you. Obedience is the only thing that can save you. If God is the one fighting

ANYONE WHO SAYS HE DOES NOT HAVE A WAR TO FIGHT IS ALREADY DEFEATED.

you, nobody can save you. If God is the one fighting you, repentance and obedience are the only ways of escape. There was no deliverance prayer that would have saved Jonah until he obeyed God. If he had continued in disobedience, he would have killed himself and others and God would have required their blood from him. God can be the source of our war.

THE TYPES OF WARFARE THAT WE FIGHT

We fight physical attacks. These come in the form of sicknesses or other physical conditions.

The mind can also be attacked. A lot of people are going through this condition now. People also suffer from emotional attacks, which result in worry, anxiety, depression, discouragement, failure etc.

There are also occult attacks. They come through human beings who employ satanic powers to attack people. This is common now in the corporate world. Many people are being attacked by their colleagues with demonic powers. Some people have underneath their clothes what they call local insurance which really is no insurance because they are afraid to die. There can be attacks based on your generations or ancestors. There can be abusive attacks and curses on a person. There could be attack on a person's marriage, business or spiritual life. All these are the kinds of attacks that can come against a person.

THE MYSTERIES OF OUR WARFARE

There are seven major mysteries of the war in which we fight day by day. The Bible says we wrestle not against flesh and blood, but against principalities, powers, rulers of the darkness of this world, spiritual wickedness in high places. These forces that we battle are invisible to the physical eyes.

1. We fight unseen foes. Angels have a lot of respect for Christians because angels can fight the foes they can see, while Christians fight the enemies they cannot see and are winning.

2. Your progress is the battle you win minus the battle you lose. If you fought four battles and lost three, it means you are not moving forward at all.

3. No one is excused from this war. Anyone who says he does not have a war to fight is already defeated. The enemy fights people with different weapons; by the time the devil changed the weapon he was using against Samson, Samson because lost because he did not understand that weapon at all. It was strange to him. He thought it was just beating this or pulling down that. Eventually, that weapon made Samson a grinder of pepper in the camp of the enemy. It is true that Samson prayed for his strength to come back, but he never received

his sight again. No one is excused from the war.

4. Daily casualties are regular occurrences. So you must decide that you will not be a casualty in the battle of life.

5. The more colourful your destiny is, the harder your battle. So, there is no use in crying. You could cry and fill buckets with your tears, that will not move God at all. What moves God is your faith and prayer. As long as you have a colourful destiny, your battle will be very hard. Joseph was a man of destiny, so his battles were hard.

6. You either fight or you perish, there is no middle ground.

7. To be a spiritual civilian is to be a casualty.

WHAT ARE THE KEYS TO SUCCESS IN THIS WARFARE ?

1. Knowledge. If you do not have the knowledge of what you are fighting, you will get into trouble. You must know who Jesus is, and also who the devil is.
2. Holiness unto the Lord.
3. Watchfulness.
4. The word of God.
5. Prayer and fasting.
6. Spiritual violence.
7. Refusal to give up. Refuse to quit.

There is something known as 24-hour breakthrough. Elisha stood by

THE PROHPET — David versus Goliath 1

Okoko-maikoooo-cheii-chei-chei what a monumental insult........

...So, they sent this little boy, to fight me Goliath the giant with great might.

Just try me and I'll show you why little boys, in God's kingdom, are called Giant-killers.
(Watch out for part 2)

the gate of Samaria, and made a declaration: "Tomorrow about this time (within 24hours) there will be a shift." The children of Israel were in Egypt for 430 years; one single night, within 24 hours, the bondage was over. Moses was roaming about in the desert, and one day, he saw a burning bush (an encounter) and within 24 hours, he had become someone who could march to the palace of Pharaoh to order him to let the people of God go.

Within 24 hours, God moved Joseph from prison to palace. That is what is called 24-hour breakthrough. It is the kind of breakthrough that will cause those who saw you a few days ago to see you and not believe you are the same person they saw.

Beloved, in order to experience breakthrough within the next 24 hours, please pray the following twenty-one prayer points violently.

PRAYER POINTS

1. Every power behind my problem, run back to hell fire, in the name of Jesus.
2. My destiny, arise and confuse my enemies, in the name of Jesus.
3. Overhauling angels, repair my life, in the name of Jesus.
4. You stubborn pursuers, hear the strong order from heaven, leave me alone by fire, in the name of Jesus.
5. O God, arise and move me to the front, in the name of Jesus.
6. Thou power of impossibility, shatter, in the name of Jesus.
7. My time of favour come, in the name of Jesus.
8. Every nonentity cage, break, in the name of Jesus.
9. My hidden glory, what are you waiting for? Manifest by fire, in the name of Jesus.
10. Every power that has placed me in an evil queue, die, in the name of Jesus.
11. What my enemy says I will not do, by fire, by thunder, by force, I will do them, in the name of Jesus.
12. My divine ability, speak for me by fire, in the name of Jesus.
13. I shall have miracle, in the name of Jesus.
14. O God, arise and tear away the garment of shame, in the name of Jesus.
15. I receive an outbreak of signs and wonders, in the name of Jesus.
16. Let all my divine helpers lose their sleep until they help me, in the name of Jesus.
17. My Father, set a table for me before my enemies, in the name of Jesus.
18. I decree fast-forward breakthroughs, in the name of Jesus.
19. Season of tribulation, go season of testimony, come, in the name of Jesus.
20. Circle of darkness, die, in the name of Jesus.
21. My problems, fall down and die, in the name of Jesus.

THE MYSTERY OF OUR WARFARE
is a message delivered at the Mountain of Fire and Miracles Ministries by the General Overseer, Dr. D.K. Olukoya.

A CALL TO SERVE

Are you a member of MFM with a burden to help the needy, are you interested in alleviating the plight of the poor or in the spread of the gospel through the sponsorshing of the publication of tracts? Your resources, time and talent can be extended to several groups that are in charge of these areas. These groups include:

o   We care Ministry,
o   Mission Outreach
o   Tracts and Publications
o   Ministry to Drug addicts
o   Campus fellowship
o   Ministry to School
o   Ministry to Glorious Children, etc.

Thus says the Lord, "Verily I say unto you, in as much as ye have done it unto one of the least of these my brethren, ye have done it unto me" Matthew 25 : 40.

WONDERFUL JESUS!

DIVINE TRANSFORMATION

I joined MFM a jobless and frustrated man. I was ejected from my apartment when I could not pay the rent. Somebody gave me a book written by the G.O and directed me to MFM. Since then my life has changed. I got four contracts at a go and this changed my fortunes. In addition, I have a regular employment which provides additional income. Praise the Lord!

Bro. Ola
MFM Ajilo-Ondo

GOD FAVOURS ME

I gave my life to Christ in 1993 and was a member of one of the biggest Pentecostal churches in Nigeria. But I still had some secret sins which I was unable to stop. Finally, I decided to go for deliverance at the MFM Headquarters Lagos. As I started, my wife telephoned me to say that armed robbers came to attack them at home. I realized it was the devil's strategy to make me forsake the deliverance programme. I prayed while on the deliverance ground and the plan of the robbers was not actualized. I was able to undergo the programme successfully and I have overcome my secret sins. Now, all the members of my family are full members of MFM. Also, before the deliverance programme, people and even customers used to run away from me but since after the programme, the whole thing has changed for good. Praise the Lord!

Bro. Ifeanyi
MFM Amichi

I HAVE THE LAST LAUGH

For three academic sessions, the devil placed embargo on my university admission. Through violent prayers and intercessions by men of God, I eventually got admission. Just then, satan afflicted my sponsor with an infectious disease which forced him out of work. With prayers by the campus fellowship and God on my side, I received favour in Christ and went through the course. Out of 800 students that sat for the examination, only 85 passed and I was one of them. Praise God Almighty!

Bro. Ibikunle
MFM Ejigbo

PERMANENT HEALING

In 1998, I had a terrible sickness, which lasted for many years. I lost so many jobs and opportuntunities as a result of the sickness, because employers could not cope with my condition. I was advised to come for deliverance and when I did, the Lord healed me. The sickness stopped. Now, I have a good job and I am enjoying good health. Praise the Lord!

Sis. Sade
MFM Egbeda

SAVED FROM ROBBERS

Recently, the vehicle in which I was travelling broke down on the way. The Holy Spirit helped us to fix it and we left the spot. Immediately we departed, a major robbery operation took place at the same spot and many lives were lost. Praise the Lord!

Bro. Ejiro
MFM Okokomaiko

MULTIPLE BLESSING

I retired from Lagos State Government service after 25 years. I prayed about the prayment of my gratuity and it was paid. My daughter had her wedding and it was successful. God also provided a new accommodation for me miraculously. I could not pay my rent completely but to my surprise, my landlord's wife gave me the money. . Praise the Lord!

Bro. Olujobi
MFM Egbe

THESE BOOKS ARE AVAILABLE FOR SALE
ASK YOUR VENDOR

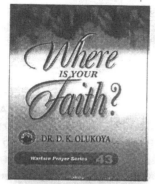

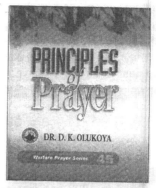

FIRE IN THE WORD is a weekly Spiritual Bulletin of the Mountain of Fire and Miracles Ministries, published by Tracts and Publications Group. All Enquiries should be addressed to The Editor, Mountain of Fire Magazine, 13, Olasimbo Street, off Olumo Road, Onike, P.O. Box 2990, Sabo Yaba, Lagos, Nigeria. Telephone 01-867439, 864631, 868766, 08023180236. Copyright reserved.

FIRE IN THE WORD

Ye Shall Know the Truth, and the Truth Shall Make You Free (John 8:32)

ISSN 978-2947-10-5 Vol. 12 No. 8 Sun. 30th Dec. '07 - Sat. 5th Jan., 2008   ₦10

THE POWER OF A PRINCE

My Year of Uncommon favour & Open Heaven Breakthroughs

Genesis 28

This message is for those who want climb higher than they have done in previous years. It is for those who want to laugh their enemies to scorn. It is also for those who want to decree a thing and it shall be established.

Genesis 32:24: *"And Jacob was left alone; and there wrestled a man with him until the breaking of the day. And when he saw that he prevailed not against him, he touched the hollow of his thigh; and the hollow of Jacob's thigh was out of joint, as he wrestled with him."* Jacob was left with one leg and he still went on struggling. Verse 26: *"And he said, Let me go for the day breaketh.*

And he said, I will not let thee go, except thou bless me."

It is strange to know that the fellow who could bless Jacob was actually trying to run away from him. Jacob had to grab him and say, "I will not let you go unless you bless me." Verse 27: *"And he said unto him, What is thy name. And he said, Jacob. And he said, Thy name shall be called no more Jacob, but Israel: for as a prince hast thou power with God and with men, and hast prevailed. And Jacob asked him, and said, Tell me, I pray thee, thy name. And he*

FIVES MINUTES OF CORRECT PRAYERS CAN CHANGE YOUR DESTINY FOREVER

said, Wherefore is it that dost thou ask after my name? And he blessed him there. And Jacob called the name of the place Peniel for I have seen God face to face, and my life is preserved."

The name Israel means, prince unto God. A prince is a king's son. A king's son has authority in his words. Great men and women queue up for an audience with the king. The appointment book of the king may be filled throughout the year but the king's son can walk right to the king without any appointment. He gains entrance to see the king anytime. He gets his requests granted without having to beg because he is a prince; the king's son.

WHAT IS THE POWER OF A PRINCE ACCORDING TO GENESIS 32?

DELIVERANCE CASE

The power of a prince is power with God and with man. And how does one become a prince with God? The same way that Jacob became one; he wrestled with God in prayers. How do we know that what Jacob was doing was wrestling with God in prayers? The book of Hosea 12:4 explains: *"Yea, he had have power over the angels, and prevailed: and made supplication unto him: he found him in Bethel, and there He spoke with us."*

Jacob wrestled in prayers and made supplications, that was how he became a prince with God. God has many friends but some are closer to Him than others. When you become a prince with God, you get direct easy connection to the throne of grace. Jacob was in a mess; he had taken his brother's birthright through deceit. He was given a very bad name at birth and was also a supplanter, a deceiver. He deceived his father, Isaac to obtain his brother, Esau's blessing and so Esau was pursuing him. He escaped to his uncle called Laban, who was more tricky than him. Laban changed his salary ten times and smuggled the wrong wife into his tent. Laban's place became unfavourable, and he could not return home because his brother Esau was waiting for him there to take revenge. Indeed Jacob was in a terrible mess. He was on the run almost all his life trying to escape from Esau whom he cheated and Laban who deceived him until one day, he met an angel passing by and the wrestling match started. Is it possible that an angle could not break away from the grip of a mere human being? Was Jacob that physically strong as to keep down an angel? The answer is "No." But with the power of prayers, he could do that. Wrestling in prayers that one night changed his life forever.

Fives minutes of correct prayers can change your destiny forever. Likewise His name was changed from Jacob to Israel, one who struggled with God and prevailed, that is, a prince with God.

Romans 15:30 says, *"Now I beseech you, brethren, for the Lord Jesus Christ's sake, and for the love of the Spirit that you strive together with me in your prayers to God for me."* Here we learn a very great lesson, which is that one can actually wrestle with God in prayers, meaning that you must not easily give up with God in prayers like many Christians do. This is an area where the olden days Christians are better than the present-day ones. They sat down and prayed until there was

YOU CAN CHANGE YOUR LIFE COMPLETELY THROUGH WRESTLING IN PRAYERS

victory. Jacob wrestled with an angel through prayers, which is more than physical wrestling. It is the kind of wrestling that brings blessings from God. It is a situation where an invisible God is faced by a visible man. So, Jacob got the title of the man who wrestled with God. When the angel screamed, "Let me go! For the day is breaking" it showed that the angel could not go until Jacob let him.

God welcomes persistent and hard fighters. True faith never gives up and that is why God is called the God of Jacob. We have many people who pray but few are wrestlers. If some people are asked to pray one prayer point for two hours, many of them will lose concentration after 10 or 15 minutes because the wrestling spirit is not in them. Men who have the wrestling spirit can take a single prayer point and pray it for hours and their minds will not wander about. So, if you find that your mind still wanders when you pray, it means you are yet to win the first battle in the school of prayers. We have many who pray but few who wrestle. Likewise there are many watchers, but few observers, there are many who look but few that see. There could be an angel of God by your side now and you may not know. Try to be a wrestler. One of our ancient fathers in the Lord used to say that the more he prayed, the better his life became. So, Paul knew what he was talking about when he said brethren should strive with him in prayer.

Abraham was a very serious wrestler in prayers. When the two angels wanted to destroy Sodom and Gomorrah, he faced them and told them that they could not destroy the righteous with the evil, and they asked him what he wanted. He asked them if they would leave the place alone if they found fifty righteous men and they agreed to leave the place if they found fifty righteous men. He went on like that until he came to ten. Abraham struggled until he got to his number. Perhaps if he had brought the number to two, those people would not have been destroyed.

Moses was another serious prayer wrestler, he

THE PROPHET

PAPA JAMES, I AM TIRED OF THIS SUFFER-HEAD AND NOT BEING FASHIONABLE AGAIN. I HOPE THIS YEAR WILL NOT BE THE STORY OF "GOD WILL PROVIDE" AGAIN O! YOU MUST DO SOMETHING QUICK.

MA JAMES, LET'S BE GRATEFUL FOR WHAT GOD HAS DONE FOR US ALL THESE YEARS, BESIDES OF WHAT USE IF WE GAIN THE WORLD AND LOSE OUR LIVES? THINK WELL AND GLORIFY GOD.

would not leave God until he received an answer. Elijah, Ezekiel, and Daniel were serious prayer wrestlers too. Prayer wrestlers do not give up until they obtain results.

When you are persistent in prayers and refuse to stop until something happens, things will begin to happen. You can change your life completely through wrestling in prayers. All those who cried unto God violently in the Bible were not disappointed. Violent prayers that are raised to the throne of God are always answered.

Perhaps you have been very worried about your situation I would like you to give God a chance to work on whatever has been disturbing you. Ask the Lord to forgive you for any sin that may hinder you from receiving answers to your prayers.

The seven prayer points below must not be taken lightly. They are Bible prayers that give instant results. Therefore, I counsel you to pray them aggressively.

PRAYER POINTS

1. My problems, fall by the sword of God, in the name of Jesus.

2. Oh God, arise and break the head of the dragon of my father's house, in Jesus' name.

3. Every anger of the enemy against my life become a point of testimony by fire, in the name of Jesus.

4. Oh stars of heaven, arise and fight for me, in Jesus' name.

5. Every assembly of violent men against me, scatter, in Jesus' name.

6. Thou powers of the night, release my virtues now, in Jesus' name.

7. Oh God, arise and perfect every thing that concerns my life, in Jesus' name.

THE POWER OF A PRINCE
is a message delivered at the Mountain of Fire and Miracles Ministries by the General Overseer, Dr. D.K. Olukoya.

A CALL TO SERVE

Are you a member of MFM with a burden to help the needy, are you interested in alleviating the plight of the poor or in the spread of the gospel through the sponsorshing of the publication of tracts? Your resources, time and talent can be extended to several groups that are in charge of these areas. These groups include:

o   We care Ministry,
o   Mission Outreach
o   Tracts and Publications
o   Ministry to Drug addicts
o   Campus fellowship
o   Ministry to School
o   Ministry to Glorious Children, etc.

Thus says the Lord, "Verily I say unto you, in as much as ye have done it unto one of the least of these my brethren, ye have done it unto me" Matthew 25 : 40.

WONDERFUL JESUS!

CHRONIC ULCER GONE

I had ulcer for many years and could not get a cure in spite of all the places I went to for healing. I was directed to this church and was counselled to go for deliverance. During the deliverance programme, especially on the third day, I vomited lumps of blood and since then I have been perfectly healed. Praise the Lord!

Sis. Josephine
MFM Ogudu/Ojota

GOD DELIVERS ME FROM EVIL BURIAL

All my businesses collapsed and I went home and met the pastor of MFM Aguleri branch. He advised that I should do a house cleansing of my father's compound. I and other members of the family went to my village and during the prayer section, my father was forced by the Holy Spirit to show where he buried a charm of greatness for 20 years in his parlour. The caldron was dug out and destroyed. He confessed that he did it so that nobody in the family, including any of his sons or daughters would be richer than him. Today, I am back to Abuja free and my business resotored. Praise the Lord!

Bro. Ikechukwu
MFM Abuja

DIVINE BREAKTHROUGH

Four years ago, I paid a large sum of money into my bank account in Abuja hoping to come to Lagos and withdraw it for my trip abroad. But when I got to Lagos, I discovered that the bank had gone distressed. Since then I have been living from hand to mouth. I met the General Overseer and he gave some prayer points to pray everyday. Also, I was always at every Breakthrough Clinic. Today, God has answered my prayers. The distressed bank has been acquired by a bigger bank and my money has been paid. I am preparing to travel abroad. Praise the Lord!

Bro. Madumere
MFM Headquarters

DIVINE TOUCH FOR SAFE DELIVERY

I thank God for His intervention during my wife's delivery. Satan tried to create a problem for my wife during pregnancy but failed. The scan reports were terrible. The doctor said she would have to undergo a caesarian session but God intervened and she was delivered safely without surgery. Praise the Lord!

Bro. Emmanuel
MFM Abule Anu

SAVED FROM ACCIDENT

Some weeks ago, on my way to Ibadan, a van carrying school children left its lane and ran into mine, on very high speed. As I shouted blood of Jesus, I saw my truck totally avoiding hitting the bus. The accident was averted. Also, since the beginning of the forty days vigil programme, God has proved Himself mighty in my life. Praise the Lord!

Bro. Peter
MFM Asoro, Benin city

GOD SAVES ME FROM PROGRAMMED ACCIDENT

I was planning to travel to the eastern part of the country, I dreamt of being involved in an accident. I went to the man of God who prayed for me and cancelled the spirit of accident. During the journey, the accident manifested physically but God delivered me. Praise the Lord!

Bro. Kayode
MFM Ikotun

DELIVERED FROM SATANIC DEPOSIT IN THE THROAT

A demonic deposit was in my throat for a very long time. I tried many things to get it without success. I went for deliverance and the evil deposit disappeared from my throat during prayers. Praise the Lord!

Sis. Bisi
MFM Abeokuta

EVER FAITHFUL GOD

I am very new in MFM. But before I came to MFM, I lost my job. Later, I went for deliverance and to my greatest surprise, I got a very good offer for employment. Praise the Lord!

Bro. Adebowale
MFM Abaranje

LOST PROPERTY RESTORED

I thank God who restored my lost property. Recently, when I was elevated, all my enemies were exposed and put to shame. Praise the Lord!

Bro. Kunle
MFM Aguda-Surulere

THESE BOOKS ARE AVAILABLE FOR SALE
ASK YOUR VENDOR

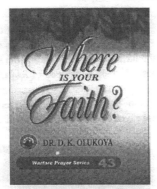

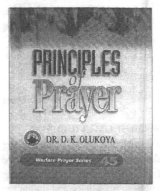

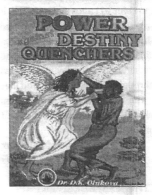

FIRE IN THE WORD, is a weekly Spiritual Bulletin of the Mountain of Fire and Miracles Ministries, published by Tracts and Publications Group. All Enquiries should be addressed to The Editor, Mountain of Fire Magazine, 13, Olasimbo Street, off Olumo Road, Onike, P.O. Box 2990, Sabo Yaba, Lagos, Nigeria. Telephone 01-867439, 864631, 868766, 08023180236. Copyright reserved.

Ye Shall Know the Truth, and the Truth Shall Make You Free (John 8:32)

ISSN 1595 - 7314 Vol. 12 No. 9 Sun. 6th - Sat. 12th Jan., 2008

THE SON OF PERDITION

My year of unprecedented greatness and unmatchable increase
Deuteronomy 28:13, Psalm 71:21, Ephesians 3:20, Psalm 92:10

Our message this week titled, "The son of perdition" is an all important one for those who are working for God in one category or the other,. This message will help them ensure that they themselves do not perish while they are trying to get others saved. In John 17:12, we see the eternal word of our Lord Jesus Christ, which says, *"While I was with them in the world, I kept them in thy name: those that thou gavest me I have kept, and none of them is lost, but the son of perdition; that the scripture might be fulfilled."*

2 Thessalonians 2:3 says, *"Let no man deceive you by any means: for that day shall not come, except there come a falling away first, and that man of sin be revealed, the son of perdition."*

Hebrew 10:39: *"But we are not of them who draw back unto perdition; but of them that believe to the saving of the soul."*

In Acts 1:17, we read what Peter says about Judas. The passage reveals how gifted Judas was. Acts 1:17: *"For he was numbered with us, and had obtained part of this ministry."* Judas was numbered with the apostles and had part of the ministry but Jesus said, *"The Son of man goeth as it is written of him, but woe unto that man by whom the Son of man is betrayed. It had been good for that man if he had not been born."* (Matthew 26:24)."

It means that it is better for a person not to be born at all than to be a daughter or son of perdition.

Many years ago, a certain man of God had a revelation, where God took him up and he saw heaven and all the beautiful things therein. He was so happy with the place that he did not want to come back but the Lord told him that He had another place to show him. So they went down and there they saw hell fire. He saw fire entering into the nostrils of men and coming out; he .saw fire looking like worms crawling in and out. He saw men and women crying and groaning in bitter lamentation. He saw many members of his church that had been buried at the cementery in hell fire; he looked at the sufferings on their faces and broke down and cried. There and then he made up his mind never to go there. As he made up his mind on that the Lord said to him, "Son, do you know why many of these people are here?" He said, "Father, it is because they were sinners." But the Lord said it was not and gave him reasons why they landed in hell fire. The reasons are as follows.

1. "This is how they do it."
2. "It does not matter. What is so serious about it."
3. "They knew the truth too late."

These are the thee major things that take men to hell fire. In fact, hell fire is truth known too late. I always pray that anyone that wants to serve God should first of all pray for the revelation of heaven and hell fire before going into the field. Ministers who have had that revelation preach the gospel effectively. The reason many ministers of God are still playing with sin is that

THE ENEMY HAS A WAY OF PUTTING SOMEBODY WHERE HE KNOWS THE PERSON WILL SOMEMESAULT

they have not seen the revelation ‹ these two places yet. When you s‹ these the pictures of heaven and hel what people are running about for i the world will lose its hold upon yo then the words of Ecclesiastes th: says vanity upon vanity, all is vani will be very clear to you. The world riches such as marriage, cars, hous‹ etc that people fight to acqui sometimes turn to big problems f‹ them.

When you see the pictures ‹ heaven and hell, your life will n‹ remain the same again. It is wh pushes the people you see shoutir and sweating inside commutter bus‹ or at the bus stops preaching tl gospel. That is why one of n favourite passages in the scriptur‹ is that which says, "Though I prea‹ the Gospel, I have nothing to glo of, but necessity is laid upon me, w‹ is me if I preach not the gospel." M‹ who have seen the two cam| conclude that it is a serious matter.

WHAT IS PERDITION?

Perdition means ruin. It means lo‹ destruction or condemnation. It mea eternal death or punishment. It is tl opposite of salvation. A close stu‹ of the Bible reveals that tl expression, "son of perdition" is us‹ to describe only two persons in t scriptures. The first person was Jud and the second was the anti-Chri That of Judas is found in John 17: and that of the anti-Christ is found 2 Thessalonians 2:3. The life of Jud .gives us a good picture of what tl son of perdition is: Judas was chos‹ as one of the disciples of Jesus. I was chosen after Jesus had done vigil to get His disciples, meaning that Jesus had prayed all night to get Judas. This is worthy of note. It is possible that somebody had interceded in prayer to get you saved, somebody might have prayed hard for you to give your life to Jesus and therefore you surrendered your life to Jesus. But the Bible says, "Let him that thinketh he standeth, take heed lest he fall."

Judas was chosen after much prayer. He was sent out as one the twelve. When Jesus said, "Behold, I give unto you power to tread upon serpents and scorpions …" and when He sent them out two by two to heal the sick and raise the dead, Judas was one of them. Many Christians today have never raised the dead or prayed for the sick to be made whole. But Judas went far, he raised the dead and prayed for the sick to be made whole. Many Christians have not got to the level Judas got to before he eventually went into perdition. Judas accompanied Jesus around, he watched and observed the character and power of Jesus. He heard Him teach, he heard Him claiming to be the Messiah. But with all these, Judas never came to full faith in the Messiah. Part of the strategy of the enemy to thoroughly disgrace and destroy Judas was to put him in charge of money; he became the treasurer. Beloved, be careful so that the post you are given does not ruin you. The seemingly exalted position that a person finds himself may be that which will close the gate of heaven against him. Perhaps you are the mother in Israel in your church, be careful so that the position does not close the gate of heaven against you. Judas was put in charge of money; the enemy is an expert at giving what he knows will destroy a person properly.

DELIVERANCE CASE

The enemy has a way of putting somebody where he knows the person will somemesault. He did it to Judas. Judas was the one who complained that some ointment was being wasted on the feet of Jesus. When Jesus entered into Jerusalem with the shout of "Hosannah" and praises from the people, the Pharisees were very envious and wanted to destroy Him. The same Pharisees wanted to kill Lazarus, because the fact that Lazarus kept walking about was a testimony that Jesus indeed is the Son of God. They did not know how to get at Jesus but Judas presented himself before them with a proposal and began to look for a moment, and a way to betray Jesus from that day.

Jesus tried so many things to stop Judas from entering into that bondage but he remained adamant. When they sat at supper and Jesus told them that one of them would betray Him only Judas was indicted but that was not enough to caution him. Jesus indicated that somebody would betray Him and Judas accepted that satan would enter into his life. Beloved, I want you to know that the devil entered into Judas in the presence of Jesus.

Judas identified Jesus with a kiss, and when they arrested Jesus, he was full of regret. He took the money back to the people but they rejected it and told him that he had delivered the person they wanted. Judas threw their money down, ran away and hanged himself. They used his money to buy a piece of land where they bury the dead. That is a short history of the life of Judas who the Bible calls, the son of perdition.

WHAT ARE THE LESSONS WE CAN LEARN FROM ALL THESE?

Judas was of a tribe close to that of Jesus. He knew Jesus Christ, he spent years travelling and walking with Jesus but money still controlled him. The enemy was able to pick him as the best candidate to betray Jesus. Judas exercised authority to perform miracles. He held an important position.

Perhaps Judas could serve as the greatest example of someone who wasted opportunity in the Bible. I am yet to see anyone who named his child Judas, because that name is synonymous with shame. If Judas had conducted himself well it was possible that in our Bible today, we would see a gospel according to Judas, but all that is left as a memorial about him is a field of blood.

Unfortunately, there are many sons and daughters of perdition in the world today. It is also sad that a lot of people who go to church do not have a vision of heaven, many are not heaven-bound. Some do not want Jesus to come now because they know that if He comes now, they will not go with Him. But the truth is that He can come at anytime.

WHO IS A SON OR DAUGHTER OF PEDITION?

There are so many of them in our world today. They are those who are chosen but are not saved. For example, when a man of God looks at a person and concludes that he or she is a wonderful brother or sister and makes him or her a house fellowship leader, or a pastor or a chorister etc., such a person has been chosen but is not really saved. He or she is a son or daughter of perdition.

A son or daughter of perdition is somebody who has been chosen but prefers to be a vessel of dishonour. He or she decides to tow the path that will not lead to good progress or honour God. Sons or daughters of perdition are the unsaved miracle workers, unsaved pastors, unsaved pastors, unsaved deliverance ministers. Nowadays, when you pick up the Bible of some pastors, instead of finding tracts what you find are complimentary cards of big men and businessmen and when you grab their phones, the numbers stored there are those of people who they get money from, it is a sign of perdition.

Sons of perdition are those who are holding important positions in church but are very far from heaven. They sing and talk about heaven but are very far from it. They sing, "You need not look for me in Egypt but that is where they are. They are foremost in stumbling; they are quick to see a backslider and to say because somebody backslid they too must backslide. A son of perdition is a strong tree in the house of God that has already fallen but is still standing. Ants have eaten up inside. Although it is standing, it is gone.

SIN NEVER DELIVERS WHAT IT PROMISES

A son of perdition is somebody who is a lost coin inside the church. The Bible talks about three types of lost entities: lost sheep, lost coin and the prodigal son. A lost sheep is easy to find because it will be crying on the streets. The lost sheep represents unbelievers who are still in the world being harassed by the devil. But there is a big problem with a lost coin.

A coin can be lost in a room for one year and no one will not know where it is. You could be sweeping the room every time but your broom will not touch it., many are lost right inside the church, they have disappeared before God. They are disobedient before God, they have deserted God; they are already disoriented. There are many people in the church who are very good actors and very good pretenders. Such people should know that the fire of God, the power of God, and His judgment will search them out. When a person refuses to repent and allows the label of the "son of perdition" to come upon him; the Bible says, it would have been better if such a person was not born.

A son or daughter of perdition is somebody who has the light of God and opportunity but abuses the privilege. Opportunity determines responsibility so if you abuse the privilege and God sees that you are not serious, one day, His judgment will come down. Any brother that beats up his wife is a son of perdition. Likewise a sister that fights her husband is a daughter of perdition.

You are a son or daughter of perdition when you see the manifestation of the power of God and still refuses to give your life to Christ.

There are many sisters who started attending Sunday school when they were three or four years old, they grew knowing about Christ but today they can give you a list of about twenty or thirty men they have slept with; they are daughters of perdition. There are pastors of perditions and bishops of perdition. They call themselves pastors and bishops but go about committing immorality. These are serious matters. The Bible says, "Let him that thinketh he standeth, take heed lest he fall." You may say, "I thank God, nobody can see me." But God sees you. God is watching, you may think you are hiding or masquerading, but masquerading is only for a while, very soon you will be seen for who you are.

A son of perdition is somebody who is nonchalant about the things of God. He has all possible spiritual advantage but is nonchalant. Such a person belongs to the category of those who make choices that lead them up to destruction. They will never know that sin never delivers what it promises.

A son of perdition is someone who cooperates with satan to get ahead. A son or daughter of perdition is somebody who is associated with Christ, or near to Christ, engaged in the ministry but not truly saved.

There are ushers of perdition, choristers of perdition, and pastors of perdition; they are just there but have not really found life, they are not born again.

A son or daughter of perdition is anyone who neglects all the obstacles that God puts on his or her way to prevent him or her from getting destroyed.

The son of perdition is someone who becomes sad but does not repent, like Judas, he was very remorseful but did not repent. Many people are in prison for committing one offence or the other, some of them are sad not because they believe that what they did was wrong but because they were caught, if they were not caught, they would not feel sorry.

A son or daughter of perdition is that person on whose heart Jesus has been knocking but he or she refuses to open. Sons and daughters of perdition are those seeking the hand of Jesus and not His face; they are only after what they can get, and not His happiness. The son of perdition is someone who has the opportunity for repentance but does not take it. Such a person refuses to destroy the spots, wrinkles and blemishes in his life.

A son of perdition is a person who rejects the correction of the Holy Spirit. The Holy Spirit is a gentlemen, if He corrects you once, twice, thrice and you keep repeating what you are saying or doing, a time will come when you will hear His voice no more, then perdition sets in.

The son of perdition is somebody who listens to anointed preachers, but remains untouched and unmoved by the Spirit of God.

A son of perdition is someone who has stopped serving God and is angry with God because God has not done what he wants Him to do.

A son of perdition is someone who never breaks down at his or her sin to ask God for forgiveness.

Sons and daughters of perdition are greedy for money; they are serving God because of money. They do praise worship but do not pray. They worship but the worship is not from the heart. They have very little contact with God after leaving the services. Some people come to church when they like and only

THE PROPHET

BRO. JOHN, WE HAVE NOT BEEN SEEING YOU AT THE FELLOWSHIP THESE DAYS, HOPE NOTHING?

AH, BRO. JOE, I AM SO BUSY THESE DAYS THAT I DONT EVEN HAVE THE TIME TO EAT NOT TO TALK OF FELLOWSHIP. IT IS LONDON TODAY, AMERICA TOMORROW MY BROTHER THE LORD IS GOOD!

REMEMBER THAT IT IS THE ALMIGHTY GOD THAT HAS GIVEN YOU POWER TO GET WEALTH AND TO EAT WEALTH SERVE THE LORD!

read their Bible when they want to preach to others. They are the sons of perdition. Anyone who comes to a Bible-believing church and hears the word of God but does not change is a son of perdition

There is a place for weeping and gnashing of teeth, there is a place known as the bottomless pit, a place of utter darkness, a place known as the palace of sorrow, where the fire is never quenched, a place where there is no rest day or night, a place where the worms do not die, a place of everlasting destruction, a place of regret and a place of suffering, that is where the sons of perdition end up.

Beloved, you had better become serious so that you do not end up in hell fire. If you remain as the son or daughter of perdition, the end will be disastrous. It is time to repent and ask God to forgive you. Do not be like the Israelites who were going about in the wilderness under God's protection but they were already under a curse of wastage; God had pronounced a curse that they were all going to be wasted. So despite this, God was still protecting them and they were eating their manna. It is just like somebody who bought a Christmas goat and was feeding the goat right from the month of June and the goat was rejoicing and dancing not knowing that its end would come in December. The Israelites were walking under God's protection in the wilderness with the pillar of fire and the pillar of cloud, but there was already a sentence of death upon them.

Those who are serious with their salvation should pray that God should show them a picture of heaven. They have seen enough of spirit husbands, masquerades and all types of terrible things, it is high time they began to see visions of heaven. Moses cried unto the Lord, and told Him that he was tired of seeing this cloud, and wanted to see Him, and Moses saw God. Now, we are under a better covenant than Moses, everybody ought to key into heaven.

Beloved, you had better be wise on time, the end of the age is practically here. If you take this issue seriously, things will change but if you take it nonchalantly, you will be writing you name down on the agenda of perdition. It does not matter whether you are a pastor, deliverance minister or General Overseer, those things are just ordinary labels and will get nobody anywhere. What is the use of your position when you are already a child of perdition and cannot key to heaven? What is the use of your post when you know that heaven is far from your vision? You must cry to the Lord for mercy.

Beloved, you have to make up your mind that things must not continue as they have been. If you do not see heaven while you are alive, you cannot see it when you are dead.

PRAYER POINTS

1. My Father, I have failed you, help me today, in the name of Jesus.

2. Satanic visions, die, heavenly visions, appear, in the name of Jesus.

3. Every power of the iniquity of my father's house, die by the blood of Jesus, in Jesus' name.

4. I shall not repeat the iniquity of my father's house, in the name of Jesus.

5. I shall not draw back into perdition, in the name of Jesus.

6. Blood of Jesus, purge my sins away, in the name of Jesus.

7. Father Lord, reveal yourself to me, in the name of Jesus.

THE SON OF PERDITION

is a message delivered at the Mountain of Fire and Miracles Ministries by the General Overseer, Dr. D.K. Olukoya.

A CALL TO SERVE

Are you a member of MFM with a burden to help the needy, are you interested in alleviating the plight of the poor or in the spread of the gospel through the sponsorshing of the publication of tracts? Your resources, time and talent can be extended to several groups that are in charge of these areas. These groups include:

o　　We care Ministry,
o　　Mission Outreach
o　　Tracts and Publications
o　　Ministry to Drug addicts
o　　Campus fellowship
o　　Ministry to School
o　　Ministry to Glorious Children, etc.

Thus says the Lord, "Verily I say unto you, in as much as ye have done it unto one of the least of these my brethren, ye have done it unto me" Matthew 25 : 40.

WONDERFUL JESUS!

DELIVERANCE FROM POISON

Through negligence I drank poison which gave me a lot of pains. I was asked to go for deliverance. I was afraid because of fasting. However, I did it by the grace of God and to the glory of God, I went through deliverance with fasting and prayers and the poison completely flushed out from my body. Praise God!

Sis. Esther
MFM Oworonshoki I

STRONGMAN DIES

After I joined MFM, I was directed to go for deliverance because of joblessness. I went for the programme and a man in my family died after confessing to witchcraft. Shortly after, his partner also died. Few months later, I got a good job where I was made the managing director. Praise the Lord!

Bro. Marvelous
MFM Morogbo

GOD OF THE SUDDENLY

I was demoted from Grade level 12 to grade level 6. I started praying about the situation. During a visit I went to Akure to see my son, I decided to go to the State Primary Education Board (SPEB) and God in His mercy, sent a man of God to me who assisted me and the demotion was cancelled and I was restored to my position. Praise the Lord!

Sis. Dorcas
MFM Ikare Akoko

GOD SAVES MY HOUSE AND PROPERTY FROM BURNING

Sometime ago, I plugged the water heater and forgot to put it off before I went to work. Before the water dried up, thre was power outage which was not restored until I came back home. Secondly, God provided a shop for me after a long search for one and the money to pay the rent. Praise the Lord!

Sis. Dupe
MFM Abeokuta

GOD DID THE IMPOSSIBLE IN MY LIFE

For good 12 years, I was a choir master in a dead church and was wallowing in abject poverty. One day, God spoke to me to go to Mountain of Fire and Miracles Ministries and very soon after I joined this church, the Lord intervened in my life and today, I can feed myself and I am doing what I thought I could never do in the next 10 years. Praise the Lord!

Bro. Segun
MFM Abule-Egba

GOD CANCELS THE VOW OF THE ENEMY

Some people boasted and vowed that I would not see the end of last year. But to the glory of God I was not consumed last year. God kept me alive till the end of the year. Praise God!

Sis. Wansoba
MFM Egbe Zonal

GOD HEALS MY SON

My son took ill to the point of death but after some intercessory prayers by brethren, he became well again. Praise the Lord!

Bro. Oluwagbemi
MFM Olowora

THE LORD SAVED US

I am a securing officer in a company. I was on duty with another colleague when armed robbers attacked the company premises. They asked us to lie down on the floor. As we did this, I went to the Lord in silent prayers of safety and protection. After a couple of minutes they departed and we thank God that we were not hurt. Praise the Lord!

Bro. Benjamin
MFM Ejigbo

OTHER HIGHLIGHTS

● Groups and individuals involved in evangelism should register for free evangelism materials at the Tracts and Publications office. Registration ends on December 13, 2007.

○ Individuals who wish to represent the Headquarters at the MFM Bible Quiz competition on the 15th December, 2007 should gather at the auditorium near the MFM Press on Sunday 9th December, 2007 at 12.30pm. There are lots of fantastic prizes to be won.

● Members should seize the opportunity of the Bookfair to purchase their Christian Literature and other materials at reduced prices.

FIRE IN THE WORD, is a weekly Spiritual Bulletin of the Mountain of Fire and Miracles Ministries, published by Tracts and Publications Group. All Enquiries should be addressed to The Editor, Mountain of Fire Magazine, 13, Olasimbo Street, off Olumo Road, Onike, P.O. Box 2990, Sabo Yaba, Lagos, Nigeria. Telephone 01- 867439, 864631, 868766, 08023180236. E-mail: mfmtractsandpublications@yahoo.com Copyright reserved.

FIRE IN THE WORD

Ye Shall Know the Truth, and the Truth Shall Make You Free (John 8:32)

ISSN 1595 - 7314   Vol. 12   No. 10   Sun. 13th - Sat. 19th Jan., 2008   ₦10

2008 AD - A YEAR OF
DRAMATIC CHANGES

My year of unprecedented greatness and unmatchable increase

Deuteronomy 28:13, Psalm 71:21, Ephesians 3:20, Psalm 92:10

Beloved, our message this week forcuses on the prophetic picture of the year 2008 AD. A careful look at it will give you proper direction for the year. God answers prayers and there is no situation that God cannot change. One key factor about this year is that it should be a year of serious minded, highly focused, and high-voltage praying.

In 2007, there were serious crises in all areas of human endeavour which seemed to defy any permanent solution. These crises invaded practically all aspects of the society and all facets of human experience, whether social, economical, political or religious. The never-ending search for solution to these problems has continued. Human theories that were heralded before are no longer effective, even psychology and education can no longer help the situation. There seem to be a global spirit of confusion and aimlessness in operation. Right from the year 2007 as well, we find various governments and politicians struggling under complex problems they could not solve. It got so bad that the relevance of education is now being questioned. Philosophical foundations are beginning to crumble and the economy is even frustrating renowned economists. So, it is clear to all that these crises have defied all human solutions. However, the year 2008 is a year of mixtures depending on which side you are.

1. It shall be a year of dramatic changes, there will be a strange shaking of people and places, that will happen by divine order.

2. This year, the old order which has not fulfilled its purpose shall be turned away to make way for the new plan of God.

3. This year, the chain of the enemy that has held many of God's people back will be broken into pieces.

4. It shall be a year of deliverance accompanied by supernatural confirmation of the Holy Ghost.

THE TREES OF THE FIELDS WILL CLAP THEIR HANDS FOR THE RIGHTEOUS THIS YEAR ACCORDING TO ISAIAH 55:12.

5. This year, many people will come into their rightful inheritance. A lot of people will get to positions where they were never expected to be.

6. This year, some people's seat that were stolen shall be mysteriously retored.

7. This year, angelic ministry will manifest openly to help God's people. Many people will see angels but will not know.

8. This year, there shall be increase in divine opportunities and harvest. All those who are running crooked businesses will go down, while those who are doing genuine businesses will come up because of the level of divine opportunities and harvest. I counsel you to sow liberally this year so that you can have a bumper harvest.

9. This year, those who have been hidden away by the enemy will begin to manifest.

10. This year shall be a year of new beginnings, new directions, regenerations and resurrection.

11. Unfortunately, it shall be a year of climate madness; unless accurate prayers are said, weather disaster will get worse.

12. This year, there shall be a rage of natural disasters. It will begin slowly, then gather speed and increase in frequency, unless we terminate it with prayer.

13. This year, there shall be a lot of aggressive political boiling in many nations.

14. This year, the camp of the enemy of those who have been praying for a long time for their deliverance to come and are living a holy life will suffer terrible destruction.

15. This year, the Almighty will silence clever political animals that are troubling the peace of Nigeria.

16. It shall be a year of massive failure for disloyal people. So, wherever you are working or rendering service to anyone do it with all your heart, be loyal. Disloyalty will not yield any good result this year, rather it will result into disaster.

17. This year, unless intensive prayers are said, there will be an emergence of new and difficult diseases that even

scientists will find difficult to understand.

18. This year, the anointing for high level of success will fall upon righteous people who are in business.

19. This year, the enemies of the righteous will be buried underneath the new wave of uncommon prosperity that God is going to give His people.

20. This year, the Almighty will give insight, foresight and prophetic precision to His people to enable them to excel. It will be very sad for anyone who is not

born-again this year, because he or she will lose to those who are born-again.

21. This year, there will be a serious transfer of wealth into the hands of God's people, especially those who have decided to be divine bankers for the Lord.

22. This year, there will be progress, provision and protection for the righteous whether the devil likes it or not. In fact, the trees of the fields will clap their hands for the righteous this year according to Isaiah 55:12.

23. This year, there will be a massive recruitment of young people into destructive associations, and very strange wastage of young lives. We need to pray hard and talk to the young ones more this year. The enemy used the whole of 2007 to perfect an agenda to waste youths this year.

24. This year, true children of God (the elect) who are scattered about in wrong churches shall begin to relocate to where they should go because the time is at hand.

25. This year, the enemy will launch heart-breaking and unbelievable attacks against marriages. We need to pray hard, meaning that this year, we should learn to control our mouth more.

26. This year, many small scale businessmen shall receive the anointing for explosive growth.

27. This year, cleverly concealed dark secrets of false prophets shall be revealed.

28. This year, concerning our nation, the arrester shall be arrested, the cap shall launch a fight against the shoes, the balloon shall slay the blower, and the habitation of the crocodile shall all of a sudden eject the crocodile. The madness of evil priests and priestesses shall manifest because the patient shall now become the doctor; the manipulator shall be manipulated and the adjuster shall be adjusted. This message for our nation is coded, I pray the Holy Spirit will give you the understanding.

29. This year, there will be a rage of silencer diseases; we need to pray against them.

30. This year, there will be a rage of the spirit, which the Bible calls "Leviathan spirit." It is an evil power in the seas. (Job 41). Job 41 gives us an understanding of this spirit. It says: *"Canst thou draw out leviathan with an hook or his tongue with a cord which thou lettest*

THIS IS NOT A YEAR TO ALLOW WORRY AND ANXIETY TO FINISH YOU OFF

down? Canst thou put an hook into his nose or bore his jaw through with a thorn?" (Job 41:1-2). Verse 34: *"He beholdeth all high things; he is a king over all the children of pride."*

There will be a rage of leviathan spirit, and one major characteristic of leviathan spirit is pride. This year, many people will exhibit foolish pride, which will put them into serious trouble. They will exhibit pride of body, intellect, sexual power, worldly things, power, money, looks and show disrespect for authorities. All forms of pride are backed up by the spirit of leviathan. It will be a terrible thing too this year because the leviathan in the sea will go into a rage, but for us here at MFM, this year is encoded in four scriptures: Deuteronomy 28:13: *"And the Lord shall make thee the head, and not the tail; and thou shalt be above only, and thou shalt not be beneath..."* Psalm 71:21: "Thou shalt increase my greatness and comfort me on every side." Psalm 92:10: "But my horn shalt thou exalt like the horn of an unicorn; I shall be anointed wiht fresh oil." and Ephesians 3:20: "Now unto him that is able to do exceeding abundantly above all that we ask or think. So for the Mountain of Fire and Miracles Ministries, it is a year of "Unprecedented greatness, and unmatchable increase."

Whatever you say, Jesus is still the answer. Prayer will work if you pray it correctly. The Holy Spirit is still available now for us to consult, God still inhabits the praises of His people, There will still be room at the cross for those who will run to the cross.

SURVIVAL STRATEGIES FOR THIS YEAR

1. Pray accurately, meaning that you could pray inaccurate prayer and enter into trouble.

2. Simplify your life. Do not live a sophisticated life.

3. You must take one day at a time. This is not a year to allow worry and anxiety to finish you off. You must obey the injunction of Jesus: "Sufficient unto the day is the evil thereof." It means you must depart from the school of worry completely.

4. Live within your budget. For example, do not plan a wedding or burial that will run you into debts. Your creditor may come with a gun or cutlass and finish you off. Cut your coat according to your cloth.

5. Watch your mouth. Listen more and talk less.

6. Read your Bible and carry it with you wherever you go.
I read the story of an Israeli soldier who was shot and he fell down. His colleagues thought he was deed but he was not. By the time they checked him, they found that the bullet hit his chest pocket where he had a Bible. The bullet penetrated through the Bible until it got to Psalm 91 and stopped. That was how God saved him.

7. Eat the right things.

8. Get organized. Organize your life well. Avoid coming late to services.

9. .Cultivate the habit of listening to messages of men of God; at least two or three per week.

10. Find time to be alone with God everyday. Do not joke with your quiet time.

THE PROPHET

David versus Goliath 3

Goliath of Gath, today, my God, whom I serve shall surely deliver you into my hands like fried chicken. And I will cut off your head.

Wonderful... satan gave me an incomplete information on how to fight JESUS people...

11. Make friends with godly people, and stop befriending those who are ungodly. You can minister to them but you do not have to join them in in their activities.

12. Memorize more scriptures this year. The more scriptures you memorize, the more your spirit man becomes strong.

13. Develop a forgiving attitude.

14. Work hard; be diligent. Do not be lazy at all.

15. Read more spiritually uplifting books. You should read at least five good books in a year. Cut down on what you spend in buying magazines that will not move your destiny forward.

16. Do not neglect the assembly of God's people, and your family altar. The Bible actually issues a curse against families that neglect their family altars. Jeremiah 10:25 says, *"Pour out thy fury upon the heathen that know thee not, and upon the families that call not on thy name for they have eaten up Jacob, and devoured him, and consumed him, and have made his habitation desolate."* Do not allow God to pour His fury upon your family.

17. Be humble. Let pride die.

18. Live a holy life. The key to tremendous enjoyment this year is holy living and aligning your life to the truth of God's word. A life of decect,hypocrisy and lack of seriousness with the Lord will lead one into trouble this year. Thank God, He will hearken to the cry of those who will humble themselves and cry to Him.

This year, we need to work harder than we did last year. We need to realize that some of the methods people think can solve problems will not solve any problems this year. Everyone needs to become a student in the school of intercession and God will help us.

PRAYER POINTS

1. God, arise and let your light shine over Nigeria, in the name of Jesus.

2. Blood of Jesus, sanitize Nigeria, in the name of Jesus.

3. Every enemy of the peace and prosperity of Nigeria, die, in the name of Jesus.

4. Every grave dug for me, scatter, in the name of Jesus.

5. Every power prolonging my problems, die, in the name of Jesus.

6. Every power challenging God in my life, die, in the name of Jesus.

7. Every native doctor assigned to waste my life, carry your load, in the name of Jesus.

8. My lost blessings in foreign lands, arise, locate me now, in the name of Jesus.

2008 AD -THE YEAR OF DRAMATIC CHANGES

is a message delivered at the Mountain of Fire and Miracles Ministries by the General Overseer, Dr. D.K. Olukoya.

A CALL TO SERVE

Are you a member of MFM with a burden to help the needy, are you interested in alleviating the plight of the poor or in the spread of the gospel through the sponsorshing of the publication of tracts? Your resources, time and talent can be extended to several groups that are in charge of these areas. These groups include:

o   We care Ministry,
o   Mission Outreach
o   Tracts and Publications
o   Ministry to Drug addicts
o   Campus fellowship
o   Ministry to School
o   Ministry to Glorious Children, etc.

Thus says the Lord, "Verily I say unto you, in as much as ye have done it unto one of the least of these my brethren, ye have done it unto me" Matthew 25 : 40.

WONDERFUL JESUS!

DELIVERANCE FROM IDOLS AND SPIRIT OF DEATH

I was a worshipper of many idols which included marine spirit for many years. Sometime ago, I was sick to the point of death and was introduced to MFM I was told of salvation and the power of Jesus to save and was prayed for. Three days later, I dropped dead in my house, and members of family rushed to MFM and called the pastor who came with his prayer warrior and they prayed for me. My family gave up on me but to their amazement, after 30 minutes, I was revived. Today, and hale and hearty and back to my business. Praise the Lord!

Bro. Okagbuo
MFM Aguleri

DIVINE HEALING

I had some swelling in my body. But during a PMCH programme, the G.O mentioned my case and I received my healing instantly. Praise the Lord!

Sis. Oladunke
MFM Headquarters

GOD GIVES ME A NEW LIFE

Since I was born, I had never experienced peace. I was living a life of fragmentation. Bus since I joined this ministry, my life has changed for good. Praise the Lord!

Sis. Okagbuo
MFM Aguleri

DIVINE INTERVENTION

Recently, as my husband was traveling to Lagos, the vehicle he boarded was involved in an accident. As victims were being rescued from the vehicle, fire broken out. But I thank God that nothing happened to my husband. Praise the Lord!

Sis. Orhiene
MFM Benin

GOD STOPS THE HUMILIATION

Soon after I gave my life to Christ, my inlaws three me out and I started sleeping at the balcony. I prayed that God should give me a house where I can stay and God did it for me. Even those who were mocking me can now see the hand of God upon my life. Indeed

God is awesome. Praise the Lord!

Sis. Josephine
MFM Ojodu

DIVINE VISITATION AFTER 19 YEARS

I thank God for the unspeakable and unexplainable gift He has given to me and my wife we were looking unto God for the fruit of the womb for sometime and within the period, we visited many places for solution but to no avail. When we joined this ministry. God answered our prayed by giving us a bouncing baby girl. Since then, long standing stagnancy has been broken. Praise the Lord!

Bro. Andrew
MFM Abule Anu

DIVINE INTERVENTION

I had accommodation problem for 20 years. But during the last 70 Days Fasting and Prayer programme. God provided my own house for me. Also, God intervened during the Tejuoso market fire disaster and prevented my shop from getting burnt. Praise the Lord!

Bro. Felix
MFM Headquarters

TOTAL DELIVERANCE

I am not literate but I used to pray for people and preach in public places some months ago, I developed internal heat and over weight this made me inactive in the work of God so I decided to go for deliverance during which I vomited strange things and also passed out slimy substance. After that, I was restored fully. Praise the Lord!

Bro. Ogbonaya
MFM Iba

ANOINTING BREAKS THE YOKE

My son's wife was sick and admitted in the hospital. Her condition was so bad that she need surgery. I prayed for her over the telephone and told her that before anything, she should use the anointing oil from Prayer City which I gave to them. After applying the anointing oil, miraculously, she was healed. Praise the Lord!

Sis. Evlyn
MFM Ojo

THESE BOOKS ARE AVAILABLE FOR SALE
ASK YOUR VENDOR

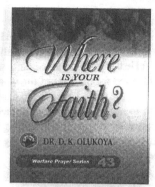

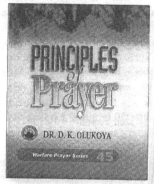

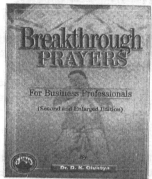

FIRE IN THE WORD is a weekly Spiritual Bulletin of the Mountain of Fire and Miracles Ministries, published by Tracts and Publications Group. All Enquiries should be addressed to The Editor, Mountain of Fire Magazine, 13, Olasimbo Street, off Olumo Road, Onike, P.O. Box 2990, Sabo Yaba, Lagos, Nigeria. Telephone 01-867439, 864631, 868766, 08023180236. Copyright reserved.

FIRE IN THE WORD

Ye Shall Know the Truth, and the Truth Shall Make You Free (John 8:32)

ISSN 1595 - 7314 Vol. 12 No. 11 Sun. 20th - Sat. 26th Jan., 2008

₦10

THE MYSTERY OF
PAIN

My year of unprecedented greatness and unmatchable increase
Deuteronomy 28:13, Psalm 71:21, Ephesians 3:20, Psalm 92:10

This week, we are looking at the message titled, "The mystery of pain." Isaiah 53:5 says, *"But he was wounded for our transgressions, he was bruised for our iniquities: the chastisement of our peace was upon him; and with his stripes we are healed."* The bottom line here is that Jesus suffered pain. Matthews 5:4 says. *"Blessed are they that mourn: for they shall be comforted."*

WHAT IS PAIN?

Pain is a feeling of being hurt, a feeling of suffering. It is an unpleasant discomfort experienced by some body who is wounded or ill. It is a feeling of discomfort.

FACTS ABOUT PAIN

1. Pain is universal. Everyone at one point or another in life experiences some pain.
2. Pain has no respect for age. Both young and old people suffer pain.
3. Pain does not discriminate. It does not matter, whether you are black or white, rich or poor.
4. It is impossible to journey through life without experiencing some element of pain and discomfort. Job 14:1 says, *"Man that is born of a woman is of few days, and full of trouble."*
5. Pain may differ from one person to another; one person may have headache while another person may have backache.
6. Pain is either acute or chronic. An acute pain happens suddenly and ends at some point. It is a kind of pain you get from a broken leg or an injury. But as the injury heals the pain goes away. But chronic pain is long-lasting.
7. You can stumble upon pain. That is, accidentally you can come across it. A lot of people are suffering from accidental pain,

PAIN IS ARROGANT, IT WILL NOT GO WITHOUT MAKING A POINT

which they stumbled upon.

8. Pain is a signal that something is wrong and needs attention. Every pain is a signal or an indication that something is wrong and needs attention. If a headache suddenly starts, the resultant pain is a sign that something is wrong and needs adjustment. If not for pain, one could break his leg and not even know that his leg is broken. A slap on the face or a blow on your nose could be ignored if not for the pain.
9. There is something known as spiritual pain. It could be a guilty conscience. It could be a broken spirit, a loss of direction or a decline of one's spiritual life or loss of spiritual gift.
10. People generally turn to pain relievers instead of pain quenchers when they feel pain. Many drugs prescribed by doctors only stop the sensation of pain while the condition that

causes the pain is still in existence. It is the tragedy of our world that the best selling drugs are tranquilizers. They just calm people down. They only remove pain but the problem remains. That is why believers must see their problems as a tree, which has fruits, leaves, branches and a root. It is a waste of time cutting off the flowers and the branches when the root is still in place.

11. Spiritual pain has pushed many people into religious cults and terrible societies. Pain is the reason you see an able-bodied man at a bar beach being bathed by a woman. Pain is the cause of such strange situations.

12. Pain is a teacher. Pain teaches people, whether they understand the lesson or not, is another matter.

13. Pain is a guardian watching over people and pegging the limit of their foolishness.

14. Pain is an invigilator, which tells us when the

DELIVERANCE CASE

time is up and we have to submit our papers for marking.

15. Pain is an adviser. It advises us to stop what we are doing now or the pain will increase.

16. Pain is a memory aid. It is an aid to our conscience.

17. Pain is independent of our sentiments. It is independent of all the sentiments you may feel.

18. Pain is arrogant, it will not go without making a point. It will make its point known, and will not go until its point is understood. It will come back again and again until the position it opposes is altered.

19. Pain is therefore both a friend and an enemy.

20. Pain can make you better or bitter. It can make you stronger or weaker.

21. Some forms of pain are directly related to our behaviour and actions.

22. Pain calls attention to the relationship between our

present conditions and our past actions.

23. Not all forms of pain are related to past sins. Job did not commit any sin yet he suffered pain. The Bible says, *"Many are the afflictions of the righteous but the Lord delivers him from them all. He keepeth all his bones that none is broken"* (Psalm 34:11).

24. Pain prompts us to take action. There are many conditions people would have ignored but because it is hurting them, they have to take action. Pain forces people to take action that they would otherwise have put off to a later date.

25. Pain prompts sacrifices for our greater good. Painful situations prompt us to make sacrifices. Before the crown, there must be a cross.

26. This is power in pain. Believers acquire considerable power while dealing with their pain. Many would not have become prayer warriors if not for the pain the enemy brought their way. So, there is power in pain. Pain has made many to focus more on the power of God. Pain has made many to recognize their weaknesses and they lean heavily on the strength of the Lord.

27. There are two categories of pain: pain God's way, and pain the devil's way. Not having sexual intercourse until after marriage could be painful but it is pain God's way. To pray from 12 to 3 am for 21days is not easy but it is having pain God's way. You can either have pain God's way or have pain the devil's way. The devil's pain is a terrible pain to have, it has thrown

EVERYONE IN THIS WORLD IS POWERLESS TO STOP CHANGE

many people into serious trouble.

28. Pain from God would yield ultimate good. The Bible says, *"Take my yoke upon you, and learn of me; for I am meek and lowly in heart: and ye shall find rest unto your souls. For my yoke is easy, and my burden is light"* (Matthew 11:29-30). Pain from God converts our corruption to heavenly purity. Pain from God converts our gloom to glory. Pain from God converts our earthly trouble to heavenly luxury. Pain from God converts our failure to success, our midnight to morning, defeat to victory, death to eternal life, warfare to triumph, struggle to success, tribulation to jubilation, fears to testimony, and pain to gain.

29. Pain from the enemy can cause insanity, it has a maddening power. When the enemy raises pain against you, then you

need to counter and deal with it. You need to reject it aggressively and insist that you will have pain only God's way. The maddening power of devil's pain pushes people to do strange things.

30. There is only one spiritual pain killer that treats the cause of pain instead of just the symptoms. Pain only listens to one voice, and that is the voice of the blood of Jesus. Jesus came to absorb the pain, punishment and suffering that we had put ourselves in. He was lashed 39 strokes of cain and was bruised. He bore pain so that you and I would not have pain. If He already bore the pain that you are supposed to have from the enemy, then there is no need for you to bear the pain anymore.

31. Most times, pain is an alarm crying for change. It could be a sign that God wants you to change something. It could be your prayer level, your Bible reading level, or your holiness level, because the only thing that is certain about life is change. Everyone in this world is powerless to stop change. Terrible pains come when you do not wish to change. Somebody who is young must anticipate getting old. So, it is foolish for the young person to think that he will never need to retire at one level in his life. The single must anticipate the possibility of being part of a couple one day. But when you make no plans and refuse to change, pain comes in as a result of that.

32. Finally, Pain is an oppressor, and the Bible says *"Oppression maketh a wise man mad"* (Ecclesiastes 7:7). When somebody who is normal begins to experience oppression, he will behave like a mad person.

Beloved, you should deal with the oppressing spirit called evil pain. If you know the Lord has been passing you through fire, water and storm in order to

THE PROPHET

remold your life, or He has been putting His finger on your pressure point and is giving you pain, that pain is a good one. But if you do not want pain God's way, you will get it the devil's way, which is very terrible and can lead to destruction. Therefore, I counsel you to pray the following prayer points with violence and anger.

PRAYER POINTS

1. Oh God, arise and place Elijah's anointing upon my life, in the name of Jesus.

2. Oh God, arise and place Samuel's anointing upon my life, in the name of Jesus.

3. Oh God, arise and place Joseph's anointing upon my life, in the name of Jesus.

4. Oh God, arise and place Moses' anointing upon my life, in the name of Jesus.

5. Oh God, arise and place Nehemiah's anointing upon my life, in the name of Jesus.

6. Oh God, arise and place Abraham's anointing upon my life, in the name of Jesus.

7. Oh God, arise and place Esther's anointing upon my life, in the name of Jesus.

8. Oh God, arise and place Joshua's anointing upon my life, in the name of Jesus.

9. Oh God, arise and place Isaac's anointing upon my life, in the name of Jesus.

10. Oh God, arise and place Daniel's anointing upon my life, in the name of Jesus.

11. Oh God, arise and place Deborah's anointing upon my life, in the name of Jesus.

12. Oh God, arise and place Paul's anointing upon my life, in the name of Jesus.

13. Oh God, arise and place Elisha's anointing upon my life, in the name of Jesus.

14. Oh God, arise and place Messianic anointing upon my life, in the name of Jesus.

15. Pain of darkness, my life is not your candidate, die, in the name of Jesus.

16. Every arrow fired to arrest my progress, backfire, in the name of Jesus.

17. Oh God, arise, buy me back, where I have sold myself, in the name of Jesus.

18. Bad luck, die, in the name of Jesus.

19. Financial grave, clear away, in the name of Jesus.

20. My hand, magnetize prosperity, in the name of Jesus.

21. I recover by fire, the lost wealth of my ancestors, in the name of Jesus.

22. Every good thing I touch become prophetic gold, in the name of Jesus.

23. I receive the power to maximize my potentials, in the name of Jesus.

24. My way, open by fire, in the name of Jesus.

25. Every disaster programmed against me and my family, backfire, in the name of Jesus.

THE MYSTERY OF PAIN

is a message delivered at the Mountain of Fire and Miracles Ministries by the General Overseer, Dr. D.K. Olukoya.

A CALL TO SERVE

Are you a member of MFM with a burden to help the needy, are you interested in alleviating the plight of the poor or in the spread of the gospel through the sponsorshing of the publication of tracts? Your resources, time and talent can be extended to several groups that are in charge of these areas. These groups include:

o   We care Ministry,
o   Mission Outreach
o   Tracts and Publications
o   Ministry to Drug addicts
o   Campus fellowship
o   Ministry to School
o   Ministry to Glorious Children, etc.

Thus says the Lord, "Verily I say unto you, in as much as ye have done it unto one of the least of these my brethren, ye have done it unto me" Matthew 25 : 40.

WONDERFUL JESUS!

DELIVERANCE FROM FAMILY IDOL

I thank God for His goodness over my life. In the last deliverance programme, I was delivered from the idol that my family members have been worshipping over the years. On the third day of the deliverance programme, after breaking my fast, I passed out some slippery substances which were evil deposits. Since then, I have become completely free. Praise the Lord!

Sis Blessing
MFM Ikare

GOD FIGHTS MY BATTLE

Dangerous charms were buried in my plot of land in order to afflict me. After some days, when I went to clear the land, I felt pain on my legs. Through the word of knowledge, I discovered that it was an evil deed. So, I presented the case to the man of God in the church. He prayed for me and anointed my legs and the pain ceased completely. God. Praise the Lord!

Sis. Victoria
MFM Asoro, Benin City

FIRE ACCIDENT AVERTED

I thank God for saving my family from fire accident. Recently, a co-tenant plugged a hot plate (stove) and went out. Somebody around who perceived that something was burning, raised alarm and the situation was put under control. Praise the Lord!

Sis. Eunice
MFM Odogunyan.

FRUIT OF THE WOMB

I got married in 2001 but could not have children. My husband and I went to the hospital for test and it was discovered that my husband had no sperm at all. We started treatment and during the last 2nd MFM International Convention, I took a bold step of faith, bought a teddy toddler and wrote the name of the baby on it. We returned to the hospital early last year, and the doctor said that we had to wait for four months. My husband and I kept praying fervently. In February last year, I took in and in August, the devil struck, I took ill and was taken to the hospital again. It was so severe that it became a mental case. I was brought down to the church and was prayed for. In October last year, I gave birth to a baby boy. Glory be to God!

Sis. Omotayo
MFM Headquarters.

GOD ANSWERS ALL

I had a terrible experience last year because I was in a state of confusion during the good part of the year. I was no longer comfortable with my job. During the Seventy Days Fasting and Prayer programme, I prayed to God to change my job. God answered my prayers by changing my job. Secondly, I prayed God to grant me journey mercy during a trip to my village, and He did. Also, I thank God for healing me of frequent malaria/fever attack. Praise the Lord!

Sis. Nki
MFM Lekki

DELIVERED FROM
THE SPIRIT OF DEATH

Before I came for deliverance in MFM, I dreamt that I saw myself in the burial ground. As I was about to run away from the burial ground, I met a mad man who forcefully slept with me. Three days later, I developed insomnia. But after the deliverance, I can now sleep very well. In fact, the semen that the mad man deposited in my body came out. Also, the pain that I used to have on the left side of my body disappeared after the deliverance. Praise the Lord!

Sis. Clara
MFM Oworonshoki.

GOD PROMOTES AND HEALS ME

I was transferred from Yola to the Head office of my company in Lagos but without promotion. I cried out to the Lord in prayers and to the glory of God, I was promoted and given an increase in salary. Secondly, a strange thing gave me stomachache for over 3 years but during the Holy Fire programme, the stomachache disappeared completely. Lastly, the Lord has increased my spiritual coast more than ever before. Praise the Lord!

Sis Eugenia
MFM Iyaiye Ojokoro

NOW ON SALE

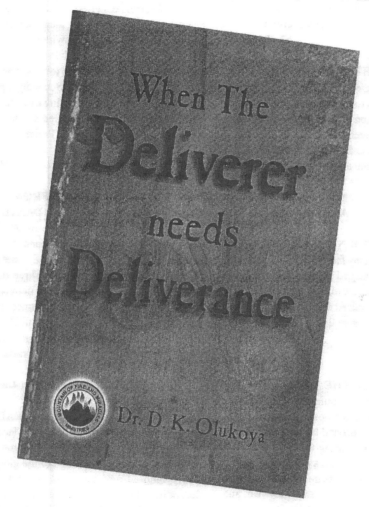

WHEN THE DELIVERER NEEDS DELIVERANCE: It is a book that described as one of the most powerful books ever written on the subject of the Christian ministry. This book is written by a minister who is well versed in the perils of the Christian ministry, the pit-fall to avoid as well as the vital areas where the gospel minister needs to be ministered to. This is indeed, a ground breaking book from the pen of an author, who has been given uncommon insights into the deep pathos as well as the heavy burdens, which the Almighty has for all cadres of Christian leadership including General Overseers, General Superintendents, Senior Pastors, Pastors, Evangelists, Christian workers and deliverance ministers. It is a manual for ministerial deliverance. This book will change your life and your ministry.

FIRE IN THE WORD, is a weekly Spiritual Bulletin of the Mountain of Fire and Miracles Ministries, published by Tracts and Publications Group. All Enquiries should be addressed to The Editor, Mountain of Fire Magazine, 13, Olasimbo Street, off Olumo Road, Onike, P.O. Box 2990, Sabo Yaba, Lagos, Nigeria. Telephone 01- 867439, 864631, 868766, 08023180236. Copyright reserved.

FIRE IN THE WORD

Ye Shall Know the Truth, and the Truth Shall Make You Free (John 8:32)

ISSN 1595 - 7314   Vol. 12   No. 12   Sun. 27th Jan. - Sat. 2nd Feb., 2008   ₦10

THE TRAGEDY OF
COVERED SIN

My year of unprecedented greatness and unmatchable increase
Deuteronomy 28:13, Psalm 71:21, Ephesians 3:20, Psalm 92:10

This week, we are looking at the message entitled, "The tragedy of covered sin." One of the most serious verses in the Bible is found in Proverbs chapter 28 verse 13: *"He that covereth his sins shall not prosper but he that confesseth and forsaketh them shall have mercy."*

Many years ago, a certain man was taken to court and charged with murdering his wife. The only witness against him in court that day was his 14 years old son. The man cried bitterly in the court room to prove that he did not kill his wife but the son insisted that he killed her. The man was sentenced to death, because of the witness of his 14 year old son. Twenty-two years later when the boy had become 36 year old, he surrendered his life to Jesus. That day, he came forward to tell the preacher that he had a confession to make. He told the preacher that 22 years ago, he was the one that killed his own mother and falsely accused his father of the crime and his father was sentenced to death.

The preacher wondered why he was making the confession. But he told him that he preferred to confess it and face the consequences than to lose his salvation. Then the preacher told him to go to the police and report himself. So, he went to the police station and confessed what he had done. He was taken back to court, where he too was sentenced to death. But he died a happy person; he died the death of the righteous (Number 23:10). If he had covered his sin he would not have prospered.

Sin is a fact of life and is the most horrible thing in the universe. In fact, if it was not for the issue of sin, Jesus had no business dying. Sin is so terrible that God had to surrender his own Son as a scapegoat so that He could be dealt with to eliminate sin. That day, where He hung on the cross, the people He came to die for were laughing Him to scorn. So, He had no comfort from those who were watching Him die. His legs were suspended from the ground and His head was not touching heaven. He was suspended in the middle. He turned to His own Father but He refused to answer and He cried out : "My Father, why has thou forsaken me?" God ran away from His own Son because of the horribleness of sin.

Sin is revealed clearly in the Bible. A policeman pursuing a thief is actually pursuing sin. Many times the medicine prescribed by doctors is against sin. The conscience is always condemning sin and God always punishes sin. The Bible says, though hand be joined in hand, no sinner will go unpunished (Proverbs 11:21). Sin is a cheat, a destroyer and a deceiver. The Bible says there is a way that seems right but the end thereof is death (Proverbs 14:12). Sin will promise you pleasure but will pay you back in the coins of pain. Sin will promise you life but will pay you back with the currency of death. Sin will promise you profit but will give you poverty. Sin is dangerous beyond description.

The Bible says sin is a violation of the law of God. Our human society may punish crime but only God can punish sin. When you refuse to conform to the law of God, you are a sinner. There is no small sin. Sin is sin. Sin is missing the mark of God for your life. Sin is when you turn aside from a straight path. Sin is when you are competing with God, that is, when God says this is what to do and you say, "No, in my own opinion this is what I believe is right." If you have the right to determine what is right or wrong then you have made yourself a god.

Sin is when men overstretch their divine limits. Sin is when you refuse to attain the divine standard God has set for you.

HIDDEN AND UNCONFESSED SINS MAKE ONE A LAUGHING STOCK BEFORE THE ENEMY.

Many people according to the record of God are supposed to be prophets, prophetesses, evangelists and pastors to the nations. They have been born again for 10 years, 15 years, 20 years, 5 years, but are yet to do what God expects them to do. They are sinners because they have refused to attain that standard He set for them.

Some years ago, a certain brother prayed about his life and the Lord showed him a vision. He said he saw a staircase which led to a high mountain and began to climb it. He stopped at number 3 out of 27. And God said to him, "Look, you have been born again for 12 years, you are expected to have climbed these 27 steps but you are still on level 3. You have one year to readjust your life if not, you will be replaced." He cried and began to work hard to see what he could do but unfortunately within the next few weeks, he died and that was the end.

God will not leave a vacuum in His programme. If He has placed you somewhere and expects you to perform and you do not, you are calling for replacement. It is sin when you refuse to attain His standard.

Concealment of sin has devastating effects. Any sin that is not confessed or that is excused will certainly invite the anger of a righteous and holy God against a person. The Bible says; "He that covereth his sin shall not prosper." Many people do not

DELIVERANCE CASE POWER PASS POWER (1)

Wait for me you bush meat

Stop in the name of Jesus. By the anointing of the Holy Ghost, upon me. I bind you with heavenly chains. I come against you with. Isa. 49:24-26.

understand what it means to cover up sin. You cover up your sin when you are making excuses. Many people do not take responsibility for their sins rather they blame others. They make excuses, and instead of blaming themselves, they cover up.

You may cover your sin by enveloping it in secrecy. You keep quiet and do not tell anyone about it. You may cover your sin with falsehood like Gehazi and it will lead to trouble. When you use a lie to cover up a lie, you will need another lie to cover up that lie and then you will become a perpetual liar. All liars shall

have their place in the bottom of hell fire.

You may cover your sin by shifting the blame to another person. But in whatever way you do it, you may be the one turning back your own prosperity. The Bible says he that covereth his sins shall not prosper but whosoever confesseth and forsaketh them shall have mercy. When Christians turn away from their sins, confess and forsake them, the power of God will move unhindered.

WHAT DOES CONFESSION MEAN?

Confession means to own up that you are guilty of an offence.

Confession means to reveal, expose, bare, unfold, uncover, or unveil. It also means to acknowledge and to plead guilty.

The folly of indulging in sin and excusing it invites trouble but when you confess your sins, you come nearer to God and get blessed. Anyone who wants to be nearer to God must not cover up anything before Him. Tell Him that innermost desire of your heart that is bad and very terrible. The reason some people are always thinking evil is that they are evil. Such people need to open up to the Lord.

The more you cover up your sin, the farther you go away from God. Do not be an hypocrite. Hypocrites cover up. They smile at people although they hate them. They pretend as if they like the people they hate. Beloved, if you are like that, please repent and open up to God. Some people came to Jesus asking Him about the people who perished and those that walls fell upon. They wanted to find out from Him what sin they committed. Jesus said, "Except you repent, you shall likewise perish" (Luke 13:5).

BENEFITS OF CONFESSION

1. Confession brings you nearer to God. The people the Bible refers to as the friends of God are those who keep very short account with God. Anytime they get into trouble with God, they get on their knees, confess their sins and tell God they are sorry. They ask for forgiveness.

2. Confession of sin makes the power of God to flow into your life.

3. A Great work of grace will come upon you.

4. Confession will turn your captivity into victory. Job chapter 42 verse 10 says, *"And the Lord turned the captivity of Job, when he prayed for his friends: also, the Lord gave Job twice as much as he had before."* When you confess your sin, God will turn your captivity into victory.

5. When you confess your sin, your spiritual battle will become the Lord's battle.

6. When you confess your sin and you are open to God, you will become a victorious wrestler.

7. When you confess your sin, you will receive deliverance from besetting sins.

8. You will receive both spiritual and physical healing, when you confess your sins.

COMPLETE ORTRUE REPENTANCE IS ESSENTIAL FOR COMPLETE DELIVERANCE

9. When you confess your sin, the Bible says, you will preserve your soul but when you refuse to confess your sin, pride will move in and destruction will follow. You will be brought down and God will begin to resist you. It will weaken your spiritual life, lead you into falsehood, worldliness and worst of all spiritual and physical poverty.

WHY DO YOU NEED TO CONFESS YOUR SIN AND FORSAKE IT?

You need to confess your sin and forsake it so that you may prosper physically and spiritually. These days, we have a lot of pretenders in the house of God. They claim to repent of their sin, yet they are not genuine. Repentance without restitution is not genuine. If you have stolen what belongs to another person, it is not enough to say, "God forgive me." You have to return what you have stolen.

Repentance without restitution is not complete. If you have sworn falsely in the past, go back and tell the truth. Do not stop with just saying, "God forgive me." This is where many people are having trouble and this is where deliverance becomes very hard work for the deliverance ministers. If you haven stolen from somebody, return what you have stolen so that God will have mercy on you.

Repentance brings deliverance. No matter the amount of noise you make on the deliverance ground, if you have cleverly hidden sins, nothing will happen. The deliverance minister may not know. The pastor may not know but the evil spirits know that you are hiding something, they will go and hide in that area where you refuse to confess and then trouble will multiply.

No one can see an evil spirit in operation unless there is complete repentance. Complete or true repentance is essential for complete deliverance. If you are not completely repentant, the evil spirits will reenter. When you drop a particular sinful activity in

your life, the enemy in that area will no longer have a legal ground to stay or enter into your life. If you have been watching terrible films, the spirit of lust will continue to pursue you. If you have been doing things you cannot tell other people, the strongman will not leave you alone. It will stick to that area of your life, where you are still not repentant.

Ignorance of the principles of deliverance has produced a lot of sorrow. An unrepentant person is a failure in the school of prayer. He is a failure in the school of spiritual warfare.

Hidden and unconfessed sins make one a laughing stock before the enemy. When you still have anger, fornication, bitterness, and evil thoughts in

your heart, you cannot ask demons to get out. They will not listen. This is why in this new year, ensure that you purge yourself and live a holy life. If you know you are playing with sin, repent quickly and run to the Lord, confess those sins and forsake them to avoid trouble.

WHAT IS REPENTANCE?

1. Repentance is total sacrifice and surrender of yourself to God.
2. Repentance is to deny yourself – you take up your cross daily and follow Jesus.
3. Repentance is to come to Jesus with the heart of "I can't do it on my own."
4. Repentance is to turn around and go in the opposite direction.
5. Repentance is to change one's mind.
6. Repentance is to have godly sorrow for sin.
7. Repentance is to put off the old man and put on the new man.
8. Repentance is a complete reversal of your attitude and values.
9. Repentance is to bury your pride.
10. Repentance is hating the bad things you once loved.
11. Repentance is for your spiritual hands to release the filthy objects they are clinging to.

THE PROPHET

What if your G.O says No?

Ooh sweet heart. Not even a worldwide G.O or 10,000 Overseers can stop or quench my love for you.

PROPHET.MO

Hmm.. Another prospective kingdom casualty case file. This brother is playing with satan's tail + everlasting fire Heb. 10:26-31; Heb. 12:15-17. Another modern Esau

Anybody who goes back to his sin never repented. If he completely repented, he would not go back to it. Unfortunately, many will learn at the gate of hell fire, they will learn the hard way.

Repentance is not the sorrow of a thief who was caught and he got terrified of the consequences. Repentance is not reluctant apology of somebody who has been proved wrong. Repentance is not when you force somebody to appologise. Repentance is not stopping a particular sin because of certain circumstances. Some people stop some bad habits for health reasons not because they are repentant. Feeling sorry alone is not repentance. When you truly repent you hate all your sins. Repentance which does not make you mourn for your sin is counterfeit repentance.

If you are not married according to the word of God, repent. If you are selfish, repent. If you drink and smoke, repent. If you have been born again for years and you are not moving forward in God, repent. If you pray to God and still consult other things, you better repent. If you check your heart and find that it is dark, you better repent. He that covereth his sin shall not prosper but if you confess and forsake them, you shall have mercy. It is good to beg for mercy now than to wait till the day of judgement when these sins are read out and then it will be too late. Talk to the Lord about your life. Do not hide anything. Tell Him about the thoughts of your heart, the kind of words you speak, the kind of places that you go, the things you do and do not want anybody to know. You have the opportunity to call for that mercy now by being open to the Lord. It would be a tragedy if you allow the enemy to waste your life because you refuse to repent. Do not allow the enemy to toy with your destiny. He will toy with it if you are living in any known sin.

Perhaps your heart is a workshop of the enemy, deal with it now. If you have not yet surrendered your life to the Lord and want to do so, say the following prayer: "Father, in the name of Jesus, I come before you today and surrender my life to You. Lord Jesus, come into my life, take control of my life as from today. I renounce the devil and his works, in Jesus' name. O Lord, wash me with your blood. Thank you Father Lord, in Jesus' name. Amen.

The Bible says He that keepeth Israel neither slumbers nor sleeps. But what can make Him to sleep or slumber on behalf of a person is when the person covers his sin. Open up to God today.

PRAYER POINTS

1. Satan, you will not write my name in your book, my name will be in the book of life, in Jesus' name.
2. Strangers hiding in my heart, scatter, in the name of Jesus.
3. Every internal warfare fashioned to destroy me, die, in the name of Jesus.
4. My Father, have mercy on me, in the name of Jesus.
5. My Father, wherever I have failed you, help me Lord, in the name of Jesus.

THE TRAGEDY OF COVERED SIN

is a message delivered at the Mountain of Fire and Miracles Ministries by the General Overseer, Dr. D.K. Olukoya.

A CALL TO SERVE

Are you a member of MFM with a burden to help the needy, are you interested in alleviating the plight of the poor or in the spread of the gospel through the sponsorshing of the publication of tracts? Your resources, time and talent can be extended to several groups that are in charge of these areas. These groups include:

o   We care Ministry,
o   Mission Outreach
o   Tracts and Publications
o   Ministry to Drug addicts
o   Campus fellowship
o   Ministry to School
o   Ministry to Glorious Children, etc.

Thus says the Lord, "Verily I say unto you, in as much as ye have done it unto one of the least of these my brethren, ye have done it unto me" Matthew 25 : 40.

WONDERFUL JESUS!

ACADEMIC BREAKTHROUGH

I am a student of the University of Lagos. During the last Seventy Days Fasting and Prayer programme, I prayed to God about my last semester exams and asked for excellence in my results. Despite the fact that I made some terrible mistakes in some papers, when the results were released, I passed excellently. I thank God for this miracle in my life. Praise the Lord!

Bro. Damilola.
MFM Egbeda

DIVINE HEALING

Sometime ago, my daughter took ill and was hospitalised. The diagnosis revealed that there was a problem with her intestine. I rejected this and prayed to God. To God's glory, she recovered miraculously. Also, I fell sick but the good Lord took control and healed me. Praise the Lord!

Sis. Akindapo
MFM Abaranje – Ikotun

GREAT DELIVERANCE

For a long time, I had some problems. There was no money for my parents to pay my school fees. One sister introduced me to MFM and some brethren prayed with me and God took perfect control. Secondly, I missed my practical exams unknowingly. I went to the man of God, and he prayed for me. To the glory of God when the results came out, I passed the examination.

Sis. Funmilayo
MFM Ijebu-Ode

DELIVERANCE FROM THE SPIRIT OF DEATH AND HELL

My daughter-in-law brought me to this church because I was not able to walk or stand due to ill-health. I took part in the deliverance programme twice and after the programme, God made me whole. I can now walk. Praise the Lord!

Sis. Onyeanwuna
MFM Upper Mission, Benin City

GOD INTERVENES

The first time I sat for the G.C.E examination I did not make the English paper and my friends started mocking me saying why has my prayer not brought me success. But I took courage and sat for it a second time and to God's glory out of four candidates that had credit in English in my centre, I am one of them with distinction in many of my subjects. Praise the Lord!

Bro. Jide
MFM Ado-Ekiti

DIVINE PROTECTION

I had wanted to board a particular vehicle, but could not. So, I boarded another one moving in front. Later, I noticed that the same vehicle I had wanted to take was involved in an accident. God delivered me. Praise the Lord!

Bro. Lawrence
MFM Omooye

GOD IS GREAT

Recently, I boarded a commuter bus at the garage and took the last space. But the Holy Spirit asked me to get down and join the next bus which was empty. To my greatest surprise, on our way to Lagos, the bus from which I came down had a fatal accident with a truck and all the passengers including the driver died. Praise the Lord!

Bro. Kehinde
MFM Ikorodu 1

WITHHELD RESULT RELEASED

About 8 years ago I completed my Masters degree programme but my result was withheld without any reason. I paid all the money I needed to pay and tried all I could but still it was not released. I decided to charge the school to court but my husband disagreed and advised that I should take it to the Lord in prayer and I did. To the glory of God, by the time I went back again my result was given to me. Praise the Lord!

Sis. Rose
MFM Agodo

DELIVERANCE FROM THE SPIRIT OF DEATH

My son who is a final year student in the university attempted suicide. In the process of committing suicide, we got into his room and saw him almost dead. I quickly took the anointing oil and applied it on him and he regained consciousness and said he shall not die. We rushed him to Prayer City for deliverance and there he confessed that he was smoking marijuana to my amazement. I thank God for his deliverance from the spirit of death. He is now normal and back to his senses. Praise the Lord!

Sis. Oluwatoyin
MFM Headquarters

NOW ON SALE

The MFM 2008 Anointed Diary is now on sale.
It is a daily devotional guide for Bible Reading
and Spiritual Warfare that will make everyday
of the year 2008 AD a victorious one for you.
Grab your copy from the vendors.

FIRE IN THE WORD, is a weekly Spiritual Bulletin of the Mountain of Fire and Miracles Ministries, published by Tracts and Publications Group. All Enquiries should be addressed to The Editor, Mountain of Fire Magazine, 13, Olasimbo Street, off Olumo Road, Onike, P.O. Box 2990, Sabo Yaba, Lagos, Nigeria. Telephone 01- 867439, 864631, 868766, 08023180236.E-mail: mfmtractsandpublications@yahoo.com Copyright reserved.

FIRE IN THE WORD

Ye Shall Know the Truth, and the Truth Shall Make You Free (John 8:32)

ISSN 1595 - 7314 Vol. 12 No. 13 Sun. 3rd - Sat. 9th Feb., 2008   ₦10

DEDICATIONS THAT SPEAK AGAINST YOU

My year of unprecedented greatness and unmatchable increase
Deuteronomy 28:13, Psalm 71:21, Ephesians 3:20, Psalm 92:10

Beloved, our message this week titled, "Dedications that speak against you" is for everyone. It is both preventive and curative. In the Book of Acts of the Apostles, some men made a vow that they would neither eat nor drink until they had killed Paul (Acts 23:12). It was the vow of the enemy! Also, in the book of Exodus, the Egyptians and Pharaoh made a vow that they would pursue, overtake and destroy. It was a vow of the enemy. But then, we can counter the vow of the enemy by praying "Counter-vow prayers."

Sometime ago, a sister ran to us for help: she was facing very terrible situations. She had three children studying in three different universities abroad. All of them came back home on the same day without anyone sending for them. Two of them were deported, and they landed on the same day. The third one said he heard a voice urging him to go home. But coincidentally or by the arrangement of the enemy, he too arrived on the same day as others. All three children came back on the same day; what a terrible situation. However, when we started praying, we discovered that all the three men had been married to family spirit wives, and the day they all came back was the wedding ceremony day. So, one way or the other, they found their way back to the country.

WHAT DOES IT MEAN TO DEDICATE A PERSON OR THING?

- It means to devote a person or thing to the worship of a spirit.
- It means to set apart for a definite purpose.
- It means to inscribe or address as a compliment to a person.
- It means to perform a ceremony of religious acceptance.
- It means to consecrate.
- It means to ordain, induct or enshrine.

The principles of heaven have been in operation since men were created. Everything man is doing now and is working well is definitely based on the principles of heaven. That is why it is often said that order is the first principle in heaven. At the same time, heaven has power to organize what is called, "organized disorder." Therefore, it means that the principles of dedication did not start with man, or the devil; it started with God. But like most things that God started, the enemy grabbed, polluted and counterfeited the act of dedication.

1 Samuel 1:11 says, *"And she vowed a vow, and said, O Lord of hosts, if thou wilt indeed look on the affliction of thine handmaid, and remember me, and not forget thine handmaid, but wilt give unto thine handmaid a man child, then I will give him unto the Lord all the days of his life, and there shall no razor come upon his head."* That was Hannah

YOU ACQUIRE THE NATURE OF WHAT YOU ARE DEDICATED TO

dedicating Samuel in advance, and immediately she said that, the stamp of heaven came upon it. Thus Samuel became a prisoner for God, a prisoner of hope. In the same vein, anyone whose parents named Samuel has become a prisoner of God because since it is the parents that did it, it is an official heavenly transaction. Anyone called Samuel, by virtue of that name must abstain from sin or sinful lifestyle if he does not want trouble. Anyone that is not serious with the Lord should not bear some Bible names because he will only put problems on himself by going about with such names.

In 1 Samuel 1:24, Hannah fulfilled her vow: *"And when she had weaned him, she took him up with her, with three bullocks and one ephah of flour, and a bottle of wine, and brought him unto the house of the Lord in Shiloh: and the child was young."* The woman could not be bothered about the age of the child. *"And they slew the bullock, and brought the child to Eli. And she said, Oh my Lord, I am the woman that stood by thee here, praying unto the Lord. For this child I prayed; and the Lord hath given me my petition which I asked of Him: Therefore also I have lent him to the Lord; as long as he liveth, he shall be lent to the Lord. And he worshipped the Lord there"* (1 Samuel 1:25-28). So, Samuel was dedicated to God- that was a spiritual transaction. Samuel was the first ruler in Israel; he was a judge and a priest. His

DELIVERANCE CASE (THE STORY OF MY LIFE • PART 1)

children did not do very well, but his own dedication endured.

Now, let us consider non-living things. 1 Chronicles 18:11: *"Then also King David dedicated unto the Lord, with the silver and gold that he brought from all these nations; from Edom, and from Moab, and from the children of Ammon, and from the Philistines, and from Amalek."* So, David gathered so many things such as spoons, golden vessels, golden apparels etc and dedicated them to the Lord. These materials were dedicated to God. It is a principle in Scriptures: when a thing has been dedicated to the Lord, God regards that thing with holy jealousy. Therefore, when somebody in the book of Daniel 5 began to mess up with those things that David had dedicated to God, the Lord defended the dedicated materials with aggression.

Daniel 5:1-4: *"Belshazzar the king made a great feast to a thousand of his lords and drank wine before the thousand. Belshazzar whiles he tasted the wine, commanded to bring the golden and silver vessels which his father Nebuchadnezzar had taken out of the temple which was in Jerusalem* (those things that David had already dedicated) *that the king and his princes, his wives, and his concubines, might drink therein. Then they brought the golden vessels that were taken out of the temple of the house of God which was at Jerusalem: and the king and his princes, his wives and his concubines drank in them. They drank wine and praised the gods of gold, and of silver, of brass, of iron, of wood and of stone."* They did not know that a particular finger had departed from heaven. Verses 5-7: *"In the same hour came forth fingers of a man's hand and wrote over against the candlestick upon the plaister of the wall of the king's palace: and the king saw the part of the hand that wrote. Then the king's countenance was changed, and his thoughts troubled him so that the joints of his loins were loosed and his knees smote one against another. The king cried aloud to bring in the astrologers, the Chaldeans and the soothsayers..."* That night, the man died. The vessels remained dedicated. No wonder, the Bible says, *"I know whom I have believed, and I am persuaded that He is able to keep that which I have committed to Him against that day"* (2 Timothy 1:12). That is how God operates. The devil copies the system, and practices the principles of evil dedication amongst men.

There are many people who do not understand what is going on in their lives. Sometime ago, when I was in England, a mother brought her five beautiful daughters to me: three of them were medical doctors, one a lawyer, and one worked in a bank. They were ages 41 and below. They were very beautiful women but had no husbands. Men would come and run away;

they would eat their food, take their money, ride in their cars, and run away. When I started praying with them, the Lord said, "Ask their mother what she knows about a waistband?" She screamed and said in her husband's family, there was a waistband, which every girl child in the family must wear and that all the five daughters wore it. She said the same fate befell any woman in the family that used it, meaning that through the waistband, all the ladies were already married off to some spirits somewhere, they have been dedicated to them. Until those things were broken, these women never moved forward. The enemy would see to it that they followed the dedication through. The reason the battle of so many people is so hard is that there are some spirits battling against them.

Deliverance is a very good process, which sometimes takes place in stages. Sometimes after a deliverance session, evil dreams could become intense because for the first time, the victim can now see what has been hiding in his life.

FACTS ABOUT DEDICATION

1. A person is a property of what he is dedicated to.
2. Dedication is outright sale, and to be free, you must be bought back. That is, you must be redeemed.
3. Whether the person who did the dedication is dead or alive, the agreement remains binding.
4. Changing a name of dedication is also a spiritual transaction. If you are bearing a name that shows that you are already connected to an idol, it is good for you to change the name. In fact, it is the best thing to do. But after changing it physically, you still have to change it in the spiritual register or the power behind the name will still be looking for you.
5. A person is married to any power to which he/she is dedicated.
6. The powers to whom a person is dedicated see to it that the contract is not broken.
7. You acquire the nature of what you are dedicated to. A person's character will conform to that of whatever idol he or she is dedicated to. For example, anyone dedicated to the god of thunder would be quick tempered.
8. Sex with a candidate of evil dedication also converts his or partner to a candidate because the Bible says, "Two shall become one."
9. All dedications have the voice of authority; they speak for or against. A person that has already been dedicated to a spirit wife may have difficulty leaving his location because the spirit wife will be crying against his moving forward. A person who is about to be ordained as a pastor could suddenly fall

PEOPLE DEDICATED TO IDOLS OBEY EVIL COMMANDS

into the sin of fornication or adultery which could result in pregnancy and a week to the ordination, a letter will come to say, "This pastor has made me pregnant." That will be the end of the ordination. So, all dedications have a voice of authority. Many cases of failure at the edge of breakthroughs happen because there is a voice that said, "No."

Practically all indigenous cultures are saturated with one form of idolatry or another. This is very clear from some of the ceremonies that are conducted. For example, during child naming ceremonies, babies are fed with dead rats. How can a person move forward when as a baby, somebody had fed him with a dead rat and alligator pepper? So, our culture is a culture of dedication to many things. Even the coronation of kings takes its root in dedication ceremonies. Burial ceremonies are not left out. All the ceremonies to initiate people into adulthood, dedication of buildings, worship centres, market places, etc are all rooted in idolatry. So if you or your parents have ever been through any of these ceremonies, know for sure that one way or the other, you have been dedicated to something. And this kind of dedication is an evil marriage.

One terrible thing about evil dedications is what you find in Psalm 106:28: *"They joined themselves also unto Baal-poer and ate the sacrifices of the dead. Thus, they provoked*

Him to anger with their inventions: and the plague broke in upon them." All kinds of terrible things happen once a person gets involved in these things. Most of what we call tradition and culture are dedications: habits of eating, drinking, and pouring of libations to the dead. These situations establish and strengthen bondage.

Once a person is dedicated to a particular power, you will notice a particular pattern of operation and herein lies the root of many problems facing Africans. For example, Africa is extremely rich, but is not benefiting from all its natural resources. It is blessed with all kinds of raw materials but other races who enslaved Africans come and buy them and sell them back to Africa. In a certain magazine, it was reported that 54 per cent of the world's gold reserve is in Africa; yet Africa does not determine the price; other nations do that. These evil dedications have

resulted in backwardness. Many parents in their ignorance have sold out their children. Many people are suffering now long after those who sold them have gone.

SIGNS OF EVIL DEDICATIION
1. **Deadness of the spiritual senses**: Victims would notice that their spiritual senses are deadened. No matter how hard they struggle, their spiritual growth will be slow; they will notice that there is a force pushing them back. They would cry and cry but find that they really cannot move. And anytime they want to make an aggressive move in their Christian life, there would be a counter-attack by forces of darkness.

2. **A victim of evil dedication easily magnetizes satanic attacks:** If a witch is supposed to attack somebody in a house and cannot find the person she is looking for, she will transfer

the attack on the body of the victim of dedication because he has a magnetizing power towards witchcraft.

3. **Poverty:** There are some gods or idols that automatically transfer poverty to people that are dedicated to them. Such people remain poor thoughout their life time.

4. **Unpardonable errors:** Victims of evil dedications make inexcusable mistakes. This is responsible for situations where a young man of twenty-two rapes a woman of eighty.

5. **Spiritual crash land syndrome:** A person dedicated to idols would suffer from "spiritual crash landing." When he goes very high in God, all of a sudden, he comes down and would not be able to explain what went wrong.

6. **Acute marital problems:** Once a person who is dedicated to an idol does not break the covenant before getting married, there will be serious problems. That is why in Mountain of Fire and Miracles Ministries, some deliverance prayers have been introduced into marriage ceremonies.

7. **Early widowhood:** Evil dedications lead to early widowhood and all kinds of moral disorders.

8. **Addiction:** It leads to destructive addiction to alcohol, tobacco etc.

9. **Untimely death:** It leads to untimely death. There are some families, where

THE PROPHET David versus Goliath 4

Listen you little mouse, that your God who sent you to fight me is weak. And I curse you in the name of my god-sango

You are under God's curse already, and within 1 minute you shall fall down and die before me, in Jesus name. Amen

somebody must die every year.

10. **Obedience to evil commands:** People dedicated to idols obey evil commands. There are people abroad who were summoned home by some strange voices.

11. **Dreams of backwardness and limitation.** They are signs of evil dedication.

12. **Rising high and falling big:** Victims rise high in life only to fall flat after sometime.

Most of the yearly pilgrimages that many people make to their towns and villages during festive periods are seasons of negotiations with evil powers and the enemy. The initiation of children into family cults, tribal marks and tattoes are forms of evil dedication. In some places, they leave the babies by the riverside for one or two weeks after birth. All these evil practices make people properties of evil spirits; wherever they go, they believe that they belong to them.

If you find that there was a time you were very ill as a young person and because of that, incisions were made on your body and face, know for sure that you have been dedicated to whatever power kept you alive at that time. Names and locations of evil dedications put people into bondage. Unreasonable ban on certain food items by some people lead to evil dedications.

WAY OUT

1. **Repentance:** Repent properly before the Lord.

2. **Examine your background:** Take a thorough look at your background; how did your great grandfather, grandfather and father die? Is there any evil pattern running in your family? How many times was your mother married? Check out all these things.

3. Personally identify any dedication that may be speaking against you, so that you can silence it and move forward.

4. Prayerfully rectify your foundation. The trouble you are in could be as a result of evil dedication. If your spouse has a background of evil dedication you are in trouble too because by that marriage, you have already dedicated yourself. But you can deliver yourself through prayers.

5. The last thing to do is to destroy every altar of satan and dedicate yourself to the Lord. One way to be free from evil dedication is by dedicating your life and everything that belongs to you properly to God.

PRAYER POINTS

1. My Father, I need help, arise and help me, in the name of Jesus.

2. Thou power of evil dedication speaking against my destiny, die, in the name of Jesus.

3. Any power pretending to be my parent in the dark, die, in the name of Jesus.

4. Any foundational dedication in my family line speaking failure into my destiny, die, in the name of Jesus.

5. Every unconscious evil dedication, die by the blood of Jesus, in the name of Jesus.

6. Every yoke of evil dedication, break, in the name of Jesus.

7. I dedicate my life and everything that is mine to the King of kings and the Lord of lords, in the name of Jesus.

DEDICATIONS THAT SPEAK AGAINST YOU is a message delivered at the Mountain of Fire and Miracles Ministries by the General Overseer, Dr. D.K. Olukoya.

A CALL TO SERVE

Are you a member of MFM with a burden to help the needy, are you interested in alleviating the plight of the poor or in the spread of the gospel through the sponsorshing of the publication of tracts? Your resources, time and talent can be extended to several groups that are in charge of these areas. These groups include:

o We care Ministry,
o Mission Outreach
o Tracts and Publications
o Ministry to Drug addicts
o Campus fellowship
o Ministry to School
o Ministry to Glorious Children, etc.

Thus says the Lord, "Verily I say unto you, in as much as ye have done it unto one of the least of these my brethren, ye have done it unto me" Matthew 25 : 40.

WONDERFUL JESUS!

GOD ALMIGHTY HEALS ME

I had an ailment which defied all medical solutions. I became worried and restless. I went to my pastor for prayer and he placed me on 21 days prayers, after which the sickness disappeared. Since then I have been hale and hearty. Praise the Lord!

Sis. Uche
MFM Agodo

POWER OF GOD MANIFESTS

A neighbour dropped feaces at my backyard with incantations pronounced on it. Some people advised me not to remove it or I would die. I prayed seriously on it, poured anointing oil on it and burnt it. To God be the glory, nothing happened to me. Praise the Lord!

Sis. Mabel
MFM Amichi

GOD DELIVERS ME FROM MULTIPLE PROBLEMS

I had attacks in my dream, which affected my career. My life was turned upside down. But during a deliverance programme, God Almighty delivered me from all these. Praise God!

Bro. Tunji
MFM Ogudu/Ojota

GOD GIVES ME BACK MY JOB

What appeared not to be a serious problem in my office led to my suspension by my boss. I decided to use the period to go for deliverance. During the period, my boss placed a notice to replace me. I called on the name of the Lord and believed nobody would take my position. After the suspension, I got my job back. Praise the Lord!

Sis. Chinyere
MMF Odogunyan, Ikorodu

TOTAL DELIVERANCE AND HEALING

I was an ulcer patient before I went for deliverance so I was afraid the ailment would be aggravated by the dry fasting involved. But to the glory of God, not only did I complete the exercise successfully, I was healed of the ulcer. Praise the Lord!

Sis. Bose
MFM Ogwashi-uku

STOMACHACHE DISAPPEARS WITH FASTING

Before I joined MFM, I found it very difficult to fast because of some stomach problems. In fact, I thought it was impossible for me to fast. However during a special programme in the church which involved dry fasting, I thought the end had come. But with prayer and encouragement from the pastor and brethren, I participated. To the glory of God and my greatest surprise, my stomach problems have disappeared. Praise the Lord!

Sis. Toyin
MFM Ado Ekiti

SATANIC POWERS DISGRACED

In my clinic a cat always appeared at night between 12.15am and 2.15am. My house fellowship members prayed at the clinic and it stopped. But one night during a woman's delivery, the cat came again. I prayed violently and three days later, it was discovered dead. Secondly, the first wife of the husband of a female patient in my clinic challenged and accused me of spoiling her plans of dealing with the woman and her child she did not want to let go. I prayed to God about it and He took control of the situation. Praise the Lord!

Sis. Christy
MFM Abule-Egba

GOD ANSWERS MY PRAYERS

On my way to Ile-Ife recently, the tyre of the vehicle I boarded burst. I thank God I was not a victim of death through the accident. I also asked God to give me a new job and He did. Praise the Lord!

Bro. Patrick
MFM Olowora

CHILDBRITH BREAKTHROUGH

I got married in 2006. Soon after I took in but lost the pregnancy two months later through a mysterious satanic attack. Two months after the attack I took in again. But suddenly I started feeling the same way I felt when I lost the first pregnancy. I came to the church and some ministers of God prayed for me. Miraculously, the Lord took me abroad and I had my baby there safely without any problem. I am back here with my baby to glorify the name of the Lord. Praise the Lord!

Sis. Angela
MFM Headquarters

NOW ON SALE

The MFM 2008 Anointed Diary is now on sale.
It is a daily devotional guide for Bible Reading
and Spiritual Warfare that will make everyday
of the year 2008 AD a victorious one for you.
Grab your copy from the vendors.

FIRE IN THE WORD

Ye Shall Know the Truth, and the Truth Shall Make You Free (John 8:32)

ISSN 1595 - 7314 Vol. 12 No. 14 Sun. 10th - Sat. 16th Feb., 2008   ₦10

The Mystery of BATTLE CRIES

My year of unprecedented greatness and unmatchable increase
Deuteronomy 28:13, Psalm 71:21, Ephesians 3:20, Psalm 92:10

Dear reader, before you go into our message for this week titled, "The mystery of battle cries," I would like you to take the following prayer points aggressively:

1. Shame, I uproot you by fire, in the name of Jesus.
2. Every power that wants me to expire before my testimony, die, in the name of Jesus.
3. Every power assigned to waste my opportunities, your time is up, die, in the name of Jesus.
4. Every arrow fired against my star, backfire, in the name of Jesus.
5. Satan, hear the word of the Lord, return my stolen virtues, in the name of Jesus.

There are mysteries about heaven that many people do not understand. One of them is this: there is no soul that ever cried to God violently and was disappointed. It is a mystery of heaven. No wonder the Psalmist says, *"When I cry unto thee, then shall my enemies turn back: this I know; for God is for me"* (Psalm 56:9). This mystery was at work when Jesus stopped within a crowd of people to attend to one man. He could not go forward when Blind Bartimaeus began to cry. He had never met Jesus before, he never listened to any of His sermons and never knew about the apostles. But he had heard about Jesus. This is the mystery of heaven that says that no soul ever utters a violent cry and is disappointed. The Bible says, "And Jesus stood still," (Mark 10:49) because moving away would have meant Jesus Himself disobeying the ordinance of heaven, so He stood still.

Right from the beginning of creation, no violent cry has been raised to the throne of God without getting an answer. *"And from the days of John the Baptist until now the kingdom of heaven suffereth violence and the violent take it by force"* (Matthew 11:12). 1 Timothy 6:12 says, *"Fight the good fight of faith, lay hold on eternal life, whereunto thou art also called and hast professed a good profession*

FAILURE TO BOLDLY DECLARE YOUR BATTLE CRY WILL GIVE YOUR ENEMY AN UPPER HAND.

before many witnesses." Believers have to fight in prayers and in faith. The Bible admonishes us to fight. We need to fight because life is a battle. The Bible says, man that is born of woman is of a few days and full of trouble (Job 14:1).

Every man or woman would fight his or her own battle. There are some battles that have sent a lot of people to early graves. If you neglect a battle you have to fight, it will kill you. If you do not stop the enemy, they will stop you. The strategy is very simple: stop them before they stop you.

SOURCES OF BATTLES OF LIFE

1. Blood pollution.
2. Success manipulation.
3. Failure of divine purpose.
4. Peppery arrows.
5. Satanic syringe.
6. Air manipulation.
7. Debts.
8. Caged finances.
9. Unexplainable hatred.
10. Incomplete victory.
11. Closure of good roads.
12. Marital distress.
13. Eating in the dream
14. Aimlessness.
15. Anti-promotion spirits.

DELIVERANCE CASE (The Story of My Life - Part 2)

16. Circle of problems.
17. Infirmity.
18. False vision.
19. Denial of access to rightful position.
20. Silencing of good things.
21. Counterfeit blessings.
22. Rain of affliction.
23. Evil observers.
24. Desert spirits.
25. Amputated breakthroughs.
26. Evil marks: Many people will not move forward until the evil spiritual marks upon them are removed. I know a lady who had thirteen failed marriage engagements because there was a mark on her. I pray that any invisible evil mark on you as you read this message shall be wiped off, in Jesus' name.
27. Business henchmen.
28. Unprofitable load.
29. Slow progress.
30. Evil deposit.
31. Satanic poison.
32. Unfriendly friends.
33. Internal suicide.
34. Counterfeit children.
35. Rejection.
36. Vagabond power.
37. Pockets with hole.
38. Demon idols.
39. Wondering stars.
40. Profitless hardwork.
41. Harassment by intelligent forces.
42. Failure at the edge of breakthrough.
43. Spiritual stagnancy.
44. Lack of helpers.
45. Circle of wastage.
46. Alive but unavailable children.
47. Evil family pattern.
48. Gradual dispossession.
49. Attack by the spirit of death and hell.
50. Spiritual blindness.
51. Disfavour.
52. Constant failure.
53. Remote controlling powers.
54. Disgrace.
55. Strange accidents.
56. Unexplainable backsliding.
57. Prostitution.
58. Mental illness.
59. Polygamy.
60. Hard life.

Beloved, at this juncture, I would like you to take the following prayer point: "Every battle assigned to stop me, I stop you before you stop me, in Jesus' name." Every battle has it's battle cry.

WHAT IS THE MYSTERY OF BATTLE CRY?

- A battle cry is a specific proclamation upon which you focus your victory.
- A battle cry is a declaration that guarantees success in battles.
- A battle cry is a deliberately chosen utterance to bring victory.
- A battle cry is an aggressive statement strategically directed to do the enemy maximum damage. The Bible says, "For this cause was the Son of God made manifest that he might destroy the works of the enemy" (1 John 3:8). So Jesus too can destroy things.
- A battle cry consists of words vomited by the Holy Ghost to send terror into the camp of the enemy.
- A battle cry is a holy cry uttered from the depth of the spirit.
- A battle cry is a prophetic pronouncement upon which victory is projected and won.
- A battle cry is an aggressive utterance, pronouncing the end result of a confrontation.

Battle cries are therefore indispensable to victory in battles, it is a sign that you have declared war. A battle cry contains a pattern of war and sets the battle in array. Even the enemies of our souls understand the power of battle cries. The enemy also has his own battle cry. But unfortunately, most children of God have none. When somebody faces you and says, "You are finished," you must not swallow it. You reject it immediately by the words of your own mouth because the person is making his or her own battle cry against you. It could be a doctor that would say, "this your ailment is incurable." Reject it outrightly. Don't ever keep quiet at battle cries, respond.

Look at the enemy making a battle cry in 1 Samuel 17:8-11, *"And he stood and cried unto the armies of Israel and said unto them, Why are ye come out to set your battle in array? Am not I a Philistine, and ye servants to Saul? Choose you a man for you, and let him come down to me. If he be able to fight with me and to kill me, then we be your servants: but if I prevail against him, and kill him, then shall you be our servants, and serve us. And the Philistine said, I defy the armies of Israel this day; give me a man, that we may fight together. When Saul and all Israel heard those words of the Philistine, they were dismayed, and greatly afraid."* It was until David came and began to reply Goliath that they regained confidence.

Spiritual battle is a matter of words. The children of darkness understand this very well. Failure to boldly declare your battle cry will give your enemy an upper hand. Goliath was only silenced when David countered his battle cry with his own prophetic one. The Bible says that in the words of a king, there is power. Battle cries are kingly words and Jesus is called, "The King of kings and Lord of lords." These other kings and lords are believers who know and exercise their authority and are living holy lives. The Bible therefore is a compendium of different battle cries. You need to identify the battle cry that suits your own situation. You need to identify

> IDENTIFY THE BATTLE CRY THAT WILL BE ALRIGHT FOR YOUR KIND OF BATTLE.

the negative battle cries that have been directed to your life and counter them with prophetic ones. You need to stop the battle cry of the enemy before it stops you.

SOME SPECIFIC BATTLE CRIES IN THE BIBLE

1. Jacob's battle cry – Genesis 32:26: *"...Let me go for the day breaketh. And he said, I will not let thee go, except thou bless me."*

2. Moses' battle cry – Numbers 10:35: "*And it came to pass, when the ark set forward, that Moses said, Rise up, Lord, and let thine enemies be scattered; and let them that hate thee flee before thee."*

3. Gideon's battle cry – Judges 7:18*: "When I blow with a trumpet, I and all that are with me, then blow ye the trumpets also on every side of all the camp, and say, The sword of the Lord, and of Gideon."* Jacob knew that he was not being blessed so his own battle cry had to do with blessings. Moses knew that they had terrible battles to fight so they needed the Lord's help.

4. Elisha's battle cry: 2 Kings 2:14: *"And he took the mantle of Elijah that fell from him, and smote the water and said, Where is the Lord God of Elijah? And when he also had smitten the waters, they parted hither and thither: and Elisha went over."* His battle cry was "Where is the Lord God of Elijah, arise and fight for me!"

5. Joash's battle cry: 2 Kings 13:14: *"Now Elisha was fallen sick of his sickness whereof he died. And Joash the king of Israel came down unto him, and wept over his face, and said. O my father, my father, the chariot of Israel, and the horse men thereof."* He knew he was in trouble and cried out.

6. Zerubbabel's battle cry: Zechariah 4:6-7: *"Then he answered and spoke unto me saying, This is the word of the Lord unto Zerubbabel saying, Not by might, nor by power, but by my spirit; saith the Lord of host. Who art thou, O Great mountain? Before Zerubabbel; thou shall become a plain; and he shall bring forth the headstone thereof with shoutings, crying, Grace grace unto it."*

THE PROPHET Power pass power (2)

This man needs urgent counselling on demonic disgrace + humiliation - Modern-day sons of Scevaa (Acts 19:12-16).

I'm back again. Shhaaan-ta-na-na-ri-va okla-okla-homma-kaka. I command you, fall down and die, in the name of Jesus Whom I serve.

7. Bartimaeus's battle cry: Mark 10:47: *"And when he heard it was Jesus of Nazareth, he began to cry out, and say, Jesus, thou Son of David, have mercy on me."*

8. Jesus' battle cry: Jesus made seven cries on the cross. That was the final cry and the termination of problems. John 19:30: *"When Jesus therefore had received the vinegar, he said, It is finished: and he bowed his head, and gave up the ghost."* Since the day He said, "It is finished," it means that all the troubles, tribulations, and problems that believers have are finished.

HOW TO UTTER AN
EFFECTIVE BATTLE CRY

1. Surrender your life to Jesus.
2. Repent of every known sin.
3. Pray to locate the particular battle cry that you need for your battles. Identify the battle cry that will be alright for your kind of battle.
4. Issue that battle cry after the order of David.

If you are issuing a battle cry and find that the battle is not moving then organize to change your battle cry, because sometimes what you see in spiritual warfare is not what you are fighting. I pray that the Lord will open your understanding to issue a correct battle cry. Jabez was in trouble for a long time until one day, when he began to pray the correct prayer, things changed for the better.

PRAYER POINTS

1. Terminators, your time is up, die, in the name of Jesus.
2. O God, arise and let my Goliath die, in the name of Jesus.
3. Failure, I fail you today by the power in the blood of Jesus, in Jesus' name.

4. My stubborn enemies, hear the word of the Lord, my problems are over, it is your turn, carry your load, in Jesus' name.
5. By fire and by thunder, enough is enough, I possess my possession, in the name of Jesus.
6. I shall not die but live to declare the works of the Lord, in Jesus' name.
7. The sun shall not smite me by day nor the moon by night, in Jesus' name.
8. My Father, arise, have mercy on me, in the name of Jesus.
9. Stones of fire arise, locate my Goliath, in the name of Jesus.
10. My mouth, release sharp arrows to the camp of the enemies, in the name of Jesus.
11. Who art thou mountain of trouble before me, die, in Jesus' name.
12. My Pharaoh, my Herod, my Haman, die, die, die, in the name of Jesus.
13. Wherever witches are gathered against me, Holy Ghost fire, scatter them, in Jesus' name.
14. Battles assigned to waste my life, I stop you before you stop me, in Jesus' name.

THE MYSTERY OF BATTLE CRIES
is a message delivered at the Mountain of Fire and Miracles Ministries by the General Overseer, Dr. D.K. Olukoya.

A CALL TO SERVE
Are you a member of MFM with a burden to help the needy, are you interested in alleviating the plight of the poor or in the spread of the gospel through the sponsorshing of the publication of tracts? Your resources, time and talent can be extended to several groups that are in charge of these areas. These groups include:

o　　　We care Ministry,
o　　　Mission Outreach
o　　　Tracts and Publications
o　　　Ministry to Drug addicts
o　　　Campus fellowship
o　　　Ministry to School
o　　　Ministry to Glorious Children, etc.

Thus says the Lord, "Verily I say unto you, in as much as ye have done it unto one of the least of these my brethren, ye have done it unto me" Matthew 25 : 40.

WONDERFUL JESUS!

GOD HAS ANSWERED MY PRAYERS

I am a degree holder but could not get a good job. I decided to start trading but along the line, the business collapsed and I was left with nothing. I was invited to the monthly programme of the church, where I made three requests to God. To my greatest surprise, all the three requests have been granted. Praise God!

Bro. Jacob
MFM Shibiri

VICTORY OVER HIRED KILLERS

A word of knowledge came from the pastor during one of our services that we should pray against hired killers and I did. Unknown to me, my daughter had a misunderstanding with someone in the office and as a result, assassins were hired against her. But God foiled and uncovered the evil plot. Secondly, an evil arrow was fired against me which resulted into rashes and sores on my legs but God intervened and healed me. Praise the Lord!

Sis. Elizabeth
MFM Ughelli

POISON NEUTRALISED

In 2005, I was poisoned and as a result, I could not sleep well. Recently, during one Wednesday service, the General Overseer mentioned my case and instantly, I received my healing. Right now I am free. Praise the Lord!

Sis. Ebun
MFM Headquarters

GOD BLESSES ME FINANCIALLY

Recently, our father in the Lord gave a word of prophecy concerning a brother at the Sunday service, and I claimed it. He said that God wanted to bless the brother financially. To the glory of God. I got a business breakthrough. Two of my clients were issued United Kingdom visiting visas for six months each. They did not hesitate to settle my fees. Praise the Lord!

Bro. Alex
MFM Upper Mission Benin city

KIDNAPPED SISTER –IN- LAW RELEASED

Last December, I received a phone call from my brother that his wife had been kidnapped. I reported the matter to the pastor who asked us to bring a dress and picture of the missing lady. We gave the items to the pastor and he prayed over them. Fourteen days later, the lady was released. Praise God!

Bro. Daniel
MFM Ikorodu 1

VICTORY OVER DREAM ERASERS

I thank God for bringing me out of idolatrous foundation into the light of Christ. Before I joined this ministry, I could not recollect my dreams. But now I can remember all my dreams vividly. My prayer life has improved and there is spiritual and physical progress in my life. Praise the Lord!

Sis. Modupe
MFM Abaranje, Ikotun

DELIVERED FROM THE SPIRIT OF DEATH

Sometime ago, the G.O called a prayer point which I prayed casually not knowing that it was meant for me. Two months later, my husband was involved in a motor accident, but he came out unhurt as he called the name of Jesus. indeed there is power in the name of Jesus. Praise the Lord!

Sis. Adesanmi
MFM Ilorin

GOD HEALS ME

Towards the end of one of our Thursday's revival services, I became very sick that I could not even stand to go home after the service. But the pastor prayed for me and I was healed and restored. I became strong enough to participate fully in the Power Must Change Hands programme at the weekend. Praise the Lord!

Bro. Ejiofor
MFM Ogwashi-Uku

DIVINE PROTECTION

I thank God for His protection over my life. On my return trip from a business journey, the vehicle I boarded had two accidents in a row. First, one of the rear tyres got removed on high speed. God took control, there was no casualty. The tyre was replaced and the journey continued. Suddenly again, the propeller pulled out and the vehicle somersaulted three times. Again God intervened and no life was lost. Praise the Lord!

Bro. Edison
MFM Ajilo Ondo

NOW ON SALE

The MFM 2008 Anointed Diary is now on sale.
It is a daily devotional guide for Bible Reading and
Spiritual Warfare that will make everyday of the year
2008 AD a victorious one for you.
Grab your copy from the vendors.

The Battle Cry Christian Ministries invites freelance Marketers all over the country who are interested in selling life-changing, fast selling Christian books by Dr. D.K. Olukoya (G.O. Mountain of Fire and Miracles Ministries): including Prayer Rain and Prayer Passport. Kindly apply in writing to the Marketing Manager, Battle Cry Christian Ministries, 322, Herbert Macaulay way, Sabo-Yaba, Lagos. Tel.: 08033044239, 01-8044415.

This is to inform our dear readers that your favourite "Sound the Battle Cry" bulletin would now come out once in two weeks; starting in February better packaged containing two messages and sold for N20. It is better value for your money!

FIRE IN THE WORD, is a weekly Spiritual Bulletin of the Mountain of Fire and Miracles Ministries, published by Tracts and Publications Group. All Enquiries should be addressed to The Editor, Mountain of Fire Magazine, 13, Olasimbo Street, off Olumo Road, Onike, P.O. Box 2990, Sabo Yaba, Lagos, Nigeria. Telephone 01- 867439, 864631, 868766, 08023180236.E-mail: mfmtractsandpublications@yahoo.com
Copyright reserved.

FIRE IN THE WORD

Ye Shall Know the Truth, and the Truth Shall Make You Free (John 8:32)

ISSN 1595 - 7314 Vol. 12 No. 15 Sun. 17th - Sat. 23rd Feb., 2008

₦10

IF YOU WANT TO BE IN GOD'S INNER CIRCLE

My year of unprecedented greatness and unmatchable increase

Deuteronomy 28:13, Psalm 71:21, Ephesians 3:20, Psalm 92:10

Beloved, our message this week entitled, "If you want to be in God's inner circle" is for the following groups of people:

a. Those who believe that miracles can still happen.
b. Those who want to win before the battle starts.
c. Those who will not elevate the words of doctors, lawyers or anybody above the words of God.
d. Those who believe that God is a God of the suddenly.
e. Those who believe that God is a God of divine intervention. That is, God is able to come through the backdoor when you are expecting Him at the front, and is able to bring tears of joy to your eyes.
f. Those who have faith in the living God and have decided that this year will not swallow anything that belongs to them.
g. Those who are bent on receiving their breakthrough this year.

Do not allow anyone to deceive you by saying that God does not have favourites because He does. The decision to be one of them or not is entirely yours. You can decide to be as close to God as you want to be. God does not push people away. He says, if you move close to me, I too will move close to you but if you move away, I too will move away. Therefore, the decision to be close to God or not is yours. What a wonderful thing it is to be in God's inner circle.

In Amos 3:7, the Bible says, *"Surely the Lord God will do nothing but he revealeth his secret unto his servants the prophets."* So, there are some people who know the programme of God. There are some people who can tell you what will happen in the next seven years. Those are God's favourites. Elisa could be called the executive man of God. He operated as if he usually sat with God in a committee, where they made decisions. Another man in the Bible called Micaiah said something that no prophet ever said in the Bible. He said, "I saw God on His throne and the committee of heaven around him, and your name Ahab was on their agenda" (1 Kings 22:19-22). He said other things done by the committee. That man was allowed to know what was going on in the highest council in heaven. What a glorious thing for a person to walk in that realm. The person would be confident and unbelief would have no place in him. People would look at him and think he is bragging. That is what happens when a person is a member of God's inner circle.

Moses prayed for some seventy elders and the Lord put the spirit of prophecy upon them and they began to prophesy. But there were two persons, who were not in that meeting but because their hearts were there, the overflow of that anointing

THERE IS ALWAYS VACANCY IN THE INNER CIRCLE OF GOD.

came upon them and they began to prophesy just like the people who were standing before Moses. Man looks at the face while God looks at the heart. However, some people rushed to Moses and asked him to stop them since they were not at the meeting but Moses shook his head and said, "Would to God that all of you were prophets then there would be no problem again" (Numbers 11:29). If everyone in the church could hear God, there would be no more problems; any time we gather, it would be to celebrate Jesus.

Unfortunately, this generation and many churches nowadays are looking at the hands of God while very few people look at His face. Anyone who looks at the hands of God alone is only expecting what He can give. Many people never look at His face to see if He has any problem, that they could help with. They will be surprised to know that God actually can do with some help sometimes. One major problem that God has is what is written in Matthew 9:37-38. *"Then saith he unto his disciples; The harvest truly is plenteous, but the labourers are few:* (but even the few labourers are fighting themselves). *Pray ye therefore the Lord of the harvest, that he will send forth labourers into his harvest."* There is plenteous harvest but very few labourers. God is looking for generals, men and women who will move this generation for

DELIVERANCE CASE (THE STORY OF MY LIFE - PART 3

Jesus. There is always vacancy for God's generals in heaven. There is always vacancy in the inner circle of God. Five hundred disciples followed Jesus at a time and out of these seventy drew close, out of the seventy, twelve were chosen and out of the twelve there were three, and out of those three, there was one called John the Beloved. You are as close to Him as you personally want to be.

Beloved, the pertinent question is: What would be written down about you when you leave this world? Will the people who attend your burial ceremony be sorry that you are dead or be happy that you are gone? Will men be able to trace your footstep on the sand of time? Many people are tired of being pushed here and there by the enemy. But the trouble is that their spiritual hands are too weak to battle with some powers. God is looking for generals, He is searching for them day and night. The Bible says, the eyes of the Lord goes to and fro throughout the whole world looking for those whose hearts are right with Him. And immediately He finds them, He conscripts them into His army.

Paul was a general in the army of God but he was beheaded. Peter was another general, who was crucified upside down. We have Martin Luther, Smith Wigglesworth, the great apostle Ayo Babalola, all these were God's Generals. God's heart cry for this generation is to have members for His inner circle. Will you be part of that inner circle or do you want to remain outside? Do you want to be among God's generals? Do you want to be in that inner caucus of the Holy Spirit? God is searching for such people day and night. They are the ones who can move their generation forward for Jesus. What testimony will you leave behind?

There are many strange things happening around us and the kind of power we carry may not match these things if we do not go higher. There is a lot of manipulation going on. There are strange things happening and God is searching for people who will curtail these forces and put them where they belong. The Bible says, "The world is waiting for the manifestation of the sons of God" (Romans 8:9). It means they are not manifesting yet. I pray that whatsoever is preventing you from manifesting as a general in the army of God will die today, in the name of Jesus.

If you want to be God's general or if He has called you to be one and you have decided to be, He will draw you into a life of crucifixion. He will put you on a very good cross and nail you there thoroughly. If He has called you into that realm and it is your desire to go in, He will draw you into a life of humility, and complete obedience would be required from you.

OTHERS MAY YOU CANNOT

If God has called you into that inner circle, He would stop you from measuring yourself by other

Christians. If He has called you into that inner circle and you want to belong, in many ways God will allow other people to do things which He will not allow you to do. Others may be pushing themselves forward wherever they are, you cannot do it because you belong to His inner circle. Others may pull strings in order to get what they want: you cannot because you belong to His inner circle. Others may be lobbying and manipulating in order to get ahead, the members of the inner circle do not do that kind of thing. In fact, if you belong to that inner circle, and you try to copy people who are manipulating and cheating, you will meet with serious failure. If you attempt to follow those who are doing the wrong things, the Lord will oppose you with a serious rebuke.

Others may be careless with the opposite sex but you cannot, if you want to be in His inner circle. Others may be sleeping around and aborting pregnancies but you cannot. If you try it you might die in the process. Others may engage in oral sex, anal sex, and all kinds of sexual perversion but you cannot. If you do, all your heavenly visions and divine dreams will vanish. Others may be stealing from God, you cannot because the hand you use in stealing God's money cannot be laid on the dead and the dead would rise up. You cannot lay it on the sick and the sick will recover. Others may be smoking and drinking secretly

but you cannot because you belong to the inner circle. Others may be addicted to their jewelry make-ups, and other jezebelian materials but you cannot because you are a general in the army of the living God. Others may require in-laws and third parties to settle quarrels between them and their spouses, you cannot because you are higher than that. Others may be boasting of their work, you cannot because you belong to the inner circle of the Almighty. Others could be boasting of their successes or achievements, the members of the inner caucus of the Almighty do not talk about such things. If they try it the Holy Spirit will seriously rebuke them. If they force themselves into it, the Holy Spirit will deal with them in a way that will make them feel bad about themselves, because they belong to a higher group. Others may abandon their spiritual lives and aggressively pursue wealth but you cannot because it is clear to you that you are not going to take anything out this world. For the Bible says, "We brought nothing into the world and it is certain that we will take nothing out of it!" God supplies the day to day needs of His favourites from His own unseen treasury, so they do not steal or cheat. The Lord may

allow others to be honoured and put forward above you but will keep you in hiding. It is a way of preparing you for the coming glory as His general. The Lord may allow others to be great while He keeps you small for now because He is still working on your life like a mechanic working on a vehicle. It is to make you explode at the fullness of time. The Lord may let others do many things and they get all the credit while you do not get any. As a general you do not worry yourself about such things. As a general in the making, God will make you work and toil without knowing how much you are doing. He will do it to make your work more precious. The Lord may even let others get credit for all the work you have done. That does not worry the general in the army of God. It is to make your reward ten times greater when Jesus comes. Others may spend a bigger proportion of their salary buying something to make them look more beautiful, but you cannot because your beauty is the glory of God. And if God wanted all those things on you He would have done so right from your mother's womb and you will be born with them. Others may be practising sex outside marriage, you cannot because if you do it, the Lord who has appointed you as soldier will demote you. Others may be chronic hypocrites, you cannot because you will be shot from both sides. Others may be sitting on the fence, you cannot because if you do, you will be twice dead. Others may be dressing to kill, you cannot because your own dressing is supposed to be the amour of God. There is no point dressing to kill physically when spiritually you are naked. Others may attach marine weave-on unto their hair, you cannot because your hair is the glory of the Lord, and the symbol of your destiny. Others may marry outside the church, with no dowry paid or engagement done, you cannot because you represent heaven on earth. Others may disobey and insult their spiritual fathers, you cannot because the Bible says, "Honour your father and your mother that your days may be long." It means that if you do not honour them, your days will be short. Others may be seeking worldly approval, you cannot because the approval of heaven is what you need, and also, the approval of men is vanity in heaven. Others may be playing

spiritual bat, you cannot because bats do not become generals. If you dress decently to church and dress indecently outside, you are a bat, you cannot become a general. Others may be comfortable without the baptism of the Holy Spirit, you cannot because that is the power of God to make you great. Others may be comfortable without any gift of the Holy Spirit, but you cannot because you will become a trunkless elephant or a weaponless soldier. Others may be happy coming to church only on Sundays but you cannot because your well will run dry. Others may be going to prostitutes, both academic and crude, but you cannot because you will mortgage your anointing on the altar of Jezebel. Others may allow all kinds of men to touch their body, you cannot allow those dirty claws of death to run through your body because you belong to the inner circle of the Almighty. Others may rush to many unbelievers because

they feel that nobody is coming to them, you cannot because that would mean casting your pearls before swine. Others may be doing what they like but you cannot do what you like anymore because the destinies of millions of people are attached to yours. If you fail, a lot of people will fail. If you refuse to gather the kind of power God wants you to gather, a lot of people will be destroyed. And when you appear at the throne of grace, the blood of many people will be crying against you.

Immediately you make a decision to be close to God, your training will start. The Holy Spirit will consider it an insult to share you with other things, and will rebuke you for indecent words or remarks that you make. The Holy Spirit will harass you when you do something wrong and may not harass other Christians for doing the same thing. The Holy Spirit will check you anytime you are going astray.

When God draws you into that inner circle, He will not excuse you for the sins others commit and go free. When God draws you close, He may not explain to you a thousand things bothering your mind immediately. When God is dealing with you, the Holy Spirit could tie your tongue, and you will not be allowed to speak when you are angry. When the Lord is dealing with you, the Holy Spirit has the right to chain your hands, close your eyes

THE PROPHET Power pass power (3)

and control you in the way that He may not control others. That is why you should not compare yourself with people. He will exercise aggressive management over your life.

Beloved, are you walking the way God wants you to walk? Is your heart right with God? Are you willing to drop everything for Jesus? Do you have hatred or anger against anyone? Are you pursuing some values in the church and another set of values outside? Are you a stumbling block to new believers

Others may be doing the wrong things but you cannot. You belong to the inner circle of the Almighty when you become God's favourite person. The Bible says Noah found grace in the eyes of God. The Bible talks about God being close to Noah, Daniel, and Joseph. Do you desire to be a general in this generation? God has set up many people as watchmen for their families. If you do not fulfill the specific purpose for which God has created you, He will order that you be cut down and replaced. Do you really want to be a friend of God? Or are you rejecting all the readjustment He is asking you to make? Are you aware that God is writing down things you will have to answer one day? Are you aware that you may be closer to hell fire than you think?

Talk to the Lord and say, "Lord, I want to be your favourite person. I want to be in your inner circle. I want to be the kind of man that could be invited into the council of heaven to see what is going on. I want my spiritual eyes to be open. I am tired of spiritual blindness. I am tired of not seeing where I am stepping into. I am tired of putting my money in the wrong things all because I cannot see. I am tired of moving with friends who want to destroy me. I am tired of seeing men just after the flesh and not for who they are. I am tired of employing witches and wizards in my business. Tell the Lord to remove anything that will prevent you from getting to His inner circle, no matter how much you love it. Do not allow the Lord to be harsh on you before you submit to Him. God bless you as you make the necessary adjustment, in Jesus' name.

PRAYER POINTS

1. Every power making my visions dark, die, in the name of Jesus.
2. Oh heavens over my spiritual vision, open by fire, in the name of Jesus.
3. Oh heavens over my spiritual vision, open by fire, in the name of Jesus.
4. Oh heavens over my spiritual vision, open by fire, in the name of Jesus.
5. Arrows of backwardness targeted against me this year, backfire, in the name of Jesus.
6. My destiny arise by fire and reject disgrace, in the name of Jesus.
7. Every dragon that does not want me to lift my head, die, in the name of Jesus.
8. Every satanic vigil organized against my progress, scatter, in the name of Jesus.
9. Mark of tragedy, die, mark of breakthrough, come, in the name of Jesus.
10. Wall of fire, envelope me and my family, in the name of Jesus.
11. I shall arise and shine, no power shall put me down, in the name of Jesus.

IF YOU WANT TO BE IN GOD'S INNER CIRCLE
is a message delivered at the Mountain of Fire and Miracles Ministries by the General Overseer, Dr. D.K. Olukoya.

A CALL TO SERVE

Are you a member of MFM with a burden to help the needy, are you interested in alleviating the plight of the poor or in the spread of the gospel through the sponsorshing of the publication of tracts? Your resources, time and talent can be extended to several groups that are in charge of these areas. These groups include:

o   We care Ministry,
o   Mission Outreach
o   Tracts and Publications
o   Ministry to Drug addicts
o   Campus fellowship
o   Ministry to School
o   Ministry to Glorious Children, etc.

Thus says the Lord, "Verily I say unto you, in as much as ye have done it unto one of the least of these my brethren, ye have done it unto me" Matthew 25 : 40.

WONDERFUL JESUS!

DOUBLE BLESSING FROM GOD

My wife gave birth to a bouncing baby girl successfully at Ondo town. I left Lagos where I was working for the naming ceremony and also to help my wife arrange certain things. By the time I returned to my place of work, I discovered that I had been sacked. I continued to pray to God for job without any positive result. One day, a friend of mine advised me to take a chair in my sitting room and ask Jesus to sit down by my side and discuss with Him face to face. I took two chairs for both of us in faith and asked Him to give me a job. To my surprise I found myself fully employed in the Vice-president's office in Abuja. Praise God!

Bro. Hammond
MFM Ondo

GOD RESTORES MY MARRIAGE

I thank God for what He has done for me. Sometime ago, my mother in-law came up one day and commanded me to get out of my husband's house without any reason. A sister that attends MFM introduced me to one of their programmes, so I attended the programme for three Sundays, after which I went through deliverance and God restored my marriage and my business. Praise the Lord!

Sis. Tope
MFM Abule-Anu

EXAMINATION BREAKTHROUGH AFTER 7 YEARS

For seven years I was battling with just one paper to pass my ICAN qualifying exams. It became so serious that I was almost discouraged. One day, the General Overseer, while ministering said that we should write out what we wanted the Lord to do for us. I committed this very case to God and when the result came out, I passed. Right now I am a qualified Chartered Accountant to the glory of God! Praise the Lord!

Sis. Tolu
MFM Headquarters

SATANIC POWERS UNSEATED

I am an importer of GSM handsets and accessories. Shortly after my consignment arrived the country, they were ceased. I visited many fellowships but there was no solution. A friend introduced me to MFM and after series of prayers, the satanic powers that held on to my goods were finally unseated by fire. Praise the Lord!

Bro. Destiny
MFM Iba

SET FREE FROM INFIRMITIES

Before I joined this ministry, I was practically surviving on drugs. My state of health was so bad that I became a regular caller at the hospital. But today I am set free and delivered. I also thank God for granting me journey mercies. Praise the Lord!

Sis. Joy

MFM Ijaiye Ojokoro

THREEFOLD MANIFESTATION OF GOD'S POWER

First, since my family and I came back from Kaduna after a long stay, God has been good to us. Secondly, my son was stooling and urinating blood, I took the case to the Lord and he was divinely healed. Thirdly, although we came back a poor family from Kaduna, God has been meeting our needs, and recently my younger brother had a successful wedding. Praise the Lord!

Sis. Ruth
MFM Apata

GOD CHANGES MY STATUS

God changed my status by providing another job that is three times better than what I had before. To the glory of God, my resumption date coincided with my birthday anniversary. I give glory to the name of Lord. Praise the Lord!

Bro. Shofoluwe
MFM Omo-Oye

DELIVERANCE FROM STOMACH ACHE AND ARMED ROBBERY ATTACK

I thank God that after deliverance a chronic stomach problem I had for a long time stopped. Secondly my baby that had not walked for a long time started walking. Thirdly, my brother who came to Lagos on a business trip was attacked by armed robbers on his way back to Port-Harcourt. When the armed robbers could not find any money on him, they decided to punish him by forcing him to eat raw pepper. In the process one of them flashed his torch on his face and recognized him. Then they ran and left him unhurt. Praise the Lord!

Sis. Pat
MFM Adaloko

DIVINE PROTECTION

I thank God for saving me from armed robbery attack. On my way home recently, I found that armed robbers were operating on my street but to the glory of God, I was not attacked. Praise the Lord!

Sis. Bolorunduro
MFM Abule-Egba

DIVINE FAVOUR

I put in a pray request for a study leave at my place of work and to the glory of God, the request was granted. Praise the Lord!

Sis. Ebun
MFM Ado-Ekiti

NOW ON SALE

The MFM 2008 Anointed Diary is now on sale.
It is a daily devotional guide for Bible Reading and
Spiritual Warfare that will make everyday of the year
2008 AD a victorious one for you.
Grab your copy from the vendors.

FIRE IN THE WORD, is a weekly Spiritual Bulletin of the Mountain of Fire and Miracles Ministries, published by Tracts and Publications Group. All Enquiries should be addressed to The Editor, Mountain of Fire Magazine, 13, Olasimbo Street, off Olumo Road, Onike, P.O. Box 2990, Sabo Yaba, Lagos, Nigeria. Telephone 01- 867439, 864631, 868766, 08023180236.E-mail: mfmtractsandpublications@yahoo.com Copyright reserved.

FIRE IN THE WORD

Ye Shall Know the Truth, and the Truth Shall Make You Free (John 8:32)

ISSN 1595 - 7314 Vol. 12 No. 16 Sun. 24th Feb. - Sat. 1st Mar., 2008 ₦10

STARS UNDER ATTACK

My year of unprecedented greatness and unmatchable increase
Deuteronomy 28:13, Psalm 71:21, Ephesians 3:20, Psalm 92:10

This week, we are looking at the message titled, "Star under attack." Psalm 19:1-6: *"The heavens declare the glory of God; and the firmament sheweth his handiwork.* (Meaning that the heavens can make a declaration over a man's life and over the earth; and the firmament reveals things; so the heavens talk and the firmament shows). *Day unto day uttereth speech,* (This confirms that the heavens speak. Each day has its own speech and these things may change from day to day and time to time) *and night unto night sheweth knowledge* (there is a mystery with the night, there are certain things that are only revealed at night. There are some prayers that are best prayed at night. Jesus said, "Would God not avenge His saints who cry to Him day and night." There are some prayers for the day and some prayers for the night. The sun, the moon and the stars speak. Verses 3-6: *"There is no speech nor language, where their voice is not heard. Their line is gone out through all the earth, and their words to the end of the world. In them hath*

he set a tabernacle for the sun, Which is as a bridegroom coming out of his chamber, and rejoiceth as a strong man to run a race. His going forth is from the end of the heaven, and his circuit unto the ends of it: and there is nothing hid from the heat thereof."

We can see that actually, the heavens do speak, but there are some satanic children who can hear them talk. The enemy does not bother with any destiny that does not bother him. He is not interested in stopping anyone whose life does not mean anything to him. But immediately he knows that your destiny is a threat to him, the battle of your life begins. Matthew 2:1-2 says, *"Now when Jesus was born in Bethlehem of Judea in the days of Herod the king, behold there came wise men from the east to Jerusalem, saying, Where is he that is born King of the Jews? For we have seen his star in the east, and are come to worship him."*

THE ENEMY DOES NOT ATTACK PEOPLE WITH INFERIOR QUALITIES.

Those men were able to locate the star of Jesus and they traced it.

Verse 7: *"Then Herod, when he had privily called the wise men, enquired of them diligently what time the star appeared."* Why did he want that information? He wanted to carry out a counter attack against the star, but the wise men did not cooperate with him. These wise men from the east were able to locate the star of Jesus among other stars, meaning that there are some men who can decode the language of heaven. Unfortunately, these men are mostly evil because Christians do not want to settle down and learn the necessary things, rather they are busy fighting themselves.

Demonic people can look at the heavens and know that a child has been born somewhere and what the child would become. If they want to extend their wickedness, they can do something to that star like as it is written in Daniel 8:9-10. Many people need to pray very hard to restore their star which has already been cast down. Daniel

DELIVERANCE CASE (The Story of My Life - Part 4)

8:9-10: *"And out of one of them came forth a little horn, which waxed exceeding great, toward the south, and toward the east, and toward the pleasant land. And it waxed great, even to the host of heaven; and it cast down some of the host and of the stars to the ground, and stamped upon them."* It cast their star down from heaven and stamped upon them so that they will not raise their heads again. At this juncture, I would like you to take this prayer point: "Any power that says I will not lift my head, die, in the name of Jesus."

It cast the stars down and to ensure that they do not rise again, it stamped on them. You may wonder whether these stars are human beings? But those ancient men understand things we do not know. Genesis says, 37:9 says, *"And he dreamed yet another dream, and told it his brethren, and said, Behold, I have dreamed a dream more; and, behold, the sun and the moon and the eleven stars made obeisance to me."* His parents understood the dream instantly. Joseph's parents knew that by the sun and the moon he was referring to his father and mother and the stars were his brethren. The interpretation was that they were human beings. The Bible says, *"There is one glory of the sun, and another glory of the moon, and another glory of the stars: for one star differeth from another star in glory"* (1 Corinthians 15:41).

When satanic powers want to finish a person they start from when the person is in the womb. If the person escapes that they could use sexual attack, if that fails, they could go for his urine, faeces, saliva, fingernail etc. When they try all these things and find it difficult to deal with the person, they now go to people who operate altars in the stars; men and women who visit the heavens.

WHY DO MEN VISIT THE HEAVENS?

1. To obtain directions.
2. To know the future, because heavens speak and heavens know.
3. To cage progress.
4. To destroy people.
5. To control situations.

6. To manipulate communities. A single man/woman in a village who can speak to the heavenlies is the controller of that village and they will fear him or her exceedingly.

7. To manipulate wealth from the heavens.

8. To gain advantage over other men.

9. To oppose God and His kingdom agenda. I pray that any power visiting the heavens against you shall be cast down and disgraced, in Jesus' name.

10. To gain political leadership.

11. To dominate.

12. To obtain protection.

13. To get provision and supply.

14. To attack the stars of others and destroy their destiny.

This issue takes you back to when you were born and when you were given your names. Many people do not know the number of names they were given on their naming ceremony day or who suggested the names. As a result of this, a lot of people go about with bewitched names thereby renewing covenants of stagnation. These men saw the star of Jesus and travelled all the way from the east, placing themselves at peril and spending a lot of money just to see the owner of the star.

In some places immediately a child is born, a spiritual investigation is carried out on the star of the child and this has been the source of many people's problems. This is why some people never went to school. Their stars were investigated and it was discovered that if they went to school they would shine. If they discover that proper marriage would make the star of a particular woman to shine, they will quickly give her a demonic boyfriend in primary school. The enemy does not attack people with inferior qualities. But if he finds that the quality of your life is superior, you will come under attack.

QUARRELS AMONG PARENTS EXPOSE THE STARS OF THEIR CHILDREN TO DANGER

A space in heaven has been allocated unto every man or woman. It is a mystery. This is why the Bible talks about "thy heaven which is over thine head." Each man/woman has a space given him/her in the heavens and in addition, every one has a star. The wise men said, "We have seen His star in the east and this is why we have come to worship Him." Sometimes when the star of a person is known to wicked people they begin to do all kinds of strange things to that star; they will begin to attack the progress of such a star and programme words into the star so that the person will not experience progress.

A lot of people are under star bondage. Your star is an embodiment of your destiny, a carrier of your destiny. There are terrible people who specialize on star attacks. A lot of things happen at naming ceremonies. If your spiritual eyes are open, you will see spiritual stars on the heads of babies, sometimes shining with different colours. Astrologers can read these stars from the palm of a person.

But we thank God that a star, which has been destroyed, can be recovered through some prayers. But if it has been cast down and trampled on, like we see in Daniel 8:9-10, you need to specially pray for a creative miracle.

The Bible talks about wandering stars in the book of Jude, meaning that a person's star can be programmed to wander about. So the person will be moving about like a vagabond, without a special aim in life.

SEVERAL WICKED THINGS THAT CAN BE DONE TO A PERSON'S STAR

1. It could be shut down: When it is shut down, the person becomes a living corpse.

2. It can be dimmed: When this happens, the person will lose his glory.

3. The star can be obstructed: When it is obstructed, stagnation will set in.

4. The star can be made to sink. When this happens, the person will be living on past glory.

5. The star can be exchanged: The attacked person will live a fake life and everywhere he or she goes there will be a road sign saying, "Road closed."

6. The star can be caged; meaning that the person can be buoyant, intelligent, but not moving.

7. The star can be tampered with: The person will be dreaming of good things but those good things will never happen physically.

THE STRATEGIES OF STAR ATTACKERS

1. Prevention of birth: They would not want the person to be born at all. Sometimes, the affected baby may refuse to cry at birth. They may seriously attack the mother.

2. Through attack in the womb.

3. Through attack as a baby: They struggle to take away what belongs to that child and transfer it to other people.

4. Quarrelsome parents: Quarrels among parents expose the stars of their children to danger.

5. Household witchcraft particularly polygamy: People who come from polygamous homes or those whose names are idolatrous need deliverance from evil star attackers.

6. They use envious enemies.

THE PROPHET

7. They cause sex with satanic agents. If you sleep with satanic agents you are in trouble, because you can lose your stars through that.

8. Dreams of spiritual thieves: When you dream of people coming to steal from you, your star is under attack.

9. Food in the dream: Eating in the dream is very bad. Sicknesses are planted in the body through it. Prayerlessness will be established, business and marriage can also be paralysed.

10. Padlock bondage: They could lock up people's stars and throw them away.

11. Construction of coffins for those who are not dead: They make tiny coffins as a symbol and bury them. It is a way of burying people's stars in mother earth.

12. Sponge used for bathing by streams organized by some prophets or prophetesses: If they have ever taken you to the stream for such baths, you need to pray hard. They might have used those sponges to wash away your glory and stars.

13. They use the hair: If you noticed some part of your hair was cut off and you could not explain how it happened, you need to pray.

14. Through naming ceremonies done with some strange items such as dead rat, alligator pepper etc.

WAY OUT

1. Repent of any sin that can hinder your prayer.

2. Identify areas in your life that you have opened to star hijackers.

3. Pray all the following star-recovery prayer points aggressively.

PRAYER POINTS

1. Every naming ceremony bondage, die, in the name of Jesus.

2. Every evil wise man pursuing my star, die, in the name of Jesus.

3. My buried glory, arise and shine, in the name of Jesus.

4. Every power that is attacking my star, I bury you today, in the name of Jesus.

5. Every star padlock fashioned against my destiny, die, in the name of Jesus.

6. My destiny, run into the strong tower of the Lord, in the name of Jesus.

7. Power to remember me fall upon my helpers, in the name of Jesus.

8. Those who do not know me shall fight for my cause, in Jesus' name.

9. Thou power of darkness hijacking my star, die, in the name of Jesus.

10. Every power that says my star will not move, your time is up, die, in the name of Jesus.

STARS UNDER ATTACK

is a message delivered at the Mountain of Fire and Miracles Ministries by the General Overseer, Dr. D.K. Olukoya.

A CALL TO SERVE

Are you a member of MFM with a burden to help the needy, are you interested in alleviating the plight of the poor or in the spread of the gospel through the sponsorshing of the publication of tracts? Your resources, time and talent can be extended to several groups that are in charge of these areas. These groups include:

o   We care Ministry,
o   Mission Outreach
o   Tracts and Publications
o   Ministry to Drug addicts
o   Campus fellowship
o   Ministry to School
o   Ministry to Glorious Children, etc.

Thus says the Lord, "Verily I say unto you, in as much as ye have done it unto one of the least of these my brethren, ye have done it unto me" Matthew 25 : 40.

WONDERFUL JESUS!

GOD OF PROMOTION

For quite some time, I could not fast or pray well. But on the last day of the last Prophetic Congress, the hand of God touched me and my prayer and fasting life was restored. Secondly, I work in a bank. During the Seventy Days Prayer and Fasting period, I was promoted with a car and a driver attached. Praise the Lord!

Sis. Oluwatoyin
MFM Headquarters

INSANITY GONE

I came for deliverance in MFM on behalf of my child who was sick and kept in the custody of a fake prophet. I thank God that during the deliverance, my child was let off the hook and was able to speak to me sensibly. Praise the Lord!

Sis. Anna
MFM Agodo

GOD SAVES ME FROM SUDDEN DEATH

Recently, I travelled to Bayelsa State from Lagos in an eighteen-seater bus. Between Okada town and Ore I slept off only to be woken by a loud bang and noise. By the time I opened my eyes, our vehicle already had a head-on collision with a Mercedes V-boot car. The driver and one other passenger died instantly while many others sustained terrible injuries. Only four of us came out unhurt. Praise the Lord!

Bro. Matayas
MFM Egbe Zonal Headquarters

EVIL PROPHECY DISGRACED

Before our wedding, members of my husband's family said if I did not get pregnant before the wedding, I would find it difficult to have a child. I rejected the evil prophecy and my husband and I agreed not to defile our bed before our wedding. We continued in prayer against the evil prophecy and thank God today, we have a baby.

Sis. Oladimeji
MFM Ikorodu 1

MONEY RECOVERED

A certain man borrowed some money from me after which he started avoiding me. I tried my best to collect my money from him but to no avail. Later, I prayed about it and went to his house. On getting there, I met him and he paid me. Praise the Lord!

Bro. William
MFM Olowora

JESUS CHRIST HEALS ME

After a medical examination, the doctor diagnosed diabetes. I felt that the stripes of Jesus that heals and my faith in Him will fail me if I continued to attend the hospital for treatment. So, I came for deliverance before my next check-up day. And when I went for the check-up, all the tests proved negative. I came out of the hospital a happy person. I am healed. Praise the Lord!

Sis. Stella
MFM Ejigbo

GOD'S DIVINE GUIDANCE

On my return journey from a trip, our bus ran into an armed robbery operation. Passengers from on-coming vehicles were robbed of their belongings but God helped the driver of our bus and he was able to avoid them. Many people were hurt while trying to escape but God guarded me home safely. Praise the Lord!

Sis. Florence
MFM Ikare

SUPERNATURAL PROMOTION

In the civil service, promotion is done every three years. Two years ago, I was promoted. A year later, I was promoted again. This year, I shall be going for another promotional interview. This implies three promotions in three years instead of one. Praise the Lord!

Bro. Openaike
MFM Abaranje

GOD GIVES ME A DIVINE TOUCH

I thank God for His love and mercies over my life. I received a divine touch during the "Igniting the fire" programme. Since then I have had turnaround breakthroughs. Also, the plans of the enemy for me to die were destroyed and God has caused me to overcome the spirit of death and hell. Praise the Lord!

Bro. Adedokun
MFM Ojo

SPIRIT OF DEATH DEFEATED

A friend in my place of work dreamt and told me that my husband and I were electrocuted. When she told me the dream I cancelled it immediately. Three days later, our NEPA meter caught fire and exploded at night. I raised alarm and cried out for help. Neighbours. came and put off the fire. I thank God Almighty that the evil dream did not manifest. Praise the Lord!

Sis. Efurien
MFM Aboru

NOW ON SALE

The MFM 2008 Anointed Diary is now on sale.
It is a daily devotional guide for Bible Reading and
Spiritual Warfare that will make everyday of the year
2008 AD a victorious one for you.
Grab your copy from the vendors.

FIRE IN THE WORD is a weekly Spiritual Bulletin of the Mountain of Fire and Miracles Ministries,
published by Tracts and Publications Group. All Enquiries should be addressed to The Editor, Mountain of Fire
Magazine, 13, Olasimbo Street, off Olumo Road, Onike, P.O. Box 2990, Sabo Yaba, Lagos, Nigeria.
Telephone 01- 867439, 864631, 868766, 08023180236.E-mail: mfmtractsandpublications@yahoo.com
Copyright reserved.

FIRE IN THE WORD

Ye Shall Know the Truth, and the Truth Shall Make You Free (John 8:32)

ISSN 1595 - 7314 Vol. 12 No. 17 Sun. 2nd - Sat. 8th Mar., 2008

₦10

DESTRUCTIVE LOCATIONS

My year of unprecedented greatness and unmatchable increase
Deuteronomy 28:13, Psalm 71:21, Ephesians 3:20, Psalm 92:10

This message is for those who need to be relocated from where the enemy has pushed them. Every man or woman is in a particular position in the spirit realm at every given time. Every man has a location, your location determines your possession. It is often said that 99 percent of success is based on correct location and the major cause of failure too is as a result of wrong location. Talent alone cannot move a life forward, other things are needed as well. Intelligence alone cannot move your life forward. You can be intelligent but not wise. You can be talented but be an absolute fool.

The problem of Adam was location. After he had eaten the forbidden fruit and God came to see him in the garden, He could not find him in his rightful position. And God began to ask. "Adam, Adam, where are you?" That is, where is your location? So, spiritually, Adam had shifted location despite the fact that he was still in the garden, moving around as usual. So, it is possible for someone to be in a location of wastage.

It is a tragedy for a man to be wasted only because he was wrongly located not because he was supposed to be wasted. Jeremiah 51:1 says, "*Thus saith the Lord; Behold, I will raise up against Babylon, and against them that dwell in the midst of them that rise up against me, a destroying wind.*" Sometimes, the wicked dies, and the righteous is also swept away in the flood that was sent against the wicked. There are many innocent citizens whose lives have been snuffed out by what is known as "Stray bullets." We see innocent people dying accidentally.

About Babylon God warned: He said He was going to send a destroying wind, which would claim two victims. First, it was going to waste Babylon because God was against Babylon. Secondly, it was going to sweep away those that dwell in the midst of them, that is its inhabitants. The people who were living there were not part of its problem but because they were there at that time, they became victims. These innocent inhabitants would be destroyed as a result of the crossfire between God and Babylon. And we are in a period of crossfire operations now. Beloved, I pray that in this season of battles, you will not be found in the wrong camp, in Jesus' name. It is not sufficient to be righteous, it is also important that you are not among those who are part of the target to be destroyed. It is good for you to be a righteous person in the right place.

Jonathan the son of Saul entered into a covenant with David. He knew

ALL PERPETUAL LATECOMERS ARE SERVING ANOTHER GOD, AND NOT THE LIVING GOD.

that David was the Lord's anointed and made a covenant with him to be his everlasting friend; yet Jonathan died fighting on the side of Saul whom God had penciled down for destruction. He was a righteous man in covenant with David, but when the sword came for his father, he was found in the midst of them that rose up against God. So he along with them were swept away by the destroying wind, he was not spared. Nowadays, such destructive wind is blowing all over the place. That is why the scriptures in Psalm 91 has become quite relevant. The shadow of the Almighty is the right place to be always. Anyone who is not there, would be hit by any destroying wind that comes. Anyone who is not in the rightful position will be a victim of the destruction that takes place. When the angel of destruction was going around Egypt to slay all the Egyptian firstborns any Israeli firstborn that went to play with his Egyptian friend in a location that was not marked with the blood of the lamb would be destroyed. Although he was an Israelite, and probably living a good life, he would be wasted in the destroying wind because he would have been in a wrong location no matter how righteous he was.

It is therefore important to locate your position in the house of God and also in the agenda of the Almighty, because when the crossfire begins and you are not

DELIVERANCE CASE (The Story of My Life - Part 5)

correctly located, you may get into trouble.

It is very sad to know that despite the number of churches we have now and the crowd that troupe into them, a lot of people are still lost right inside the church. Some people inside the church can also be likened to a letter properly enveloped, stamped and posted, but which got lost in transit. They can be compared to the Israelites who left Egypt but got lost in the wilderness — they could not reach the promised land. Many are known by God and many are known with God but they do not have God. Many are running the business of God without knowing the God they are running His business. There are plenty who come to church but have really never met the Lord — they have not had an encounter with God therefore they are wrongly positioned. Many are married to church activities and programmes, but do not know the God whom they serve. Many have become what we call "almost there" Christians — they are not really there. They believe that they have to

be born again, sanctified and also receive the baptism of the Holy Ghost but have failed to live the right life.

The kind of words coming to many today is the kind of words God spoke to Eve in the garden of Eden: "Woman, what hast thou done?" Meaning that if you know the implication of what you have done, you will be sorrowful. Now everybody is in trouble because of she did. Many come to church and have a form of godliness, but they are like a cake not turned, they are religious and zealous but do not know the power of God. Many are very familiar with church programmes but far from God and His righteousness. An almost there Christian is not a Christian. He or she is not far from the kingdom of God but he or she is not there- it is a dangerous and destructive position to be. Jesus looked at a certain man and said: "Thou art not far from the kingdom of God," but he never entered there. The fact is that almost

there is not there. If you almost received the baptism of the Holy Ghost, you did not get it. Many people are almost where God wants them to be spiritually but are not there. It is a destructive position. You need to take a stand quick. The middle position is a dangerous location to be. A child of God should not go to a location that has been marked for destruction. It is an insult on your salvation if you enter a bus, and sleep off as a result of incantations.

If something was supposed to carry 2000 volts of electric power, and it has only 10 volts, even a small boy will play with it because of low power. Fire has levels. When you strike a matchstick you will get fire, but a small boy can blow it out. Fire from firewood is also a form of fire, but somebody can pour water on it and that will be the end of the fire. The candle fire is fire but any small wind can put it off. Somebody with the candle-fire and the matchstick fire could be boasting that he has the fire of God but that is a low level of fire. At the same time the gas cooker fire is another fire entirely. It cannot be blown out. The fire used by welders is another form of fire. So fire has levels. Luke 3:16 says, *"John answered, saying unto them all, I indeed baptise you with water, but one mightier than I cometh, the latchet of whose shoes I am not worthy to unloose: he shall baptise you with the Holy Ghost and with fire."* The passage is talking about two different kinds of baptism: baptism of the Holy Ghost and baptism of fire. Woe befalls any witchcraft power that would touch a man or woman that is baptised with fire. But when there is no fire, they have a field day.

THOSE WHO ARE WRONGLY POSITIONED

1. The Almost there: The first group of people in the house of God who are wrongly located are the "Almost there" people. It is a destructive location to be. The destroying wind can sweep them away at any time. They could board a commuter bus that the enemy has decided to waste it's occupants, and because they are wrongly positioned, they will be swept away.

2. People in the dark regions: The second group of people in the house of God who are wrongly located are those in the dark regions. It would surprise you to know that among the children of God, there are some who are sitting and abiding in the region of darkness.

They know they have familiar spirit but are not making any effort to get delivered. They know they have witchcraft spirit and are not taking any steps to be free. They are in the dark regions, they are lost and anything can happen. They can get into the crossfire of the Almighty.

3. Those who sit at the back: In the house of God, there some people who prefer to sit at the back whether they come early or late. They have chosen a permanent seat at the back. Even when they come early they still want to sit at the back. They do not want to look at anybody straight in the eye and will not come to the front at all. It is a very sad situation to be.

4. Those who sit in the veranda: There are also those who sit in the church veranda. They do not like entering into the auditorium. If you ask them to come inside they will come up with various excuses such as there is no space inside again, it is hot inside or I am alright here. To be a veranda Christian is a big problem.

5. Church nannies: There are also people in the church of God who could be called church nannies. They come to church to play with children. They may not be their

ONCE YOUR LOCATION IS WRONG, AND THE ALMIGHTY CANNOT FIND YOU, YOU WILL BE WASTED

children but they will be busy playing with them. While the service is going on, they are playing with their neighbour's child who has come for service. I pity such people because they come and do not gain anything. It is a destructive location.

6. Perpetual late comers: They wake up when the praise worship has ended. They are careful to keep appointments with their friends or business partners and never get late to their place of work. But to them God's house is secondary. All perpetual latecomers are serving another god, and not the living God. People like that are in a destructive location.

7. Strange pastors' associates: They are close to pastors but are not born again. They are close to the truth but the truth is not in them. They carry the bag of the man of God but there is no bag of the Holy Spirit in their lives. They are like closed bottles thrown into the midst of an ocean. Although they are in the midst of the ocean, no water can get inside them. They are in a destructive location. Such people should pray not to become like Gehazi.

8. The troublemakers: We have those who come to the house of God to make trouble, they always create headache for the pastors and those who are supposed to look after their soul.

The Lord is sounding this warning because the wind that is blowing now will blow away anyone who is not correctly located. The message for the end time is not a message of "You are going to be great, you will rise up, I see you at the top etc." That is not the message for this season. The correct word for this season is the scripture that says: "And now also the axe is laid to the root of the trees, therefore any tree which bringeth not forth good fruit is cut down and cast into the fire"(Matthew 3:10). Do not allow God to cut you off. God wants you to bring forth fruit of repentance.

Some people have been coming to church for a long time but you cannot see the mark of God upon their lives. They do not communicate with God, they have no relationship with God. There are some who do not like listening to messages while some are only interested in prayers. Many come but they lack stamina. They cannot

really pray for long – it is a wrong location to be. Some are completely indisciplined. They do not want to be controlled. Some sisters complain that something is walking about in their heads. That should be expected when they have all kinds of attachments on their heads.

Sometime ago, a white woman who is a member of MFM Overseas wrote me a letter, asking why black sisters copy white women, and are not happy with what God has given to them. She wondered why some paint their faces so much and attach things to their nails. The reason we warn against the use of jewelry and attachments to different parts of the body is that those things hinder deliverance. And the fact that when some people comply and pray they have testimonies shows that those things can hinder deliverance. Sometimes, you see some sisters going back to those things again,

and when you ask them why, they would say they saw a female pastor wearing trousers and all kinds of things on television. The question is: are the names of these people written in the book of life? There are some people who are easily angered, it is a wrong location to be. Anger is a destroyer, it can open door to so many things. Men and women who are sexually loose are in the wrong location.

Psalm 71:3 says: *"Be thou my strong habitation, whereunto I may continually resort: thou hast given commandment to save me; for thou art my rock and my fortress."* It means that if I am inside a vehicle, He has given commandment to that vehicle to save me, if I am passing by a building about to collapse, He has given commandment that I must pass before it collapses. Food poison cannot affect me because He has given commandment that the poison should go somewhere else. If Mr. Pestilence is moving all over town and gets to my house, He would tell him to pass over. This commandment cannot work for somebody who is wrongly located.

In the midst of destructions happening around, for example, petrol pipe vandalization in which a lot of people get roasted by fire, you would be surprised to know that there are Christians amongst them. Also, you could have Christians in vehicles that run into the lagoon. The cause of all these is wrong location.

THE PROPHET | David versus Goliath 5

...I THINK IT'S TIME TO TEACH YOU CHURCH-RAT AN EVERLASTING LESSON

YOU BETTER START RUNNING, BECAUSE YOUR OBITUARY IS AS CLOSE AS YOUR TWO FRONT TEETH. BIG-FOR-NOTHING

Once your location is wrong, and the Almighty cannot find you, you will be wasted. If you are not where you are supposed to be, you will be wasted. Anywhere you cannot do the will of God is not the right place for you. If you are not located where God wants you to be spiritually, an arrow can fly against you.

The rate at which people are running after money these days is alarming. Many are becoming experts at looking for money in the wrong location. You must understand that once you have another god besides God, you are wrongly placed and anything can happen to you at any time. People may gather and begin to wonder how it happened but heaven is saying, "Where art thou? because you were not found where heavens put you. Where heavens expected you to go, you were not found in that location. You need to understand where you are.

Beloved, are you wrongly located? Spiritually are you no where to be found? Anyone who is not serious with his spiritual life is writing a letter to the destroying wind. If you know that your ways are not right with God and you do not repent and change quickly, you are writing a letter to the destroying wind. If God is saying, Where art thou and cannot locate you, He will declare your position vacant in heaven. Will you allow Him to do that? If you do not have the fire you are supposed to collect, you are wrongly located. If the kind of anointing you are supposed to carry is not upon your life, you are wrongly located. If the kind of prayer God expects you to pray to move His hands is not coming from you, you are wrongly located. If you keep falling into sin and coming out, you are wrongly located.

If Peter did not come to fish the day Jesus met him, he would be wrongly located. Jesus told His disciples to go to the upper room until they were filled with power. He sent them to a location. If anyone of them refused to go to the upper room, when the day of Pentecost came and fire fell, he would miss it. God told Jonah to go to Nineveh and prophesy against it but he boarded a boat for Tarshish, he went to the wrong location and it was not a pleasant experience. Beloved, do not allow the enemy to waste you. Make sure you are in the right location always.

PRAYER POINTS

1. Boat of Jonah carrying me away, catch fire, in the name of Jesus.
2. Anointing of bad location upon my life, die, in the name of Jesus.
3. Power to be in the right place at the right time, come upon my life now, in the name of Jesus.
4. My Father, deliver me from wastage, in the name of Jesus.
5. Dark authorities assigned to waste my calling, scatter, in the name of Jesus.
6. Evil location assigned to magnetize me, scatter, in the name of Jesus.
7. My Father, if I am wrongly located, relocate me by fire, in the name of Jesus.
8. Every power writing my name in the book of demotion, die, in the name of Jesus.
9. Hunters of my soul, die, in the name of Jesus.
10. Power of God, baptize me, in the name of Jesus.

DESTRUCTIVE LOCATIONS

is a message delivered at the Mountain of Fire and Miracles Ministries by the General Overseer, Dr. D.K. Olukoya.

A CALL TO SERVE

Are you a member of MFM with a burden to help the needy, are you interested in alleviating the plight of the poor or in the spread of the gospel through the sponsorshing of the publication of tracts? Your resources, time and talent can be extended to several groups that are in charge of these areas. These groups include:

o   We care Ministry,
o   Mission Outreach
o   Tracts and Publications
o   Ministry to Drug addicts
o   Campus fellowship
o   Ministry to Schools
o   Ministry to Glorious Children, etc.

Thus says the Lord, "Verily I say unto you, in as much as ye have done it unto one of the least of these my brethren, ye have done it unto me" Matthew 25 : 40.

WONDERFUL JESUS!

GOD PROVIDES FOR ME

My mother died and I had no money for the burial expenses. I prayed that God should see me through. And miraculously, God raised helpers for me. I had enough to go home and do the burial and came back with many things without borrowing from anybody. Praise the Lord!

Sis. Elizabeth
MFM Ojo

WONDERFUL GOD

I thank God for journey mercies and the purpose of the journey was fulfilled. I also thank God for providing a new job for my daughter after she resigned from her former employment with faith that God would provide a better one for her. Praise the Lord!

Sis. Ifidon
MFM Alagbole

DELIVERANCE ROM KIDNAPPERS

I got a phone call while writing an examination that one of my daughters was missing and could not be reached on phone. I started praying and confessing Exodus 14:14 within me. By the grace of God, she later came home to narrate how she boarded a passenger bus which was stopped by some armed uniform men who claimed to be policemen and that the bus was a stolen one. Unknown to them, they were ritual kidnappers. They took her and other passengers to their slaughter camp in a jungle where they were taken away one after the other, until it got to her turn as the last person. Their huge tall boss came out, looked her round and told her to thank her God and ordered her to be released immediately and she was dropped at the nearest bus stop. Praise the Lord!

Bro. Raymnd
MFM Omiyale Ejigbo

POWER IN THE ANOINTING OIL

I was formerly a muslim and had a lot of disorderliness in my life. Even before I got born again, somebody introduced the anointing oil to me. I took it with faith and immediately the unexpected began to happen. I started to vomit some substances in liquid form and in great volumes. The following day, I vomited two long worms. Later, I gave my life to Christ and I am fully alright now. Praise God!

Sis. Jesubukola
MFM Aguda

DIVINE INTERVENTION

I used to suffer attacks in my dream and was always having had dreams. I also suffered memory loss and swollen legs. I came for prayers and God healed my dream life and swollen legs. Today, I am completely free. Praise the Lord!

Bro. Ezekiel
MFM Oworonshoki

WONDERFUL GOD

Few years ago, my sister who lives in London had some problems. Since then I started having problems too. I did many entrance exams which I failed. When my sister came from London, someone introduced us to MFM Prayer City and we went there for the deliverance. Since then things have been moving on smoothly for us. Praise the Lord!

Bro. Olamide
MFM Upper Mission. Benin City

THE LOST ITEMS RECOVERED

I lost my purse containing some reasonable sum of money and also my handset. All effort to get them proved abortive. So, I went to God in prayers while some brethren also prayed about it. To my surprise, somebody brought the purse with the whole amount and my handset to me. Praise the Lord!

Sis. Esther
MFM Ughelli

DELIVERED FROM THE POWER OF DEATH

Recently, I was sent to the bank to do some transaction on behalf of my company. I completed the transaction and went back to my office. But on getting there, an armed robbery operation was taking place in our premises, our God intervened and nobody was killed and the money I collected from the bank was not taken from me. I bless the name of the Lord for His deliverance upon my life. Praise the Lord!

Bro. Olamuji
MFM Ogudu/Ojota

NOW ON SALE

The MFM 2008 Anointed Diary is now on sale.
It is a daily devotional guide for Bible Reading and
Spiritual Warfare that will make everyday of the year
2008 AD a victorious one for you.
Grab your copy from the vendors.

FIRE IN THE WORD, is a weekly Spiritual Bulletin of the Mountain of Fire and Miracles Ministries, published by Tracts and Publications Group. All Enquiries should be addressed to The Editor, Mountain of Fire Magazine, 13, Olasimbo Street, off Olumo Road, Onike, P.O. Box 2990, Sabo Yaba, Lagos, Nigeria. Telephone 01- 867439, 864631, 868766, 08023180236.E-mail: mfmtractsandpublications@yahoo.com
Copyright reserved.

FIRE IN THE WORD

Ye Shall Know the Truth, and the Truth Shall Make You Free (John 8:32)

ISSN 1595 - 7314 Vol. 12 No. 18 Sun. 9th - Sat. 15th Mar., 2008

₦10

LICENCE TO KILL

My year of unprecedented greatness and unmatchable increase
Deuteronomy 28:13, Psalm 71:21, Ephesians 3:20, Psalm 92:10

1 John 3:8 says, *"He that committeth sin is of the devil; for the devil sinneth from the beginning. For this purpose the Son of God was manifested, that he might destroy the works of the devil."* This scripture says that Jesus Himself is a destroyer, and came purposely to the earth to do some works of destruction.

I would like you to consider the following questions: What do you do when you have an enemy who has vowed to drink your blood? What do you do when you discover that you have been swallowed half way? What do you do if the greatest gathering of witches and wizards have been assigned to kill you? What do you do when dark powers have taken an oath to destroy you? What do you do, when you know that the spirit of Saul is pursuing your David? What do you do when you know that the spirit of Cain is out to eliminate you? What do you do when you are aware that your name has been circulated among spiritual assassins?

What do you do when you know through your dream that there is poison circulating in your blood? What do you do when you face an enemy that has vowed to die unless he gets you? What do you do when you face an enemy that has sold his or her soul to satan? What do you do when the arrows of death have entered into your liver as it is written in the book of Proverbs? What do you do when you have been openly threatened with destruction? When

somebody looks at you in the face and says: "Your mother will regret the day you were born?" What do you do when you cry for help, and the enemy scares the helpers away? What do you do when you have been boxed to a corner in the battle of life? What do you do when you are being tormented by very clever enemies? What do you do when the enemy is bent on turning your joy to sorrow?

Sometime ago, a certain lawyer went to the court to argue a case, which he won brilliantly. But the lawyer arguing for the other side was very angry. Immediately they finished, he walked to him and gave him a heavy slap right there in the courtroom. They held him back, cautioned him, and promised to discipline him but the harm was already done. By the time the lawyer that won the case got home, the first person he met at the door was his wife. He embraced her, but she just slumped in his hands to his amazement. The daughter ran towards him asking what happened to mummy and as he touched her she also slumped. So right there at his door step, he was looking at the corpses of his wife and daughter. The son too came but he refused to touch him and screamed and ran until he was brought for prayers. If he had touched the boy too that

BELIEVERS ARE ANOINTED TO KILL EVERY POWER THAT IS WORKING AGAINST THEIR DESTINY AND EVERY POWER THAT WANTS TO KILL THEM

would have been it. What do you do when you are faced with such a situation? What do you do when the enemy has blocked all the escape routes?

SOME HARD FACTS ABOUT YOU AND YOUR BATTLES

There are certain hard facts that you must know about yourself and the battle of life.

1. If you do not kill, you will be killed. The Bible says, *"For this cause was the Son of God made manifest that He might destroy the works of the devil."* If you do not destroy these things, they will destroy you.

2. God Himself is the ultimate killing machine. God has killed people with flood and burning sulphur and has also buried people instantly. God has killed people with fire and has sent plagues upon the Egyptians. It was God Himself that afflicted some people in the Bible with leprosy. He has in time past sent curses, confusion, diseases, drought and other things in order to kill. He was the One that allowed the wife of Lot to become a pillar of salt. He was the One that allowed the ground to open up and swallow Korah, Dathan and Abiram. He was the One that allowed Uzziah to be killed, the man that touched the ark. He was the One that killed the baby of Jeroboam, God was the person that drowned the Egyptian army.

3. Your major mission on earth is to kill. Majority of those who are in hell fire now got there because they refused to kill one thing - sin.

DELIVERANCE CASE (The Story of My Life - Part 6)

4. There are dark angels and agents of darkness who have your name and address, and they want to kill you. You would be deceiving yourself to think that serpents and scorpions have come to play with you.

5. There are killing agents all around us. Malaria is a killing agent, HIV is a killing agent. Antibiotics which are prescribed by doctors are for killing all the killing agents in the blood. If you do not kill them they will kill you. The antibiotic is a killer.

6. Believers ought to have voices that can kill both spiritually and physically. In our church in Port-Harcourt a certain woman got home from the Anointing Service and anointed her house. A serpent came out from under the chair and she shouted, "Be arrested and go into the toilet, in Jesus' name." The serpent did a roundabout turn and went into the toilet. It was there until people came around and killed it. So you should have a voice that can kill both spiritually and physically. That is why you must be careful what you say with your mouth. Christians must be careful what they say about their countries. You can use your voice to kill a nation or make it to live.

7. There are many things around which must be killed. To kill here means to put an end to something, to terminate, to destroy the essential quality of a thing, to cause something to stop action, to check the flow of a particular current into a particular place, to consume totally, to deprive something of life, to delete, to rub off, to cut off, to destroy a thing or cause it to expire. It also means to eradicate or to terminate a function, meaning that something could still stand and be breathing but it has been killed. Something can still sit down and be watching, but it has been killed.

Exodus 7:1-2: *"And the Lord said unto Moses, See, I have made thee a god to Pharaoh: and Aaron thy brother shall be thy prophet. Thou shalt speak all that I command thee: and Aaron thy brother shall speak unto Pharaoh, that he send the children of Israel out of his land."* So, Moses got to Egypt and became a god unto Pharaoh. Believers are supposed to be feared. Witches should run away when they appear; and wizards should not operate until they leave a place. Demons are supposed to run away from Christians instead of the reverse that we have now. Moses went to Egypt and started a killing mission; wonder after wonder, signs after signs and miracles after miracles. He started the battle with the serpent playing on the floor. Later, he moved the battle to the waters, later to the air; then to the heavenlies. Pharaoh still refused to let them go until God killed all the firstborns in Egypt including cattles. If they were not killed, the people of Israel would not have been set free.

Elijah too came on a killing mission. He said: "If I be a man of God, let fire come down," and he roasted 102 persons. He was respected. He also took 850 prophets of Baal and Baalim and slaughtered them. Peter spoke words to Ananias and Supphira, and they were no more. Luke 10:19 says, *"Behold, I give unto you power to tread on serpents and scorpions, and over all the power of the enemy…"* To tread on means to kill. When you kill every power of the enemy, they will not be able to harm you.

9. Jesus Himself gave us an example; He spoke words to the fig tree, and by the following morning, it was dried up (Matthew 21:19-21).

10. Hebrew 2:14 says, *"Forasmuch then as the children are partakers of flesh and blood, he also himself likewise took part of the same; that through death he might destroy him that had the power of death, that is, the devil."*

It means that our mission on earth really is to be anointed to kill, to be programmed to kill, to be re-organized to kill, and to be rearranged to kill. It is for us to receive power to kill satanic elements, sicknesses, pain, oppressions, satanic opposition, cancer, ulcer, demotion etc. So, anything that wants to kill your calling, marriage, prayer, anointing, promotion, advancement, or destiny, you better kill it. If you do not kill it, you will be killed. That is the truth. Believers are anointed to kill every power that is working against their destiny and every power that wants to kill them.

If you want to fly a plane, drive a vehicle, run ship services, carry a gun etc, you need a license. No matter how weak, slender, slim or hungry a traffic police man looks and no matter how fat and comfortable you are in your car; once he says stop you must obey because he has the license to stop you, he has the

authority to stop you. You need to collect that license so that your voice will carry the power of God; your voice will carry the living word that can speak life to dead situations and your voice will carry the power to root out, to pull down, to destroy and to speak death into any situation that is organized to kill you.

To use your license, you must pray some kind of prayers, which are known as killing prayers. When you find yourself in a dangerous situation where the enemy wants to kill you, you must use your most potent weapon.

ANALYSIS OF KILLING PRAYERS

1. The first kind of killing prayer can be found in Ezekiel 5:10. These prayers may sound rather unkind or unfriendly but if you do not kill, you will be killed. These prayers are not targeted against human beings, but against what the Bible calls "Every power of the enemy- the serpents, and scorpions." Ezekiel 5:10: *"Therefore the fathers shall eat the sons in the midst of thee, and the sons shall eat their fathers; and I will execute judgments in thee, and the whole remnant of thee will I scatter into all the winds."* The first kind of prayer is to command the enemy to kill themselves. You find

MAJORITY OF THOSE WHO ARE IN HELL FIRE NOW GOT THERE BECAUSE THEY REFUSED TO KILL ONE THING - SIN

the same thought in Isaiah 49:26: *"And I will feed them that oppress thee with their own flesh; and they shall be drunken with their own blood, as with sweet wine and all flesh shall know that I the Lord am thy Saviour and thy Redeemer, the mighty One of Jacob."* This one is very blunt. You can pray like this: "Every agent of death delegated against my life, drink your own blood and eat your own flesh, in the name of Jesus." It is a very effective prayer.

2. Luke 18:3: *"And there was a widow in that city; and she came unto him, saying, Avenge me of mine adversary."* That prayer is very powerful. The second prayer you ought to pray is to cry unto God to avenge you of your adversary. You can say: "God, arise and avenge me of my adversary, in the name of Jesus."

3. The third kind of prayer is found in Ezekiel 16:23: *"And it came to pass after all thy wickedness, (woe, woe unto thee! saith the Lord God;)"* The third kind of prayer is to command woe unto all your enemies. You can say, "Woe unto the vessel that the enemy is using to do me harm, in the name of Jesus."

Ezekiel 16:27: *"Behold, therefore I have stretched out my hand over thee, and have diminished thine ordinary food, and delivered thee unto the will of them that hate thee, the daughters of the Philistines, which are ashamed of thy lewd way."* The fourth kind of prayer is to command your enemies to be delivered into the hands of their own enemies. You can pray a sample prayer like this: "Let the enemy of my enemies rise up and consume them, in Jesus' name."

5. Judges 5:20: *"They fought from heaven; the stars in their courses fought against Sisera."* The fifth kind of prayer is to command heavens to fight for you, And a sample prayer is: "O heavens, fight for me, in the name of Jesus." Fighting from heaven is like applying computer knowledge. Very soon Christians who do not know how to fight from heaven will find themselves at the back, because that is the latest technology. The fellow who can fight from heaven have control of all other things. There is a lot of talk about terrorism now, but the truth about it is that guns and physical weapons will not solve that problem, because there are people who programme themselves into the heavenlies before those who

will fight the battle wake up. They programme enchantments into the heavens even before believers wake up. If you do not know how to dismantle them, you are wasting your time. How do you fight an enemy who has attached a bomb to himself and is ready to die? The only answer is fighting from the heavenlies.

6. Ezekiel 20:38: *"And I will purge out from among you the rebels, and them that transgress against me: I will bring them forth out of the country where they sojourn, and they shall not enter into the land of Israel: and ye shall know that I am the Lord."* The sixth kind of prayer is to ask God to sanitize and purge your household so that satanic agents hiding there will be exposed.

7. Ezekiel 20:47 *"And say to the forest of the south, Hear the word of the Lord; I will kindle a fire in thee, and it shall devour every green

tree in thee, and every dry tree; The flaming flame shalt not be quenched, and all faces from the south to the north shall be burned therein."* The seventh kind of prayer is to command all the trees cooperating with your enemies to be roasted by the fire of God. You can say: "Every tree of darkness working against my destiny, receive the fire of God, in the name of Jesus."

8. Ezekiel 21:32: *"Thou shalt be for fuel to the fire; thy blood shall be in the midst of the land; thou shalt be no more remembered: for I the Lord have spoken it."* You can command the enemy to be fuel for divine fire, in Jesus' name.

9. Ezekiel 30:8: *"And they shall know that I am the Lord when I have set a fire in Egypt, and when all her helpers shall be destroyed."* You can command the helpers of your enemies to be destroyed, in Jesus' name.

10. Ezekiel 29:3-4: *"Speak, and say, Thus saith the Lord God; Behold, I am against thee, Pharaoh king of Egypt, the great dragon that lieth in the midst of his rivers, which hath said, My river is mine own, and I have made it for myself. But I will put hooks in thy jaws, and I will cause the fish of thy rivers to stick unto thy scales and all the fish of thy rivers shall stick unto thy scales."* The tenth kind of prayer is to command the hook of the Lord to kill every power from the waters working against your destiny, in Jesus' name.

11. The eleventh kind of prayer is found in Ezekiel 32:22: *"Asshur is

| THE PROPHET | David versus Goliath 6 |

there and all her company: his graves are about him: all of them slain, fallen by the sword." You can ask the Lord to prepare their graves.

12. The twelfth kind of prayer is found in Jeremiah 14:16: *"And the people to whom they prophesy shall be cast out in the streets of Jerusalem because of the famine and the sword; and they shall have none to bury them, them, their wives, nor their sons, nor their daughters: for I will pour their wickedness upon them."* You can ask God to pour their wickedness back on them, in Jesus' name.

13. The thirteenth kind of prayer you could pray is in Jeremiah 17:4: *"And thou, even thyself, shalt discontinue from thine heritage that I gave thee; and I will cause thee to serve thine enemies in the land which thou knowest not; for ye have kindled a fire in mine anger, which shall burn for ever."* Command your enemies to serve their enemies so that they will be kept busy and have no time for you.

14. The fourteenth kind of prayer you could pray is found in Jeremiah 23:15: *"Therefore thus saith the Lord of hosts concerning the prophets; Behold I will feed them with wormwood, and make them drink the water of gall."* Ask the Lord to feed them with wormwood and let them drink the water of gall.

15. The fifteenth kind of prayer is in the book of Jeremiah 50:29: *"Call together the archers against Babylon; all ye that bend the bow, camp against it round about; let none thereof escape: recompense her according to all that she hath done..."* Command all the host of the Lord to turn against them.

16. The sixteenth kind of prayer is found in the popular Psalm 68:1: *"Let God arise, let his enemies be scattered."*

Isaiah 44:25 says, *"That frustrateth the tokens of the liars..."* Command frustration upon the enemy. "And maketh diviners mad," command madness upon the enemy. "And turneth wisemen backward." Command their wise men to become backward. "And maketh their knowledge foolish." Command their knowledge to become foolish. You command frustration, madness, backwardness and foolishness upon them. These are fours ways in that verse to pray to kill every power that wants to kill the good things in your life.

10 KILLING PRAYER POINTS

1. I stand on the platform of Calvary and decree my breakthrough, in the name of Jesus.

2. Powers of darkness in my family line, die, in the name of Jesus.

3. Fountain of failure, I sentence you to death, in the name of Jesus.

4. Fountain of infirmity, die, in the name of Jesus.

5. Any power that wants to kill my prayer life, die, in the name of Jesus.

6. Every power that has vowed to die instead of seeing my miracle, die, in the name of Jesus.

7. Every snake anointed by a native doctor to fight me, die, in the name of Jesus.

8. Bullet from heaven, kill every serpent and scorpion working against my destiny, in the name of Jesus.

9. Thou killing incantation, backfire, in the name of Jesus.

10. Every stronghold of satan in my body, die, in the name of Jesus.

LICENCE TO KILL

is a message delivered at the Mountain of Fire and Miracles Ministries by the General Overseer, Dr. D.K. Olukoya.

A CALL TO SERVE

Are you a member of MFM with a burden to help the needy, are you interested in alleviating the plight of the poor or in the spread of the gospel through the sponsorship of the publication of tracts? Your resources, time and talent can be extended to several groups that are in charge of these areas. These groups include:

o   We care Ministry,
o   Mission Outreach
o   Tracts and Publications
o   Ministry to Drug addicts
o   Campus fellowship
o   Ministry to Schools
o   Ministry to Glorious Children, etc.

Thus says the Lord, "Verily I say unto you, in as much as ye have done it unto one of the least of these my brethren, ye have done it unto me" Matthew 25 : 40.

WONDERFUL JESUS!

GOD'S ULTIMATE GIFT

For a very long time, I was looking for a piece of land to buy, which would not involve me giving alcohol to anybody. In one of our programmes in the church, the pastor gave a word of prophecy that somebody would bring something to a brother which the brother had been longing to have. A week later, somebody invited me to come and buy a land. I paid for the land and got all the documents for it. Furthermore, nobody asked me for any alcoholic drink. Praise God!

Bro. Adeusi
MFM Ikare

DELIVERANCE FROM WITCHCRAFT SPIRIT

My first daughter was initiated into witchcraft and since then it has been disturbing her. Somebody introduced me to this church, and we went through deliverance. After the programme, my daughter became completely delivered from the spirit of witchcraft. Secondly, I introduced my husband to this church, he too went through deliverance and since then, his life has been experiencing bountiful testimonies. Praise the Lord!

Sis. Ikati
MFM Ogudu/Ojota

GOD HEALS ME

Sometime ago, I had an attack in the abdomen and went for a scan test which detected ovarian mass. Four days after the scan, the ovarian mass moved from the right to the left making me very uncomfortable. I decreed God's word against the pain, came for deliverance and got divinely healed. Praise the Lord!

Sis. Busola
MFM Owutu/Ikorodu

EYE PROBLEM DISAPPEARS

For sometime, I could not see clearly due to eye problem. But after a short prayer in MFM, I was healed, Now, I can see clearly. Praise the Lord!

Bro. Andrew
MFM Shibiri

STOLEN CAR RECOVERED

My husband was attacked by armed robbers while returning from a vigil. His official car and everything he had were stolen. He was worried and downcast when he came home. Later, we went into serious prayers telling God not to allow the prayers at the vigil to be in vain. The following day, we received a telephone call that the car was abandoned along Abeokuta expressway. Indeed God is faithful. Praise the Lord!

Sis. Olayinka
MFM Omiyale-Ejigbo

VICTORY OVER SATANIC DREAMS

I am 92 years old. Recently, I had a dream where some people came to strangulate me and when I wanted to shout the name of Jesus, they warned me not to call that name. Suddenly God gave me the power and boldness and I was able to shout the name of Jesus and the dream cleared. Recently too, when I was about stepping out of the house, I experienced an evil wind that almost blew me down. When I shouted the blood of Jesus, everything ceased and I am well. Praise the Lord!

Sis. Janet
MFM Headquarters

DELIVERED FROM EVIL BIRD

An evil bird used to come into my room every night to disturb me. I decided to go for deliverance and to the glory of God, on the night of the first day of deliverance, the fire of God burnt the evil bird to ashes. Since then my business has started to prosper and I was also delivered from spirit husband. Praise the Lord!

Sis. Afolayan
MFM Apata

DELIVERED FROM THE GRIP OF DEATH

For about two months I was struck by sickness to the point of death. Throughout the period, I was confined to my house. But I resisted the attack through prayers. I declared that I shall not die but live. My prayer was answered and to the glory of God, I am now hale and hearty. Praise the Lord!

Sis. Omotenola
MFM Kwale

EVIL BIRD DIES

We had been praying about an evil bird that usually came crying every night at our residence. As the fire of God descended, the bird came into the room where we were praying and God empowered us to kill it. The bird was set on fire and roast to ashes. We were thus delivered from the menace of this evil bird. Praise the Lord!

Sis. Akinmolayan
MFM Ijebu-Ode

MOUNTAIN OF FIRE AND MIRACLES MINISTRIES
8, Maitama Sule Street, Off Awolowo Ikoyi, Lagos.

JOIN US AT MFM IKOYI BRANCH AS WE EVANGELISE THE GOSPEL OF OUR LORD JESUS CHRIST AND DO SOUL WINNING.

Date: ▶ **21st -24th March 2008.**

Venue: ▶ **MOUNTAIN OF FIRE & MIRACLES MINISTRIES**
8, Maitama Sule Street, Off Awolowo Ikoyi, Lagos.

JESUS IS LORD!

FIRE IN THE WORD, is a weekly Spiritual Bulletin of the Mountain of Fire and Miracles Ministries, published by Tracts and Publications Group. All Enquiries should be addressed to The Editor, Mountain of Fire Magazine, 13, Olasimbo Street, off Olumo Road, Onike, P.O. Box 2990, Sabo Yaba, Lagos, Nigeria. Telephone 01- 867439, 864631, 868766, 08023180236.E-mail: mfmtractsandpublications@yahoo.com Copyright reserved.

FIRE IN THE WORD

Ye Shall Know the Truth, and the Truth Shall Make You Free (John 8:32)

ISSN 1595 - 7314   Vol. 12 No. 19   Sun. 16th - Sat. 22nd Mar., 2008   ₦10

HE SHALL ARISE

My year of unprecedented greatness and unmatchable increase
Deuteronomy 28:13, Psalm 71:21, Ephesians 3:20, Psalm 92:10

Psalm 68:1-2: *"Let God arise, let his enemies be scattered; let them also that hate him flee before him. As smoke driven away, so drive them away; as wax melteth before the fire, so let the wicked perish at the presence of God."*

This passage carefully describes the way they will scatter. They will flee as smoke is driven away, as wax is melted before fire and perish in the presence of God. All these will happen when God arises.

God has enemies. There are people who hate God with perfect hatred. So if God has enemies, you cannot be an exception. Do not deceive yourself by thinking that you have no enemies. Those who nailed Jesus on the cross were His enemies and not His friends. And what did He do for them to treat Him that way? He was healing the sick, raising the dead, setting the oppressed free, and teaching the word of life. For good works, they nailed Him on the cross. Indeed, they were His enemies.

Mark 4:35 says, *"And the same day, when the even was come, he saith unto them, Let us pass over unto the other side."* The decision to pass over unto the other side was not that of the disciples. It was Jesus' decision and the will of God for them to cross over.

Verses 36-39: *"And when they had sent away the multitude, they took him even as he was in the ship. And there were also with him other little ships. And there arose a great storm of wind, and the waves beat into the ship, so that it was now full. And he was in the hinder part of the ship, asleep on a pillow; and they awake him, and say unto him, Master, carest thou not that we perish? And he arose, and rebuked the wind, and said*

THE MASTER MAKES A DIFFERENCE IN THE STORM.

unto the sea, Peace be still. And the wind ceased, and there was a great calm."

Two things were clearly mentioned in the foregoing: there was a rebuking of the wind and there was a speaking unto the sea. So whatever demon or power causing the trouble was in the wind. Therefore, He rebuked that wind, turned back to the sea and said, "Peace be still." The wind ceased and there was a great calm.

In verse 37, there arose a great storm and in verse 39, Jesus arose. Before God arose, there was a joyful gathering of the enemy. Before God arose, there was a rising up of powers, principalities, rulers of darkness of this world and spiritual wickedness in high places. Before God arose, there was mockery by the enemy. Before God arose, there was boasting and threatening by the enemy. Before God arose, the enemy had concluded plans for disgrace. Before God arose,

DELIVERANCE CASE (The Story of My Life - Part 7)

there was serious advancement of the forces of the enemy. Before God arose, there was a show of power by the enemy marching up and down. Before God arose, evil kings and thrones were having a field day. Before God arose, sickness was boasting with its terminating agenda. Before God arose, there was darkness and confusion. Before God arose, the enemy had moved to bury the destiny of many. Before God arose, it was impossible for God's people to possess their possession. Before God arose, the strongman was guarding his palace and his goods were in peace. Before God arose, wickedness was entrenched in multiple places. Before God arose, the Red sea was boasting, and Pharaoh, the stubborn pursuer was rejoicing. Before God arose, the walls of Jericho pursued their evil agenda. Before God arose, Goliath was boasting. Before God arose, many thought that it was finished.

Jesus was in the boat yet a great storm arose. The people were doing the will of God, they were not committing sin; because it was God who said, "Let us cross over." But the storm arose and did some revival.

Dear reader, I pray that any satanic revival going on in your life shall be quenched, in the name of Jesus.

Before Jesus arose, there was a lot of confusion in that ship, but after Jesus arose, the storm died. It had to go down because the Master arose, and there could not be two captains on the same sea. Jesus could not be there and the storm and waves would be speaking.

The Master makes a difference in the storm. The storm may be rising against you, now, never mind, the Master shall arise and there will follow a great calm. The calm will be so serious that you will wonder whether there was ever a storm. The Bible says, "The thief cometh not but for to steal, and to kill and to destroy." That is the coming of the thief. But thank

God there is a second coming: "But I am come that they might have life and that they might have it more abundantly" (John 10:10).

Often the devil takes a great shot at us in a hurry. He rises first with his storms and God in His own wisdom and amazing way, allows the devil to do the preliminary shooting and stirring of evil storms before He shows up with His glorious peace. It is often said that the darkest hour of the night is just before morning. Psalm 30:5 says, *"For his anger endureth but a moment; in his favour is life; weeping may endure for a night, but joy cometh in the morning."* Every night is therefore an assurance that the morning is coming.

The storm arose despite the fact that Jesus was there, it had no respect for Him. But then the storm died to rise no more. The sea of Galilee where that miracle took place is now reputed to be one of the calmest seas in the world. There has never been another storm on it since Jesus said: "Peace be still."

There was a certain sister, a medical doctor who kept failing a qualifying examination. She failed the sixth time and only had one more chance. She prayed and fasted for three days without food even to the examination hall. She saw some of the very brilliant students too. They were meant each to come and examine a patient lying on bed, after which they got the professors' verdict. Generally in medicine, anyone who fails will know. On that day, each student went in and came out crying, they were fourteen of them. When it was her turn, she went in shivering. The examiner asked her a question which she did not understand and in her confusion, she held the patient with one hand and with the other one checked her wristwatch to

WHAT YOU NEED TO DO FOR GOD TO ARISE IS TO CALL UPON HIM

see how many minutes left before she was thrown out. But immediately she did that, all the professors shouted, "That is it! You got it!" She was actually meant to check the patient's pulse first which other students did not do. That was how she passed the examination. And God made her to pass in such a way that proved that she had no hand in it.

Jesus was in the boat, and men waited for His move in that desperate hour. He too waited on the men to move in prayers so that He could move on their behalf. It was a very strange position. It was when they cried unto Him that He arose.

Beloved, you must understand that witches can never repent. Buying gin, kola-nuts, alligator pepper, cock and hen and going to a village to beg a witch is a complete waste of time. The Bible says, they will never repent. All the bad spirits in actual sense are defying God, they are not going to make peace with God at all because they know they are going to hell fire. They said to Jesus, "What have you to do with us?' Have you come to punish us before our time?" They knew where they were going but decided not to go down without fighting. These bad powers have gone beyond reconciling with God. They will never agree to submit, they can never be pacified. The only language they understand is what Jesus did to the wind: He rebuked the wind.

What do you do when you are already thinking of giving up? What do you do when there are so many questions in your mind but few answers? What do you do when you feel there is no need to try anymore? What do you do when circumstances are screaming at you to give up? What do you do when even your close family members are saying you will never make it? What do you do when you face satanic persecution? What do you do when they invite you to join their dark club because of your situation? What do you do when fresh arrows are fired at you everyday? What do you do when trials and discouragement seem to follow you everywhere you go?

Sometime ago, in London, a hefty looking man came for counselling and wept like a baby. He said he got married to a woman who gave birth to triplets, and a year later, the woman died. He brought the children to see me. They had wrecked their father. All his family members ran away. Anyone who came to their house had an accident on departure or lost all his wealth. He said it got so bad that his letters to family members were read by outsiders so that they (family members) would not get into trouble. I asked the children what they wanted to do and they replied: "Man of God, it is too late." Then I told them that they had left somebody out of the issue, and that was Jesus who would deliver their daddy from their hands.

The world is a strange place, where no one should sit around and play with his or her life. The expression, "Let God arise" in Psalm 68 was written by David when the ark was being taken back to Jerusalem. However, David was not the first person to say, "Let God arise." The originator of these words was

THE PROPHET | David versus Goliath 7

NO WAY. I SHALL NOT DIE BUT LIVE... SAITH THE LORD...

CHEiii !!! I MISSED. WHAT AN ACROBATIC DIVE. THIS IS AN UNBELEIVABLE MARSHAL ART...

FWWHHiii

Moses. Any time the ark of God was being moved, the battle cry was: "O God arise, and let your enemies be scattered." Immediately, the priest heard this, he would run into the holy of holies, carry the ark, follow the crowd and they would begin to move. They cry of "Let God arise," in those days was a cry for change, a progress move. Do you want to move forward? Then cry to Him to arise. And when God arises, angels will fight your battle, your enemies will begin to fight themselves, things will begin to happen at a fast pace, your oppressed life will receive freedom, and those who want to destroy you will find you indestructible and become your friends. Those who threw Shadrach, Meshach and Abednego inside fire eventually asked them to come out.

Psalm 50:15 says, *"And call upon me in the day of trouble: I will deliver thee, and thou shalt glorify me."* What you need to do for God to arise is to call upon Him. To call means to talk loudly, to speak in a loud distinct voice so as to be heard at a distance. To call is to make a request or demand. To call is to utter a cry. A call can involve shouting, yelling, or screaming. There are different forms of making a call. The way you call will determine the response.

Psalm 9:19 says, *"Arise, O LORD; let not man prevail: let the heathen be judged in thy sight."*

Call upon the Lord today and He will deliver you.

PRAYER POINTS

1. O God, arise and let the voice of my enemy die, in the name of Jesus.

2. O God, arise and let every power that does not want to see my joy die, in the name of Jesus.

3. O God, arise and let every power behind my problems die, in the name of Jesus.

4. O God, arise and let the strongman delegated against my career, die, in the name of Jesus.

5. The voice of man will not prevail over my destiny, in the name of Jesus.

6. This week, my breakthroughs must manifest by fire, in the name of Jesus.

7. O God, arise and let satanic storms in my life die, in Jesus' name.

HE SHALL ARISE

is a message delivered at the Mountain of Fire and Miracles Ministries by the General Overseer, Dr. D.K. Olukoya.

A CALL TO SERVE

Are you a member of MFM with a burden to help the needy, are you interested in alleviating the plight of the poor or in the spread of the gospel through the sponsorshing of the publication of tracts? Your resources, time and talent can be extended to several groups that are in charge of these areas. These groups include:

o   We care Ministry,
o   Mission Outreach
o   Tracts and Publications
o   Ministry to Drug addicts
o   Campus fellowship
o   Ministry to Schools
o   Ministry to Glorious Children, etc.

Thus says the Lord, "Verily I say unto you, in as much as ye have done it unto one of the least of these my brethren, ye have done it unto me" Matthew 25 : 40.

WONDERFUL JESUS!

GOD ANSWERS MY PRAYER

I graduated from the university in 1996. I wrote application letters to different companies but could not get a job. I decided to teach in a private school for about a year but I noticed that in the school, most of the teachers made the same decision but were not able to fulfil it. I decided to resign from the school and prayed to God to take control of my situation. Some days after my prayers, I was employed in a better company. Praise the Lord!

Bro. Olusegun
MFM Olowora

MENSTRUAL PAIN GONE

I suffered menstrual pain for ten years but after participating in a deliverance programme organized by the church, I was permanently healed. Also God in His infinite mercies delivered me from eating in the dream and my brother won a case in human court. Praise the Lord!

Sis. Best
MFM Iba

DIVINE RESTORATION

My son who is 4 years old was breathing through his month instead of his nose. This bothered us and we sought for medical help. The doctor we consulted told us that the child would undergo surgery at a cost of four hundred thousand Naira (N400, 000). We consented to this but on the day of the surgery the doctor complained that the child had low blood level and we were given other appointments twice in two months. After the second appointment, we decided to go to God in prayer for His divine intervention God heard our prayer as the blockage melted away on its own. The child can now breath normally as confirmed by the same doctor who wanted to do the surgery. Praise the Lord!

Bro. Toyin
MFM Abule Egba

THE GREAT HEALER

My husband had ulcer for sometime and all attempts to get him healed with western medicine proved abortive. But after prayers by men of God, the ulcer disappeared. He was healed miraculously to the glory of God. I also thank God for His love and mercy over my life and family. Praise the Lord!

Sis. Bello
MFM Abaranje

ANOINTING BREAKS THE YOKE

I had eye problem for a long time and was constantly on drugs. It got to a point, I started feeling uncomfortable because the drugs were no longer working. There were times I could not sleep. But when I started using the anointing oil from MFM, the eye problem disappeared completely. I can now sleep well. Secondly, recently, I came out on the street and saw a young lady naked. She was going mad and people were running away from her. I wanted to run too but a voice spoke to me and I quickly ran back home and picked a skirt and a blouse and anointed them. When I brought the clothes, the crowd that had gathered said that she was violent and would tear the clothes. I went straight to her prayed for her and she said Amen. She collected the clothes and as soon as she wore them, she became normal. Praise the Lord!

Sis. Mary
MFM Headquarters

EVIL PATTERN BROKEN

For about two years a teacher died every term in the school where I work. It was revealed to me and another teacher that an arrow of death was fired at our school. We prayed in the staffroom and at the assembly ground against the evil trend and God answered us. The arrow of death has gone back to the sender. Praise the Lord!

Sis. Rose
MFM Ibillo

ISSUE OF BLOOD CEASES

For five years, I had an issue of blood which refused to stop. But when I joined Mountain of Fire and Miracles Ministries and went through series of deliverance, God answered me and the long term bleeding stopped. Praise the Lord!

Sis. Comfort
MFM Aboru

GOD RESTORES MY MARRIAGE

I had serious problems in my marriage for over eight years. The situation caused separation between me and my husband. However, after series of fervent prayers, my marriage has been restored to the glory of God and to the shame of the devil. Praise the Lord!

Sis. Ajoke
MFM Lekki

NOW ON SALE

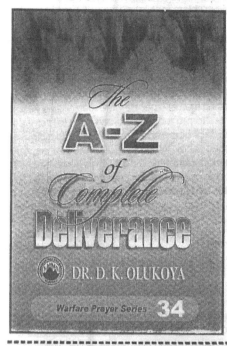

At last! The two long awaited books are back on the stand. Ever potent for all your deliverance and prosperity needs. Hurry now for your copies Stock is limited. Price N170 each.

Hello Children!

Your popular Spiritual tonic "Junior Fire in the Word" is on the stand again. It is still as refreshing as ever. Now you have more opportunities to win Fanstastic prizes every month as you send in your entries Hurry grab your copy from the vendors. The price is still N20.

FIRE IN THE WORD, is a weekly Spiritual Bulletin of the Mountain of Fire and Miracles Ministries, published by Tracts and Publications Group. All Enquiries should be addressed to The Editor, Mountain of Fire Magazine, 13, Olasimbo Street, off Olumo Road, Onike, P.O. Box 2990, Sabo Yaba, Lagos, Nigeria. Telephone 01- 867439, 864631, 868766, 08023180236.E-mail: mfmtractsandpublications@yahoo.com Copyright reserved.

FIRE IN THE WORD

Ye Shall Know the Truth, and the Truth Shall Make You Free (John 8:32)

ISSN 1595 - 7314 Vol. 12 No. 20 Sun. 23rd - Sat. 29th Mar., 2008

₦10

MEMBERS OF DANIEL'S BAND

My year of unprecedented greatness and unmatchable increase
Deuteronomy 28:13, Psalm 71:21, Ephesians 3:20, Psalm 92:10

In this message we shall look at the characteristics of those who belong to Daniel's band by considering the words of a hymn writer in his song titled, "Dare to be a Daniel." The song says: "Standing by a purpose true." That means members of Daniel's band must be people who are standing by a purpose and are pursuing that purpose. It continues, "Heeding God's command;" members of Daniel's band are those who heed God's commandment. "Honour them, the faithful few." Unfortunately, the members of Daniel's band are few.

The chorus says, "Dare to be a Daniel; dare to stand alone." It is a challenge.

Beloved, it is not easy to stand alone. Eagles do not fly in flocks. Those who want to fly high do not flock, they must stand alone. Men and women who have changed things were people who were going the opposite direction. It is not easy to be a lone ranger. The chorus of that song says, "Dare to stand alone. Dare to have a purpose firm. Dare to make it known." It means, take your stand. Let people know what you believe. Do not be an hypocrite. That is, the way you look in the church should not be different from the way you look outside. Let people know what you believe. When they know what you believe, they know your stand, and know what to bring before you.

The second stanza of that song says, "Many mighty men are lost, who could not stand, but they would have been a host for God if they first joined Daniel's band." Since they did not join Daniel's band, they could not stand. Stanza three: "Many giants, great and tall; who are boasting all over through the land, headlong to the end they would fall if Daniel's band confronted them." The giants that are moving all over the place are doing so because they have not seen a Daniel's band to confront them. Beloved, do you want to belong to Daniel's band.

There are many people who come to the MFM but unfortunately, many are really not members of MFM. Attendance does not make one a member. One becomes a member when the church is inside him or her. Many people are at MFM but are not in MFM. Many people rush to MFM to quench the fire of the enemy, but God is not looking for bench warmers. He is not looking for those who are not serious with their salvation. When we do exactly what God wants us to do, there will be miracle galore.

Many years ago, I took some questions to the Lord: I told Him that we have people who come to MFM and are still committing fornication, there are people there who tell lies, there are sisters there who dress like Jezebel in the streets, and there are witches and wizards there also. The Lord said, "They are

ANY LIFE THAT IS YIELDED TO GOD IS AUTOMATICALLY DEDICATED TO QUALITY.

not members. Do not worry yourself about them." The Lord said they only come to make the halleluyah loud."

You must decide whether you want to belong to Daniel's band or not, that is whether you want to do what God wants you to do or not. Those who wear indecent clothes are not members, they are just coming to collect miracles. They fail to understand that if they would follow the total teaching of MFM, God will bombard them with miracles. It is surprising to see people come to the church wearing what they call "spaghetti," which exposes their body. It is also shocking to see men wearing chains, I wonder if they are slaves. Do you want to be in Daniel's band? Dare to be a Daniel, dare to stand alone, dare to have a purpose firm, dare to make it known.

Beloved, I would like to let you know that when you are on the Mountain of Fire, you are on the mountain-top. When you climb to the mountain-top, fire will come upon you, and when you receive the fire, you become a power generator.

Every member of MFM should be able to know what to do in any given situation because it is a do-it yourself ministry. As a member of MFM, even if you have to refer people to the General Overseer or pastors, you ought to have given them a first aid. If you are not able to do so, it means you are not part of MFM yet. The Mountain of Fire and Miracles Ministries is a

DELIVERANCE CASE (THE STORY OF MY LIFE - PART 8)

do-it yourself ministry, where people are not made slaves to pastors, prophets or any other person. You ought to be able to pray by yourself and get results. If you want to be in Daniel's band, you must know what you are doing.

DIFFERENT CLASSES OF SOLDIERS

There are different kinds of soldiers. Some soldiers are drivers, some are nurses; some are dentists; doctors, musicians, stewards etc. But when there is war, there are some soldiers who go to the warfront, they are called combatant soldiers. That is where MFM belongs.

During the Nigerian civil war, a certain woman went to the market, and found a grenade by the side of the road, and because she was a civilian, she did not know that it was a bomb. She put it on her basket of yams for her children to play with as toy. But on the way, it got detonated and in the explosion, her head went one way while her basket of yams went another way. A soldier will never

do that because he will know that it

is a dangerous weapon.

People complain about certain things we warn about in MFM because they are civilians. A Christian soldier can recognise a satanic weapon when he sees one. Some people were given two holes in their ears by their parents, not knowing the implication of that, they added extra holes. When we scream danger, such people do not understand. Many who think their hair is too short attach something to it so that it will be very long, when those who know the danger scream danger, they wonder what is wrong. I pray that God will open the understanding of many people in Jesus' name.

CHARACTERISTICS OF DANIEL'S BAND

Psalm 8:9 says, *"O LORD our Lord, how excellent is thy name in all the earth!"* Our God is the supreme

excellence, God is not a failure. The first man in the Bible that had a qualification of the spirit of excellence was Daniel. The first thing you need to pray into your life if you want to be part of Daniel's band is found in Daniel 5:12: *"For as much as an excellent spirit, and knowledge, and understanding, interpreting of dreams, and showing of hard sentences, and dissolving of doubts, were found in the same Daniel, whom the king named Belteshazzar: now let Daniel be called, and he will show the interpretation."*

Daniel 6:3: *"Then this Daniel was preferred above the presidents and princes, because an excellent spirit was in him..."* These passages are emphasizing excellence. That is the first thing you must have to be in Daniel's band.

In those passages, the Bible puts together the things that constitute excellence:
1. Knowledge
2. Understanding.
3. Interpretation of dreams.

4. Dissolving of hard sentences.
5. Dissolving of doubts. These are things that make up an excellent spirit according to the Bible.

It is not everybody that would be born a prophet or a powerful person. In fact, the number of those born with these qualities is very few. But like Daniel, you can pray any good thing into your life. You cannot read anywhere in the Bible that God called Daniel to be a prophet like He did to Isaiah, Jeremiah, Elisha and Elijah. For Daniel there was no such call, he prayed himself into position, he prayed himself into relevance. You too can pray good things into your life and pray yourself into position. You can pray yourself into a situation where things will change. The more you pray, the more you discover, and the more you discover, the more you recover, and the more you recover, the more direction you have, and the more direction you have, the more success you have, and the more success you have the better your destiny becomes.

The first man in the Bible with the qualification of excellence was Daniel. He was the person God used for the salvation of the magicians. The king had decided to kill all of them but Daniel went to God and got the solution. He was the same person that lions could not devour. He was a bold and fearless man, his life was yielded to God. And any life that is yielded to God is automatically dedicated to quality. Only the best is good for your life. The

Bible says let your light so shine that God may be glorified in your life. The Lord is calling you to pray the spirit of excellence into your life so that you can belong to Daniel's band, so that you too can be a spiritually knowledgeable person.

1. Knowledge: Knowledge is the enemy of ignorance. It is the only thing that can kill or damage ignorance.

A certain big man in Lagos had a dream, where he saw himself in a church, and a funeral ceremony was being conducted for somebody. As the people were singing a hymn, he sang along with them joyfully. But something said to him. "You are singing, but who died?" So he looked at the back of the pamphlet and saw his own picture there. Then he shouted, "Stop singing, I am not dead." But they just continued singing and told him it was late since he already sang with them. Before that week ran out, his wife and six children perished in a car accident along with the driver. He became destablished and was fainting. They put him in a vehicle to take him to the hospital, and the vehicle also had an accident and he died instantly. So within a week, the whole family was wiped out because of ignorance. If he had

ANYTHING YOU WEAR THAT DOES NOT GLORIFY GOD WILL PUT YOU IN TROUBLE

some knowledge of spiritual warfare, immediately he had that dream, he would have risen up and said: "Father, in the name of Jesus, I scatter the evil congregation I saw now. Let the pamphlet be roasted with fire. I shall not die but live to declare the works of God." That simple two or three minutes operation would have saved his life and that of his family.

To be in Daniel's band you must be a man or woman of knowledge. Knowledge, they say is power. Knowledge will move you forward. Knowledge will do great things to your life. The Lord is calling for the people of excellence now to belong to Daniel's band. Do not worry about those who are looking at you and are saying you look dull and unexciting. Understand that the people in darkness have no right to tell you who are in the light how to run your life. When the same people run into trouble, they run back to those they deride. Knowledge is part of the spirit of excellence. When God begins to do a great thing in a person's life, the first thing that enters his or her spirit is knowledge.

2. Understanding: The second thing you should imbibe which is part of the spirit of excellence is understanding. Do not be shallow in your understanding of the things of God. Pray to be able to understand your Bible and the deep teachings thereof, be a person of understanding.

3. Interpretation of dreams:

The third thing, which is a constituent of the spirit of excellence is interpretation of dreams. We spend a lot of our time dreaming. A lot of people will bring dreams to you or you may dream dreams yourself. You ought to be able to sit down and decipher or decode these dreams. Your dream is a spiritual monitor that tells you what goes on in your life in the spirit realm.

4. Dissolving of doubt:

You should be able to dissolve any doubt that anyone could have.

The Lord is calling for excellence. By excellence, we mean the very finest, the very best of its kind. Would to God that all Christians would have this spirit of excellence within them. Then you will understand deeply why the Lord has called you, you will know what you are doing and things will be clear to you.

Wanted! Member of Daniel's band. Dare to be a Daniel, dare to stand alone. In his own time, Daniel stood alone, his life was strange, his behaviour was strange, his prayer life was strange, the way he talked was strange. Everything about him was strange. Daniel did not join the crowd, he remained alone. When everyone was forbidden to pray, he prayed, and when he was thrown into the lion's den, the Lord delivered him. The king came to inquire of him and said, "Daniel, servant of the living God, is your God whom you serve day and night able to deliver you from the lions?" He answered "Live long O king, the Lord has already delivered me." And those that threw him into the den were eaten up by the lions. Would to God that all Christians were like that. The world is going one way, we should go God's way. We do not have to copy them, they should copy us. Light does not copy darkness.

Beloved, you must be careful not to copy Christians who are worldly because you do not know their department in God's army. The combatant ones know what they are doing. That is why the major pastors who are having breakthroughs are still those who believe in holiness within and without. It is very sad to know that a lot of present-day believers know the Bible but do not know God. They know how to claim it and receive it, but are not taught about the evil power of their father's house. They are not taught that they are basically Africans and their fathers worshiped idols and that the idols are crying. Do not wait for the enemy to use you as a bad example, do not wait till the enemy messes you up.

You must get your bearings. A time will come when the money some people are running after so much that they do not have time for God will be put it in their hands and they will not be able to close those hands. The members of the public that they want to please now and show that they are stylish will look at their corpses and run away because of the stench. They will be surprised to see that those they were trying to please will be the first to rejoice at their death. Do not allow your job or business to debar you from serving the Lord, because if you

die, another person will take over. Even the children you think you are working for will start fighting over the properties after

| THE PROPHET | David versus Goliath 8 |

MY GOD SHALL COVER ME WITH HIS FEATHERS, AND UNDER HIS WINGS SHALL I TRUST... PSM 91:4

NONESENSE. IF NO BE SAY I NEVER CHOP THIS MORNING, I FOR DON FINISH YOU KPATA-KPA-TA...

you have gone, and may even kill themselves because of the property. Therefore, this is the time to readjust your life and destiny by declaring for Daniel's band. Do not bother about man's approval but God's approval. They can call you all sorts of names but as far you know where you are going, you should not be bothered.

The safest way you can preserve your life in this kind of environment is to remain as pure and clean as God made you and shun every form of artificiality. Any attempt to modify the image of God is artificiality. Anything that you wear that does not glorify God will put you in trouble. The church of God is not a fashion parade centre, but a place where you bring the power of God down. We must try and follow the pattern of God. God told Moses to ensure that he followed the laid down pattern. If Moses did not follow that pattern, miracles would not have happened. Christians who dress indecently and use demonic materials are not helping the power of God to manifest more. Make up your mind whether you want to be in Daniel's band or not.

Beloved, stand against the following seven curses through the prayer points below.

1. Death curse: You may not believe it, but someone, somewhere is wishing you were dead. That wish is a curse! Stand against it.
2. Sorrow curses.
3. Tragedy curses.
4. Demotion curses. If your husband is running after a strange woman, it is demotion for you. You need stand against it.
5. Curse of blockage. You need to kill financial, marital and academic blockage.
6. The curse of infirmity. There are powers that will be happy to see that you are not able to walk again.
7. Curse of death and hell. Stand against the powers of darkness that want you in hell fire. The enemies of the soul of man issue curses day and night that make people to fall into unpardonable errors. You must stand against them.

PRAYER POINTS

1. Every power issuing death curses against me, appear, in the name of Jesus.
2. Every power issuing death curses against me, die, in the name of Jesus.
3. Every power troubling my destiny from my sleep, die, in the name of Jesus.
4. Every sorrow curse targeted against me, backfire, in the name of Jesus.
5. Every power of Balaam cursing my destiny, die, in the name of Jesus.
6. Every owner of the load of tragedy, carry your load, in the name of Jesus.
7. Arrows of demotion, backfire, in the name of Jesus.
8. Every gathering of the strongman at the gate of my breakthrough, scatter, in the name of Jesus.
9. Every curse of blockage, by the blood of Jesus, die, in the name of Jesus.
10. My gun of prayer, fire, in the name of Jesus.
11. Anything that is removing excellence from my life, die, in the name of Jesus.
12. Anyway I have cooperated with my enemies, O Lord, forgive me, in the name of Jesus.
13. O Lord, open my eyes, I do not want to be spiritually blind, in Jesus' name.
14. O Lord, teach me deep and secret things, in the name of Jesus.

MEMBERS OF DANIEL'S BAND
is a message delivered at the Mountain of Fire and Miracles Ministries by the General Overseer, Dr. D.K. Olukoya.

A CALL TO SERVE
Are you a member of MFM with a burden to help the needy, are you interested in alleviating the plight of the poor or in the spread of the gospel through the sponsorshing of the publication of tracts? Your resources, time and talent can be extended to several groups that are in charge of these areas. These groups include:
o   We care Ministry,
o   Mission Outreach
o   Tracts and Publications
o   Ministry to Drug addicts
o   Campus fellowship
o   Ministry to Schools
o   Ministry to Glorious Children, etc.
Thus says the Lord, "Verily I say unto you, in as much as ye have done it unto one of the least of these my brethren, ye have done it unto me" Matthew 25 : 40.

WONDERFUL JESUS!

SATAN PUT TO SHAME

I delivered my third child through a caesarean section. I became afraid to get pregnant again, but unknowingly I got pregnant again. My husband and I agreed to abort the pregnancy but the pastor warned us against such a step. He continued to counsel and pray for me. Sometimes, he held vigils with my family. Fear of death further gripped me when at the ninth month, there was no sign of labour. But with encouragement and prayers by the pastor and other brethren, I was delivered safely to the glory of God and to the shame of satan. Praise the Lord!

Sis Huonyemesi
MFM Ogwashi-Uku

GOD BLESSES MY FAMILY

I thank God for blessing my family with a child. When I was six months pregnant, I had a dream where two nurses were attending to me in the hospital. They told me to push but I told them that it was not yet time. I narrated the dream to the minister of God and we cancelled the dream together. To the glory of God, I was delivered safely of a baby girl. Praise the Lord!

Sis Ezekiel
MFM Oyo

SEVEN YEARS OF BARRENNESS BROKEN

I thank God Almighty for giving me the privilege to worship in MFM. I was married for seven years without a child. Somebody invited me to MFM Lagos, during the end of year programme. At the programme, the G. O. made a proclamation that changed my life. God opened my womb and since then I have been giving birth to children. When I got back home, my family members stopped me from worshipping in MFM. But now that bondage is broken and I am back to MFM, God's favour is upon my life. Praise the Lord!

Sis Uzoma
MFM Amichi

STRANGE WOMAN DISGRACED

My husband abandoned me and my child for a strange woman. I did all I could to get him back but did not succeed. All the communication links to him were disconnected. My efforts proved abortive. But during the Women Deliverance programme at the Prayer City, the G. O. gave a word of knowledge concerning my situation and I claimed it. On getting home from the Prayer City, I received a call, behold, it was my husband begging me to forgive him. That was how we were reunited. Praise the Lord!

Sis Adaeze
MFM Agodo

SAFE DELIVERY

I thank God for granting me safe delivery during childbirth. After normal birth that lasted less than ten minutes, the devil had other evil plans which manifested through unexplainable severe bleeding and the arrow of untimely death. Through prayers and divine grace of God, the Lord gave me victory to the shame of the enemies. Praise the Lord!

Sis Chinyere
MFM Headquarters.

I GOT PREGNANT IN SPITE OF FIBROID

When I got pregnant, I discovered that I had a lump in my womb. A scan test revealed many fibroids in my womb. The doctor then recommended that I got rid of the pregnancy so that he could remove the fibroids. My husband and I rejected the idea. We then began to pray and to the glory of God, I gave birth to a bouncing baby after I had gone through a deliverance programme. We substituted the termination of the pregnancy with a deliverance programme and it paid off. Praise the Lord!

Sis Olatunji
MFM Ikorodu 1

VICTORY OVER EVIL SPIRIT

I was experiencing spiritual attacks in my place of work. It got so bad that the devil was constantly ministering to me to resign my appointment. But God delivered me. Secondly, I had a vision that the spirit of death and hell was after my life. To God's glory, I was delivered through aggressive prayers. Thirdly, God expanded my wife's business and gave us victory over chronic enemies. Praise the Lord!

Bro Bayo
MFM Igando

MIRACLE BABY

My wife's pregnancy was overdue. Naturally, we were worried but we continued in our prayers to God. Some people were asking us to try other means but we rejected the counsel. In agreement with our pastor, we prayed on the anointing oil and I used it to rub my wife's stomach. Not long after, she put to bed but the placenta refused to come out. We were referred to another hospital but I refused believing that God would complete His job. God did it and both my wife and baby are well. Praise the Lord!

Bro Damian
MFM Ojo

Join us and **BUILD** for the Lord

THE PRAYER CITY DELIVERANCE STADIUM AND INTERNATIONAL CONFERENCE CENTRE

₦35,000,000,000

To be a part of this project, send your donation* to the Regional Overseer/Pastor or to the Secretariat
Prayer City Partners and Friends
i/c The Office of the G.O.
13, Olasimbo Street, Onike-Yaba, Lagos.

Mode of payment

Any Branch of Oceanic Bank International Plc. Nationwide
Account No.: 0801101006463
Name of Account: MFM-Prayer City Partners and Friends

For further information contact
08055145040, 08023128677,
08034934848, 08023261588
email: info@mfmprayercity.org
website: mfmprayercity.org

FIRE IN THE WORD, is a weekly Spiritual Bulletin of the Mountain of Fire and Miracles Ministries, published by Tracts and Publications Group. All Enquiries should be addressed to The Editor, Mountain of Fire Magazine, 13, Olasimbo Street, off Olumo Road, Onike, P.O. Box 2990, Sabo Yaba, Lagos, Nigeria. Telephone 01- 867439, 864631, 868766, 08023180236.E-mail: mfmtractsandpublications@yahoo.com Copyright reserved.

FIRE IN THE WORD

Ye Shall Know the Truth, and the Truth Shall Make You Free (John 8:32)

ISSN 1595 - 7314 Vol. 12 No. 21 Sun. 30th Mar. - Sat. 5th Apr., 2008

OPEN MY EYES, OH LORD

My year of unprecedented greatness and unmatchable increase
Deuteronomy 28:13, Psalm 71:21, Ephesians 3:20, Psalm 92:10

Our message this week is titled, "Open my eyes, O Lord." It is one of the greatest prayers you can pray for yourself. Psalm 119:18 says, *"Open thou mine eyes, that I may behold wondrous things out of thy law."*

Certain things become clear from this scripture: The Psalmist is not talking about the physical eyes. He is talking about the eyes that would allow you to see wondrous things. From this scripture, you can see that if those eyes are not open, there are certain things you will not see, there are certain things you will miss and there are certain things you will not understand. Kings may pass before you, you will not know. Angels may sit beside you and you will not know.

Luke 24:31 says, *"And their eyes were opened, and they knew him; and he vanished out of their sight."* Jesus walked with them several miles, He opened scriptures to them and explained to them about Christ but they did not understand. They saw Jesus and did not know it was Him. They were asking Jesus if He was a stranger in Israel, until their eyes were opened.

Luke 6:39: *"And he spoke a parable unto them, Can the blind lead the blind? Shall they not both fall into the ditch?"* Many people were led by blind people before, and they fell into the ditch. Deliverance is what will get such people out.

Revelation 3:17 says, *"Because thou sayest, I am rich, and increased with goods, and have need of nothing, and knowest not that thou art wretched, and miserable, and poor, and blind and naked."* So, the fact that you have riches, and are increased with goods does not mean that all is well. The Bible says, there is wretchedness and blindness and poverty. It means that a person could be blind without knowing that he or she is blind spiritually. There are many watchers but very few observers. There are many that look but only few see. It is a tragedy that most of the major prophetesses or prophets that can really see now are very old people. The question is, what is happening to the young ones? Why is the Lord not opening their eyes? Why can't they see? Eyes have great power because they are the conveyors of the soul. Eyes gather information and transmit it to the spirit world.

LEVELS OF SIGHT (KINDS OF EYES)

1. Natural eyes or physical eyes: Jesus says it is better to pluck out the natural eyes if they will take you to hell fire. Anybody who cannot see physically now will see on the resurrection morning if he is born again. But if he can see now and end up in hell fire, he is a blind person.

2. Mental eyes: The Bible says in 2 Corinthians 4:4; *"In whom the god of this world hath blinded the minds of them which believe not lest the light of the glorious gospel of Christ, who is the image of God,*

PANIC AND FEAR ARE NORMALLY CAUSED BY SPIRITUAL BLINDNESS

should shine unto them." The Bible says that the enemy does not want them to see or understand the gospel.

3. Spiritual eyes: Ability to see spiritual things. Spiritual eyes enable one to see spiritual things. This is where the problem lies.

There are many living dead in our midst, they only see with the physical eyes. Many things are not clear to a lot of people that is why they misbehave. Many things are strange to many people that is why they go into what they should not go into. The living dead only see with their physical eyes.

2 Kings 6:8-12 says *"Then the king of Syria warred against Israel, and took counsel with his servants, saying, In such and such place shall be my camp. And the man of God* (which is Elisa) *sent unto the king of Israel, saying, Beware that thou pass not such a place; for thither the Syrians are come down. And the king of Israel sent to the place which the man of God told him and warned him of, and saved himself there, not once nor twice. Therefore the heart of the king of Syria was sore troubled for this thing; and he called his servants, and said unto them, Will ye not show me which of us is for the king of Israel?"*

Here was a king who was planning against his enemy but discovered that anything he planned one way or the other came to the knowledge of the enemy. Israel knew what the king was planning. So, he was suspicious of his

DELIVERANCE CASE (THE STORY OF MY LIFE - PART 9)

lieutenants and began to ask who among them was a spy. Verses 12-16 says, *"And one of his servants said, None, my Lord, O king: but Elisa, the prophet that is in Israel, telleth the king of Israel the words that thou speakest in thy bed chamber. And he said, Go and spy where he is, that I may send and fetch him. And it was told him, saying, Behold, he is in Dothan. Therefore sent he thither horses, and chariots, and a great host; and they came by night, and compassed the city about. And when the servant of the man of God was risen early and gone forth, behold, an host compassed the city both with horses and chariots. And his servant said unto him, Alas, my master! How shall we do? And he answered, Fear not: for they that be with us are more than they that be with them."*

That servant could not see that those that were with them were more than the enemies. He would have thought that the old prophet was going crazy. 2 Kings 6:17-19 says, *"And Elisha prayed, and said, Lord, I pray thee, open his eyes, that he may see. And the Lord opened the eyes of the young man, and he saw; and, behold, the mountain was full of horses and chariots of fire round about Elisha. And when they came down to him, Elisha prayed unto the Lord, and said, Smite this people, I pray thee, with blindness. And he smote them with blindness according to the word of Elisha. And Elisha said unto them, This is not the way, neither is this the city; follow me and I will bring you to the man whom ye see. But he led them to Samaria."*

These scriptures make us to understand that spiritual blindness is a spiritual entity. It can be removed from a person and can also be put on a person. The prayer of Elisha for that boy was, "Open my eyes, O Lord, in the name of Jesus."

Apart from the physical realm, there is also the spiritual realm for God is a Spirit. Panic and fear are normally caused by spiritual blindness. We notice in those scriptures that Elisha did not panic because he had already seen the chariot of fire surrounding him. So, he was not afraid but others were afraid. The servant could not see the spiritual world. The Syrians too, had eyes but could not see Elisha, meaning that Elisha lived in both the spiritual and physical world.

Spiritual blindness is a disaster. Many people ought to pray and pray before they take some steps. We must recover from spiritual blindness. What the servant of Elisha saw was fear, but his master saw faith. The prophet trainee feared failure, suffering, and death. I pray that the Lord will open your eyes. When the Lord opens your eyes, things will begin to happen.

We can see a mystery about the prophets of old. We see a man standing and praying a double-barrelled prayer: He turned to his own servant and said: "O Lord, open his eyes." And he turned to the enemy and said, "O Lord, send blindness." So, he was opening eyes and sending blindness at the same time. His servant's eyes were opened, while his enemies' eyes were shut.

CONSEQUENCES OF SPIRITUAL BLINDNESS

Christians need to understand some secrets and mysteries. But spiritual blindness is the big problem.

When you are spiritually blind, you will marry the wrong person. When you are spiritually blind, you will employ a witch as your house girl. When you are spiritually blind, you will board a vehicle that has been marked for accident. When you are spiritually blind, your dreams will become an avenue for the enemy to attack you because they know you cannot see them.

When you are spiritually blind, you will ask for revelation and get an attack. When you are spiritually blind, where you should get comfort, you get discomfort, where you should get plenty, you get lack. Where love should envelope you, there will be hatred. When you are spiritually blind, the Lord will set a table before you in the presence of your enemies but with your own legs you will kick away the table. When you are spiritually blind, your enemy will prophesy over your head and you will be saying Amen! Amen!! When you are spiritually blind, where you are supposed to receive acceptance, you will be rejected. When you are spiritually blind, you will fail where success is meant to be very easy. When you are spiritually blind, instead of freedom, there will be bondage.

Spiritual blindness makes people to be careless. Anyone who is spiritually blind will face hardship. When you are spiritually blind, you will frown at those you should smile at. When you are spiritually blind, you could chase away your angel of blessing. When you are spiritually blind, instead of promotion, there will be demotion.

WHAT HAPPENS WHEN YOUR EYES ARE OPEN?

When your eyes are open, things are made clear. Nobody can deceive you. Your dreams will have meaning. You will avoid unnecessary injury. When your eyes are open, you will be able to expose truth and error. There will be revelation. When your eyes are open, darkness will be defeated, and then angels of darkness will fear you because they know you can see. When your eyes are open, guidance is provided for you, and your safety is assured. You know when to move and when not to move. When your eyes are open, you prevent catastrophe and you are empowered.

WHAT YOU NEED TO SEE WHEN YOUR EYES ARE OPEN

When your eyes are open, you are supposed to see the following five things or you become a failure:

1. Who you are: The earlier you see that, the better. Do you really know who you are? Do you really understand yourself? It is a tragedy

IT WOULD BE A TRAGEDY IF YOU ARE PRAYING SO HARD BUT MISS THE RAPTURE

for the enemy to know who you are and you do not. You must tell the Lord to show you who you are. If you do not know who you are in life, you will fail. Jacob knew that he was failing and cried out. He cried out until the angel said, "Actually, you are supposed to be Israel but was named Jacob. Since you have decided to know yourself, this is who you are, you are a prince." You need to pray really hard to find out who you are.

Perhaps the person you think is your father is not really your father. This could be the reason why things are not working well with you. Perhaps you are answering the wrong name. You need to identify the deepest root of your failure. If you do not know who you are, you do not know anything. If you do not discover what you are supposed to be doing here, you do not know anything. It is possible to be born again, sanctified, Spirit-filled, and a pastor without knowing who you are. The most horrible form of ignorance is the ignorance of oneself. Until you discover who you are, you can never achieve your greatest goal in life. Inability to discover who you are will put you at the bottom of the ladder. You need to pray hard. Many come to this world, but are not present. They arrived on earth but did not show up, and so most of the people you see are not real people. Most people you meet are people who are what people say they are or what their parents want them to become or what the environment has made them to become or what they made themselves or what the enemy has made them and not what God made them. If you are to be effective, you must really know who you are. You can know who you are through prayers.

2. God: Isaiah said, "I saw the Lord," and right from that day, his life was never the same. When you see and know your God, the Bible says, you will do exploit. You need to know the God you serve.

3. The enemy: When the enemy is coming, you will know that it is the enemy, and know what to do.

4. Your purpose: A lot of people come to the world without knowing what they are doing there. If all there is to life is to get married, have children, get certificates, die and go, then life is an empty bubble. You need to know what you are doing.

5. Where you are going: Now that you are here, where next? This world is a temporary place. There

is still another country. But this is where you will decide what to do, whether to go to the beautiful country or to another place.

The last thing we are waiting for now, which may happen at anytime is the rapture. We can see all the signs. Lack of holiness, lukewarmness, lack of commitment, lack of Bible study, increase in knowledge, etc are signs of the end of the age.

You need to know where you are going. You need to know why God brought you here. You need to know that you are here for a purpose. The Bible says within a twinkle of an eye, the last trumpet shall sound. It would be a tragedy if you are rich and do not hear the trumpet. It would be a tragedy if you are married, and have everything you desire but do not hear the trumpet. It would be a tragedy if you are coming to a Bible-believing church and do not hear the trumpet. It would be a tragedy if you

are praying so hard but miss the rapture. Anyone who has ever had a vision of rapture and did not go with it is in serious trouble. If you have never seen anything about heaven in your dreams then there is a problem.

The rapture of the church will be worldwide for there are true believers scattered all over the world. The Bible says, "One shall be taken and the other shall be left." All true believers shall be taken. Every country will experience chaos on that day. Governments will move in as fast as possible to prevent anarchy and terror. Many of them will struggle to put strong measures in place to address the chaos that will happen. But they will not succeed because millions of people will suddenly disappear from the face of the earth within a twinkle of an eye from all works of life. People will be missing. The roads, streets, and airports will be in shambles. All the engineers, bus drivers, pilots and multitudes of private car owners would be cut off, and there will be crashes of planes and vehicles. A lot of people in those planes and vehicles will not have time to repent before they land in hell fire. It will take weeks to unscramble the mangled cars and aircraft. And the remaining millions of people will be wailing and will be dazed by what would have taken place just as they screamed during the time of Noah. When Noah was warning that there was going to be rain, they did not believe him, but all of a sudden, it happened. You may say, "I don't believe this kind of superstition."

THE PROPHET | David versus Goliath 9

What you believe does not matter because it shall surely happen. Many key persons will disappear and communication will be in a mess. Emergency shelter and first aid will not solve the problem. The Red Cross will be completely useless. The opportunists will move in; looting and killing people. They will believe that there is nothing anybody can do to arrest them. There will be complete breakdown of law and order. It is then many will understand what we have been saying. Many will rush to the church. The churches will be filled to the brim but then it will be too late.

Whatever will tie you down to this world when the trumpet sounds is already there now unless you deal with it. There are many people now who open their Bibles only during church service. If not for the enemies pursuing some people they will never come to a place like MFM because they do not like the way they look, the way they dress, and the way they do anything. They just like the prayers. At the MFM, we are going to heaven and assembling are together candidates who want to make heaven.

Your sugar daddy and fornicating boyfriend will glue you down here when the trumpet sounds. Your anger, malice and pride will prevent you from making rapture. Once you do not go with rapture, your going to church is in vain. You need to pray that whatsoever will glue you down should release you now. Is it money? It will grow wings and fly away. Is it beauty? Beauty is vain. If you say, "I cannot be serious now because of my husband," that husband will turn back at the grave yard. I want you to understand that it is a serious matter. Whatever is going to glue you down is already inside you unless you cry out to God for deliverance.

PRAYER POINTS

1. Anything in my life that will hold me down for the antichrist, die, in the name of Jesus.
2. Every filthiness in my heart, blood of Jesus, purge it out, in the name of Jesus.
3. Thou power of God, open my eyes, in the name of Jesus.
4. O Lord, with a word, let my problem disappear, in the name of Jesus.
5. O God, arise and laugh my enemies to scorn, in the name of Jesus.
6. O Lord, let your chariot of fire appear in my situation, in the name of Jesus.
7. Every enemy that has outnumbered me, receive double disgrace, in the name of Jesus.
8. Every covenant of darkness attached to my eyes, break, in the name of Jesus.
9. I use the padlock of heaven to lock up tragedy, disappointment, failure and death, in the name of Jesus.
10. Any particular house in my place of birth that is cooking my destiny, receive the fire of God, in the name of Jesus.
11. O wind of God, arise by fire, reverse every curse working against me and bring me blessings, in the name of Jesus.
12. Every power summoning me for evil, answer your own summon, in the name of Jesus
13. Every fetish power targeted against me, die, in the name of Jesus.
14. Thou power of almost there, your time is up, die, in the name of Jesus.
15. Every lost blessings of my ancestors, I recover you by fire, in the name of Jesus.

OPEN MY EYES, O LORD
is a message delivered at the Mountain of Fire and Miracles Ministries by the General Overseer, Dr. D.K. Olukoya.

A CALL TO SERVE

Are you a member of MFM with a burden to help the needy, are you interested in alleviating the plight of the poor or in the spread of the gospel through the sponsorshing of the publication of tracts? Your resources, time and talent can be extended to several groups that are in charge of these areas. These groups include:

o   We care Ministry,
o   Mission Outreach
o   Tracts and Publications
o   Ministry to Drug addicts
o   Campus fellowship
o   Ministry to Schools
o   Ministry to Glorious Children, etc.

Thus says the Lord, "Verily I say unto you, in as much as ye have done it unto one of the least of these my brethren, ye have done it unto me" Matthew 25 : 40.

WONDERFUL JESUS!

THE SPIRIT OF DEATH FAILS

A new convert came to stay with us. At night, I discovered that he had stopped breathing. I immediately alerted my husband and we started praying, telling God to take control. God answered our prayers, and he came alive. Praise the Lord!

Sis Ugo
MFM Omiyale Ejigbo

DIVINE HEALING

I had a swollen knee which defied all manner of treatment. The pain on the knee cap made it difficult for me to bend and walk. During one of our programmes I took the matter to God in prayers and I received total healing. Praise the Lord!

Bro Ochuko
MFM Ughelli.

GOD TOUCHES MY SON

I struggled to educate and send my son abroad. As soon as he got there, he forgot me and was saying negative and very uncomplimentary things about me. I cried to the Lord and He answered me. My son now sends things to me without my asking at least, once in three days. Praise the Lord!

Sis Victoria
MFM Asoro

GOD GRANTS ME JOURNEY MERCIES

My brother's wedding date was fixed and the venue was in Imo State. Two weeks to the day, I started having dreams of accidents. I started fasting and I prayed the prayer of agreement with my wife. And God granted me journey mercies. Praise the Lord!

Bro Austin
MFM Egan

GOD RESTORES MY DREAM LIFE

My dream life was turbulent. This prompted me to go for deliverance. Immediately after the programme, God restored my dream life and now I remember my dreams. Praise the Lord!

Bro. Oluwole
MFM Abule Anu

DELIVERANCE FROM LONG-TERM SICKNESS

I was afflicted with a mysterious sickness for many years. However, after undergoing a prayer and fasting programme here, the sickness disappeared and I have been made whole. Praise the Lord!

Bro. Boniface
MFM Adaloko

SAFE DELIVERY

I thank God for His mercies over my life. Recently, a pregnant sister in my house started having labours pains. I gave her the anointing oil and prayed for her and after sometime, she gave birth safely. I thank God for saving the baby because it was premature. God perfect His work in the life of the family. Praise the Lord!

Sis. Banjoko
MFM Ijebu Ode

DELIVERED FROM TWELVE YEARS ASTHMA

After I gave a testimony of what God did in my life, that night, the Lord Jesus visited me in my sleep and carried out a spiritually surgery on me. When I woke up, asthma of over 12years disappeared. By the same visitation, the poverty of several years came to an end. Praise the Lord!

Bro. Odumosu
MFM Ijaiye Ojokoro

RELEASE FROM PRISON BY GOD

Some amount of money was missing in my place of work and all the workers were arrested and put in prison. My colleagues were all released on bail after their relatives gave money to the police. I did not have anybody to come to my rescue. I cried out unto the Lord after they had transferred me to Kirikiri maximum prison. The Lord heard me and the culprit was caught. Then I was released without paying a dime. Praise the Lord!

Sis Ifeoma
MFM Ajangbadi

DIVINE HEALING

I had some health problems and the doctor told me to stop eating some things. When I got back home, I started eating those things and the problem came back. I took the matter to God in serious prayers and I started eating those things the doctor said I should not eat. To the glory of God, all the problems have disappeared. Praise the Lord!

Bro. Kunle
MFM Shibiri

GOD OF ALL IMPOSIBILITIES

My younger sister was due for marriage and my family members continued postponing the date severely. I cried unto the Lord for divine intervention and God responded by providing somebody who sponsored the marriage ceremony. Also, God provided a befitting job for my husband. Praise the Lord!

Sis Shofoluwe
MFM Omo-Oye

FIRE IN THE WORD, is a weekly Spiritual Bulletin of the Mountain of Fire and Miracles Ministries, published by Tracts and Publications Group. All Enquiries should be addressed to The Editor, Mountain of Fire Magazine, 13, Olasimbo Street, off Olumo Road, Onike, P.O. Box 2990, Sabo Yaba, Lagos, Nigeria. Telephone 01- 867439, 864631, 868766, 08023180236. E-mail: mfmtractsandpublications@yahoo.com Copyright reserved.

FIRE IN THE WORD

Ye Shall Know the Truth, and the Truth Shall Make You Free (John 8:32)

ISSN 1595 - 7314 Vol. 12 No. 22 Sun. 6th - Sat. 12th Apr., 2008

The Shrine
OF THE FLESH

My year of unprecedented greatness and unmatchable increase
Deuteronomy 28:13, Psalm 71:21, Ephesians 3:20, Psalm 92:10

A shrine is not a strange thing to an average person living in Africa because in many of the communities, there are shrines where people worship every time. God is in the business of disqualifying men and women when they do not meet His standard. This is because everyone has this personal shrine which he or she worships everyday. Some people spend hours in the bathroom every morning trying to worship this shrine. Some people feed this shrine at least three times everyday. This shrine complains at every little inconvenience. It hates any form of discomfort.

The most difficult thing in life is for one to know oneself. It is true that the easiest person to deceive is oneself. And the worst fraud is to deceive oneself. But it is surprising to know that many people actively deceive themselves. Some know within them that they are not on the path to heaven at all, yet they pretend.

The chief usher of a certain church came to me crying, that God had taken away his peace. He told me that any time they finished counting the offering in his church, the pastor would pick all the fifty naira notes for himself. He watched the pastor do this for about three years, expecting him to fall down and die, but found that the man was getting fatter instead. Therefore, he decided to be picking the twenty naira notes after the pastor had picked the fifty naira notes. But the first day he did it, an angel appeared to him in the dream and said, "Son, you have just started a process that your generation coming will also reap the punishment because you are stealing from the Lord." He told the angel that the pastor too was doing it. God told him that the pastor was just a temporary staff. It was then he ran to me. What pushed that man to do that kind of thing was the shrine of the flesh.

Ninety per cent of what many people carry about are materials used to worship this shrine: a comb to comb the hair of the shrine, a mirror to watch the shrine very well, lipstick to give it read colour, and sometimes, you find a very tiny Bible hiding in their midst.

If you want an increase of Christ in your life, there must be a decrease of self. Somebody once said that madness is to increase your speed where you have already lost your way. Many are saying they want Nigeria or the world to change, but few people are ready to change themselves. The command now is loud and clear: "Lay aside the shrine called self or God will lay you aside."

There are many people who are busy comparing themselves with others forgetting that the Bible says the battle is not to the strong, neither the race to the swift. God has an agenda for your life. You must

> THE DEVIL COMES IN WHEN WE OPEN THE DOOR THROUGH OUR UNCRUCIFIED FLESH

understand that life is not about how fast you go but how well you do it. Lay that shrine aside, let God use you, so that God does not lay you aside. At this juncture, I would like you to make the following confession: "I live to die, I die to live; the more I die, the more I live." This is why Paul said, "I die daily." The more the shrine of the flesh dies, the more of God rises up in your life. The flesh is our greatest enemy. Our greatest enemy is not the devil, witches and wizards; but this shrine, which we carry about. Temptations are effective because of our sinful nature, the sin in us welcomes them, and they start causing problems for us. Immediately you are able to put Mr. Flesh in its proper place, demons will run away from you. There will no longer be a ladder for them to climb in to work in your life.

A certain man was in big trouble and believed the whole world was against him because he lost his job five times, his wife ran away, somebody impregnated his daughter that was in the secondary school, and he became so depressed. He cried to the Lord in desperate prayer to deliver him. And the Lord appeared to him and he was very happy because he wanted the Lord to sympathize with him, promote him, give him justice and deliverance from all his troubles. But to his amazement, the Lord pointed at him and said, "Your problem is rooted in you and not your enemy." This is the hardest part of Christian life. Many people are not willing to admit

DELIVERANCE CASE

that they are their own problem. The Lord told him that he was only deceiving himself by blaming the devil. The Lord said further, "Son, listen to me well, I am the Almighty, I am not struggling with the devil. I desire that your flesh be in submission to my Spirit. I want to dethrone you from the centre of your life and be your Lord. Your flesh is doing more to hinder my work than any evil power you are praying against. So, the devil is not the issue as much as the power of your flesh." The man was dazed because he thought the Lord would deal with witches and wizards on his behalf. But the Lord told him that he was the problem.

Our toughest battle is with the flesh. Galatians 5:17 says, *"For the flesh lusteth against the Spirit, and the Spirit against the flesh; and these are contrary the one to the other: so that ye cannot do the things that ye would do."* This fight between the flesh and the spirit is so serious that if the flesh is not put under control, one will not be able to fulfill one's destiny. When there is no food for the shrine called flesh, its power goes down. And when Mr. Flesh is very

weak then the spirit can rise. That is the secret of fasting. Fasting does not change God. But when you begin to fast, the flesh becomes a weak king and the spirit begins to rise. Then you are able to pray more and get results.

The devil comes in when we open the door through our uncrucified flesh. People come to programmes and get blessed but because Mr. Flesh is uncrucified, they get the miracles and lose them. Some lose their miracles right from the car park, while some lose theirs at home. After a very powerful prayer meeting, Mr. Flesh waits for people at different points. It could be at home, where he will push somebody to provoke them and they will get angry and misbehave and that will be the end of the breakthrough they have received. Some come to prayer meetings and instead of sitting down and interceding, praying that the Lord should visit them, they would be listening to the gossips of a friend, analyzing everything and everybody.

The devil is always looking for open doors. He knows the limitations of his power. Jesus said the prince of this world came and found nothing in Him. The devil had no access to Jesus because He was dead to self. He was dead to its desires and agenda. Is lust still in the laboratory of your heart? It means there is something in you that needs to die. If it does not die, you are not going anywhere. Even if God has decided to use you but your flesh is still on the throne of your life, you will be disqualified or at most be a temporary instrument or you become like a tout at the bus-stop calling for passengers while he goes nowhere. Or you become a human signboard, which does not leave where it is.

The powers of darkness operate the most powerful X-ray machines that exist. Immediately they set eyes on a person, they can tell the spiritual level of the person. That is why they said to the sons of Sceva, "Paul we know, Jesus we know, but who are you? Your names are not here, you have no authority." No matter what powerful name you give yourself, they know you. You may be a very powerful singer, but you could be just a temporary vessel.

Sometime ago, in one of our stations abroad, as I told the congregation to rise up and sing a song, the Lord said: "Son look at that man who is going to play the keyboard very well." I looked at him and he was very handsome man. The Lord said, "He would pollute this meeting if you do not stop him." I thought of how I was going to embarrass the man, but I had to listen to my Master. So, I told the pastor to remove the man from the keyboard. "Ah! We hired him and we have paid," the pastor said. "Put your church organist there," I replied. The pastor told me that the church organist was not as good as this man. But I insisted he put the church organist there. After the service, the man came to me and demanded why he was embarrassed at the service. I asked him the following question as led by the Holy Spirit: "When last did you visit a prostitute?" His eyes blinked at my question and then he understood why I asked him to leave and he asked for help. Here was a man who seemed to be serving God but was dishonest inside. There are many like that. Beloved, if you are like that, how long will you act? Won't you cry to the Lord that the shrine of flesh that has been controlling your life should dry up and die?

The scanning machine of darkness can detect the smallest compromise you make. They can see those cleverly concealed evil habits that others cannot see. This is why the prayers of many people are not effective. The devil will defeat any Christian whose flesh is not crucified with ease. The devil is looking for houses to dwell in and any area of your life that is not submitted to God would be taken over by him for a residence. The human life is like a large mansion. God will take residence of the room you give to Him. The one you do not give to Him, He leaves it to you; and Jesus is knocking at the door looking for serious people. The fact remains that the absence or scarcity of the power of God in this generation is not the fault of God, but the unavailability of yielded, ready vessels. Whatever area of your life you submit to the devil, the devil will use it. If you submit your hair, ears, thoughts, marriage, job, house, ambitions, certificate or voice, he will use it.

From Galatians 5:24, we understand that we need to pray some surgical prayers. Some things have to be cut down, some things have to die. Christians need to get to that level, where they no longer fall into temptation, a level where they are completely dead to temptation. If you are still blaming other people for your shortcomings, then you are not ready for change yet. But when you point the accusing finger at yourself, then you are

THE SHRINE OF SELF IS THE TOOL THE DEVIL USES TO GET CONTROL OF PEOPLE'S LIVES

getting somewhere. Those who are still having evil affections and lust, are not of Christ, they have not crucified the flesh. That is what the scripture is telling us.

Somebody tempted Peter with money. He said to Peter, "Take this money and give me this gift also, that on whosoever I lay my hands on would receive the Holy Spirit." Peter looked at him and said, "Your money perish with you." Peter was able to say so to him because there was nothing in Peter that would respond to the sensation and temptation of money.

I want you to know that the enemy can detect the smallest unfaithfulness and falsehood in your life. You may tell a man of God a lie, and God may not even tell him that you are telling a lie, but the enemy knows and will use it against you. Peter had allowed God to crucify that area of his life that was yielding to money. The flesh enables a man to engage in activities contrary to the Holy Spirit. The flesh will not improve, it is rotten to the core. And most of the problems we have are brought upon us by this shrine. It is responsible for rash decisions, plain disobedience and irrational thinking. The most difficult problem of man is to point accusing fingers to himself.

THE FLESH IS VERY DANGEROUS AND HAS NO MERCY.

The flesh is a harder problem to deal with than the devil.

We fight four basic enemies:

1. **Sin.** The Bible says, *"And she shall bring forth a son, and thou shall call his name Jesus. For he shall save his people from their sins"* (Matthew 1:21).

2. **The world.** The Bible says, *"In the world you shall have tribulations, but be of good cheer for I have overcome the world"* (John 16:33).

3. **The devil.** But the Bible says, *"Resist the devil, and he will flee from you"* (James 4:7).

4. **The shrine called flesh.** To this one, there is no promise at all. You need to fight it to a standstill. That is why you must deal with all self-righteousness and selfishness. Selfishness is when self is on the throne. It breeds indiscipline, boasting, stubbornness, rebellion, covetousness, laziness, restlessness, and

procrastination. If you do not pull down the power of this shrine, the Lord will disqualify you from the battlefront. He has to do that or you will become a casualty.

Many years ago, an old white man preached a message titled: "How to be miserable." According to him, if you want to be miserable, do the following things:

• Always be thinking about yourself alone. Do not think of helping others.

• Always be talking about yourself and your achievements.

• Use the word "I" as often as possible.

• Mirror yourself continually in the opinion of others.

• Always listen greedily to what they say about you.

• Always be suspicious.

• Expect to be appreciated for everything you do.

• Be jealous and envious.

• Be sensitive to any small insult. Never forgive anyone who criticizes you.

• Love yourself supremely above others.

• Allow yourself to be on the throne of your life.

If you feed your flesh, it will get stronger and if you feed your spirit, your spirit will get stronger. Jesus said, "The flesh profiteth nothing." You must not underestimate the power of the flesh. If you do, you would be captured before you know it.

The shrine of self is the power of sin which functions against the law of God. The shrine of self is the one that forbids the practice of spiritual good. The shrine of self is that which the Bible says cannot please God. The shrine of self is the tool the devil uses to get control of people's lives. The shrine of self is that which gives legal ground to satanic activities in our lives. The shrine of self is the empty way of life we received from our ancestors. The shrine of self is the producer of evil works within. This is why repentance destroys its work. When you repent, you destroy the works of Mr. Flesh. The shrine of self is the one that gets angry. The shrine of self is the one that engages in impure thoughts. The shine of self has the capacity to specialize in people's lives. Beloved, do not rejoice and start saying, "I only tell lies. I don't commit fornication," because the shrine might have decided to specialize in that area of

THE PROPHET | David versus Goliath 10

your life. There is no difference between a witch and a fornicator. They are both students in the training school of the flesh. And the Bible says both of them shall not inherit the kingdom of God.

Occasional anger is the work of the flesh. Jealousy, fighting, selfishness, tribalism etc will all lead to the same place. If you have a mango tree in your house and do not want it to produce fruits again, the solution is to uproot it. Many people have not done certain things because there is no opportunity for them to do them. Mr. Flesh can keep quiet for one week or more and you begin to thank God. But it can rise again when you provoke him. This is why a pastor can give his wife a serious beating. The reason some people do not commit fornication is that they have not found somebody who will submit to them. The day they find one, Mr. Flesh that has been lying low will come up. The reason some people are not in prison for stealing or embezzlement is that they have never worked in a place where they have access to a lot of money, the day they come across it, Mr. Flesh will come up. This is why you must not joke with the flesh. That is why drastic measures must be taken against the flesh, it has to be dragged to the cross and nailed there. The cross too like Mr. Flesh has no mercy. Jesus died on it. Once you get to the cross, you die to the flesh. The flesh is able to allow some scattered victories here and there before attacking again.

WAY OUT

You must decide that this shrine must be destroyed, and that you are not going to worship or feed it again. You must decide to pray the prayer of Zechariah who said: "That which must die, let it die." That is, let the flesh die. Pray that God should get a good nail and nail you to His cross, so that whatever anyone does against you will not affect you. And focus on hearing the Lord say, "Well done, thou good servant, enter into the joy of your master." Anything that will not allow you to hear this from the Lord is the shrine of self.

It is a pity that what is going to affect some people in ten years time is already in them. The sin that they will commit and annoy God is already inside their lives. You need to render the flesh dead so that if you were getting

angry before, you become unprovokable. Until the flesh dies, you cannot become what God wants you to become. There are some pastors who are proud. They do not understand the word of God which says, "What do you have that you did not receive?" If you received it from God, why are you behaving as if you did not receive it? The flesh must die so that you can walk freely with the Holy Spirit.

PRAYER POINTS

1. Power of the cross, crucify my flesh, in the name of Jesus.
2. Every power of the flesh in my destiny, die, in the name of Jesus.
3. Anything in my life that has not manifested now but will manifest in the future to destroy my life, die, in the name of Jesus.
4. Any material from my body in the kingdom of darkness, disappear by fire, in the name of Jesus.
5. Every ladder used by the enemy to climb into my life, be roasted, in the name of Jesus.

THE SHRINE OF THE FLESH
is a message delivered at the Mountain of Fire and Miracles Ministries by the General Overseer, Dr. D.K. Olukoya.

WONDERFUL JESUS!

SERPENTINE SPIRIT DESTROYED

I always dreamt about snakes right from my childhood. This spirit was tormenting my life. Later, I discovered that the problem came into my life through incisions made on me by my parents. I came here for deliverance and after the programme, I was set free. Praise the Lord!

Sis Benedicta
MFM HQ Benin City

GOD GIVES ME MULTIPLE BREAKTHROUGHS

I thank God for giving me the strength to undergo the deliverance programme with fasting and prayers. Secondly, the Lord has given me victory in my dream life. Thirdly the Lord gave me financial breakthrough. Lastly, the Lord has given me favour in the sight of men and God. Praise the Lord!

Sis. Sanni
MFM Oworonsoki

MULTIPLE VISA GRANTED

Before I came for prayers, things were not working out in my life. But since I came to MFM, things have been going on well. Recently, I applied for a UK visa and got six months multiple visa. I give God the glory.

Bro. Nelson
MFM Kampala Uganda

PROMOTION LETTER RECEIVED

I had a terrible dream about my promotion letter which I told my pastor. He prayed with me. Later, I had another dream where I was harvesting groundnut and somebody tried to stop me from taking it. But I refused saying that the groundnut was mine. When I got to the office that week, I was given my promotion letter. Praise the Lord!

Sis Komolafe
MFM Ikare

GOD GRANTS US VISA TO USA

Sometime ago, two of my brothers got admission to study abroad and with all the documents presented at the embassy, they were not given visas. We started prayers, the pastors and ministers prayed with us. I thank God that after persistent prayers, they were given visas and the two of them have travelled abroad. Praise the Lord!

Sis Kemi
MFM Lekki

GOD TRANSFORMS MY LIFE

I was facing a chain of terrible problems. I trusted in God, started praying violently and God began to reveal secret things about my life to me. In a dream, God took me to my village where I saw a huge snake and He gave me the strength and courage to cut off its head. Since then my life has changed for the better.

Bro James
MFM Ojo

JESUS THE GREATEST HEALER HEALS MY GRANDCHILDREN

One of my grandchildren suddenly became paralysed and could not walk again. I brought him to church and the man of God prayed for him. To the glory of God, he is now well and can walk again. Soon after, the second one in Warri was returned to me sick. After diagnosis, nothing was found, yet he was seriously sick. I brought him also to the church for prayers and to the glory of God, he is also healed now. Praise the Lord!

Sis. Chukwuedo
MFM Asaba

DIVINE HEALING

My child was sick with high fever between March and April 2005. We went to various hospitals but there was no solution. We also prayed in my former church but there was still no improvement. The Spirit of God ministered to me to come to Mountain of Fire and Miracles Ministries. When we came, we were placed on deliverance by the pastor. After the programme, my child received his healing. Praise the Lord!

Sis okoro
MFM Ughelli

GOD RESTORES MY WIFE'S BUSINESS

My wife's business has not been moving fine since we moved into this district. But during the "Pray your way to 2003" it was ministered to me by the Holy Spirit to take a handful of sand from the Prayer City and sprinkle it on her shop. To the glory to God, since then there has been improvement in the business. Praise the Lord!

Bro Victor
MFM Olowora

GOD IS GOOD

I finished my secondary school since two years ago and was waiting for my Jamb result. With continuous prayers, just recently I got my result and have been admitted into the University of Ilorin. I thank God for everything. Praise the Lord!

Sis. Kolawole
MFM Aguda

Join us and **BUILD** for the Lord

THE PRAYER CITY DELIVERANCE STADIUM AND INTERNATIONAL CONFERENCE CENTRE

N35,000,000,000

To be a part of this project, send your donation* to the Regional Overseer/Pastor or to the Secretariat

Prayer City Partners and Friends

i/c The Office of the G.O.

13, Olasimbo Street, Onike-Yaba, Lagos.

Mode of payment

Any Branch of Oceanic Bank International Plc. Nationwide
Account No.: 0801101006463
Name of Account: MFM-Prayer City Partners and Friends

For further information contact
08055145040, 08023128677,
08034934848, 08023261588
email: info@mfmprayercity.org
website: mfmprayercity.org

FIRE IN THE WORD, is a weekly Spiritual Bulletin of the Mountain of Fire and Miracles Ministries, published by Tracts and Publications Group. All Enquiries should be addressed to The Editor, Mountain of Fire Magazine, 13, Olasimbo Street, off Olumo Road, Onike, P.O. Box 2990, Sabo Yaba, Lagos, Nigeria. Telephone 01- 867439, 864631, 868766, 08023180236.E-mail: mfintractsandpublications@yahoo.com Copyright reserved.

FIRE IN THE WORD

Ye Shall Know the Truth, and the Truth Shall Make You Free (John 8:32)

ISSN 1595 - 7314 Vol. 12 No. 23 Sun. 13th - Sat. 19th April, 2008

WITHOUT STRENGTH BEFORE
THE PURSUER

My year of unprecedented greatness and unmatchable increase
Deuteronomy 28:13, Psalm 71:21, Ephesians 3:20, Psalm 92:10

amentation 1:6 says, *"And from the daughter of Zion all her beauty is departed: her princes are become like harts that find no pasture, and they are gone without strength before the pursuer."*

What a tragic lamentation. The runner is in big trouble because he is being pursued but has no strength. Somebody that is pursued cannot relax. If he has no strength then he is already a prey, a casualty. A runner that has no strength is as good as being in prison because it is only a matter of time before he or she is caught. When a person that is pursued has no strength before the pursuer, it means he or she is running in vain, he or she is engaged in a useless exercise. Somebody who has no strength before the pursuer is as good as gone. Unfortunately, this is the situation of many people. They have accumulated enemies from their fathers' houses, mothers' houses, their inlaws and their places of work. They have accumulated these arrays of pursuers but then they have no strength.

Beloved, are the things pursuing you catching up with you? Are you pursued by anger, lust, fear, evil dream, familiar spirits, witches, bad luck, poverty, lukewarmness,

backsliding, worldliness, immorality, and unseriousness, and are they catching up with you? Think about it. Are those things that were never close to you dominating you now? You need to pray. Are the old sicknesses that went away when you surrendered your life to Jesus coming back now? There is a spiritual rule that does not change. It says, if you go back to your old sin, your old problem will come back. Jesus said to the man by the pool of Bethesda, "Sin no more lest a worse thing come upon you." So old sin, old problem.

The truth is that as a Christian, you ought to be the pursuer and not the pursued. Have you started to lose stamina in prayer? Were you the kind of person who could fast for three or seven days and nobody would know you were fasting? But now you are losing stamina? Have you started to faint in your resistance to satan? Are the kind of sin and thoughts that never use to cross your mind now staging a throne in your heart? Then you are becoming powerless before the pursuer. The powerlessness of our present generation of Christians is alarming and **NO DEMON CAN COME AND BE PRESSING YOU DOWN ON YOUR BED WHEN GOD IS CLOSE TO YOU**

terrible. It is time to decide that you must take your rightful position, that is being the pursuer and not the pursued. So, you need power to contend with and to subdue the powers of darkness. Nowadays, men and women are going deeply into the occult to receive power. Unless Christians are able to contend with their power, there will be problem.

There is a rule in the spirit world which does not change. It says, when a greater power comes across a lesser power, as a matter of necessity, the lesser power must bow. If you are without strength before a strong pursuer then there is trouble.

HOW TO PURSUE THE PURSUER

There is only one key to pursue the pursuer and it is found in Psalm 51:17 which says, *"The sacrifices of God are a broken spirit: a broken and a contrite heart, O God, thou wilt not despise."* This key is a broken and a contrite heart. There is no way God will reject the cry of those who have a broken spirit and a contrite heart. It means there are people that God despises. That is why the Bible says, *"They will call upon me but I will not answer"* (Proverbs 1:28). "They will call upon me when they need help

DELIVERANCE CASE (The Story of my life - Part 11)

and I will turn my face away!" But if you have a broken spirit, God will not despise your cry. In Psalm 34:18, we can see those that God is close to; those who are the friends of God. You can be the friend of your pastor or General Overseer but if you are not a friend of God, you are wasting your time.

Psalm 34:18 says, *"The Lord is nigh unto them that are of a broken heart; and seeth such as be of a contrite spirit."* Many people are talking what they do not practise. Many carry the Bible but the Bible is not in their heart. And the enemy can see all the hypocrisy and acting. The enemy has powerful X-ray and scan machines through which he can see Christians who are serious and those who are not serious. If you are being pursued by an enemy that is stronger than you, you are already a prey. The Bible says, "Finally, my brethren be strong in the Lord..." (Ephesians

6:10). It did not say be strong in gossiping, be strong in backbiting or be strong in pride." It says, "Be strong in the Lord and in the power of His might" because our enemy is strong. It is this enemy the Bible refers to as the strongman. That strongman is not of God, it is a negative strongman.

Our lives must demonstrate the power of God, and for that to happen, we must be broken. The Lord is close to those who are broken. They are the kind of people He wants. If you are not broken then you will be without strength before the pursuer. But if you are of a broken heart, the Lord will be close to you and His power will be following you around. The people of darkness will see it and run away. When God is with you, they will run away from you. No demon can come and be pressing you down on

your bed when God is close to you. Spirit spouse, witches, familiar spirits and household wickedness cannot harm somebody that is broken because God is with the person. When God is with you, wherever you go, He goes. Where you sit down, He sits down because He is always close to those that are broken.

WHAT IS BROKENNESS?

Brokenness is the taming of the soul. When a soul is tamed by God, it is said to be broken. Many souls are not tamed that is why you see many people talking carelessly. That is why many people are getting angry and fighting. When your soul is not tamed, you will be cursing people and your tongue will be very acidic. Brokenness is giving abundant room to the Holy Spirit to operate in your life. It is complete submission and obedience to God.

Brokenness is for you to die and for Christ to live in you. And you become like a small Jesus moving about. Brokenness is inner transformation by God. Brokenness is total elimination of the flesh in your life and complete enthronement of God in your heart. Brokenness is to allow God to make you what He wants. The Lord is nigh unto those that are of a broken heart. He is glued to them.

When you are broken, there are things you do not do, and there are things that do not happen to you. A broken person does not act in anger. The fact that you lose your cool means you are still without strength before the pursuer. The fact that you get into sin quite easily and jump out again to repent shows that you are without strength. The power of a broken life cannot be contested. Any unbroken area of a life is enough to make the enemy come in easily. You cannot fight an enemy that is stronger than you. If you can allow God to break you down, and all the activities and powers of the flesh die in your life, you will find life a lot easier. And you will begin to pursue the powers that have been pursuing you.

FACTS ABOUT
SPIRITUAL WARFARE

1. You must deal with the devil and his cohorts.

2. You must take control of your mind. It is not every battle that is with the devil and his cohorts alone. You must establish a solid immigration control at the door of your mind. And anyone or anything that approaches that door of your mind without the appropriate documents is sent back to the sender. All the terrible evil thoughts must be sent out. It is part of warfare.

3. You must crucify the flesh. The big truth is that satanic attack cannot prosper in a life that does not cooperate with it. If your flesh cooperates with the devil, the devil will attack you. If you are dead to sin, the enemy will run away from you. Dead men do not respond to temptation. Dead men do not commit fornication. Dead men do not abuse people. Dead men are not capable of responding to somebody who is abusing them or who is talking rubbish to them.

Herein lies the power of a broken man. When we live a life of brokenness, no weapon formed against us can prosper. All the prayer against the devil will be to no avail, if one is not broken. In such cases, the devil is not the real enemy, the enemy

WHEN YOU KEEP FRIENDS WHO ARE NOT GODLY, THEN YOU ARE NOT BROKEN

is the flesh which many people have refused to surrender to the Holy Spirit.

When you are living a broken life, there is no wizard or witch that can eat your flesh. You will cease to become raw material for satanic attack. When you are living a broken life, you will know the secret of God. He will talk to you. When you are living a broken life, you become immune to satanic arrows. When you are living a broken life, you will permanently trample upon serpents and scorpions. You become a terror to demonic forces. And when you go home to be with the Lord, the demonic forces will be rejoicing that you have gone. When you live a broken life, you will offer no cooperation to the devil. You will reject sin in all its ramifications. When you are broken, you will offer no protection to the enemy. The power in a broken life is tremendous. Therefore, you do your spiritual life a lot of havoc if you are not broken. When you are broken, you will survive and record testimonies every time. You must cry out to the Lord, that the serpent of sin must die so that brokenness will manifest in your life.

Once you are living in any known sin, be assured that you are an enemy of the cross. If you are living in any known sin, you are without strength before the pursuer, no matter how hard you pray. You need to be broken.

SIGNS OF UNBROKENNESS

1. If you are stubborn, unteachable and close-minded, you are unbroken.

2. When your bad behaviour does not prick your conscience anymore, you are unbroken.

3. When you do not have godly sorrow for the sins you commit and do not break down and cry or feel sorry, you are unbroken.

4. When you are not sensitive to your own spiritual weakness and you are not sensitive to the fact that you are not praying enough or reading your Bible enough, and you are not doing what the Lord wants you to do, you are not broken.

5. If your heart is so hard that the word of God cannot penetrate it, you are unbroken and will be powerless before the pursuer.

6. If you consciously disobey God, you are unbroken.

7. If you are a hypocrite, you are unbroken.

8. If you are not humble, you are unbroken. If you are proud and think you are very important, remember that nobody is indispensable to God. If you are never deeply sincere with what you say, or you are even a Jezebel pursuing people to make them fall, you are unbroken. If you exhibit a lot of unloving characteristics, you are not broken.

9. When you keep friends who are not godly, then you are not broken.

The kind of friends you keep, the very manner in which you speak, the way you spend your leisure time, the way you use your money, the things you wear, the kind of music you listen to, the kind of things you talk about, the kind of books your read and the way you make your money, show whether you are broken or not.

WHAT DOES THE LORD WANT YOU TO DO?

He wants you to get broken so that you can be what He wants you to become. A certain man of God changed his own country. He noticed that whenever he saw sinners in the street, he did not get worried whether they were saved or not. So, he knew that something was wrong with him. He went to the mountain and prayed one prayer point for seven days. The prayer point was: "O Lord, break me!" By the time he prayed this for seven days, something happened. He became a changed man. When he rose up and began to minister, things began to happen. We need to call ourselves to order. Pride must go. All kinds of evil speaking must

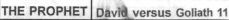

THE PROPHET David versus Goliath 11

go. All unloving characteristics must go. If you say things to other people and later begin to regret it, then you are not broken. You will be without strength before the pursuer.

Unfortunately, there are many unbroken pastors, unbroken ushers, unbroken choristers and unbroken workers in the church. A man is nothing without God. You must allow the Lord to lay you out on His stretcher, take you to His operating theatre and carry out a surgical operation on your life.

Samson was a child of promise, a child whose birth was prophesied by angels. He was destined to be a winner even before he was born. But because of the unbroken area of his life, he lost everything. He became blind. The strongman that the Philistines feared became somebody who was grinding pepper in the midst of the Philistines. Eventually, he died with his enemies. Although, he killed more enemies at his death he died with them.

Beloved, you need to cry to heavens to deliver you from unbrokenness so that you will fulfill your divine destiny.

PRAYER POINTS

1. O Lord, break me, in the name of Jesus.
2. My Father, help me, I do not want to be a negative example. in the name of Jesus.
3. Thou power of failure at the edge of success, your time is up, die, in the name of Jesus.
4. Thou power of poor finishing, die, in the name of Jesus.
5. Heavenly fire, arise, attack poverty in my life, in the name of Jesus.
6. Thou strongman troubling my life, die, in the name of Jesus.
7. Every habitation of wickedness in my dwelling place, scatter, in the name of Jesus.

8. Mirror of darkness fashioned against me, explode in the face of your owner, in the name of Jesus.
9. Thunder of God, lightning of God, arise in your anger, scatter every witchcraft gathering troubling me, in the name of Jesus.
10. All round success, pursue me and locate me, in the name of Jesus.
11. My Father, make my life a success story, in the name of Jesus.
12. Every satanic decree against my advancement, die, in the name of Jesus.
13. I, (mention your name) will fulfill my destiny at the appointed time, in the name of Jesus.
14. Every uncompleted good project in my life, be completed by fire, in the name of Jesus.
15. I shall walk, I shall run, I shall fly as an eagle this year, in the name of Jesus.
16. My spiritual legs, hear the word of the Lord, move me forward by fire, in the name of Jesus.

WITHOUT STRENGTH BEFORE THE PURSUER

is a message delivered at the Mountain of Fire and Miracles Ministries by the General Overseer, Dr. D.K. Olukoya.

WONDERFUL JESUS!

I NOW ENJOY DIVINE HEALTH

I thank the Lord Almighty for His healing power upon my life. Before I joined MFM, I used to be sick always. But since I joined this church, I have been enjoying good health to the glory of God. Praise the Lord!

Sis Adewole
MFM Alagbole

GOD RESTORES MY MENSTRUATION

I appreciate God for His mighty power of restoration. For six years I menstruated only four times in a year. But when I came for the deliverance programme here, God restored and perfected it to His glory. Praise the Lord!

Sis. Aregbeshola
MFM Headquarters

MERCIFUL GOD

Since 1998, my boss who is a woman has been attending promotion interviews to no avail. Though she is a muslim, she nevertheless asked for my prayers concerning progress in her work. I prayed and to God's glory, she passed and has been promoted this month. Also, I thank God for granting my family and journey mercies. Praise the Lord!

Sis. Adedeji
MFM Abaranje

DELIVERANCE FROM EVIL DEPOSITS

I was afflicted with stomach ulcer for many years. I got introduced to this church and went for deliverance. On the third day of the programme, I vomited blood and some black objects. Since then, I have been made whole and the satanic affliction has disappeared from my life. Praise the Lord!

Sis Josephine
MFM Ogudu/Ojota

GOD SAVES MY BROTHER FROM POISONED FOOD

My brother went to a friend's house and was poisoned through food. He was meant to die but God restored him when I gave him anointing oil which made him to vomit everything. Praise the Lord!

Bro. Israel
MFM Morogbo

GOD OF PROTECTION HAS ALSO GIVEN US A BABY GIRL

I give thanks to God Almighty for His protection over my life and for giving my younger brother a bouncing baby girl. Praise the Lord!

Sis. Victoria
MFM Ayetoro.

SATANIC COBWEB DISAPPEARS

During a prayer session, God opened my eyes and I saw that cobwebs were being removed from my face and all parts of my body. Since that day, all the problems in my life have disappeared completely. Impossibilities have now become possible. Praise the Lord!

Sis. Olabode
MFM Igando

BLEEDING OF MANY YEARS STOPS

I have been bleeding for many years and this affliction brought me a lot of suffering. I was introduced to this ministry and was also counselled to go for deliverance. God visited me after the programme. The bleeding stopped and I was made whole. Praise the Lord!

Sis Sheri
MFM Aboru

GOD HEALS ME

I was suffering from diabetes for years until I passed through deliverance in this church and the Lord healed me. He is indeed the Healer. Praise the Lord!

Sis. Christy
MFM Sapele

GOD SAVES US FROM UNTIMELY DEATH

I thank God for what He has been doing in my life since the day I promised never to patronize any herbalist. In my dream, I saw my brother with a withered hand and both of us started praying about it. God answered our prayer by restoring the hand. And the person behind the problem died. God also saved another brother of mine from sudden death. Also, I had backache. I prayed and God healed me. Praise the Lord!

Sis Sola
MFM Ijebu

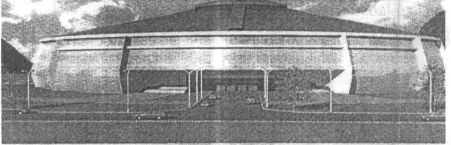

FIRE IN THE WORD, is a weekly Spiritual Bulletin of the Mountain of Fire and Miracles Ministries, published by Tracts and Publications Group. All Enquiries should be addressed to The Editor, Mountain of Fire Magazine, 13, Olasimbo Street, off Olumo Road, Onike, P.O. Box 2990, Sabo Yaba, Lagos, Nigeria. Telephone 01- 867439, 864631, 868766, 08023180236.E-mail: mfmtractsandpublications@yahoo.com Copyright reserved.

FIRE IN THE WORD

Ye Shall Know the Truth, and the Truth Shall Make You Free (John 8:32)

ISSN 1595 - 7314 Vol. 12 No. 24 Sun. 20th - Sat. 26th Apr., 2008

ORGANISE A FIGHT AND GAIN INDEPENDENCE

My year of unprecedented greatness and unmatchable increase
Deuteronomy 28:13, Psalm 71:21, Ephesians 3:20, Psalm 92:10

This week, we would consider the message titled, "Organize a fight and gain independence." It is for those who want to recover what the enemy has stolen from them. It is also for those who want to be champions.

Revelation 12:7-8 says, *"And there was war in heaven: Michael and his angels fought against the dragon; and the dragon fought and his angels. And prevailed not; neither was their place found any more in heaven."*

Our key phrase is "And there was war in heaven..."

The Bible is a military book. And right from the first page to the last, it is filled with wars and battles. Also, therein you find things like fiery darts of the enemy, the shield of faith and the armour of Christians. You also read about the Lord of Sabaoth, the Lord of hosts, the Lord, the man of war, etc. The summary of the Bible is this: God created man and placed him in the garden called, the Garden of Eden. This garden is somewhere in the south of Asia, not too far from the northern part of Africa. Man sinned in that garden and fell from what God designed him to be. Immediately man fell in the garden, God inaugurated a plan for man's ultimate redemption. And like everything in the world, God started from somewhere. He had to first of all call out Abraham to form a nation. Abraham is not Israel; he was called out to form the nation of Israel, to form a nation through which the redemptive plan of God would be accomplished. God brought Abraham out of Babylonia down to the land of Canaan. Abraham's descendants migrated to the land of Egypt and there they grew to become a nation. These descendants of Abraham stayed in Egypt for over four hundred years until they were led out of Egypt under the direction of Moses, back into the promised land of Canaan. It is part of the tragedy of scriptures that where the first fathers left and went to Egypt was where they were trying to go back to and it took them forty years to do so. And in the course of about four hundred to five hundred years, under the reign of David and Solomon, the nation became a great and mighty kingdom. Then at the close of Solomon's reign, the anointing and power of strange

YOU MUST FIGHT TO ENLARGE YOUR COAST

women was great enough to break the kingdom. Just as many people today are suffering because of polygamy and nothing else. The kingdom was divided in the hand of Solomon's son. There was a northern part consisting of ten tribes and a southern part consisting of two tribes. The northern part is often referred to as Israel and the two tribes as Judah.

This kingdom of Israel consisting of ten tribes only lasted for about two hundred years and were taken captive by Assyria in 721BC. The southern part, Judah, lasted for about a hundred years longer than Israel and by 600BC, they were taken captive by Babylon; a spiritual insult indeed. A remnant of those taken captive returned to their homeland to reestablish their national life and soon after that, the Old Testament closed. All these periods involved battles. The Old Testament closed and four hundred years later, Jesus the Messiah of the Old Testament prophecies came and it was through Him that mankind was to be redeemed and recreated. He died for the human sin and rose from the dead. Then He commanded His disciples to spread the story of His life and power to all nations. And they

DELIVERANCE CASE (THE STORY OF MY LIFE - PART 12)

HE POURED THE WATER ON HIS VOMIT

"...WHEN I COME BACK TO MY SENSES THIS MALLAM WILL SMELL PEPPER. I WILL NOT MAKE THE MISTAKE I MADE IN MY LAST STREET FIGHT; WHERE ONE STRAY-DEADLY BLOW LANDED ON MY MOUTH AND EVACUATED MY FRONT —— TWO TEETH, ALL BECAUSE I WAS TOO DRUNK TO SIGHT THE BLOW!.

THE TEETH I LOST THROUGH ALCOHOL HAS REALLY DEFACED ME. WHO WILL EVER BELEIVE I HAVE A MASTERS DEGREE FROM A RENOWNED UNIVERSITY? I NEED HELP!

went into every direction spreading the good news. They went to Asia Minor; Greece, Rome and with that the Bible and the New Testament closed.

That in a nutshell is a summary of the Bible, but every step of the way was a battle. Life itself is a battle and we need to fight. The Bible says, "And there was war in heaven and Michael and his angels fought." It was not the devil that started the fight, Michael and his angels did. Sometimes, we wait for the enemies to start fighting, whereas here Michael and his angels started the fighting first. They fought against the dragon and his angels. They too fought but did not prevail. The Bible says, they shall fight against you but shall not prevail.

WHY DO YOU NEED TO ENGAGE IN SPIRITUAL FIGHT?
You fight:

1.   To defend yourself.
2.   To deliver yourself from the oppressors.
3.   To recover what belongs to you that has been taken by another.

One of the saddest moments I have ever had was the day two people among others wanted to see me. One young lady was sitting at the front and the other an elderly woman at the back. The young lady was looking at the face of the elderly woman. She recognized her as the woman who gave birth to her when she came back to the world the third time. This woman did not know and she was looking at her. The younger lady was now born again and did not die again. But she remembered the havoc she caused that woman; how she wasted all her money before she died.

Here they were sitting close to one another, one knew the other but the other did not know that she was her destroyer many years ago. You need to organize a fight to take back what has been taken from you by another.

4. Some people have not suffered any losses because there is nothing to lose and they have never acquired what belongs to them anyway. You must fight for that also. When somebody has nothing for the thief to steal, what is there to lose?

5. You must fight to enlarge your coast. You must fight and overpower surrounding foreign powers so that you can enlarge your coast. If you want the Lord to enlarge your coast, then let the territory bow to you.

6. Pull down the servants that are riding on the horse of your destiny. If you do not force them down, they will continue to ride on it. The Lord destroyed the

Egyptian army in the Red Sea; this was a battle won supernaturally. The Lord asked Moses to hold up his hands, and as he held them up, the battle of the Amalekites was destroyed. The battle was won supernaturally. God Himself has made the stars and heaven to fight against people in the Bible. God made the men of Israel to shout against the wall of Jericho and the battle was won supernaturally. There was a particular battle by Jehoshaphat and the Lord told him that he would not need to fight in the battle but that He the Lord would do the fighting. And He did the fighting.

7. You fight when you come under attack. There comes a time in the life of a Christian when he or she comes under the enemy's fire.

If you have a colourful destiny, be sure that from time to time there will be attacks against your life. Sometimes, when some Christians are under attack, they make the wrong decisions and trouble happens. In Exodus 14, we see a beautiful example of people who came under attack. Israel was born in the cradle of miracles, they marched forward only to find that they could march no further, and there was no way of escape anymore

whereas it was the pillar of God that was leading them, yet the pillar brought them to the jaws of destruction. In front was the Red Sea and by the sides were a lot of barriers of rocks and mountains, which human strength could not surmount and at the back was a deadly enemy pursuing them with rage. They were either to develop wings and fly or go right into the Red Sea. Every child of God must always identify with this situation, which the Israelites faced. The devil kept many people somewhere making bricks, fetching water and hewing wood. But all of a sudden they escaped from the clutches of the enemy, and before they knew it, fresh terror gathered around them again. The success of the attack of the enemies depends on what happens during the first few moments of that attack. Unfortunately, many people respond wrongly to attacks.

WHAT TO DO WHEN YOU COME UNDER SUDDEN ATTACK

1. Do not panic. If you panic, you will make destructive

DEAL WITH ANY SIN IN YOUR LIFE BEFORE YOU ORGANIZE SPIRITUAL WARFARE

mistakes. The Bible says, God is our strength in the time of trouble and the name of the Lord is our strong tower. Do not allow your mind to be troubled. Be calm before the Lord.

2. Listen carefully to the inner voice of your spirit when you come under sudden attack. The Bible says, when the enemies come against you, like a flood, the Spirit of the Lord shall raise a standard against them.

3. Seek godly counsel. Do not take advice from unbelievers around you because there is no system in the world that does not occasionally experience crisis. Any working system must occasionally experience crisis here and there. So do not be ignorant. There must someone, somewhere who can help you with the information that will help your life because every adversity is the enemy's reaction to your progress. It is the attempt of the enemy to steal your blessings.

4. Organize a fight. You have to fight back. That is why we must learn spiritual violence. Know that satan loves fearful people but real fighters intimidate him.

HOW TO ORGANIZE A FIGHT

1. The first thing to do is to gather your weapons. Be like

David. He called himself into the fight and organized the fight himself. He gathered five smooth stones: did not behave like Saul. Those stones represent our spiritual weapons.

Why did David choose five stones? He chose five stones in case he missed any. So by his calculation, Goliath should not take him more than five stones and he held those five stones. You too as a believer must know your weapons of warfare: the word of God, fire of God, angels of God, blood of Jesus, thunder and lightning, praises and testimonies. You must know all these weapons very well. When you use the first weapon and it does not bring you any result, go to the second weapon.

2. Soak yourself in the scriptures because the mind is like a garden, which will grow any seed you plant in it. When you begin to plant words spoken by God into your mind, you are sowing life, energy and hope into your spirit. Be a scripture addict. Do not be so ignorant of scriptures that the only thing you know how to do is to pray. Immediately you begin to pray and the devil comes and finds that the word of God is not in you, he will give you a knock on the head because the only thing he fears terribly is when a person says, "it is written." You must know what is written to be able to say it is written. You have to be a scripture addict.

3. Be tough. You must be tough. Life itself is a battle. The Bible says, "The violent taketh it

by force." If you want to organize a fight, you must never give up. When you persevere, the enemy will be destabilized. Determine to go the whole distance. Once the God of Abraham, Isaac, Jacob and Paul is your God, then you will certainly overcome.

4. You must listen to God carefully. You must be able to say like the scripture says, "Is there any word from the Lord?" If there is no word from Him, ensure that you get a word from Him. If He says, "My son or my daughter, arise and begin to fight," then you start fighting.

What do you do when you know there is war against you and you do not know how to fight? What do you when you know there is a battle you have been fighting and have had enough of that battle?

1. The first thing to do in order to organize a successful warfare is to repent of all known sins. God does not talk to unrepentant sinners. If God is refusing to talk to you about your own situation then you need to repent. You should sit down and analyse your life. Deal with any sin in your life before you organize spiritual warfare. If you do not deal with the sin in your life, the moment you begin to pray, the enemies will telephone their headquarters to find out if they should leave or not. If there

THE PROPHET | David versus Goliath 12

AA AAh.! GOLLIATH. WORLD-WIDE CHAMPION. WERE IS YOUR 'god'? PSM 2:9 THOU SHALL BREAK THEM WITH A ROD OF IRON,.... PSM 17:17 - GOD DELIVERED ME FROM MY STRONG ENEMY..

OOOOAh.! SANGO, BEEZEBUB, BAAAL, OBATALA, DARK QUEEN INTERCONTINENTAL DEMONS. WERE ARE YOU? SAVE MEE...!

PSM 2:9; PSM 17: 7; PSM17:13.

is still sin in your life, they will ask them to stay there. So, you have to repent of all known sins. The enemy has X-ray eyes to know those who are sinners and those who are not. You may be hiding something in your room and think that nobody sees you. The devil sees you and knows that you are deceiving yourself. Deal with all known sins.

2. Seek the face of the Lord.

3. Pray specifically and orderly. To pray orderly means to pray about one thing at a time. Do not lump prayers together, ask one question at a time.

Begin to war by the weapon of prayer. After you have done all these for a while, sit down and review the progress you have made. If you find that you are not making much progress, go back and review it from the beginning again. After you have reviewed it again, you can now change your realm of prayer. If you were praying with one day fasting, you can increase it to two days or three days or seven days.

PRAYER POINTS

1. Every power that has vowed to waste me, what are you waiting for? Die, in the name of Jesus.

2. Within seven days, let my stubborn oppressors be buried, in the name of Jesus.

3. Everything stolen from my life while I was in my mother's womb, I recover you by fire, in the name of Jesus.

4. Foundational arrows of affliction, die, in the name of Jesus.

5. Every power stealing my position, die, in the name of Jesus.

6. Every power that does not want me to arise and shine, your time is up, die, in the name of Jesus.

7. Power of the valley of my father's house, die, in the name of Jesus.

8. Power of satanic bus-stop, die, in the name of Jesus.

9. Point to the heavenlies and pray this: My voice, disrespect every attack, in the name of Jesus.

10. Every dream attack, backfire, in the name of Jesus.

11. I barricade myself and family with the blood of Jesus, in the name of Jesus.

12. My Father, appear in my dream, in the name of Jesus.

13. Every ancestral strongman in the heavenlies, die, in the name of Jesus.

14. Every ancestral strongman in the waters, your time is up, die, in the name of Jesus.

15. I fire back every arrow of clever attack, in the name of Jesus.

16. I refuse to be wasted, in Jesus' name.

ORGANISE A FIGHT AND GAIN INDEPENDENCE

is a message delivered at the Mountain of Fire and Miracles Ministries by the General Overseer, Dr. D.K. Olukoya.

A CALL TO SERVE

Are you a member of MFM with a burden to help the needy, are you interested in alleviating the plight of the poor or in the spread of the gospel through the sponsorshing of the publication of tracts? Your resources, time and talent can be extended to several groups that are in charge of these areas. These groups include:

o   We care Ministry,
o   Mission Outreach
o   Tracts and Publications
o   Ministry to Drug addicts
o   Campus fellowship
o   Ministry to Schools
o   Ministry to Glorious Children, etc.

Thus says the Lord, "Verily I say unto you, in as much as ye have done it unto one of the least of these my brethren, ye have done it unto me" Matthew 25 : 40.

WONDERFUL JESUS!

GOD GIVES ME A SON AFTER FOUR GILS

I thank God for giving me a baby boy. I was not even willing to have another baby, but as the Lord would have it, I got pregnant and unexpectedly it was a baby boy. Praise the Lord!

Sis. Tayo
MFM Aboru

DELIVERED FROM UNTIMELY DEATH

I am very grateful to God for delivering me from untimely death. Recently, in Benin City I was driving on the highway when suddenly I discovered that a trailer which had no rear light was reversing. I almost ran into it but God took control and swerved my car away. However, the front of the car was damaged. Fortunately, a policeman witnessed the incident and pursued the trailer to the next checkpoint. He was made to pay for the damage done to my car. I thank God for preserving my life and those who were with me in the car. Praise the Lord!

Bro. Olukunle
MFM Ijaiye Ojokoro

GOD DELIVERS MY BROTHER FROM A CRIME HE DID NOT COMMIT

Two months ago, robbers came to where my brother was working and went away with a huge sum of money. Two weeks later, my brother made a mistake by supplying goods without collecting money for them. This made his boss to say that he was involved in the initial robbery and vowed to jail him. I thank God for His intervention and His favour upon him. Praise the Lord!

Bro. Augustine
MFM Ijaiye

DELIVERANCE FROM THE SPIRIT OF UNTIMELY DEATH

The Lord delivered one of my sons from the spirit of untimely death after series of prayers. The Lord also provided free accommodation for me through a brother. One of my brothers gave his life to Jesus and thereafter God began to prosper his business. He has also started to build his own house. Praise God!

Bro Madaach
MFM Iba

DIVINE FAVOUR

Somebody called my husband and said to him, "Pastor, you will need a car to move around easily for your work can you come to my house? When he got there, the key of a car was handed over to him. Praise God!

Sis. Adedini
MFM Agbeleka

SUCCESS IN EXAMINATION

I had a wicked lecturer in the tertiary institution I attended. He said that no student would come out in flying colours in his course. I took this to God in prayer and prepared very well for the examination. To the glory of God, I came out as the best student in that course. Praise God!

Bro. Olorundara
MFM Ikare

GOD SAVES MY HOUSE FROM FIRE OUTBREAK

Recently, I left home when there was power outage for a vigil. But I inadvertently left my heater plugged to electricity. When power was restored, the heater exploded into flames and my neighbour broke open my door and put off the fire. Praise God!

Bro. Michael
MFM Ughelli

SPIRIT OF DEATH AND HELL DESTROYED

In my place of work, I was fired an arrow of infirmity and immediately, I was taken to the hospital where the doctor told me that my case was beyond any solution and that I would die. I rejected the statement and told him that I will live. Unfortunately, I died. But a woman accidentally stumbled on my body in the mortuary and discovered that I breathing, and she prayed for me. To the glory of God, two days later, I was revived and have been hale and hearty ever since. This is the awesome power of God. Praise God!

Bro. David
MFM Igando

Join us and BUILD for the Lord

THE PRAYER CITY DELIVERANCE STADIUM AND INTERNATIONAL CONFERENCE CENTRE

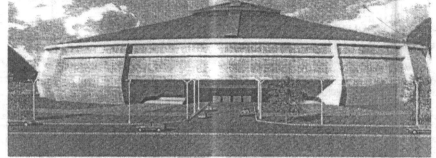

₦35,000,000,000

To be a part of this project, send your donation* to
the Regional Overseer/Pastor or to the Secretariat
Prayer City Partners and Friends
i/c The Office of the G.O.
13, Olasimbo Street, Onike-Yaba, Lagos.

Mode of payment

Any Branch of Oceanic Bank International Plc. Nationwide
Account No.: 0801101006463
Name of Account: MFM-Prayer City Partners and Friends

For further information contact
08055145040, 08023128677,
08034934848, 08023261588
email: info@mfmprayercity.org
website: mfmprayercity.org

FIRE IN THE WORD is a weekly Spiritual Bulletin of the Mountain of Fire and Miracles Ministries, published by Tracts and Publications Group. All Enquiries should be addressed to The Editor, Mountain of Fire Magazine, 13, Olasimbo Street, off Olumo Road, Onike, P.O. Box 2990, Sabo Yaba, Lagos, Nigeria. Telephone 01- 867439, 864631, 868766, 08023180236. E-mail: mfmtractsandpublications@yahoo.com Copyright reserved.

FIRE IN THE WORD

Ye Shall Know the Truth, and the Truth Shall Make You Free (John 8:32)

ISSN 1595 - 7314 Vol. 12 No. 25 Sun. 27th Apr. - Sat. 3rd May, 2008

THOUGH HAND JOIN IN HAND

My year of unprecedented greatness and unmatchable increase
Deuteronomy 28:13, Psalm 71:21, Ephesians 3:20, Psalm 92:10

The title of our message this week is, "Though hand join in hand." I would like you to read it very carefully because it addresses the root of man's problem and the reason why many people are going through one ordeal or another. Proverbs 11:21 says, *"Though hand join in hand, the wicked shall not be unpunished: but the seed of the righteous shall be delivered."*

Though hand join in hand means no matter how tight the cooperation may be, no matter how smart they are, no matter how cleverly they are concealed, no matter the walls they have built, no matter their technique of hiding, no matter the kind of meeting they have held, no matter the agreement between them, the wicked shall not go unpunished.

When sin is the driver, you can be 100 per cent sure that shame is at the back seat. The worst enemy of man is his sinful heart propelled and fueled by Mr. Flesh.

Sometimes, sin hooks a man in the process of trying to obtain something he does not have, when he is afraid that he may lose something he already has. I want you to understand that there is no small sin. When you come to the service and disturb others from concentrating, you are a sinner. There is no small sin. The consequences of what you may consider as a small sin may be immeasurable. If you are sinning because you want to make some profit, you are wasting time because

you cannot profit by sin, it is impossible. Anything you gain from sin would be taken back from you by sin. And you would pay back with interest. Sin is like a small child playing with a snake, the child may find the snake very beautiful and interesting. But the snake only remains interesting as long as it has not done its worse.

Everyone has power to choose his or her sins but nobody has power to chose the consequences of those sins. Every sin has a consequence and punishment assigned to it. So, once you commit a sin, punishment is automatic. And when sin enters, it will cause the cup of joy to leak. Therefore, as soon as the seed of sin is sowed, judgment is sure. Unfortunately, the Bible says, "...One sinner destroyeth much good" (Ecclesiastes 9:18). The sin of one person can bring tragedy to many. Everybody in the boat of Jonah would have been killed because the Lord was not ready to negotiate with him at all. Perhaps you are the Jonah in your family. That is you are the reason why waves and storms are blowing across your family. Perhaps God has brought you up to do something there which you have neglected and since you are not doing the will of God, the evil and mad wind of life is blowing against your family.

PRICES OF MATERIALS MAY RISE AND FALL BUT THE WAGES OF SIN REMAIN THE SAME

People make a mistake by thinking that sin is judged the way it appears. Sin is not judged the way you see it, but the way God sees it. And when God wants to start His judgment, where He would start may be very strange to you. For example, when God wants to judge the sin of an armed robber, He would not start and end with the armed robber alone. He could begin His judgment with the mother of the armed robber who was a fornicator or an adulterer. From there, He could move to the person who was selling him Marijuana, and from there to the woman who had the bar where he was drinking pepper soup and alcohol and from there to the person who introduced him to robbery. So, God packs so many people together when He begins to judge a sinner. He will not judge according to your opinion. You may say, "In my own opinion, I don't think what I have done is that bad, after all everybody is doing it." You may be very wrong because you might have caused more harm than anyone else who did it.

The repercussions of the same sin committed by two or more different people may be completely different. For example, if God ordains a sister to be a prophetess and decrees that through her shall be a seed that shall save Africa. And that sister commits only one abortion to remove that seed, the repercussion of her sin would be greater than some women who will do twenty abortions because their

DELIVERANCE CASE (THE STORY OF MY LIFE - PART 13)

seeds would have been for a different purpose.

Prices of materials may rise and fall but the wages of sin remain the same. The Bible says, "The wages of sin is death." (Romans 6:23). The most expensive thing in the world is sin because for the purpose of sin, God allowed His own Son to be killed. Many people are now becoming new sinners. There are new sinners every day; academic sinners, intellectual sinners, brainy sinners, psychological sinners, etc. But there is no new sin. Sin is still the same.

Beloved, I want you to understand that wickedness never goes unpunished. Though hand join in hand, no sinner shall go unpunished. The pleasure of sin is paid with sorrow. And any sin you cover up will eventually bring you down because sin is the greatest of all detectives. The Bible says, "Be sure that your sin will find you out"(Numbers 32:23). A certain man strangulated a young girl after raping her. He dragged her body to a bush path and walked home. His wife noticed that his coat was a bit rough

and that he had lost one button. Innocently, she told him that one button was missing from his coat and demanded to know what happened. He knew surely well that the button must be at the site where he killed the girl. So, he lost his peace. Policemen arrived at the site of the murder, saw the girl's body and began to look for clues around. Only one of them found the button and hid it in his pocket. It was not in the newspapers that a button was found at the site of the murder. But the man still had no peace. Something kept reminding him of the button. He became very restless. Two months later, he decided to go to the site to look for the button. Immediately, he arrived there looking at the ground, the police arrested him. They said, "We know what you are looking for. You are looking for your button." And he said, "Yes." His sin eventually found him out. The Bible says, "Your sin shall find you out." It is the greatest detective. The children

you had outside wedlock, which you are hiding from your legally married spouse will grow and eventually come back and destroy the family. Your sin will find you out.

Every sin, no matter how little has consequences. Even the misuse of the tongue has consequences. You must understand this very well. Number 12:1 says, *"And Miriam and Aaron spake against Moses because of the Ethiopian woman whom he had married; for he had married an Ethiopian woman."* They just spoke against Moses, they did not fight him and something happened.

Numbers 12:9-14 says, *"And the anger of the Lord was kindled against them; and he departed. And the cloud departed from off the tabernacle; and, behold, Miriam became leprous, white as snow: and Aaron looked upon Miriam and, behold she was leprous. And Aaron said unto Moses, Alas, my lord, I beseech thee, lay not the sin upon us, wherein we have done foolishly, and wherein we have sinned. Let her not be as one dead, of whom the* flesh is half consumed when he cometh out of his mother's womb. And Moses cried unto the Lord, saying, Heal her now, O God, I beseech thee. And the Lord said unto Moses, If her father had but spit in her face, should she not be ashamed seven days? Let her be shut out from the camp seven days, and after that let her be received in again."

It was this Miriam that put Moses in the river, when he was a baby. She was also the person that called the attention of the daughter of Pharaoh to Moses. Numbers 12:15 says, "And Miriam was shut out from the camp seven days; and the people journeyed not till Miriam was brought in again." God disciplined Miriam and Moses cried, "Heal her now O Lord." God said, "Yes, I can forgive but forgiveness does not eliminate discipline." God dealt with her for seven days. She would have died but the Lord just had mercy.

2 Samuel chapter 12 tells us a story about David. One day, David, instead of going to battle, was lazing about. Eventually, he saw Bathsheba, another man's wife, having a bath. He took her and killed her husband. And the Prophet of God came unto David. 2 Samuel 12:7 – 16 says, "And Nathan said to David, Thou art the man. Thus saith the Lord God of Israel, I anointed thee king over Israel, and I delivered thee out of the hand of Saul; And I gave thee thy master's house, and thy master's wives into thy bosom, and gave thee the house of Israel and of Judah; and if that had been too little, I would moreover have given unto thee such and such things. Wherefore hast thou despised the commandment of the Lord, to do evil in his sight? Thou hast killed Uriah the Hittite with the sword, and hast taken his wife to be thy wife, and hast slain him with the sword of the children of Ammon, Now therefore, (No. 1) the sword shall never depart from thine house; because thou hast despised me, and hast taken the wife of Uriah the Hittite to be thy wife. (No2) Behold I will raise up evil against thee out of thine own house, (No3) I will take thy wives before thine eyes, and give them unto thy neighbour; and he shall lie with thy wives in the sight of this sun. For thou didst it secretly: but I will do this thing before all Israel, and before the sun. And David said unto Nathan, I have sinned against the Lord. And Nathan said unto David, The Lord also hath put away thy sin; thou shalt not die. Howbeit, because by this deed thou hast given great occasion to the enemies of the Lord to blaspheme, the child also that is born unto thee shall surely die. And Nathan departed unto his house. And the Lord struck the child that Uriah's wife bare unto David, and it was very sick. David therefore besought God for the child; and David fasted, and went in, and lay all night upon the earth." But the child still died. God forgave David his sin. The forgiveness removed the condemnation and the sin in the record of God. But it did not eliminate the discipline. It did not remove the consequences. Thou hand join in hand, no sinner shall go unpunished.

A person who commits adultery, and after contacting HIV begins to call upon God to forgive and heal him would be forgiven and will make heaven. But the consequences of his sin which is HIV will still punish and kill him.

Sometime ago, at a pastors' conference, there was an argument between two pastors. One of them was so annoyed that he said he would drop the Bible and deal with the other one. After the conference, the vehicle he boarded was involved in a nasty accident and everybody in that vehicle except him walked out without any scratch. He broke his two legs. At the Orthopaedic hospital where he was admitted, he asked the Lord why that had to happen to him and the Lord said, "You said you would drop the Bible and you did. You really dropped it." The pastor said, "But I have asked you to forgive me." And God said, "Yes if not you would have died. The Bible has been your support and shade and you said you will drop it." He still has a bad leg today as a testimony to the discipline that he received.

FORGIVENESS DOES NOT FREE ONE FROM ACCOUNTABILITY

God has facility to forgive every sin but no one can tell the extent of the consequences. There is nothing anyone can do about it. The consequence will take its toll.

According to the book of Revelation, after you have read through the whole of the Bible and decide to continue to do evil, you are free to do so. But it says, "Behold, I come quickly and my reward is with me."

Samson's hair grew again but his eyes never got opened. Abraham brought forth Ishmael, and the consequences are clearly seen now. God may forgive sin but it will have consequences. Unfortunately, some of these consequences may remain with a person throughout his life. So, every sin you are living in today is a foundation for your generation. The sins will find you out and find out members of your generation. That is why we have to be very careful. If Gehazi had known that collecting money from Naaman would affect his offspring, he would not have done it. Through his action he planted an evil seed for his generation.

Every sin you commit will find you out. You cannot be cleverer than sin. It will eventually find you out. When you ask God to forgive you, He will and you will make heaven. But the forgiveness sometimes does not free you from the consequences of your actions. There are some wrongs you may do which could be redressed. For example, if you steal somebody's money, and you repent and make restitution by returning the money, your punishment will be limited because the wrong has already been corrected. But there are some sins that cannot be righted

Forgiveness does not free one from accountability. David committed the sin of sexual immorality, deception and murder, and when the consequences started, under the banner of sexual immorality, his own son raped his own daughter. His own son Absalom was sleeping with his wives on the roof top. David practised deception. His son Absalom too deceived him. David killed only Uriah but he lost three children. He lost the baby that resulted from the adultery, Amnon and Absalom. These were the consequences. So, if you do not want your children to become robbers, do not train them with stolen money. If you do not want your children to have broken home, do not beat up your spouse before them. If you do not want your children to go into drugs, do not get involved in drug business yourself. If you do not want somebody to mess up your own daughter, do not mess up somebody else's daughter.

MERCY OF GOD

Sometimes, when people commit sin, they would say, "Blood of Jesus." The blood of Jesus does not eliminate the consequences of sin. It would only remove the condemnation. The only thing that can eliminate the consequences of sin is the mercy of God. The trouble with the mercy of God is that it is not guaranteed. The Bible says, "I will have mercy on whom I will have mercy" (Romans 9:15). That is, that mercy is not guaranteed. You may ask God to have mercy on you, and He would say, "Not today."

Beloved, I would like you to know that sin is success in nothing. It is self-inflicted nonsense. It invites

THE PROPHET David versus Goliath 13

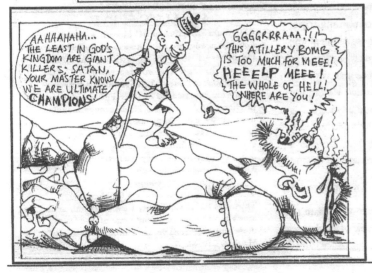

death. Sin obscures the soul. Sin can sometimes come as a friend, but the longer you stay in sin, the less and less it bothers you. Then you become hardened if you do not quickly run out of it. If you take a frog and throw it into boiling water, it will jump out. But if you put a frog in a kettle of cold water and put the kettle on fire and begin to warn it little by little, the frog will not jump out. It will be enjoying the warmth of the water until it is boiled to death. That is what sin does. Only one leak in a ship is enough to sink the whole ship. One sin can destroy a person totally. Do not compare yourself to other people. Your life is different likewise your destiny. So, do not copy others. Do not follow a multitude to commit sin. One little sin can cause great trouble. The sin you consider small and light could send you to the tail of destiny. We need the mercy of God. We need to cry to Him for mercy. Mercy is obtained in the prison of discipline. If you want to obtain mercy today, tell God the truth. If you tell Him the truth, you stand a better chance of receiving mercy. Though hand join in hand, no sinner will go unpunished.

Many people need to sort out themselves with the Lord. Why should you repeat the errors that have killed many people? The Bible says, "These things were written for our learning that through the comfort of the scriptures we might have hope. Keeping evil friends, drinking, smoking, inordinate affection, unholy relationship, lying, malice, grudges, pride etc have their consequences. To open your mouth and say that you are tired of prayer has its own consequences. Rumour mongering, gossiping, slander and all forms of misuse of the mouth have their consequences. There are consequences also for allowing your talent to lie fallow. The man with one talent in the Bible did not commit murder. He did not commit fornication neither did he rape anybody. His offence was that he did not use his talent. He buried it and because of that he went to hell fire. There is a consequence for running away from the agenda of God for your life. Trying to pay somebody back in his own coin has its consequences.

It would be a sad thing if you appear at the gate of life, and your name appears on the book of the house fellowship and the register of your church but it is not found in the Book of life. The Bible says, "One book shall be opened and other books too shall be opened, and then another book shall be opened which is the book of life. If your name is found in all those other books and because of one little sin, it is not found in the Book of life, what do you do? Do not end up living a wasted life. You should cry to the Lord from the bottom of your heart for His mercy. The Bible says, "Though hand join in hand, no sinner shall go unpunished." It did not say no sinner shall go unforgiven.

PRAYER POINTS

1. My Father, have mercy on me today, in the name of Jesus.
2. Blood of Jesus, clear away every sin that wants to destroy my destiny, in the name of Jesus.
3. Personal spiritual chains, ancestral chains, break, in the name of Jesus.
4. Every ancient prison door in my family line, break, in the name of Jesus.
5. Every gap between where I am and where God wants me to be, close by fire, in the name of Jesus.

THOUGH HAND JOIN IN HAND

is a message delivered at the Mountain of Fire and Miracles Ministries by the General Overseer, Dr. D.K. Olukoya.

A CALL TO SERVE

Are you a member of MFM with a burden to help the needy, are you interested in alleviating the plight of the poor or in the spread of the gospel through the sponsorshing of the publication of tracts? Your resources, time and talent can be extended to several groups that are in charge of these areas. These groups include:

o We care Ministry,
o Mission Outreach
o Tracts and Publications
o Ministry to Drug addicts
o Campus fellowship
o Ministry to Schools
o Ministry to Glorious Children, etc.

Thus says the Lord, "Verily I say unto you, in as much as ye have done it unto one of the least of these my brethren, ye have done it unto me" Matthew 25 : 40.

WONDERFUL JESUS!

GOD SAVES ME FROM UNTIMELY DEATH

Recently, after service on a Tuesday, as I was crossing the Ojota expressway, I fell down at the centre of the road. But I thank God that an on-coming vehicle stopped without injuring me. Finally, I thank God for healing me during our last 2-days crusade. I used to urinate four times before day break. But now, the frequent urination has stopped. Praise the Lord!

Sis. Oyebanjo
Children Department

GOD HEALS ME

I thank God for my life. Recently, I had an accident but the Lord delivered me. I am now hale and hearty. Also, I thank God for the release of my result which was seized two years ago after serious prayers. Praise the Lord!

Sis. Uju
MFM Ogudu Ori-oke

GOD REMOVES THE STUMBLING BLOCK ON MY WAY

I thank God for His mercy, faithfulness and favour over my life. I came to Nigeria from Maryland, USA two months ago. I had a problem with my travelling documents. Since then I joined the church. Through prayers, the problems were removed. All my papers are okay now and there is no problem again. Praise the Lord!

Sis. Olayemi
MFM Prayer city

GOD DELIVERS ME FROM THE SPIRIT OF DEATH AND SPIRIT WIFE

I thank God for deliveramce from the spirit of death and spirit wife. I used to drink and eat in the dream and all efforts to stop these habits were to no avail. But when I went for deliverance, the Spirit of God filled me. I received the power of God and my problems have ceased. Praise God!

Bro. Emeka
MFM Mushin

GOD PROVIDES A CAR FOR ME

I thank God for the salvation of my soul and for His goodness upon my life and family. Since I joined this church, the Lord has been good to me. Recently, He blessed me with a car. Praise the Lord!

Bro. Iyabo
MFM Okerube

GOD DISGRACES THE STRONG WOMAN OF MY FAHTER'S HOUSE

I went to the Prayer City to seek God's face concerning my life. During the deliverance, the Lord revealed to me in a vision the strongman of my father's house and through prayers given to me, I conquered the woman. Secondly, I sought employment for seven years without result. Recently, God perfected everything in my life by giving me a good job. Thirdly, a friend of mine who had twins through a ceasarian section had complications. I went to her and anointed her. To the glory of God, she gave birth to a bouncing baby girl without operation. Praise the Lord!

Sis. Titilayo Oni
MFM Dopemu

GOD DELIVERS ME FROM STROKE AND UNTIMELY DEATH

I thank God for His goodness over my life. He healed me of stroke of four years. Secondly, He saved me from untimely death. The vehicle we travelled with from Abeokuta to Lagos had its front tyre removed while on top speed. But God averted a serious accident. Thirdly, I thank God for saving my daughter that was carried away by flood during a rainfall. She was pregnant and on her way to church the rain began. God sent helpers to rescue her. Praise the Lord!

Sis. Beatrice
MFM Ojota

NOW ON SALE

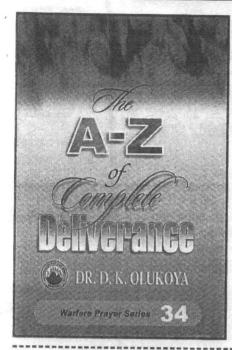

At last! The two long awaited books are back on the stand. Ever potent for all your deliverance and prosperity needs. Hurry now for your copies Stock is limited. Price N170 each.

Hello Children!

Your popular Spiritual tonic "Junior Fire in the Word" Is on the stand again. It is still as refreshing as ever. Now you have more opportunities to win Fanstastic prizes every month as you send in your entries Hurry grab your copy from the vendors. The price is still N20.

FIRE IN THE WORD, is a weekly Spiritual Bulletin of the Mountain of Fire and Miracles Ministries, published by Tracts and Publications Group. All Enquiries should be addressed to The Editor, Mountain of Fire Magazine, 13, Olasimbo Street, off Olumo Road, Onike, P.O. Box 2990, Sabo Yaba, Lagos, Nigeria. Telephone 01- 867439, 864631, 868766, 08023180236.E-mail: mfmtractsandpublications@yahoo.com Copyright reserved.

FIRE IN THE WORD

Ye Shall Know the Truth, and the Truth Shall Make You Free (John 8:32)

ISSN 1595 - 7314   Vol. 12   No. 26   Sun. 4th - Sat. 10th May, 2008

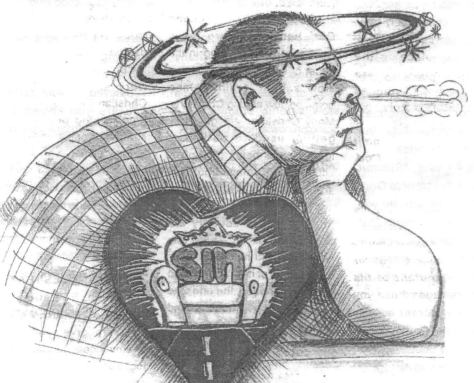

When the ENEMY is ALREADY INSIDE

My year of unprecedented greatness and unmatchable increase
Deuteronomy 28:13, Psalm 71:21, Ephesians 3:20, Psalm 92:10

Our message this week is titled, **"When the enemy is already inside."**

Ephesians 4:27 says, *"Neither give place to the devil."* It means that it is possible for somebody to allow the enemy into his or her life. And if you give place to the enemy, he will definitely stay. That is why the passage says, "Do not give place to the enemy." Many people are looking for their enemies outside. Unfortunately, the enemy is already inside.

James 4:7 says, *"Summit yourselves therefore to God. Resist the devil, and he will flee from you."* It means that if you do not resist the devil, he will stay with you. 2 Corinthians 2:11 says, *"Lest satan should get an advantage of us: for we are not ignorant of his devices."* It means that if you are ignorant of the devices of satan, he will take advantage of you. Ignorance is no excuse in the spiritual world. If you do not have knowledge about the devices of the enemy, he will take advantage of you.

Going by current events, it is clear that our generation is living in the dark. We have many beautiful and powerful inventions but most of them are being turned around to destroy people, including those who invented them. It is clear the enemy has really worked hard to promote ignorance even in the church of God. Unfortunately, the words of Jesus are still ever true today: *"Men love darkness rather than light, because their own deeds are evil"* (John 3:19).

Nowadays, among Christians there are many prodigals who are living in the midst of swine. There is also a slow satanic brainwashing going on now among Christians. Many Christians are gradually getting used to darkness. Ignorance is being promoted. Little by little, many churches are making sin to appear very light. Gradually, things like fornication and adultery are being swept aside. There has never been so much darkness in the minds of men and women than now. Indeed, the end time is here. The crime wave is mind boggling. Television sets have introduced Sodom and Gomorrah into every sitting room. Many people who call themselves Christians are grieving the Holy Spirit because they do not want to offend the wicked. They do not want to be

IF YOU GO TO BED ANGRY, THE DEVIL WILL BECOME YOUR BED FELLOW.

seen as peculiar and strange people. Many believe that merging with darkness can change darkness. If they are not careful, they will be the ones that will be changed. The early church did not dim their light to match the world in which they were living. A good study of the Acts of apostles reveals that everywhere Paul went, he was troubling the powers of darkness.

Beloved, in your place of work are you known as a Christian? Perhaps you know how to sing praise worship songs but your lifestyle does not portray Christ. It is a tragedy. We need to pray hard because many people are looking for their enemy outside but the enemy is already inside. When the enemy is already inside, many things go wrong.

WHAT DOES IT MEAN TO GIVE PLACE TO THE ENEMY?

1. To give place to the enemy means to give any sin a foothold in your life. Many years ago, a certain brother was brought to church for prayers. He had a very strange sickness. He fell sick anytime he got to the examination hall to write an examination. He could write any other thing without any problem but not examinations. When he was brought to me, the Holy

<u>DELIVERANCE CASE</u> (THE STORY OF MY LIFE - PART 14)

Spirit said. he had given a particular sin a foothold in his life. But if he confessed it, he would be free. I told him what the Lord said but he said, "No! No! By the grace of God, I am born again, sanctified, baptized in the Holy Spirit, and living a pure life." I said, "That means the Holy Spirit is lying." He said no. By the time we prayed, the Lord revealed what he was doing. He had a next door neighbour who was a fornicator. Anytime he was in the act, the brother would go to the keyhole and be peeping to watch him. I confronted him with that and he said, "Yes sir, you are right sir." Here was a man who claimed to be born again and sanctified, peeping into the room of fornicators. But immediately he confessed the sin and got broken down in the spirit, his hands stopped shaking during examinations. Many people are looking for the enemy outside but the enemy has already entered inside.

2. To give place to the enemy is to allow the enemy to gain entrance into your life. For example, some sisters would see a saloon named, "Hot head or Mermaid" and would still enter there to do their hair. Later, they would be complaining of bad dreams. Of course they would have bad dreams. They submit their hair to people who would not ordinarily have access to their hair. And through that means, they steal their virtues and divert their glory.

3. To give place to the devil means to eat at the dining table of darkness. Those who are addicted to partying should pray that they do not end up eating poison. They have to be very careful. When somebody who was sick and was healed by a herbalist holds a party through which he or she distributes his or her problems, many people will go there to eat the food. What

happens is that the problem will be automatically transferred to them.

4. To give place to the enemy is to allow the enemy to construct a building in your life. If you do not want the building to continue, you break it down and stop the construction.

5. To give place to the enemy is to allow a satanic exchange of your destiny. A destiny can be changed. When somebody goes to a fortune teller to foretell his future and the fortune teller sees that he has a colourful destiny, he will end up stealing his virtues.

Sometime ago, a certain woman followed her friend to a herbalist. When they got there, the herbalist shifted his interest to her instead of her friend who actually wanted to see him. The herbalist said to her, "Madam, you have a wonderful destiny, a beautiful destiny and you have many stars. Can you give me some?" And she foolishly said,

"Yes Baba." And right from that day, her fortunes began to go down.

6. To give place to the enemy is to engage in fornication or adultery. It is deceit of the highest order to think that somebody who is sleeping with you outside marriage loves you. In fact, such a person is your greatest enemy.

7. To give place to the enemy is to allow anger to control you. Anger is an expensive luxury. Anger reveals our true nature. Anger and temper shorten life. Your anger is a weapon for your opponent. And he who angers you conquers you. Once the enemy sees that anger is your weakness, like Moses, he will use it against you.

Anger is temporary madness. If you go to bed angry, the devil will become your bedfellow. You are as big as what makes you angry. An angry person manages everything badly. When you get angry at somebody, you are trying to use fire to quench fire, which does not work. The truth about life is that the emptier the pot, the quicker the boiling. Little quantity of water will boil over quicker than a lot of water. Angry people are normally very empty people. Anger is so bad that more than any other thing, it has opened doors to the enemy to operate in people's lives. It has opened doors for the enemy to destroy marriages and all kinds of things. Many marriages would have still been in place today if not for anger. Anyone who gets angry to the level where his or her body begins to vibrate is finished.

8. To give place to the enemy is to show unforgiving attitude towards others. When you do not forgive others, the demons called tormentors will be released to torment you.

9. To give place to the enemy is to harbour hatred against anyone. Hatred is like burning the house because you want to kill the rat. Hatred is self- punishment. In the school of deliverance, hatred is the handcuffs of demons. Once you have hatred in your heart, the enemy has already handcuffed you. Hatred hits a person harder than his or her object of hatred. Two people who hate each other cannot claim to love God. It is not possible. So hatred is like cancer. And the Bible says that hatred is murder. So, if you hate anybody, you are a murderer.

WHEN YOU FAIL TO CONTROL YOUR TONGUE, YOU GIVE THE ENEMY A PLACE

10. To give place to the enemy is to take what does not belong to you. When you engage in stealing, you give place to the enemy. In fact, most nations are nations of thieves. The spirit of "I saw, I coveted. I took and I hid" has taken over the lives of many people. Although people try to avoid the raw word stealing, the scriptures cannot be broken. Men have tried to use other words to cover up stealing. They call it 'fiddling' or 'pilfering.' In Nigeria, it is called 'embezzlement.' In some places, it is called 'creative accounting.' But as far as the word of God is concerned, if you are jealous of people who have stolen, you are a thief. If you are secretly admiring those who cheated and got away with it, you are a thief. If you are only scared by the consequences of being discovered, that is why you do not steal, you are a thief. Any pastor ministering for gain is a thief. If you are using your company supplies without permission, for example, papers, postage stamps, pens, envelope, telephone etc without permission, you are a glorious thief. When somebody lends something to you and you refuse to return it or you are carefully hoping that the person will forget, you are a thief. Every form of fraud or cheating during

examination is stealing. If you hit a parked vehicle somewhere and quickly run away because you do not want the owner to know or because you do not want to bear the cost of its repairs, you are a thief. If you appropriate something kept in your care for your own selfish purpose, you are a thief. That would give the enemy a chance to devour your blessings. When you fail to return a lost item to the owner, you are a thief. If you read stolen books, you will fail. When you purposely go to work late and collect full pay, you are a thief. When you convert things that belong to your company to personal use without permission, you are a thief. If you spend the time you are supposed to do your work in the office reading the Bible, you are

a thief. As a bachelor, if you claim to be married with children in order to evade tax or get some benefits, you are a thief. A pastor who steals money from the church purse is a thief and is inviting the leprosy of Gehazi.

11. To give place to the enemy is to harbour abominable materials in your possession.

12. To give place to the enemy means to fail to tame your tongue. The tongue has the power of life and death. You can kill yourself as well as others with your mouth. When you fail to control your tongue, you give the enemy a place. That was what happened to prophet Isaiah. His tongue had a problem, so the angel of God had to put coals of fire on it.

13. To give place to the enemy means to fail to control

your appetite. Gluttony and careless eating will give the enemy access to your life.

14. To give place to the enemy means to give in to worry and anxiety. The Bible says, "Let not your heart be troubled, believe in God and believe also in me" (John 14: 1).

15. To give place to the enemy is to run the race God did not ask you to run. When you get involved in what you should not tamper with, the enemy has the right to ensnare you.

16. To give place to the enemy is to eat the bread of sorrow.

17. To give place to the enemy is to allow bitterness into your life. Do not be bitter against anyone.

18. To give place to the enemy is to open your mind to wandering spirits. There are many people who do not concentrate during prayers. They give place to wandering spirits.

19. To give place to the enemy is to continue in the iniquity of your father's house.

20. To give place to the enemy means to trivialize the things of heaven.

21. To give place to the enemy means to be sucking from the breast of familiar spirits. That is your best friends

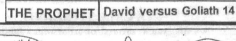

THE PROPHET | David versus Goliath 14

are those who are possessed or those who have questionable character.

22. To give place to the enemy means to be warning yourself in the fire of the enemy. That is you move close to the enemy because of the benefit you will get.

23. To give place to the enemy means to engage in any form of deception.

24. To give place to the enemy is to allow the flesh to control your life. When Mr. Flesh is on the throne of your life, your enemy will do anything to you.

25. To give place to the enemy is to make your head a landing place for curses.

26. To give place to the enemy is to allow the enemy to find a place in your life. Jesus said, "The prince of this world cometh unto me and findeth no place in me."

27. To give place to the enemy is to place your head on the lap of Delilah.

28. To give place to the enemy is to live a powerless life.

29. To give place to the enemy is to live a life that lacks the fire of the Holy Ghost.

30. To give place to the enemy is to show no resistance to the enemies that are fighting you.

Beloved, when the enemy is already inside, other evil visitors will enter easily. When the enemy is already inside, there would be a bad aura around you. Good things would be diverted from you. You will make unpardonable mistakes. You would pray only to have temporary relief because they are already inside. They just wait a little bit and start again. When the enemy is already inside, they would create a ladder for future attacks.

HOW TO DEAL WITH THE ENEMY THAT IS ALREADY INSIDE

1. Repent of every known iniquity and sin.

2. Hate the enemy with perfect hatred.

3. Quote the words of God against the enemy. Tell them that it is written and they must release you.

4. Openly rebuke them. Curse them in the name of the Lord.

5. Pray uprooting prayers because many of them have been in place for years. They need to be uprooted.

PRAYER POINTS

1. Every stranger of darkness in the temple of my life, die, in the name of Jesus.

2. Every arrow of witchcraft in my life, die, in the name of Jesus.

3. Plantation of failure in my spirit man, your time is up. Therefore, die, in the name of Jesus.

4. Every environmental witchcraft, die, in the name of Jesus.

5. Every satanic exchange of my destiny, be nullified, in the name of Jesus.

WHEN THE ENEMY IS ALREADY INSIDE

is a message delivered at the Mountain of Fire and Miracles Ministries by the General Overseer, Dr. D.K. Olukoya.

A CALL TO SERVE

Are you a member of MFM with a burden to help the needy, are you interested in alleviating the plight of the poor or in the spread of the gospel through the sponsorshing of the publication of tracts? Your resources, time and talent can be extended to several groups that are in charge of these areas. These groups include:

o   We care Ministry,
o   Mission Outreach
o   Tracts and Publications
o   Ministry to Drug addicts
o   Campus fellowship
o   Ministry to Schools
o   Ministry to Glorious Children, etc.

Thus says the Lord, "Verily I say unto you, in as much as ye have done it unto one of the least of these my brethren, ye have done it unto me" Matthew 25 : 40.

WONDERFUL JESUS!

DELIVERED OF STRANGE OBJECTS

Before I came to this church some months ago, I was always uncomfortable. But when I came here and went for deliverance, I vomited some substances that looked like blood and a small object that looked like a tennis ball came out of my body. Since then the discomfort has stopped and I am alright now. Praise the Lord!

Sis. Chiagozie
MFM Headquarters

GOD VINDICATES ME

Recently, I was given a query in my place of work without any just cause. I answered it and prayed that God should take control. To the glory of God, the issue died down without human assistance. Praise the Lord!

Bro. Adegbaso
MFM Owo

JESUS THE GREAT HEALER

Recently, I met a small girl that was very sick. Her mother told me that she had been taken to three native doctors but there was no solution. I asked all the people in the room to leave for a while. I prayed for the girl and gave her a spoonful of the anointing oil. I anointed the room also. After a few hours, the girl was revived to the glory of God. Praise the Lord!

Bro. Ainabor
MFM Jattu

20 YEARS HIGH BLOOD PRESSURE GONE

I thank God for my deliverance. I had high blood pressure for twenty years. During this period, I had difficulty with breathing. But after deliverance in this place, the Lord healed me. My blood pressure is now normal and I am hale and hearty. Praise the Lord!

Sis Ebun
MFM Festac Town

EVER FAITHFUL GOD

Recently, I got information that my mother was terribly sick. On my way to see her, I got involved in a motorcycle accident. But the Lord delivered me and I came out unhurt. Also, when I got to my mother and prayed for her, the Lord took control and healed her. She is now alright. Praise the Lord!

Sis. Akindayo
MFM Abaranje

DELIVERANCE FROM SPIRIT HUSBAND

During a deliverance programme in this church, God opened my eyes spiritually and I saw the spirit husband that was tormenting my life. He came naked and demanding for sex. I rebuked him in the name of the Lord and I saw him walk out of my life. Also during my vigils, I vomited a lot of things. Now my life has changed for the best. Praise the Lord!

Sis. Blessing
MFM Abeokuta

SAVED FROM ARMED ROBBERS

Recently, I boarded a bus which unknown to me was filled with armed robbers. They searched me and found the money I had on me which was quite a substantial sum. They counted the money and surprisingly gave it back to me. When we got to a certain bus stop, they stopped the vehicle and asked me to get off. That was how God saved me. Praise the Lord!

Bro Humphrey
MFM Egbeda

GOD HEALS ME

I went to the hospital for medical check up and the doctor diagnosed high blood pressure. I prayed against it and the Lord healed me. Now my blood pressure is normal. Praise the Lord!

Sis. Mercy
MFM Lekki

POWER MUST CHANGE HANDS MAGAZINE IS OUT AGAIN!

YOUR LONG AWAITED QUARTERLY MAGAZINE POWER MUST CHANGE HANDS IS OUT AGAIN WITH A BANG.

WITH A COPY OF THIS EDITION IN YOUR HAND, THE ENEMY IS IN TROUBLE.

IT IS TITLED, "THE ENEMY MUST EXPIRE."

HURRY NOW FOR YOUR OWN. COPIES ARE LIMITED. PRICE IS N100 ONLY.

Hello Children!
Your popular Spiritual tonic "Junior Fire in the Word" Is on the stand again. It is still as refreshing as ever.
Now you have more opportunities to win Fanstastic prizes every month as you send in your entries
Hurry grab your copy from the vendors.

The price is still N20.

FIRE IN THE WORD, is a weekly Spiritual Bulletin of the Mountain of Fire and Miracles Ministries, published by Tracts and Publications Group. All Enquiries should be addressed to The Editor, Mountain of Fire Magazine, 13, Olasimbo Street, off Olumo Road, Onike, P.O. Box 2990, Sabo Yaba, Lagos, Nigeria. Telephone 01- 867439, 864631, 868766, 08023180236. E-mail: mfmtractsandpublications@yahoo.com
Copyright reserved

FIRE IN THE WORD

Ye Shall Know the Truth, and the Truth Shall Make You Free (John 8:32)

ISSN 1595 - 7314 Vol. 12 No. 27 Sun. 11th - Sat. 17th May, 2008

THE CAPTIVES OF THE MIGHTY &
THE PREY OF THE TERRIBLE

My year of unprecedented greatness and unmatchable increase
Deuteronomy 28:13, Psalm 71:21, Ephesians 3:20, Psalm 92:10

saiah 49:25-26 says, *"But thus saith the Lord, Even the captives of the mighty shall be taken away, and the prey of the terrible shall be delivered: for I will contend with him that contendeth with thee, and I will save thy children. And I will feed them that oppress thee with their own flesh; and they shall be drunken with their own blood, as with sweet wine: and all flesh shall know that I the Lord am thy Saviour and thy Redeemer, the mighty One of Jacob."*

Isaiah 14:14-17 says, *"I will ascend above the heights of the clouds; I will be like the most High. Yet thou shalt be brought down to hell, to the sides of the pit. They that see thee shall narrowly look upon thee, and consider thee, saying, Is this the man that made the earth to tremble, that did shake kingdoms. That made the world as a wilderness, and destroyed the cities thereof; that opened not the house of his prisoners?*

In Isaiah 49: 25-26, two powers are identified. The Bible talks about the first power called the mighty. The mighty holds people captive and the mighty deals terribly with people. The second power is called the terrible.

Sometime ago, a certain man had a dream in which he fought with somebody, who had a knife. And the person used the knife on him. By the time he woke up, there was fresh blood on his bed. That was an attack by the mighty. Also, there was the case of a sister who used to be seen fighting herself and shaking things off her body. There were bites all over her body. Something was biting her, the physical signs could be seen. But no one saw what was biting her. Doctors could not help her. The situation continued until she was taken to a man of God, who prayed some simple prayers and she was delivered. The power behind such a case is **SEXUAL LOOSENESS CAN MAKE ONE A CAPTIVE FOREVER**

called the terrible. It is a dangerous thing to be in the custody of these two powers.

WHO ARE THE MIGHTY?

The mighty means the forceful, the powerful, enormous power and strong forces that can scare away potential helpers. It means powerful darkness that is not easy to penetrate and powers that are strong enough to contend with your angels of blessing. It is the kind of powers that confronted the angel bringing down the blessings of Daniel. They are the powers called the mighty.

They are the powers that argue with deliverance ministers; they always refuse to taken instructions. The mighty are the powers that threaten somebody who is trying to help another person that is their victim. They are the Goliath and Pharaoh like forces. They are the forces that scare small prophets. High level witches and wizards and aggressive strongmen are part of the

DELIVERANCE CASE (The Story of My Life - Part 15)

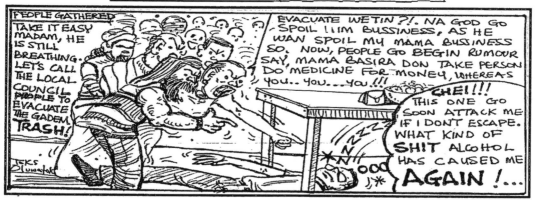

mighty. They are the multiple spirit husbands/spirit wives. A lot of people are under this kind of captivity. That is why the Bible talks about the captives of the mighty.

At this juncture, I would like you to take this prayer point: "The agenda of the mighty for my life, die, in the name of Jesus."

WHO ARE THE TERRIBLE?

The terrible means powers that are formidable in nature. They are the powers that cause intense fear. They are extremely bad and frightful forces. They are horrible, violent and iron-like enemies. They are the terrifying enemies that tear to pieces. They are what the Bible calls the terrible.

THE MIGHTY AND THE TERRIBLE

The mighty and the terrible are the following forces:

The drinkers of blood and eaters of flesh. The vampire and cannibal spirits. The fact that somebody is walking about does not mean that he is alive. He might have been eaten up by these forces. There is a revival of these satanic powers in these last days. They are the powers of stubborn witchcraft and familiar spirits. They are the occult powers. They deal terribly with anyone who was in their camp and wants to break free. They are the spirits of death and hell. They are the star hunters. They introduce vagabond spirits.

They are the rock and forest spirits. They are the stubborn stronghold and generational principality.

The Bible has about eight names for them.

THEIR NAMES ACCORDING TO THE BIBLE

1. The snare of the fowler.
2. The noisome pestilence.
3. The terror by night.
4. The arrows that fly by day.
5. The pestilence that walketh in darkness.
6. The destruction that wasteth at noon day.
7. The lion and the adder.
8. The young lion and the dragon.

Anyone under their bombardment and attack will experience certain things: People would be scared to pray with the person. The person's prayer partner will always be sick because the mighty and the terrible are dealing with him. That is why it is important to pray for our pastors. Sometimes after a service, a demon waits for them at home to challenge them because of the people they prayed for or assisted in one way or another to solve their problems. Pastors who do not know what to do under such circumstances get into serious trouble.

- When you have an enemy that scares away your friends, you need to pray against these powers.

- When you begin to notice that your former friends are becoming your aggressors, you are inside the cage of the terrible and the mighty.

- A healthy person who wakes up with a fearful life-threatening medical condition is a captive of the mighty and a prey of the terrible.

- Horrible dreams that makes one to wake up sweating is a sign that a person is under attack by these powers.

All the aggressive and terrible spirit husbands and spirit wives are sponsored by the mighty and the terrible.

Seeing dead relatives in the dream, chain of bad luck, evil family pattern, hearing strange voices, dreaming and forgetting, suicidal thoughts and all kinds of medical surgical operations are signs that someone is under the captivity of the mighty and the terrible. Please take the following prayer point: "Thou power of God, bury the terrible that is harassing my destiny, in the name of Jesus."

WHAT FACILITATES THE ATTACK OF THE MIGHTY AND THE TERRIBLE?

1. Sexual immorality: Anytime you commit a sexual sin, you open the door of your life to the mighty and the terrible.

WHEN YOU NOTICE THAT PRAYER HAS BECOME HARD WORK FOR YOU, THE MIGHTY AND THE TERRIBLE ARE CLOSE BY

Sexual looseness can make one a captive forever.

2. Food: Be careful where you eat. The food gate gives access to the mighty and the terrible.

3. Mouth: The way you use your mouth can attract the mighty and the terrible.

4. Unholy love for money: When you do anything unclean to get money, you give access to the mighty and the terrible.

5. Quest for popularity: When you want to be popular by all means, you will be caged.

6. Ancestral or generational hook: This is a situation where there is already the presence of the mighty and the terrible in a family line. So, they just transfer it to the children to be harassing them too.

7. Prayerlessness: This is where Christians should be very careful. As a Christian if you begin to notice that when you desire to pray, you cannot, you need to be careful. They are close by. If you find that your appetite for prayer just goes down, watch out for these powers. If you find that

something always takes up your prayer time, it means that these powers are close by. If you find that your former strength for prayer has gone, you need to rediscover it. If you used to tarry before the Lord in patience but now you find that you are not patient enough, you rush through your prayer and Bible reading in the morning, it means the enemy is close by.

If you begin to discover that the power and grace to fast is gone and sleep is replacing your prayers, the enemy is close by. The mighty and the terrible will catch you. If you depend on your prayer partner who is weak or does more gossiping than

praying, you are in trouble. What you have is a gossiping partner.

If you find that something binds your mouth when the Lord asks you to pray at night, then something is wrong. The mighty and the terrible are either close by or have captured you.

When you notice that prayer has become hard work for you, the mighty and the terrible are close by. You need to release yourself by fire. If not you are writing a very wonderful love letter to the mighty and the terrible.

What these two powers do in a life depend on some things.

1. The level of secret sin. If your secret sin is high, they will

not leave you alone. No matter how many songs you sing, you will not be free until you come to the Lord with an open account. So, a particular terrible power can be in a person's life for 40 or 60 years, if the person is living in secret sin. Therefore, the deeper your secret sin, the stronger the mighty and the terrible become in your life.

2. Family background. These powers are strengthened by the kind of family background you come from. If your family background is polluted and dirty, they will harass your life.

3. Your past life. The mighty and terrible will harass you if you have previously consulted them for assistance. You will fight a hard battle before they can leave you alone.

This calibre of spirits can set themselves against God and against Jesus. They are higher than all the small demons that are cast out during deliverance.

WAY OUT

1. You need to completely repent of any sin that can keep them in your life.

| THE PROPHET | David versus Goliath 15 |

2. You need to unbind your spirit man from prayerlessness. You need to pray to that level where praying becomes a thing of joy.

3. You must wage war against the mighty and the terrible. Pray confrontational prayers.

There was a certain sister, who could not explain how she spent her salary. She earned a big salary, which used to finish within a twinkle of an eye. One day, she got angry in the spirit. She collected the salary, put it on the floor, took a cutlass and was cutting around the money as she prayed: "You evil hands holding my money, I cut you into pieces, in the name of Jesus." That was all she said. In the evening, she got a message that an invisible hand had cut off her own grandmother's hands in the village. Since then her salary became useful to her.

Ask the Lord to forgive you any sin that would keep the mighty and the terrible in place before you take the accompanying prayer points violently because the issue at hand is a very serious one.

PRAYER POINTS

1. Every captive power drinking the blood of my destiny, die, in the name of Jesus.

2. Every terrible power planning to waste my life, die, in the name of Jesus.

3. Every padlock of darkness caging my breakthrough, break, in the name of Jesus.

4. Organized wickedness targeted against my life, backfire, in the name of Jesus.

5. O God of signs and wonders, appear, in the name of Jesus.

6. O God of the suddenly, appear, in the name of Jesus.

7. Miracle power of the Most High, locate me this week, in the name of Jesus.

8. O heavens, open and release my prosperity, in the name of Jesus.

9. Thou power of financial affliction, die, in the name of Jesus

10. Every owner of the load of poverty, carry your load, in the name of Jesus.

THE CAPTIVES OF THE MIGHTY AND THE PREY OF THE TERRIBLE

is a message delivered at the Mountain of Fire and Miracles Ministries by the General Overseer, Dr. D.K. Olukoya.

A CALL TO SERVE

Are you a member of MFM with a burden to help the needy, are you interested in alleviating the plight of the poor or in the spread of the gospel through the sponsorshing of the publication of tracts? Your resources, time and talent can be extended to several groups that are in charge of these areas. These groups include:

o   We care Ministry,
o   Mission Outreach
o   Tracts and Publications
o   Ministry to Drug addicts
o   Campus fellowship
o   Ministry to Schools
o   Ministry to Glorious Children, etc.

Thus says the Lord, "Verily I say unto you, in as much as ye have done it unto one of the least of these my brethren, ye have done it unto me" Matthew 25 : 40.

WONDERFUL JESUS!

DIVINE HEALING

Sometime ago, I had an emergency call concerning my child who was seriously ill. I made a covenant with God and prayed for divine intervention. Thereafter, the Lord healed her. Secondly, I thank the Lord for journey mercies. Praise the Lord!

Sis. Olufunmilayo
MFM Idimu

GOD PROVIDES MY OWN WORKSHOP

I am a mechanic by profession. I came to MFM through a very good friend. I learnt how to pray and later went for deliverance. I participated in the last 70 Days Fasting and Prayer programme. Immediately after the programme, my miracles started manifesting although I had no workshop of my own and not many instruments to work with. Miraculously, I met a brother who allowed me to use his workshop and tools and I was able to start some savings. All of a sudden, a man invited me to join him in his workshop. Unfortunately, he died the second day. But his family asked me to continue to work there. After sometime, they transferred the place to me. Praise the Lord!

Bro. Godwin
MFM Yopougon, Cote D'Ivoire

POWER OF PRAYER

Recently, my mother was sick and rushed to the hospital. I was led by the Spirit not to allow my children see her in the hospital. After praying for her, she received her healing. But my sister's children went to visit her and one of them became terribly sick. I visited her and saw her lying down lifeless. I knew it was an attack. I prayed the kind of prayer that I have never prayed before in my life. During the prayer, the Holy Spirit led me to pray some scriptural prayers which I did. To the glory of God, the girl was revived. Praise the Lord!

Bro. Abraham
MFM Orisunbare

THE LORD REVIVES ME

I was seriously sick for eleven months and most people thought I would not survive. However with prayers from the brethren, the Great Physician delivered me from the valley of the shadow of death. I am now very well. Glory be to God!

Bro. Mbido
MFM Yaounde, Cameroon

DIVINE INTERVENTION

For sometime I had problems settling my children's school bills. I even had to withdraw them from their former school due to accumulated bills. I took the matter to God in one of the Power Must Change Hands Programmes. To my greatest surprise, their father who had been away for a long time suddenly surfaced and cleared the backlog of fees. Praise the Lord!

Sis. Lola
MFM Headquarters

DELIVERED FROM UNTIMELY DEATH

I thank God for His goodness and mercy upon my family. My son fell from a storey building but did not die. God in His mercy positioned my cousin who caught him. Praise God!

Sis. Annas
MFM Owerri I

GOD SHOWERS HIS FAVOUR ON ME

I thank God for His favour upon me. Information got to me that pieces of land were being allocated to people in Asaba. I quickly left Lagos for Asaba. But when I got there, I could not get any. I was told that the land was for those living in Asaba and not for those living outside. I took the matter to the Lord at one of the MFM branches in Asaba for His intervention. To the glory of God, I went back and was given a piece of land. Praise God!

Bro. Okechukwu
MFM Headquarters

GOD HEALS

God delivered my daughter and healed her perfectly. God also delivered me from the spirit of untimely death and put an end to sickness, sorrow and poverty in my family. Praise God!

Sis. Durojaiye
MFM Headquarters

DELIVERANCE FOR MY FAMILY HOUSE

I thank God for proving Himself in my family life. We have a landed property in Lagos which we could not let out for a long time. It was difficult because an evil embargo was working against the property. But now, the embargo has been lifted by the Lord and we have rented the place out. Praise the Lord!

Sis. Victoria
MFM Ventana, Ibafo

POWER MUST CHANGE HANDS MAGAZINE
IS OUT AGAIN!

YOUR LONG AWAITED QUARTERLY MAGAZINE POWER MUST CHANGE HANDS IS OUT AGAIN WITH A BANG.
WITH A COPY OF THIS EDITION IN YOUR HAND, THE ENEMY IS IN TROUBLE.
IT IS TITLED, "THE ENEMY MUST EXPIRE."
HURRY NOW FOR YOUR OWN.
COPIES ARE LIMITED.
PRICE IS ₦100 ONLY.

Hello Children!
Your popular Spiritual tonic "Junior Fire in the Word"
Is on the stand again.
It is still as refreshing as ever.
Now you have more opportunities to win Fanstastic prizes every month as you send in your entries
Hurry grab your copy from the vendors.

The price is still N20.

FIRE IN THE WORD, is a weekly Spiritual Bulletin of the Mountain of Fire and Miracles Ministries, published by Tracts and Publications Group. All Enquiries should be addressed to The Editor, Mountain of Fire Magazine, 13, Olasimbo Street, off Olumo Road, Onike, P.O. Box 2990, Sabo Yaba, Lagos, Nigeria. Telephone 01- 867439, 864631, 868766, 08023180236. E-mail: mfmtractsandpublications@yahoo.com
Copyright reserved.

FIRE IN THE WORD

Ye Shall Know the Truth, and the Truth Shall Make You Free (John 8:32)

ISSN 1595 - 7314 Vol. 12 No. 28 Sun. 18th - Sat. 24th May, 2008

WHEN THE ROOT
IS INJURED

This week, we are looking at the message entitled, "When your root is injured."

Deuteronomy 29:18 says, *"Lest there should be among you man, or woman, or family, or tribe, whose heart turneth away this day from the Lord our God, to go and serve the gods of these nations; lest there should be among you a root that beareth gall and wormwood."*

Romans 11:16 says, *"For if the firstfruit be holy, the lump is also holy; and if the root be holy, so are the branches."* It means that if the root is dirty or unclean, so the branches will be.

Job 29:17 says, *"And I brake the jaws of the wicked, and plucked the spoil out of his teeth."*

There was a certain woman that was worshipping a snake and the snake made her very, very rich. She had an altar in the bedroom where she kept the serpent. She had a house help and other people working with her but none of them knew that she had a serpent in the house. The serpent had a regular feeding time and the woman was a government official. One day, she went out on official assignment and could not meet up with the serpent's meal time. When the serpent became very hungry and did not find food, it crawled out of her bedroom into the sitting room. The woman's houseboy who did not know about it, killed it, thinking it was an ordinary snake. Immediately the serpent died, the woman who was on official assignment died inside the plane. Her soul was already tied to that serpent and she died as soon as the snake died. But the story did not end there. The woman had three daughters, whose ages were 41, 39, and 36. They all had one strange problem. Anytime they went to bed at night to sleep, they would feel something cold lying beside them. They never could see what this cold thing was until they started praying, and the Lord told them that it was a serpent that stayed with them every night.

The more you pray, the more you discover and the more you discover, the more you recover and the more you recover, the more your progress will manifest.

WHEN THE ENEMY INJURES THE ROOT OF A PERSON'S LIFE, MANY THINGS WILL GO WRONG

There are some prayers somebody would pray and what he never thought lived in his house would manifest.

WHAT IS A ROOT?

A root connotes many things. It also includes the origin or source of a thing or person. It is the base, anchor, beginning or centre of a thing. Whether a person is born again or not, if his parents give him a good inheritance, he will accept it. Likewise, he can inherit something that is bad. The fact that a person is born again does not remove a bad inheritance unless the person deals with it practically with the tool of his salvation. A student in the university, who has already failed his course before he surrendered his life to Jesus will not automatically pass because he is born again. Salvation gives Christians facility to disgrace any power that wants to disgrace them.

A certain boy had a dream in which he was wearing an academic gown and graduating from the university. He had that dream when he was 6 years old but never realized the dream until thirty years later. He fought for thirty years before he could

DELIVERANCE CASE (THE STORY OF MY LIFE - PART 16)

realize that dream because his root already had an injury.

A certain sister had a very strange sickness and medical science could not help her. She became very thin. Different kinds of tests, including Hiv were carried out on her but they all proved negative. One day, some prayer warriors surrounded her and began to pray and God opened the eyes of one of them, who saw a thin sickly goat tied to a tree. And as they continued the prayer, the face of the goat changed to that of the sister. The goat with the human face then spoke and said, "Help me! My uncle tied me here! Help me! Help me!" That revelation only came after prayers but the sickness had wasted her time, destiny and life for 16 years.

Wickedness can be on the surface and it can be underground. Underground wickedness is the greatest source of sorrow because the foundation or root is the most critical part of a structure. The enemy knows that once the root has a problem the whole of the plant is in trouble. The enemy knows that no matter how attractive the branches, leaves and flowers of a plant is, it cannot stand when the root is sick. The enemy knows that there is a relationship between the root of a life and the destiny of that life because the root includes the foundation of a life.

When the enemy injures the root of a person's life, many things will go wrong.

SIGNS OF A SICK ROOT

1. Lack of spiritual growth: A person whose root has been injured could be in an environment where everybody is filled with the Holy Spirit but will not receive. He or she will not partake of the blessings.

2. Lack of understanding of oneself: An affected person will not understand what is happening to him or her.

3. Resistance to miracles.

4. Problematic career: No matter how the person struggles, he or she would not make head way.

5. Poor health: The enemy knows that when the health of a person is very poor, there is very little the person can really perform. If Joseph was bed ridden, he would not have been able to interpret any dream in the prison. The infirmity could have prevented him from fulfilling his destiny.

6. Very low resistance to sin: People who have sick root backslide easily. They are

quick to rebel against the word of God.

7. Unfruitful spiritual life: Affected persons never succeed in converting anybody to Christ.

8. Confusion and frustration: This is rampant abroad. You find men who want to become women and women who want to become men. It is a sign that there is problem in the root.

9. Fears and worries: An affected life would be filled with fears and worries. The fear would be so much that sleeping and going out alone would be a problem.

10. Affected persons have bad habits. For example, addiction and obsession of every kind.

11. Inability to resist temptation: Victims of injured root fall easily to any temptation.

12. Failure to receive and flow in the Holy Spirit: They find it difficult to receive the baptism of the Holy Spirit and to flow in the power of God.

13. Continuous sorrow and grief: There is no end to sorrow in the lives of those suffering from injured root.

14. Chronic hopelessness: They are always hopeless.

15. Lack of confidence in anybody: They find it hard to trust anyone.

16. Withdrawal from people: They are lone rangers. They do not like to mix with people.

17. Suicide tendency: They always talk about ending it all. They always feel like dying.

18. They feel like walking away to a place nobody knows.

19. Bitterness: People with sick root harbour bitterness and malice in their spirit.

20. A life of struggle. Victims of a sick root have to fight and struggle before they make any small progress. They fight hard to go to school, fight hard to get a job, fight hard to find a spouse, to hire a house etc. They fight hard for every little thing they get.

21. People with sick root are candidates of problem expanders, who find it easy to expand any small problem they have.

WHEN A PERSON'S ROOT IS INJURED, DESERT SPIRITS WILL MOVE IN.

22. Progress arrest: An affected person will notice that his progress is arrested. No matter how much the person struggles to move, there will be something resisting him.

23. A person with an injured root is a candidate of star hijackers.

24. A person with a sick root would be followed about by invisible persons. Anything the person does, these invisible persons will be spoiling it.

25. A person with a sick root would be a victim of money swallowers.

26. The person would also be a victim of head manipulators who do all kinds of terrible things against the head. For example, memory loss, inability to concentrate, noises in the ear, mind wandering etc.

27. Poverty: People with injured roots are usually swallowed up by poverty. They always run into debts no matter what business they do.

28. People with sick root are prey to satanic ministers. They go from one prophet to another, both genuine and fake ones, asking for

prayer. Whereas, if they would sit down and recover their destiny, they would discover that they are hundred times better than those people they are going to. They become servants of satanic ministers.

29. Harassment by coffin spirits: They are usually pursued by the spirit of death. They see this evil spirit in their dreams and smell death even physically. There are infirmities that are unto death and there is a sleep unto death, these coffin spirits sponsor them.

30. Aimlessness: A person with a sick root would be roaming around not really catching anything from the ocean of life.

31. Vagabond anointing: Such a person would be moving about from place to place. If it is a woman, she could be moving from one husband to another, or a man from one woman to another. The person can be moving from one city to another and from one job to another.

32. Attack by rock spirits: People who come from rocky places need to pray hard about their root.

33. Desert spirits: When a person's root is injured, desert spirits will move in and dry up everything the person is doing.

34. Evil marks: A sick root stands a person out negatively. Anywhere the person goes there will be problems.

35. Unprofitable load: A person with a sick root would carry evil load. He or she may be unconscious of it.

36. Marital turbulence: Spiritual marriage, whether spirit wife or spirit husband is a sign that there is a problem in the root.

ROOT WORKERS

There are some powers in the satanic kingdom called the root workers. They work on the root. Once they have messed up with the root of a person's life, they do not bother the person too much. The person may be very rich they are not worried because the root of the person is already in their hand, and it is just a matter of time before everything crumbles. The forefathers of many people have seen to it that terrible foundations were laid for everybody in their line. These terrible foundations must be dismantled before they can move forward.

HOW TO DEAL WITH ROOT WORKERS

1. The first thing to do is to carry out personal spiritual mappings. Find out either through talking to the elders or through prayers who were your parents to the third and fourth generation. What

| THE PROPHET | David versus Goliath 16 |

Psalm 125:1: "They that trust in the Lord shall be as mount Zion, which cannot be removed, but abideth for ever."

names did they bear? Did they bear the names of market days, the names of yam festivals or the names of the god of iron or any oracle? When you were young, did your father use to go out every night to come back very early in the morning? Where was he going? What were their occupations and what activities did they carry out? What are the kinds of gods they worshipped or served? How did they give names to their children? You need to make these enquiries.

2. Bring repentance unto the Lord. Ask for forgiveness for playing into the hands of the enemy.

3. Wage war against the root workers who spoil things. Cause a repair to happen by the power in the blood of Jesus.

Beloved reader, if you have not surrendered your life to Christ, that is, you are not born again, you cannot repair your injured root. Salvation is only through our Lord Jesus Christ. If you want to give your life to Christ, make the following confessions: "Lord Jesus, I come before you today, I surrender my life to you. I know that I am a sinner, forgive my sins and wash me with your precious blood. Take absolute control of my life. Thank you Lord Jesus, in Jesus' name. Amen.

Please take the following prayer points aggressively because the issue at hand is a very serious one.

PRAYER POINTS

1. Every root worker of my father's house, die, in the name of Jesus.

2. Every root worker of my mother's house, die, in the name of Jesus.

3. The root of my life, receive the touch of fire by the blood of Jesus, in Jesus' name.

4. Hand of God, arise from heaven and write the obituary of root workers, in the name of Jesus.

5. I shall not pay any ancestral debt, in the name of Jesus.

6. Every serpent and scorpion in my foundation, die, in Jesus' name.

7. Thou coffin power in my foundation, hear the word of the Lord, die, in the name of Jesus.

8. Every angry power that pursued my parents, my life is not your candidate. Therefore, die, in the name of Jesus.

9. Every power hunting for my star, your time is up, die, in the name of Jesus.

10. Thou power of the emptier, your time is up, die, in Jesus' name.

11. Every arrow of infirmity of my father's house, die, in the name of Jesus.

12. Every arrow of delay in the root of my life, die, in the name of Jesus.

WHEN THE ROOT IS INJURED

is a message delivered at the Mountain of Fire and Miracles Ministries by the General Overseer, Dr. D.K. Olukoya.

A CALL TO SERVE

Are you a member of MFM with a burden to help the needy, are you interested in alleviating the plight of the poor or in the spread of the gospel through the sponsorshing of the publication of tracts? Your resources, time and talent can be extended to several groups that are in charge of these areas. These groups include:

o   We care Ministry,
o   Mission Outreach
o   Tracts and Publications
o   Ministry to Drug addicts
o   Campus fellowship
o   Ministry to Schools
o   Ministry to Glorious Children, etc.

Thus says the Lord, "Verily I say unto you, in as much as ye have done it unto one of the least of these my brethren, ye have done it unto me" Matthew 25 : 40.

WONDERFUL JESUS!

DELIVERANCE FROM CON-MEN

I became a member of MFM a year ago. About a month ago, a sister of mine requested that I should assist her friend by using my television set as surety for her to collect her parcel from Germany. I fell for it not knowing that it was a set up. Eventually, I took the matter to the police station. God intervened and I was able to my recover television set. Praise the Lord!

Bro. Patrick
MFM Ibadan

POWER AGAINST SPIRIT HUSBAND

I was fed in the dream after which I started having problems. I had pain all over my body and my menstruation stopped. I went for deliverance at the Prayer City and on the second day of the programme, I had a dream in which I was given a sword with which I destroyed a man that came to defile me. I woke up to see my menses restored. Praise the Lord!

Sis. Ngozi
MFM Itire/Ijesha

DIVINE PROVISION

My husband was umemployed for two years. During one of the G.O's ministrations at the Prayer City, he prophesied that the Holy Spirit was distributing presents. I claimed job employment for my husband and to God be the glory, he is now gainfully employed. Praise the Lord!

Sis. Cecillia
MFM Ijegun

GOD HEALS ME OF ASTHMA

After undergoing a deliverance programme, God healed me of asthma which had been disgracing me. God has removed an evil load from my life and has set me free. God has also given me peace like never before in my life and marriage. The things my wife and I quarrelled over before, we now resolve amicably. Whenever I came from work before, I was afraid but now even without money, I feel confident. Praise the Lord!

Bro. Godwin
MFM Ishashi

ACUTE STOMACH ACHE GONE

For a long time, I was been suffering from acute stomach ache. I was advised to go for deliverance and I did. During the spiritual exercise, I passed out so many strange things after which I felt light in my body. To the glory of God, that put an end to the long term stomach problem. Praise the Lord!

Sis. Stella
MFM Jos

FOREIGN BENEFITS

During the 70 Days Fasting and Prayer programme last year, I specifically asked God for foreign benefits even though I did not know how it would come. However, God granted my prayer when one of my friends who had been abroad for a long time sent a large sum of money to me. Praise God!

Sis. Tessy
MFM Dopemu

TENANT TURNS LANDLORD OVERNIGHT

Recently, my brother inlaw asked me to follow an agent to inspect a property. Thereafter he asked if I liked it. When I said yes, he bought the fenced house worth N1.5m for me and my family. The agent handed over the keys and documents to me. That was how the God of MFM made me a landlady overnight. Praise God!

Sis. Joy
MFM Igboelerin

A DEAD CHILD RAISED BACK TO LIFE

Recently, a pupil from my school was hit by a motorcycle rider after school hours. The girl was unconscious and did not respond to treatment. We rushed her to a nearby hospital and in the process she died. But I was troubled in my heart. I started praying with some brethren as the child was being carried away from the hospital. And suddenly, the child started breathing and was resuscitated. Right now the child is alive to the glory of God. Praise the Lord!

Bro. Williams
MFM Ikare

POWER MUST CHANGE HANDS MAGAZINE
IS OUT AGAIN!

YOUR LONG AWAITED QUARTERLY MAGAZINE POWER MUST CHANGE HANDS IS OUT AGAIN WITH A BANG.

WITH A COPY OF THIS EDITION IN YOUR HAND, THE ENEMY IS IN TROUBLE.
IT IS TITLED, "THE ENEMY MUST EXPIRE."
HURRY NOW FOR YOUR OWN.
COPIES ARE LIMITED.
PRICE IS ₦100 ONLY.

Hello Children! Your popular Spiritual tonic "Junior Fire in the Word" Is on the stand again. It is still as refreshing as ever.
Now you have more opportunities to win Fanstastic prizes every month as you send in your entries
Hurry grab your copy from the vendors.
The price is still N20.

FIRE IN THE WORD, is a weekly Spiritual Bulletin of the Mountain of Fire and Miracles Ministries, published by Tracts and Publications Group. All Enquiries should be addressed to The Editor, Mountain of Fire Magazine, 13, Olasimbo Street, off Olumo Road, Onike, P.O. Box 2990, Sabo Yaba, Lagos, Nigeria. Telephone 01- 867439, 864631, 868766, 08023180236. E-mail: mfmtractsandpublications@yahoo.com Copyright reserved.

FIRE IN THE WORD

Ye Shall Know the Truth, and the Truth Shall Make You Free (John 8:32)

ISSN 1595 - 7314 Vol. 12 No. 29 Sun. 25th - Sat. 31st May, 2008

WOUNDED IN THE
HOUSE OF MY FRIEND

My year of unprecedented greatness and unmatchable increase
Deuteronomy 28:13, Psalm 71:21, Ephesians 3:20, Psalm 92:10

This week, we are looking at the message entitled, "Wounded in the house of my friend."

Zechariah 13:6 says, *"And one shall say unto him, What are these wounds in thine hands? Then he shall answer, Those with which I was wounded in the house of my friends."*

A careful look at the scripture in the foregoing gives us certain information:

1. Someone was wounded.
2. This person knew the origin of the wound.
3. The wound came from an unexpected quarter.
4. He knew that his wounds came from his friends.

Daniel 2:22 says, *"He revealeth the deep and secret things; he knoweth what is in the darkness, and the light dwelleth with him."*

There are certain things that are deep and secret, which can only be revealed by God. I Kings 14:1-3 says, *"At that time Abijah the son of Jeroboam fell sick. And Jeroboam said to his wife, Arise, I pray thee, and disguise thyself, that thou be not known to be the wife of Jeroboam; and get thee to Shiloh: behold, there is Abijah the prophet, which told me that I should be king over this people. And take with thee ten loaves, and cracknels, and a cruse of honey, and go to him; he shall tell thee what shall become of the child."*

The child of Jeroboam was sick and was not responding to treatment. Jeroboam did not know what to do. So, he decided to go and find out from the prophet what

was wrong. He wanted to know the source of the sickness. But because he had offended the God of Israel and could not face the prophet, he asked his wife to go there in disguise. I Kings 14:4 says, *"And Jeroboam's wife did so, and arose, and went to Shiloh, and came to the house of Ahijah. But Ahijah could not see; for his eyes were set by reason of his age."*

They were so far from the God of Israel they did not even know that it was not necessary to disguise because the prophet was already blind.

I Kings 14:5 says, *"And the Lord said unto Ahijah, Behold, the wife of Jeroboam cometh to ask a thing of thee for her son; for he is sick; thus and thus shalt thou say unto her; for it shall be, when she cometh in, that she shall feign herself to be another woman."* "Before the wife of Jeroboam could call, the Holy Spirit had revealed to the prophet that somebody was coming there in disguise.

1 Kings 14:6-13 says, *"And it was so, when Ahijah heard the sound of her feet, as she came in at the door, that he said, come in, thou wife of Jeroboam; why feignest thou thyself to be another? For I am sent to thee with heavy tidings. Go, tell Jeroboam, thus saith the Lord God of Israel, fore as much as I exalted thee from among the people, and made thee prince over my people Israel, and rent the kingdom away from the house of*

YOUR PARENTAGE WILL DETERMINE THE BATTLE YOU FIGHT

David, and gave it thee; and yet thou hast not been as my servant David, who kept my commandments, and who followed me with all his heart, to do that only which was right in mine eyes; But hast done evil above all that were before thee; for thou hast gone and made thee other gods, and molten images, to provoke me to anger, and hast cast me behind thy back: therefore, behold, I will bring evil upon the house of Jeroboam, and will cut off from Jeroboam him that pisseth against the wall, and him that is shut up and left in Israel, and will take away the remnant of the house of Jeroboam, as a man taketh away dung, till it be all gone. Him that dieth of Jeroboam in the city shall the dogs eat; and him that dieth in the field shall the fowls of the air eat; for the Lord hath spoken it. Arise thou therefore, get thee to thine own house: and when thy feet enter into the city, the child shall die. And all Israel shall mourn for him, and bury him: for he only of Jeroboam shall come to the grave, because in him there is found some good things toward the Lord God of Israel in the house of Jeroboam."

So, the origin of the sickness of that child was the punishment which God had planned for the whole house of Jeroboam. And the punishment was that none of them would be buried properly except this particular little child who had some good things in him. So, God wanted to remove him out of the way before He dealt with the rest of them.

DELIVERANCE CASE (The Story of My Life - Part 17)

SOME STATEMENTS OF FACT

1. There are some things known as problems. Problems are universal entities. They do not recognize racial or tribal influence. They differ as you go from one part of the world to another. It could be suicide, expression, alcoholism, etc. And there are particular sets of spirits responsible for these problems. In Africa, you find a lot of poverty, witchcraft attacks, backwardness, sicknesses, etc. So, problems are universal.

2. Problems are no respecters of person. They come without anyone's invitation. Therefore, the whole world is filled with men and women struggling to solve one problem or another.

3. Behind every problem, there is a spiritual force. Sometimes, we waste our time fighting human beings when we should be fighting the spirits behind our problems. When Jesus told His disciples that the Son of man would go to Jerusalem and die and would be buried and would rise on the third day, Peter said, "Far be it from you Lord. You are not going to die like that." It was Peter speaking but there was a force behind what he

was saying. That force was not of God. So, Jesus had to turn back and rebuke satan. He said, "I rebuke you satan." There are voices that can speak to us, which are not backed by the power of God. Behind every problem, there is a spiritual force. The truth is that the enemy has moved, tied down, loosened and has gone from street to street, family to family, community to community, race to race and tribe to tribe in order to harass and intimidate people. He has moved to shatter, detain, afflict, and wound people.

There are people who hear strange commands and begin to obey them. Many years ago, a certain fine-looking man was brought to our meeting. He qualified as a medical doctor but some hefty men had to be beside him always because he used to run all of a sudden without anybody pursuing him. He would run until he got tired and fall down. He would rest for some time, stand up and start running again. I asked the people who brought him if he was like that before he went to the university and they said no. They

told me the problem started when he got his first job. After some prayers, he regained consciousness a little bit and I asked why he was running. He told me he used to hear one voice, which would say to him, "Run!" And he would begin to run. A power was issuing an evil command to him and he could not resist it.

Apart from strange voices that issue evil command to people, there are also strange entities that follow people about. Some of the victims of these evil followers can see them, while some cannot. They follow people when they go for business to spoil things for them.

4. Every righteous man or woman will at one time or another in life, face the plot of the wicked. It happened to Joseph and Joseph triumphed. It happened to Daniel. Some people conspired against him and he was thrown into the lions' den but he triumphed. It happened to Shadrack Meshack and Abednego but they triumphed too. So, the enemies of Joseph and Daniel only rejoiced for a while. Their joy was cut off. The lions' den and furnace of fire were God's instruments to bury their enemies. So, what the enemy put

forward as an instrument of warfare against the righteous was used to destroy the enemy. You must understand that once you remain righteous the way God wants you to remain; you will never be defeated by the enemy. The Bible says, "Many are the afflictions of the righteous, but the Lord delivers him from them all." The righteous would one time or another face the plot of the wicked but the wicked will not succeed. Their instruments of wickedness will be to their own destruction. This is the stand of the scriptures.

5. The attack of the enemy can take three forms:

i. There is something the Bible calls the fiery darts of the enemy. The enemy fires this kind of evil arrows into the life of a person to last for a while. He just punishes the person for a while, releases the person and returns again. Many people are facing these fiery darts now.

ii. The enemy can have a foothold in a person's life. That is why the Bible says, "Give no place for the enemy." It means you must never allow the enemy to move freely in your life. The foothold of the enemy can keep a person from moving forward.

iii. The enemy can have a stronghold in a person's life. A stronghold can run from generation to generation. It can affect so many things. Abraham at one time in his life told Abimelech a lie. He said that his wife was his sister. Forty years later, Isaac the son of Abraham told the same lie to Pharaoh. He said that his wife was his sister. Sixty years

later, Jacob the son of Isaac and his mother deceived Isaac. Eighty years later, Laban deceived Jacob. Hundred years later, Jacob himself was deceived. One hundred and twenty years later, Reuben slept with his father's wife. One hundred and forty years later, Judah slept with his daughter in law. It went on like that. That is what is called a stronghold. This stronghold of deception, lying and iniquity was going across generations of a particular lineage. So, a stronghold is a very terrible thing. That is why the Bible says, *"For though we walk in the flesh, we do not war after the flesh: (for the weapons of our warfare are not carnal, but mighty through God to the pulling down of strongholds;) casting down imaginations, and every high thing that exalteth itself against the knowledge of God, and bringing into captivity every thought to the obedience of Christ"* (2 Corinthians 10:3-5).

In military terms, a stronghold refers to a place that is fortified. It refers to a kind of area that cannot be easily penetrated. It is a place that provides sure safety for the enemy. When the enemy of a person is hiding inside a stronghold, there is a serious problem. The enemy uses strongholds to keep people from enjoying abundant life. He uses it to

IF GOD WANTED PEOPLE TO BE SMOKING CIGARETTES, HE WOULD PUT CHIMNEYS ON THEIR HEADS FROM THEIR MOTHERS' WOMBS

hinder prayers, and maturity, and to keep people from being effective for the Lord. He also uses it to downgrade or demote destinies. The stronghold of the enemy is the reason many Christians suffer from defeat over and over again even when to the best of their knowledge they are doing everything right.

6. Your parentage will determine the battle you fight. It would be foolish for anyone to think that the battles from his home will not affect him. It would be foolish to think that the enemy of your parents will leave you alone. If the Israelites did not go to Egypt, they would not have had any cause to pass through the Red sea. It was their parents that went to Egypt and that action of their parents subjected them to some hardship.

7. If there is any problem in your life, it shows that you have something worth contesting for. So, you need to fight to free yourself.

8. The solution to any crisis you are going through is embedded in the crisis itself. This is why you must pray and roar in desperate prayer like a wounded lion or a mad prophet and tell your problems to reveal their origin or source and the solution. Those are the two commands to give to them.

Many people run away from crisis point because they do not know that the place of rest is the point of victory. Until victory is complete, there would be warfare. Some also do not know that there is a treasure even in the trouble they are going through. There is a miracle in the garden of your misery. There is a treasure in the garden of your trouble. There is a possibility in the garden of your problem. There is triumph in the garden of travail. And there is prosperity in the garden of poverty. There is honour in the garden of humiliation. So, the answer to every trouble is in the trouble itself, meaning that every problem comes with its seed of solution inside it.

Romans 8:28 says, *"And we know that all things work together for good to them that love God, to them who are the called according to his purpose."* It means that as a child of God, opposition will work for your good. That is why you need to cry out to God to show you the answer. Running away from your trouble may be running away from your breakthrough. You can turn every pressure the enemy places upon you to power. God is able to pinpoint for you the origin of your problems and the solution if you will go to Him in desperate prayers.

9. The worst thing anyone can do to himself is to wage war against himself. Unfortunately, many people an unconsciously doing that; they are assisting the enemy to fight them harder. If God opens your spiritual eyes and you see what a mermaid spirit looks like, when you see somebody who dresses like a mermaid, you will scream. Unfortunately, ignorance is no excuse. Sometime ago in Ghana, a boy came for prayers. He needed deliverance from witchcraft attacks. After the prayers, we noticed that he had a necklace on and we asked him to remove it. He refused and said he had been wearing it right from the day he was born. He said that the native doctor told him that if he removed it, he would die. But looking at him, I knew that what he had on was the instrument of his attack. I convinced him to remove it and to his amazement, he found that he was still alive after he obeyed. I told him that the thing needed to be destroyed. He first of all resisted but eventually agreed and we destroyed it. When we cracked open the pendant, we saw the following three words clearly written on a piece of paper, "I love satan." That was what he had been wearing since he was born.

Sisters, who dress indecently in the name of fashion, need to wake up so that they will not wage war against themselves. Some people are waging war against their breakthroughs and are praying against an enemy that they are already hanging on their bodies. If God wanted people to punch their ears and wear things on them, He would punch the ears from their mothers' wombs. Likewise if God wanted people to be smoking cigarettes, He would put chimneys on their heads from their mothers' wombs.

The early Pentecostal fathers in Nigeria uniformly banned jewelry from their churches because it invited demons. And the most effective ministers now are those who believe in holiness within and without. The practice of ear-piercing started with slavery. In those days, if you punched one ear, It showed that you belonged to one slave master. If you punched the two, you belonged to two slave masters. So, when the slaves were being set free, it was customary for them to cover the holes in order to hide the slavery. So, ear-piercing is even bad enough because the origin is in idolatry. Decorating these holes is even worse.

We cannot serve God well when we encumber ourselves with these things. If you bake a cake and put an emblem of idolatry on it, you are partaking in idolatry. Many people

THE PROPHET | David versus Goliath 17

Psalm 9:3:"When mine enemies are turned back, they shall fall and perish at thy presence"

hang crosses on their necks, when Jesus is no longer on the cross. Many do not know that there are different types of crosses, and that crosses with holes on top of them are witchcraft crosses called hank. Anyone who wears that kind of thing is a modern idol worshipper. The Bible says, "You shall not make to thyself any graven image" (Exodus 20:4). So, do not be the one waging war against yourself. If you are stylishly worshipping idols, you will be blocking your own breakthrough. Idol worship is not only when you physically carry idols or bow down to a particular thing. But when you design something in the shape of an idol, it is idol worship. These days, even Christians are wearing clothes designed with the eyes of serpents, stars, half a moon etc on them. All these strange objects find their way into Christian homes. Many Christians are wearing rings that carry strange patterns, and they do not understand the language the rings are speaking to them. Many of these rings and earrings are testifying even against the people wearing them. It is foolishness for a Christian to buy a vest bearing a sign he does not know or understand and wears it. Such a person may be cursing himself stylishly. Christians should avoid these kinds of things. A believer is not a wig wearer. If God has given you short hair, glorify Him for it. A believer does not put on long nails. If God had decreed that your nail would be short for you to have a breakthrough, keep it short the way He wants it. A believer does not buy extra things to attach to his or her hair. Certainly, a believer does not punch holes in the nose or mouth. If you do those things, you are waging war against yourself.

10. We do not choose our enemies, battles or struggles. But we can choose our weapons of retaliation.

The Lord is able to reveal deep and secret things. He knows what is in the darkness and the light dwells with Him.

Beloved, please pray the following prayers from the bottom of your heart. Perhaps, you have been wounded in the house of your friend, who you did not know was your terrible enemy. Perhaps too, you do not even know the root of what you are going through. You have to pray aggressively.

PRAYER POINTS

1. Every power that must die for my breakthrough to manifest, die, in the name of Jesus.

2. Every enemy of my appointed time, die, in the name of Jesus.

3. O mountain that boasted against me, your time is up, scatter, in the name of Jesus.

4. My problems, face the anger of the finger of God, in the name of Jesus.

5. Every arrow of unfriendly friends, backfire, in the name of Jesus.

6. Every magnet of darkness in my life, die, in the name of Jesus.

7. Jesus Christ my deliverer, knock out every darkness in my life, in the name of Jesus.

8. Jesus Christ my deliverer, knock out every darkness in my life, in the name of Jesus.

9. Jesus Christ my deliverer, knock out every darkness in my life, in the name of Jesus.

10. Every power assigned to kill my joy, what are you waiting for? Die, in the name of Jesus.

11. Let the enemy enter into the grave he has dug for me, in the name of Jesus.

12. Every power assigned to kill my joy, what are you waiting for? Die, in the name of Jesus. Amen.

WOUNDED IN THE HOUSE OF MY FRIEND

is a message delivered at the Mountain of Fire and Miracles Ministries by the General Overseer, Dr. D.K. Olukoya.

A CALL TO SERVE

Are you a member of MFM with a burden to help the needy, are you interested in alleviating the plight of the poor or in the spread of the gospel through the sponsorshing of the publication of tracts? Your resources, time and talent can be extended to several groups that are in charge of these areas. These groups include:

o   We care Ministry,

o   Mission Outreach

o   Tracts and Publications

o   Ministry to Drug addicts

o   Campus fellowship

o   Ministry to Schools

o   Ministry to Glorious Children, etc.

Thus says the Lord, "Verily I say unto you, in as much as ye have done it unto one of the least of these my brethren, ye have done it unto me" Matthew 25 : 40.

WONDERFUL JESUS!

GOD HEALS

I thank God for His mercy and protection over me. I took ill and the doctor diagnosed typhoid but after the treatment I still felt unhealthy. So, I decided to take part in the weekend deliverance after which I became alright. Also, God helped my husband to complete a project he had been doing for some years. Praise the Lord!

Sis Oke
MFM Oyo

DELIVERANCE FROM SPIRIT HUSBAND

My life was badly tormented by spirit husband. I went for deliverance and things changed for good. God repaired my marriage that had been damaged and gave me business breakthroughs. Praise the Lord!

Sis. Ogechi
MFM Festac

GREAT DELIVERANCE

I started worshipping in this church since October 2005. During one of the vigils, the Lord delivered me from the spirit of death that has haunted me for over five years. A dead woman that used to appear to me in my dreams vanished ever since. The Lord also promised through a word of prophecy to recover all my lost blessings. Praise the Lord!

Bro. Andrew
MFM Okokomaiko

CHEST PAIN OF OVER TEN YEARS GONE

I had serious chest pain for over ten years. During a 5 day prayer vigil organized by our branch, the pastor gave a word of prophecy that someone who was suffering from chest pain would be healed. Before the end of the programme, the Lord healed me. I started eating things that I could not eat when the pain was on. Praise the Lord!

Sis. Patricia
MFM Amichi

MISSING IN-LAW APPEARS BY FIRE

My sister in-law who was staying with me suddenly disappeared from home without any trace. It was a big problem because there was no trace of her whereabout. However, during a three-day vigil organized by the church, I wrote a prayer request concerning her case and to the glory of God, she has returned home safely. Praise the Lord!

Sis. Odumosu
MFM Ijebu-Ode

MIRACLE WORKING GOD

There was a trend of untimely death in my village. My brother and I decided to take it to God in prayers, God answered and asked us to pray and fast concerning it. We did and God took control of the situation. Also, through the fasting and prayer programme, God elevated my brother in his ministry. Praise the Lord!

Sis. Patrick
MFM Itire/Ijesha

DELIVERED FROM SUDDEN DEATH

Recently, on my way to work in the morning, the commuter bus I boarded had break failure. There was panic and many passengers were injured. But I had no single scratch on my body by the time the bus came to a halt. Praise the Lord!

Sis. Rufai
MFM Ejigbo

SAVED FROM ARMED ROBBERS

Recently, I boarded a vehicle which had armed robbers on board. They robbed all the other passengers on the way but God protected me. I got down safely and my money was not stolen. Praise the Lord!

Sis. Patrick
MFM Shibiri

TOTAL DELIVERANCE

For 4 years, after school I was unemployed. I used to eat in the dream and have all manner of oppressive dreams. I decided to go for deliverance and after that, I got employed in a bank. Also, the bad dreams have long stopped. Indeed God has been faithful. Praise the Lord!

Sis. Winifred
MFM Alapere

DELIVERANCE BY FIRE

Last year in my dream, a snake bit me and quickly disappeared before I could make effort to kill it. Since then I became stagnant both physically and spiritually. I thank God that during Pray your way to 2008 programme, the General Overseer mentioned my case and after the prayer, I was delivered completely. Praise the Lord!

Bro. Raymond
MFM Ijede

POWER MUST CHANGE HANDS MAGAZINE
IS OUT AGAIN!

YOUR LONG AWAITED QUARTERLY MAGAZINE POWER MUST CHANGE HANDS IS OUT AGAIN WITH A BANG.

WITH A COPY OF THIS EDITION IN YOUR HAND, THE ENEMY IS IN TROUBLE.

IT IS TITLED, "THE ENEMY MUST EXPIRE."

HURRY NOW FOR YOUR OWN. COPIES ARE LIMITED. PRICE IS N100 ONLY.

Hello Children!

Your popular Spiritual tonic "Junior Fire in the Word" Is on the stand again. It is still as refreshing as ever.

Now you have more opportunities to win Fanstastic prizes every month as you send in your entries

Hurry grab your copy from the vendors.

The price is still N20.

FIRE IN THE WORD, is a weekly Spiritual Bulletin of the Mountain of Fire and Miracles Ministries, published by Tracts and Publications Group. All Enquiries should be addressed to The Editor, Mountain of Fire Magazine, 13, Olasimbo Street, off Olumo Road, Onike, P.O. Box 2990, Sabo Yaba, Lagos, Nigeria. Telephone 01- 867439, 864631, 868766, 08023180236.E-mail: mfmtractsandpublications@yahoo.com Copyright reserved.

FIRE IN THE WORD

Ye Shall Know the Truth, and the Truth Shall Make You Free (John 8:32)

ISSN 1595 - 7314 Vol. 12 No. 30 Sun. 1st - Sat. 7th June, 2008

REPOSITIONING PRAYERS

My year of unprecedented greatness and unmatchable increase
Deuteronomy 28:13, Psalm 71:21, Ephesians 3:20, Psalm 92:10

Beloved, our message this week is entitled, "Repositioning prayers."

This is a destiny-changing message and I would like you to read it carefully.

Before you go further, I would like you to take the following prayer points aggressively:

1. My stones of prayers, locate the forehead of my Goliath, in the name of Jesus.

2. Taproot of failure working against me, dry up, in the name of Jesus.

3. My brain, receive divine fertilizer, in Jesus' name.

Psalm 92:10 says, *"But my horn shalt thou exalt like the horn of an unicorn: I shall be anointed with fresh oil."*

Some people are born out of position. That is, the position, circumstances, and environment surrounding where they were born do not position them for success. Such people are already aligned for failure or destiny abortion.

There is a divine position, where God has destined everyone to be. But unfortunately, many are born out of such divine positions. If you are supposed to start a journey from the west, and somebody positions you in the east then, you have started your journey on a deficit.

Many are experiencing pain now because they wish to prosper but they are in a position contrary to prosperity. Therefore, they are struggling and fighting. If somebody was meant to be a professor of Chemistry, but his father who was a native doctor had a different idea, and began to teach him incantations so that he could take over from him, his destiny would be diverted. The anointing of the native

YOUR PAST MISTAKES SHOULD NOT CONTROL YOUR LIFE

doctor would possess him. But if he had memorized incantations and had become a native doctor and all of a sudden, realized that, that should not be his position, he would try to readjust himself. But as soon as he tries to reposition himself, there would be problems.

Likewise somebody, who was meant to be an engineer, but somebody else decides to teach him the family business which is the business of wood. (Anyone that must deal with wood has to be very, very careful because, as he is cutting down witchcraft trees, the spirits there will be troubling his life). All of a sudden he finds out that he was not supposed to be in the wood business and as he wants to reposition himself, problem starts.

If somebody was destined to be an agricultural expert and somebody else convinces him to go into transport business, such a

DELIVERANCE CASE (THE STORY OF MY LIFE - PART 18)

person will have problems. Anybody that wants to go into transport business must be very prayerful because he would be transporting both evil and good everyday.

I came from a very poor home but I made up my mind that I was not going to be poor. But I did not know how to get out of poverty. I was always hoping that one day, someone preaching in the church would say something that could help me. But nothing was ever said to make me understand what I should do. But one day, in the classroom, an Indian teacher who was just meant to teach Mathematics, but sometimes would talk about other irrelevant things said, "If you

want to escape poverty, work hard at your studies." From that day, I started studying very hard. There was a time I read from 9 pm - 3 am everyday for a whole year and by the time the School certificate results were released, I had a distinction. It was possible simply because one man said, "If you want to escape poverty, study hard." Working hard at my studies helped me to reposition myself.

Poverty has pushed a lot of people to live in the kind of environment that has made their children to be polluted.

There is something called repositioning stress.

There is something called repositioning struggle and there is also something known as repositioning maneuvers. For every new level that God wants to move you to, there is a new challenge. So there is no shortcut to success.

HARD FACTS ABOUT LIFE

i.   Your past mistakes should not control your life. It is true you have made some mistakes. But by the grace of God, you have to stop living a life of error.

ii. Push out the boundaries established in your own mind on how far you can go. If you are tired of depending solely on your salary or you are tired of being tired, or you have a job, but not a career then you must push out those boundaries.

iii. There are many things in life that limit people, but you can only correct what you are willing to confront. Many people are not willing to confront their weaknesses and limitations. It is hard work for many people to confront their weaknesses and inconsistencies.

iv. It is an error to believe that it is when you cheat others or do some demonic things that you can get rich, because that way, you will invite all kinds of things into your life and will not prosper.

v. You are not supposed to live your life dancing to someone else's drum. The drum that you are supposed to dance to is that of the Holy Spirit for your destiny.

vi. Victory can only be accomplished, when there is a conflict.

Beloved, the expression "Born to win" means "Born to fight," because there were no winners who were not fighters. For you to be a winner, you must fight. If you are not moving forward, you are moving backwards. There is no other way. He who has a battle to fight and does not know he has a battle is in as much danger as the one who knows and does nothing.

It is a tragedy for you to know you have a battle to fight but do not even know the enemy to fight. If a little boy at the age of three begins to practise something, you can imagine how good that child would be when he gets up to fifty in that thing. When at the age of fifty, somebody is just registering for the General

YOU CAN PRAY YOURSELF INTO THE CORRECT POSITION IF YOU ARE DETERMINED

Certificate Examination, there is a problem.

Begin now to pray to reposition yourself. The Bible says that the earth is the Lord's and the fullness thereof. Whatever God empowers you to do, do it as a believer. It is advisable to become a landlord because it is difficult for you to gather wealth when you do not own a house.

I had a schoolmate who has a PhD in Geology. Being a sophisticated woman, she had a very good car. She said, "Well, I am learned and rich. So, I don't need to learn how to drive. I can always employ a driver." She did not bother to learn how to drive. She employed one driver and as she was going to the office one day, her driver brought out his chewing stick and began to chew it as he was driving. Occasionally, he would wound down the glass and pour out saliva. The woman said, "Stop doing that, you are embarrassing me.

Remove that chewing stick immediately." And the driver said, "Madam, if you don't want me to use my chewing stick, I will park this car now." When the woman insisted that he dropped the chewing stick, he got angry and drove to a very far place outside town, parked the car and walked away. The woman was there for five hours. She could not do anything until a kind-hearted person came and drove her home. She still did not learn how to drive until one day, her new driver took her vehicle somewhere and was using it for commercial purposes. One

of the passengers, who happened to be the woman's friend accosted him. And when the woman heard what happened, she had to go and learn how to drive. Something pushed her to learn how to drive.

There are many people who need to learn what they have never learnt before. Likewise, there are many who have learnt so much that they need to unlearn so many things.

Moses was born in a hut, he was supposed to be positioned as the deliverer of the people of Israel. But he started struggling, because

where he was, was not his place of destiny. He had to be pushed out. However, the Almighty God through the burning bush, repositioned him at the age of eighty.

That is why the following prayer point is indispensable. It says, "O God, let me find my direction while the sun is still shining, and not when it is setting, in the name of Jesus."

The prayer points below are not ordinary prayers. They are prayers vomited by the Holy Ghost to reposition you.

Perhaps by birth, environment, parentage or career, you have been wrongly positioned, and nothing is working, I counsel you to give God the chance through the weapon of prayer to reposition you. Allow Him like Daniel, who prayed himself into relevance. You can pray yourself into the correct position if you are determined.

THE PROPHET | David versus Goliath 18

PRAYER POINTS

1. O God, arise and align me to your divine agenda, in Jesus' name.
2. O God, arise and pluck me into your divine calendar, in the name of Jesus.
3. My Father, let me walk in your timing, in the name of Jesus.
4. My days, cooperate with the Almighty, in the name of Jesus.
5. Arrows shot at my position while I was in the womb, die, in the name of Jesus.
6. Dragon of frustration assigned against me, die, in the name of Jesus.
7. Every wind blowing me out of divine position, die, in the name of Jesus.
8. You child of the devil occupying my seat, clear out, in the name of Jesus.
9. Multiple rivers of income and cash, locate my life. in the name of Jesus.
10. People and resources assigned to move me forward, appear, in Jesus' name.
11. Power to excel in productivity, fall upon me now, in the name of Jesus.
12. Power of greatness, come upon my life, in the name of Jesus.
13. Power of inspiration, come upon my life, in Jesus' name.
14. Power of uniqueness, come upon my life, in Jesus' name.
15. Power of vision, come upon my life, in Jesus' name.
16. Power of wealth, come upon my life, in Jesus' name.
17. Power of intelligence, come upon my life, in Jesus' name.
18. Power of success, come upon my life, in Jesus' name.
19. Power of wisdom, come upon my life, in Jesus' name.
20. Power of knowledge, come upon my life, in Jesus' name.
21. Power of advancement, come upon my life, in Jesus' name.
22. Power of benefits, come upon me, in the name of Jesus.
23. Power of promotion, come upon me, in the name of Jesus.
24. Power of opportunities, come upon me, in the name of Jesus.
25. Power of understanding, come upon me, in the name of Jesus.
26. Power of problem-solving ideas, come upon me, in the name of Jesus.

REPOSITIONING PRAYERS

is a message delivered at the Mountain of Fire and Miracles Ministries by the General Overseer, Dr. D.K. Olukoya.

A CALL TO SERVE

Are you a member of MFM with a burden to help the needy, are you interested in alleviating the plight of the poor or in the spread of the gospel through the sponsorshing of the publication of tracts? Your resources, time and talent can be extended to several groups that are in charge of these areas. These groups include:

o   We care Ministry,
o   Mission Outreach
o   Tracts and Publications
o   Ministry to Drug addicts
o   Campus fellowship
o   Ministry to Schools
o   Ministry to Glorious Children, etc.

Thus says the Lord, "Verily I say unto you, in as much as ye have done it unto one of the least of these my brethren, ye have done it unto me" Matthew 25 : 40.

WONDERFUL JESUS!

GOD RESTORES MY MARRIAGE

After the 70 Days Prayer and Fasting programme, my husband who abandoned me and my children for four years called for reconciliation. This is how God restored my marriage. Praise the Lord!

Sis Alimi
MFM Aboru

DIVINE DELIVERANCE FROM DEATH

My daughter was in a bus travelling to Ibadan from Ife. At Ikire township, the bus stopped and parked. Somebody came to her and told her to get out of the vehicle and she obeyed immediately. A few minutes later, a big lorry ran into the bus and two other buses. In the process, 72 people were killed. I thank God for saving my daughter. Praise God!

Sis. Gbojubola
MFM Ajilo, Ondo

DELIVERED FROM THUNDER STORM

There was a heavy downpour, which was accompanied by a terrible thunder storm. The situation was so bad that I felt the presence of the thunder at my bedside. I thank God that it did not harm me. Secondly, I was served a court summon concerning my accommodation. I took it to God in prayer and even wrote a prayer request to the church because I did not want any court case with anybody. One day, when I returned from the church, the landlord called me and told me that my name had been withdrawn from the list of other tenants, that were charged to court. My God set me free. Praise the Lord!

Bro. Jonathan
MFM Apata

GOD THE GREAT HEALER

I was sick to the point of death for three weeks. I prayed to God to give me strength to undergo a deliverance programme and God did. During the deliverance programme, after the first day, when I entered into my kitchen, I was stung by a scorpion and all my toes were swollen. I applied the anointing oil on it and on the second day of the programme, all the poison of the scorpion were flushed out by the blood of Jesus and I received total healing. Praise the Lord!

Sis. Kehinde
MFM Abaranje

GOD REMEMMBERS ME

After passing through a deliverance programme in this church, all those who had forgotten me in my family began to remember and assist me. Praise God!

Sis. Victoria
MFM Sapele

GOD MY SURE AND TRUE HOPE

I lost my immediate elder brother in February 1996 to a very strange sickness. Few months later, I was retired from one of the first generation banks where I was working. Incidentally, the first job I did after retirement was not paid for. So I was faced with a lot of challenges including training my children. These situations brought me to MFM. However, God saw me through and all my children have completed their university education, gone through the NYSC programme and are now working. God has been so good; my last child even got a job just two weeks after completing his NYSC. Praise God!

Bro. Adekoya
MFM Headquarters

DIVINE HEALING

I had asthma for over a year. Every month, I spent about 65 per cent of my salary on drugs. Later, I went for weekend deliverance and to my greatest surprise, the asthma has disappeared and I do not use drugs any more. Praise God!

Sis. Tope
MFM Ogudu-Ojota

GOD SAVES ME FROM SUDDEN DEATH

I was travelling home with a bus when suddenly an an-coming vehicle collided with the bus. Some people sustained injuries but to the glory of God, I came out unhurt. Praise the Lord!

Sis. Temitope
MFM Olowora

Junior Fire in the Word

"Ye shall know the truth and the truth shall set you free" John 8:32 Vol. 24

The following winners of the Junior Fire in the Word crossword puzzle and quiz should collect their gifts at the Tracts and Publications office, MFM International Headquarters, Lagos.

Name	Age	Branch
1. Esther Ayomide Garba	10	Headquarters
2. Ruth Igbe	10	Ajegunle 3
3. Godwin Akinbule	9	Ajegunle 2
4. Precious Owolabi	8	Oworon 1
5. Babatunde Olufunke	9	Gasline, Sango Ota

**Hello Children!
Your popular
Spiritual tonic
"Junior Fire in the
Word"
Is on the stand again.
It is still as refreshing
as ever.
Now you have more
opportunities to win
Fanstastic prizes every
month as you send in
your entries
Hurry grab your
copy from the
vendors.
The price is still
N20.**

Junior Fire in the Word

"Ye shall know the truth and the truth shall set you free" John 8:32

HOW TO GET GOD'S QUICK HELP

FIRE IN THE WORD, is a weekly Spiritual Bulletin of the Mountain of Fire and Miracles Ministries, published by Tracts and Publications Group. All Enquiries should be addressed to The Editor, Mountain of Fire Magazine, 13, Olasimbo Street, off Olumo Road, Onike, P.O. Box 2990, Sabo Yaba, Lagos, Nigeria. Telephone 01- 867439, 864631, 868766, 08023180236.E-mail: mfmtractsandpublications@yahoo.com Copyright reserved.

Ye Shall Know the Truth, and the Truth Shall Make You Free (John 8:32)

ISSN 1595 - 7314 Vol. 12 No. 31 Sun. 8th - Sat. 14th June, 2008

DON'T DIE BEFORE YOUR TIME

My year of unprecedented greatness and unmatchable increase
Deuteronomy 28:13, Psalm 71:21, Ephesians 3:20, Psalm 92:10

Our message this week is titled, "Don't die before your time."

A lot of people claim they cannot die until their time comes. But what does the Bible say? The Bible makes us to understand that we can lengthen or shorten our lives according to the way we live and the way we believe. That is why any enemy that is not afraid of dying is indeed a great enemy. The way you believe is very important.

The Bible says King Asa died before his time. Let us see why he died in 2 Chronicles 16:12: *"And Asa in the thirty and ninth year of his reign was diseased in his feet, until his disease was exceeding great: yet in his disease he sought not to the Lord, but to the physicians."* (The Bible did not say it was a sin for him to seek the physicians but he did not bother to seek the Lord at all). Verses 13-14: *"And Asa slept with his fathers, and died in the one and fortieth year of his reign. And Asa slept with his fathers, and died in the one and fortieth year of his reign. And they buried him in his own sepulchres, which he had made for himself in the city of David, and laid him in the bed which was filled with sweet odours and divers kinds of spices prepared by the apothecaries' art: and they made a very great burning for him."*

King Asa died before his time. The Bible gave the answer in a very short sentence: "In his disease he sought not to the Lord," but to the physicians and therefore he died.

Anyone that puts his total hope on a doctor and believes that the doctor is the alpha and omega and believes anything he says from his book is hundred percent correct on his life, such a person will die before his time.

The Bible says something very interesting in Ecclesiastes 8:13: *"But it shall not be well with the wicked, neither shall he prolong his days, which are as a shadow; because he feareth not before God."*

The wicked will not be able to prolong his days because he does not fear God. Proverbs 10:27 also says, *"The fear of the Lord prolongeth days. But the years of the wicked shall be shortened."*

King Asa committed the agenda of his life to the hands of the doctors and refused to pray. He did not know that there is no medical X-ray or device that can detect the arrow of witchcraft. He did not know that doctors themselves find some cases absolutely mysterious. Sometimes, some doctors who are honest own up that some cases are not medical problems. They advise people in such conditions to go and pray. There was the case of a sister that was menstruating maggots. Her

WHEN CHRISTIANS DO NOT OBEY GOD, THEY INVITE THE ENEMIES TO SHORTEN THEIR DAYS.

doctor told her it was not a medical problem and counselled her to go and pray.

Jesus knows that men could die before their time. The fact that Jesus raised people from the dead and gave others powers to do so shows that many people die untimely.

The devil went to the meeting of the children of God and was roaming around there. When the Lord asked him what he was doing there, he said he was roaming around. Then the Lord said, "Have you seen my servant Job?" The devil said, "Yes, let me deal with him and he will deny you." The Lord said, "Go but do not touch his life." Beloved, the enemy has power to shorten life and to kill.

All the people Jesus raised from the dead were young people. Lazarus was a young man and had not lived out his days when he died. It is very sad to note that nowadays, young people are dying at an alarming rate.

Sometime ago, at a crusade, a mother brought her 6 years old daughter who had high blood pressure. I was thoroughly taken aback. I asked her about herself and she said that she and her husband, the girl's father, were fine.

The son of the widow of Nain in the Bible was a young man. He had not lived out his days. Jesus had to intervene. The daughter of Jairus that died, was a young lady. She had not lived out her life before she died. Jesus raised her to life so that

DELIVERANCE CASE (THE STORY OF MY LIFE - PART 19)

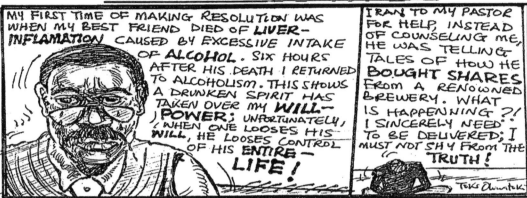

MY FIRST TIME OF MAKING RESOLUTION WAS WHEN MY BEST FRIEND DIED OF LIVER-INFLAMATION CAUSED BY EXCESSIVE INTAKE OF ALCOHOL. SIX HOURS AFTER HIS DEATH I RETURNED TO ALCOHOLISM. THIS SHOWS A DRUNKEN SPIRIT HAS TAKEN OVER MY WILL-POWER; UNFORTUNATELY, WHEN ONE LOOSES HIS WILL, HE LOOSES CONTROL OF HIS ENTIRE - LIFE!

I RAN TO MY PASTOR FOR HELP, INSTEAD OF COUNSELING ME, HE WAS TELLING TALES OF HOW HE BOUGHT SHARES FROM A RENOWNED BREWERY. WHAT IS HAPPENNING ?! I SINCERELY NEED TO BE DELIVERED; I MUST NOT SHY FROM THE TRUTH!

she could live out her days and possess her possessions. Any power that does not want you alive by any method is not the kind of thing to joke with.

Peter called Dorcas back to life so that she would finish her assignment. The devil has come to steal, to kill and to destroy. Unfortunately, many people have been turned over to satan to die an early death. It was not the will of God for Korah, Dathan and Abiram to die in the wilderness but they stood in the way of the work of God. Those men and their family members died before their time. It was not the will of God for Ananias and Sapphira to fall down inside the church and die, but they told lies to the Holy Spirit and died before their time.

Let us consider the deep scripture in Deuteronomy 17:20: *"That his heart be not lifted up above his brethren, and that he turn not aside from the commandment, to the right hand, or to the left: to the end that he may prolong his days in his kingdom, he, and his children, in the midst of Israel."*

Jeremiah 21:8 says, *"And unto this people thou shalt say, Thus saith the Lord; Behold, I set before you the way of life, and the way of death."* Two ways are laid down in that passage. The choice of where you follow becomes a personal decision. When God withdraws His blessing from people and they walk right into judgment, they die before their time. When there is no protection, satan kills them.

The Bible says, the angel of the Lord encamps roundabout those that fear Him to deliver them. So, if you do not fear the Lord, his angels will not surround you. Therefore, satan can kill you off. Thank God because He has kept millions from dying before their time. We can see that in Psalm 103 verse 3-5: *"Who forgiveth all thine iniquities; who healeth all thy diseases; Who redeemeth thy life from destruction; who crowneth thee with lovingkindness and tender mercies; Who satisfieth thy mouth with good things; so that thy youth is renewed like the eagle's."*

As long as you walk straight with the Lord, you have nothing to fear. But when a person veers off to the right or to the left, His protection is taken away. Then the enemy can move in and kill the person.

Some people are following terrible traditions; they say it is God's will when people die before their time. This is not true. Some people die because they rebel against the Lord. All those who died in the days of Noah died before their time. All those who died in the wilderness when Moses was taking them to the Promised Land died before their time. Certainly, the wife of Lot died before her time. When Christians do not obey God, they invite the enemies to shorten their days. The Lord does not want us to die before our time. Many people die before their time because their faith has been injured or killed. Unbelief can make people to die before their time.

Many times, pastors go to the cemetery and say, "The Lord has given and the Lord has taken, precious is the death of the saints in the sight of the Lord." But unfortunately, most of the time, the people have died before their time. A good soldier is always a loss to the army when he dies an early death.

God is not a God of the dead but a God of the living. Many believers die before their time because they fail to take a divine insurance. The Bible says no evil shall befall you neither shall any plague come near your camp. When you have weapons and do not use them, anything can happen, you should make use of your divine insurance.

POWER OF THE TERMINATORS

There are some powers known as terminators. Their job is to terminate. If you do not arrest them, you will be terminated.

1. **Power of sexual immorality.** This is the first major terminator that has killed so many people prematurely. Anyone that gets involved in sexual immorality is writing a letter to Mr. Death and shifting the protection of the Almighty away from his life. Sometime ago, one man and his wife came for counselling. They wanted to know if they should take one boy of seventeen to court or not. They said they sent their daughter who was fifteen years old to school and instead of her to go to school and focus on her studies, she was

busy keeping a boyfriend. Eventually, she got pregnant. And for some strange reasons, the boy went to a chemist and got syringes and the girl allowed herself to be injected by the boy who did not have any nursing or medical training. The girl could not tell her parents what she was going through until she was about to die, then she decided to tell her parents everything. So, the parents wanted to know whether they should take the boy to court or not? But taking him to court would not have brought their daughter back. She was dead unfortunately and had gone to hell fire. Many people who are playing at the edge of hell fire should stop it because they are writing a letter to hell fire. When you are writing an unchristian letter to anyone, you are looking for trouble. People must conduct themselves well so that they do not get into trouble. That is why the first advice to people when they get born again is to put away any boyfriend/girlfriend they may have. If they do not keep them off, they are looking for trouble. These days, there are so many terrible films in the streets, and they are ways of death.

2. **Oppression.** When something is oppressing you on a regular

THE LAW OF DEATH IS STRONG BUT THE LAW OF THE SPIRIT OF LIFE IN CHRIST JESUS IS STRONGER.

basis, in the dream or physically, make sure you pray until that oppression is lifted away. When something begins to press you down, know that the thing does not have a good agenda. You must quickly deal with it before it deals with you at a weak hour.

3. **Infirmity.** The devil is a good distributor of infirmity. The best prayer for infirmity is for it to go back to the sender because you did not initiate it. It is not your own, so it should go back to its sender.

4. **The spirit of death and hell.** This is the spirit that can envelope a person and snuff life out of the person.

5. **Witchcraft power.** This terminator has now become an institution all over the world. Witchcraft powers are responsible for a lot of strange and terrible things happening in our world today. There are a lot of terrible things happening now and we need to arrest them. Gone are those days when witches were only old people with gray hairs. These days, they are young, intelligent and focused. They are older than their parents. We need to understand that there are terminators around.

6. **Evil pronouncement:** Wrong use of the mouth will invite death. The Bible says that death and life are in the power of the tongue. When people make evil pronouncements against you and you accept them, you will soon be terminated.

7. **Familiar spirits.** Many people are possessed by familiar spirits unconsciously. They made covenants that involved when they would die without knowing. Some would make covenants that immediately after their wedding, they would die and it will happen that way. Some people sign covenants with the devil that they will die at 30 or 40. But the trouble is that some of these people do not know that such an agreement is in place. That is why it is good to pray that any unconscious covenant should be broken, in the name of Jesus.

8. **The triangular powers.** The triangular powers is what is known as the sun, the moon and the stars. The Psalmist says the sun will not smite you by day nor the moon by night. In some religions, all they do is to programme the moon, the sun and the stars to serve their purpose. Some people understand these things while many are very ignorant about them.

9. **Fear and worry.** These two things are the most silent and most horrible terminators, which go together. The minds of many people are so worried and stressed up, whereas the Bible says, "Let not your heart be troubled, believe in God, believe in me also" (John14:1). Worry and fear are silent killers.

Worry is taking salary advance from the devil. Worry is believing that God is not on your side again. Immediately fear and worry move in, faith jumps out.

The Bible says, "Be careful for nothing."

10. **Tragedy activators:** They are responsible for accidents, calamities etc.

11. **Drinkers of blood and eaters of flesh:** The Bible says, "When my enemies and my foes came upon me to eat up my flesh, they stumbled and fell" (Psalm 27:2).

There are some powers that eat flesh and drink blood.

Sometime ago in Canada, I came across a journal which featured the story of a certain man whose greatest ambition since he was 12 years old was to eat a whole human being and he had been trying to get somebody to eat. He even went to the mortuary but was driven away. So, he began to offer money to people who would not mind to be eaten up. One day, at the age of 39, he found a man who was fed up with life. This fellow collected the money, spent it and came back to be eaten. He quickly slaughtered the man and kept the corpse inside his big freezer and was eating it gradually. He used some for sandwich, some for barbecue until somebody reported him to the police.

There was also a 14 year old boy who believed that he would not die if he ate the heart of a man. One day, he invaded the house of one old woman with a knife when her grandchildren had gone out, killed her, cut out her heart and ate it.

12. **Spirit of murder:** We have this all over the place. This terrible spirit works through hired killers, armed robbers, etc.

13. **The spirit of suicide.** This is responsible for people killing themselves.

14. **The curse of family destruction.**

15. **Evil covenants.** Somebody can form a covenant with some

| THE PROPHET | David versus Goliath 19 |

powers consciously or unconsciously.

16. Evil summon. This is commonly used in our environment.

17. Bad food.

18. Personal curses: Many people curse themselves when they make terrible pronouncements about themselves.

19. Environmental wickedness.

20. Poison. It could be physical or spiritual poison.

21. Ancestral bondage.

These are the powers of the terminators. Their job is not to steal. Their job is to kill.

HOW TO PROLONG YOUR LIFE

1. Repent of your sin and give your life to Jesus Christ.
2. Receive deliverance through prayer. That is pray to destroy the power of the terminator.
3. Receive deliverance through obedience
4. Receive deliverance through faith.
5. Receive deliverance through the anointing of the Holy Spirit.
6. Receive deliverance by saying what God says. Do not say what the enemy is saying, or what your body is saying.
7. Receive deliverance through the atonement. Healing is in the atonement.

It is true that there is a law of gravity, but there is also a law of the spoken word. This power made the iron head to come up. Indeed there is a law of nature, but there is a law of faith which is stronger. The law of the spirit is stronger that any law. The stormy sea was real but faith was more powerful. Darkness is real but when the sun rises, darkness flees. The law of death is strong but the law of the spirit of life in Christ Jesus is stronger.

8. Prolong your life through the leading of the Holy Spirit. Get guidance from God on anything you want to do. Do not do things that you are not supposed to do. I counsel you to memorise Psalm 91 if you have not done so and make sure you confess it everyday, especially before you leave home.

PRAYER POINTS

1. Any power operating against my life form any tree, your time is up, die, in the name of Jesus.
2. Any power that wants me to die before my time, what are you waiting for? Die, in the name of Jesus.
3. Angels of fire, pursue my pursuers, in the name of Jesus.
4. Thou power of the night flying for my sake, die, in the name of Jesus.
5. Every covenant of untimely death, break, in the name of Jesus.
6. Any witchdoctor consulting against me, I bury your power, in the name of Jesus.
7. I shall not die before my time. My testimonies must appear, in the name of Jesus.
8. Every terminator of my father's house, die, in the name of Jesus.
9. I shall not de but live and declare the works of God. I take divine insurance against every attack of tragedy and every attack of the enemy. It shall be well with me. It shall be well with my life. It shall be well with my going out and coming in. The sun shall not smite me by day, nor the moon by night. Whenever I enter a place, darkness shall flee. Any child of the devil in my environment, your secrets shall no longer be covered, in the name of Jesus. Thank you Lord.

DON'T DIE BEFORE YOUR TIME

is a message delivered at the Mountain of Fire and Miracles Ministries by the General Overseer, Dr. D.K. Olukoya.

A CALL TO SERVE

Are you a member of MFM with a burden to help the needy, are you interested in alleviating the plight of the poor or in the spread of the gospel through the sponsorshing of the publication of tracts? Your resources, time and talent can be extended to several groups that are in charge of these areas. These groups include:

o We care Ministry,
o Mission Outreach
o Tracts and Publications
o Ministry to Drug addicts
o Campus fellowship
o Ministry to Schools
o Ministry to Glorious Children, etc.

Thus says the Lord, "Verily I say unto you, in as much as ye have done it unto one of the least of these my brethren, ye have done it unto me" Matthew 25 : 40.

WONDERFUL JESUS!

SUCCESSFUL SURGERY AND ACADEMIC SUCCESS

I went for a surgical operation at the General Hospital Lagos. God in His infinite mercy saw me through. This took place a week to my final examination. Secondly, after the operation, I went for my final examination at LASU and passed all my papers. Praise the Lord!

Bro. Adewunmi
MFM Headquarters

GOD GRANTS ME PEACE

I came to Lagos from Benin to collect my documents to enable me travel abroad. But unfortunately, the person who had my documents travelled and I became stranded. Before now, I was involved in a lot of things including cultism. I was part of a group that poured fuel on a church and set it ablaze but the church did not burn. Ever since, all my businesses went down. I did not have peace. Through divine intervention, I came here for deliverance. The minister told me to confess my sins to God which I did. I thank God that as soon as I did that, my peace was restored. Now I have peace of mind. Praise the Lord!

Bro. Obaro
MFM Olowora

GOD RESTORES MY GLORY

For sometime, I was doing menial work which was not the right job for me. Somebody then introduced me to MFM. The pastor and members prayed for me and taught me how to pray on my own. God restored my glory by giving me a good job befitting my status. Praise the Lord!

Bro. Gideon
MFM Ibadan 2

DIVINE HEALING

For sometime, a voice was telling me that I would die. Recently, when I got home from work, I suddenly took ill. I stooled severally but to the glory of God, after I took the anointing oil, the stooling ceased and I was totally healed. Praise the Lord!

Sis. Sarah
MFM Ijaiye Ojokoro

DIVINE HEALING

Sometime ago, I was so sick that I could not go anywhere and I was fast losing weight. I was always at home. But one day as I was reading and meditating on a particular scripture that I love so much, God gave me a command to say, "You mountain, go out, in Jesus' name." As I was saying it, suddenly a dark object came out of me and I became well and regained my weight. Secondly, God delivered me from a fire disaster. I lit a candle and forgot to put it off. It started to burn, but God intervened and quenched the fire and it could not spread. Also, God granted me journey mercies. Praise the Lord!

Sis. Ifeoma
MFM Headquarters

GOD RESTORES MY HEALTH

I had waist pain for a long time. It was so bad that I could not bend. One day, the pastor announced that people were needed to clean and wash the new branch of our church. I said within me that I would do the work whether the waist pain liked it or not. To my amazement, the waist pain disappeared after sweeping the church. Praise the Lord!

Sis. Ejiro
MFM Uwelu Benin

I GOT A BETTER JOB

I was working like an elephant but eating like an ant. Then the Holy Spirit told me to go for deliverance. This I did and the Holy Spirit revealed to me that I would get a very good job. I give glory to the Almighty God because His word has come to pass. I now have a very good job which has made me very comfortable. Praise the Lord!

Bro. Oluyemi
MFM Ijegun

VICTORY OVER UNTIMELY DEATH

I praise the name of the living God who sustained the life of my mother-in-law. We got a call recently that she was very ill. The following day, we arranged for her to be brought to Lagos. We then took her to the hospital with the help of God and intercession by brethren and she was restored. Praise the Lord!

Bro. Awosolu
MFM Ibafor I

GOD PROTECTS MY FAMILY FROM ROBBERY ATTACK

Recently, some armed robbers came to our neighbourhood but my family and I were not hurt. That was not the first time but God has been merciful. I also thank God for the salvation of a friend of mine who lives in England. Praise the Lord!

Sis. Nku
MFM Lekki

DIVINE HEALING

God saved me from the spirit of death and hell. I was sick for a long time but during a service, the General Overseer mentioned my case. He said that there was somebody at the meeting whose life had been turned upside down but the person had received God's attention. Immediately, I was made whole. Praise the Lord!

Sis. Nimota
MFM Aguda

MOUNTAIN OF FIRE AND MIRACLES MINISTRIES
SCHOOL OF SUCCESS

THIS SCHOOL IS A MUST FOR
THOSE WHO SEEK
ANOINTING FOR HIGHER CALLING.

SESSION:
NOVEMBER 2008
FOR WHO:
PASTORS, FIELD PASTORS, SENIOR PASTORS,
DELIVERANCE PASTORS, DELIVERANCE MINISTERS.

QUALIFICATIONS:
SCHOOL OF BIBLICAL STUDIES
SCHOOL OF DELIVERANCE
SCHOOL OF MINISTRY
SCHOOL OF ANOINTED LEADERS
SCHOOL OF SUPER DELIVERANCE

AND AT LEAST SEVEN YEARS MINISTERIAL
OR PASTORAL
WORKING EXPERIENCE WITH MFM.
APPLICANTS SHOULD APPLY
THROUGH THEIR REGIONAL
OVERSEERS OR HEADS OF DEPARTMENTS
TO THE GENERAL OVERSEER

NOT LATER THAN 31ST AUG. 2008 WITH ATTENDANCE
CLEARANCE FROM EACH OF THE SCHOOLS ATTENDED

MOUNTAIN OF FIRE AND MIRACLES MINISTRIES
SCHOOL OF DEEP DELIVERANCE

THIS IS A MUST FOR THOSE WHO SEEK
ANOINTING FOR HIGHER CALLING IN THE
MINISTRY OF DELIVERANCE.
SESSION:
NOVEMBER 2008
FOR WHO:
PASTORS, FIELD PASTORS, SENIOR PASTORS,
DELIVERANCE PASTORS, DELIVERANCE MINISTERS.
QUALIFICATIONS:
SCHOOL OF BIBLICAL STUDIES
SCHOOL OF DELIVERANCE
SCHOOL OF MINISTRY
SCHOOL OF ANOINTED LEADERS
SCHOOL OF SUPER DELIVERANCE

AND AT LEAST SEVEN YEARS MINISTERIAL
OR PASTORAL
WORKING EXPERIENCE WITH MFM.
ALL MINISTERS SHOULD APPLY
THROUGH THEIR REGIONAL
OVERSEERS OR HEADS OF DEPARTMENTS
TO THE GENERAL OVERSEER

NOT LATER THAN 31ST AUG. 2008 WITH
ATTENDANCE CLEARANCE FROM EACH OF
THE ABOVE SCHOOLS.

MOUNTAIN OF FIRE AND MIRACLES MINISTRIES
SCHOOL OF ANOINTED LEADERS

FOR THE INCREASE AND CONTINUOUS FLOW
OF THE ANOINTING
SESSION:
NOVEMBER 2008
FOR WHO:
PASTORS, FIELD PASTORS, SENIOR PASTORS,
DELIVERANCE PASTORS, DELIVERANCE MINISTERS.
QUALIFICATIONS:
SCHOOL OF BIBLICAL STUDIES
SCHOOL OF DELIVERANCE
SCHOOL OF MINISTRY

AND AT LEAST FIVE YEARS MINISTERIAL
OR PASTORAL WORKING EXPERIENCE WITH MFM.

ADMISSION IS STRICTLY BY NOMINATION
BY THE SENIOR OR REGIONAL OVERSEERS OR
HEADS OF DEPARTMENTS TO THE GENERAL OVERSEER
NOT LATER THAN 31ST AUGUST 2008 WITH PROOF OF
ATTENDANCE FROM EACH OF THE ABOVE SCHOOLS.

MOUNTAIN OF FIRE AND MIRACLES MINISTRIES
SUPER DELIVERANCE COURSE

THIS IS THE COURSE THAT WILL LAUNCH YOU INTO
THE HIGHER REALM OF DELIVERANCE MINISTRY
SESSION:
NOVEMBER 2008
FOR WHO:
PASTORS, FIELD PASTORS, SENIOR PASTORS,
DELIVERANCE PASTORS, DELIVERANCE MINISTERS.
QUALIFICATIONS:
SCHOOL OF BIBLICAL STUDIES
SCHOOL OF DELIVERANCE
SCHOOL OF MINISTRY
SCHOOL OF ANOINTED LEADERS

AND AT LEAST SIX YEARS MINISTERIAL
OR PASTORAL WORKING EXPERIENCE WITH MFM.

ADMISSION IS STRICTLY BY NOMINATION
BY THE SENIOR OR REGIONAL OVERSEERS OR
HEADS OF DEPARTMENTS TO THE GENERAL OVERSEER
NOT LATER THAN 31ST AUGUST 2008 WITH PROOF OF
ATTENDANCE FROM EACH OF THE ABOVE SCHOOLS.

Ye Shall Know the Truth, and the Truth Shall Make You Free (John 8:32)

ISSN 1595 - 7314 Vol. 12 No. 33 Sun. 22nd - Sat. 28th June, 2008

HEAVEN & HELL

My year of unprecedented greatness and unmatchable increase
Deuteronomy 28:13, Psalm 71:21, Ephesians 3:20, Psalm 92:10

This week, we are looking at the message entitled, "Heaven and hell."

John 14:1-2 says, *"Let not your heart be troubled; ye believe in God, believe also in me. In my Father's house are many mansions: if it were not so, I would have told you. I go to prepare a place for you."*

Hell is hot, heaven is sweet and the cross is the only thing between them. Where you go depends on which side of the cross you are. True believers in Christ are admitted into heaven while unbelievers are consigned to hell. Both places are eternal. If you are in, you are in and all their inhabitants are not transferable. Heaven is a place of eternal bliss with God, angels and saints of all ages. But hell is a place of eternal torment where according to the Bible, the worms die not and the fire is not quenched.

HEAVEN.

1 Corinthians 2:9 says, *"But as it is written, Eye hath not seen, nor ear heard, neither have entered into the heart of man, the things which God hath prepared for them that love him."*

This scripture tells us that there is a glorious end to those who die in Christ. The Bible makes us to understand that our sojourn on earth is not the end of everything. For those who do their work well the way God wants them to do it, their abode here is temporary. The lives of Christians on earth is a probationary period. God is putting them under probation to see where they will qualify for. So, anything anyone is doing without heaven as the focus is a waste of time. Anyone who seldom thinks about heaven is not likely to make heaven. Those who want to get there are always thinking about the place. They see their sojourn here as temporary and that they are going to a better country, where things are better than what it is here.

The road to heaven is never overcrowded because only a few number of people find it. Anyone who does not bear the cross on earth will not wear the crown. That is why it is good for every Christian to have a revelation of heaven. And after he or she has seen the beauty and grandeur of the place, he should also have a revelation of hell fire. And when the person has seen the horribleness of the place, he will make up his mind where he will like to go. It is good to see those two places. When that happens, the message of "Don't backslide" becomes unnecessary.

FACTS ABOUT HEAVEN

1. It is a place prepared by Christ Himself like we see in John 14:1-2.

2. It is a glorious city; it has pure gold and clear glass.

3. The place is known as the New Jerusalem. The river of life is there to ensure everlasting life. The throne of God will occupy the central place.

A NICE KIND MAN CAN GO TO HELL FIRE.

4. It is a place of godliness, meaning that no unclean thing shall be allowed to get inside. Revelation 21:27 says, *"And there shall in no wise enter into it anything that defileth, neither whatsoever worketh abomination, or maketh a lie; but they which are written in the Lamb's book of life."*

Heaven is so holy and beautiful that no sinner and no unclean person shall be permitted to enter there. Many people will be surprised to see some people they never thought would go there, and many people they thought would not make it would be there. Man only looks at the face but God looks at the heart.

Heaven is a place of unity. It is a place of perfection and joy. There is no sickness there. Somebody who has no eyes or legs in this world need not worry if he is sure of heaven because by the time he enters into life, all those things will be complete. There is no pain or death there. There is no thirst or hunger there. There is no sin there. There would be no night there. The tree of life would be there to ensure abundant life. All tears would be wiped away in heaven. However, the place is only for those who are born again. Those who have a living experience of Jesus as their Lord and Saviour. Those who do not do anything unless the Holy Spirit directs them to do it. Those who are happy reading their Bible, praying and fellowshipping with their Father. Those who are not tired of coming to the presence of the

A FRIEND ONCE TOLD ME JOKINGLY THAT, HE KNEW I WILL NOT BECOME SOMEBODY IN LIFE; BECAUSE OF THE WAY MY CALABASH WAS SMASHED AT A GYRATION CEREMONY, BY THE SUPREMOST-CHIEF OF THE PALMWINE DRINKERS CLUB IN THE UNIVERSITY.

ITS BEGINNING TO DAWN ON ME THAT, THOSE THINGS DONE JOKINGLY THEN WERE "NONENTITY AND VAGABOND" COVENANTS BEFORE A DEMON CALLED BACCHUS: THE EGYPTIAN god OF WINE; WHAT MADE ME JOIN THE CHILDREN OF BACCHUS?

Lord always. Those who have experienced God.

THE CROSS

The cross is the only ladder tall enough to reach heaven. There is no church that can throw you into heaven. There is no spiritual father or spiritual mother that can throw anyone into heaven. Every man must work out his own salvation with fear and trembling. Your position cannot take you into heaven. Your pastoral collar or ecclesiastical dress cannot take you to heaven. There are many people who would have made heaven easily if not for church posts. Some people will receive lashes from the Lord for accepting a post they knew they were not qualified for. There are many men and women who are still involved in occult practices, although they are pastors in their churches. The cross is the only ladder tall enough to reach heaven. No other ladder can get anyone there. As far as you get on that cross, and die there, you are on your way to heaven. But if with the slightest provocation, you run mad with anger, you are not on

the cross yet, and you are not going to heaven. Until you die on that cross, God does not want to have anything to do with you.

One open secret is that if you are on your way to haven, you will be busy looking for other people to take there. If somebody is not on his way to heaven, such a person will not witness to anybody, he will not be interested in winning souls for the Lord.

The way to heaven is too straight for the man who wants to walk crookedly. Once your way is crooked, you cannot walk there. Therefore, your greatest business in life is to prepare for the next life. Anything you are doing here that leaves you unprepared for heaven is a waste of time. Many people have to work harder than they doing are now if they want to make heaven. Many, who are deaf and dumb to the Holy Spirit have to pray for that deafness and dumbness to depart from their lives. Many who are going to church but their lives are not changing need to have the

touch of heaven for their lives to change, they need to cry to the Lord for a change. There are many people who want to belong to the world and still practise Christianity. Such people are not serious yet about heaven. The Bible, which is the book of God is the standard. It is not a Nigerian book, neither is it an American or British book. What the book is saying will not change. It will never bend to suit anybody rather everyone is supposed to conform to it. Some people say they can dress the way they like because they see some men and women of God dress like that. I ask them one question: "Have they looked at the book of life and found their names there?" It is better to do what God asks you to do than to copy others who will lead you astray.

A song writer says the way to heaven is a narrow pathway, where there can be no crookedness. For those who will make heaven, their yes must be yes and their nay must be nay. A man who finds heaven will find wealth and health and other things but men who run after such things first before heaven never find them. They only get into more and more trouble. Anyone who engages in sex outside marriage or extramarital affairs is in the broad way and is going to hell fire. If you are still pampering your anger or lust and the trumpet sounds, there will be no room for you to change. Stealing, lying malice, etc are things that can place you in the broad way.

Once you are sure that you are on your way to heaven, you do not have to worry about the cares of this world because that promise is always true: "Seek ye first the kingdom of heaven and his righteousness, and all these things shall be added unto you." (Matthew 6:33).

Psalm 37: 25 says, *"I have been young and now am old; yet have I not seen the righteous forsaken, nor his seed begging bread."* These are words of scriptures that can never be broken. Anyone who is not sure whether he will make heaven if the trumpet sounds now is not ready at all. Set your affection on things above.

FACTS ABOUT HELL FIRE

Hell fire is a place of unquenchable fire, a place of thirst, misery and pain. It is a place of frustration and anger, a place of separation. And a place of undiluted divine anger. It was originally prepared for satan and his host, meaning that anyone who goes there is a trespasser. It is a place created for all eternity. It is a place of consciousness; people there will know what they are doing. It is a place of torment, darkness and eternal separation from loved ones. It is a place of no return that torments the memory. It is a place of unsatisfied desires. Any Christian that ends up in hell fire will suffer a lot because the devil and his demons will be too happy to deal with him or her. Ritual killers, witches and wizards will deal with the person terribly. That is why Paul cried out in Hebrews 10:38-39: *"Now the just shall live by faith: but if any man draw back, my soul shall have no pleasure in him. But we are not of them who draw back unto perdition; but of them that believe to the saving of the soul."* So when you turn back, you go into perdition.

The issue of heaven has nothing to do with the names people bear. Those names are just like labels on the bottle. One day, the labels will be torn off and they will be seen for what they are. Then it will be clear the kind of spirit they are operating.

Hell fire a place where the wicked shall be turned into, a place where soul and body will be in suffering. The question is, are you in the narrow way or the broad way? The way in which you are travelling will decide your destination.

Luke 16:19-28 says *"There was a certain rich man, which was clothed in purple and fine linen, and fared sumptuously every day: And there was a certain beggar named Lazarus, which was laid at his gate, full of sores, And desiring to be fed with the crumbs which*

WHEN YOU HAVE NO HUNGER FOR GOD, YOU ARE STILL NOT READY FOR HEAVEN

fell from the rich man's table: moreover the dogs came and licked his sores. And it came to pass, that the beggar died, and was carried by the angels into Abraham's bosom: the rich man also died, and was buried; And in hell he lift up his eyes, being in torments, and seeth Abraham afar off, and Lazarus in his bosom. And he cried and said, Father Abraham, have mercy on me, and send Lazarus, that he may dip the tip of his finger in water, and cool my tongue; for I am tormented in this flame. But Abraham said, Son, remember that thou in thy lifetime receivedst thy good things, and likewise Lazarus evil things: but now he is comforted, and thou art tormented. And beside all this, between us and you there is a great gulf fixed: so that they which would pass from hence to you cannot; neither can they pass to us, that would come from thence. Then he said, I pray thee therefore, father, that thou wouldest send him to my father's house: For I have five brethren; that he may testify unto them, lest they also come into this place of torment."

The rich man in the above passage can be described as a very nice person. He did not want members of family to suffer. So, a nice kind man can go to hell fire. A perfect gentleman, morally correct can land in hell fire.

Luke 16:29-31 says, *"Abraham saith unto him, They have Moses and the prophets;* (that is their Bible); *let them hear them. And he said, Nay, father Abraham: but if* one went unto them from the dead, *they will repent. And he said unto him, If they hear not Moses and the prophets, neither will they be persuaded, though one rose from the dead."*

This was not a parable told by Jesus. Both men actually existed. That is why verse 19 says there was a certain rich man and verse 20 says, there was a certain beggar.

It is very dangerous to go on without being sure of your salvation. If you are not sure whether you are on your way to heaven or hell, it means that you are on your way to hell.

WHY THE RICH MAN WENT TO HELL

There are always two groups of people: candidates of heaven and candidates of hell fire. The rich man did not go to hell fire. Is it because he was rich? Abraham too was very rich yet he was in heaven. A rich man can make heaven if the money

does not become an idol to him. He did not go to hell fire because he was well dressed. Being well dressed is not a sin as far as the person's nakedness is not exposed. He did not go to hell because he ate good food. Food is only useful to the physical body. He did not go to hell fire because he had a beggar at his door for there is no human being that can look after all the beggars in the world.

Why did this man go to hell fire? The answer is found in verse 30: *"And he said, Nay, father Abraham; but if one went unto them from the dead, they will repent."* The man went to hell because he was always saying "No" to the things of God. We can see how he argued. Some people like this rich man always argue with God. Whenever God says, "Do this like this," they will do it in another way. Thousands and thousands of Christians want deliverance but do not want to keep the word of God.

Somebody who spends the least time on the things of God cannot make heaven. The person is a candidate of hell fire. Candidates of hell fire are known by the way they spend their time.

Beloved, it is time to make up your mind. Do you really have time for Jesus because each day we spend on earth takes us nearer to heaven or hell? The rich man opened his eyes and found himself in hell fire. Death is a leveler. Death cannot be bribed. Lazarus opened his eyes and found himself in the bosom of Abraham. There is nothing like purgatory, it is either you go to heaven or hell. Can you account for the way you spend your days? Do you still have time for anger, moodiness, gossiping and complaining? Do you say useless things and make purposeless visits? Do worldly things take more and more of your time? Do spiritual things take less and less of your time? The item that takes most of your time indicates where your heart is. Candidates for hell will say no to Jesus on the use of their time. They will refuse to give their lives completely. Life is a one way street. There is no repentance in the grave. If you keep saying no to what the Holy Spirit is telling you, you will end up in hell like the rich man in Luke 16.

WHO ARE THOSE WHO WANT TO GO TO HEAVEN?

There are certain signs by which they are known:

1. They do the will of their Father always. They will not allow the

THE PROPHET | David versus Goliath 21

foolish things of this world to prevent them from getting to their Father. Doing God's will comes natural to them. And once God says something, it is settled.

2. Their affection is above. There is no way the world can cage them.

2. They are fools for Christ. Isaiah 35:8 says, *"And an highway shall be there, and a way, and it shall be called The way of holiness, the unclean shall not pass over it; but it shall be for those; the wayfaring men, though fools, shall not err therein."*

3. They live holy lives. Hebrews 12:14 tells us, *"Follow peace with all men, and holiness, without which no man shall see the Lord."*

Where are you going? Is it heaven or hell? Psalm 116:15 says, *"Precious in the sight of the Lord is the death of his saints."* This is very deep. It means that some deaths are useless before God. This is the time to check up where you belong. When you begin to feel a secret selfish pride, you are not on your way to heaven yet. When you begin to feel important and independent, it means you are not on your way to heaven yet. When you begin to feel bitterness over what some people have said or done against you, you are not on your way to heaven yet. When you have no hunger for God, you are still not ready for heaven. When you do not witness to people to get born again, you are not on your way to heaven. Unteachable spirit is a sign that a person is not on the way to heaven yet. When you manifest a desire to attract attention to yourself, or you always complain, grumble and nag, you are not on your way to heaven yet. When you are compromising your attitude because nobody can see you, then you are not on your way to heaven yet. When you are selling your virtues, you are not on your way to heaven yet. It is not a sign of spiritual maturity to live above your experience. If you are still saying no to Jesus, this is the time to cry to Him. The invincible hands of death may come at any time. The fact that somebody is healthy now is not a security. The fact that there is no physical danger now is not a security. The arrows of death fly unseen at noon day. The sharpest eyes cannot see it. This is why you need to decide where you go. Confess both your secret and open sins to the Lord. Do not wait for judgment to catch up with you before you begin to repent. It may be too late. Know for sure that no matter how clever you are, your sins will eventually find you out. It will locate you where ever you are. It may take time. It is the greatest detective. Whatsoever is killing the fire of God in your soul is not something to joke with. Whatsoever is elevating carnality above spirituality for you is not something you should joke with. Be wise and choose heaven.

PRAYER POINTS

1. Any power that wants me to perish, blood of Jesus, arrest it, in the name of Jesus.

2. My Father, if I am travelling on the wrong road, deliver me, in the name of Jesus.

3. Every bewitchment upon my destiny, die, in the name of Jesus.

4. O God, arise, and separate my portion from friends who want to lead me astray, in the name of Jesus.

5. Any sin in my life, blood of Jesus, kill them, in the name of Jesus.

6. Thou power of the night working against my destiny, I bury you, in the name of Jesus.

7. Any power reciting evil against me, die, in Jesus' name.

HEAVEN AND HELL

is a message delivered at the Mountain of Fire and Miracles Ministries by the General Overseer, Dr. D.K. Olukoya.

A CALL TO SERVE

Are you a member of MFM with a burden to help the needy, are you interested in alleviating the plight of the poor or in the spread of the gospel through the sponsorship of the publication of tracts? Your resources, time and talent can be extended to several groups that are in charge of these areas. These groups include:

o   We care Ministry,
o   Mission Outreach
o   Tracts and Publications
o   Ministry to Drug addicts
o   Campus fellowship
o   Ministry to Schools
o   Ministry to Glorious Children, etc.

Thus says the Lord, "Verily I say unto you, in as much as ye have done it unto one of the least of these my brethren, ye have done it unto me" Matthew 25 : 40.

WONDERFUL JESUS!

GOD MAKES ME A MYSTERIOUS WONDER

I am a student of Mass Communication. When I went for my industrial attachment in a television house, I discovered that one needed to get recommendation from an influential person to get placement. I did not know anyone. However, I remembered that I wrote down the telephone number of a certain former Minister of Communication, which I came across in one of the dailies. I called the number severally but there was no response. But after a recent message by the General Overseer titled, "Lord, make me a mysterious wonder," I prayed and called the former Minister's number again. This time around, he picked my call and I introduced myself and told him my problem. He said that he did not know me and could not recommend me. But strangely he asked me to wait. Two minutes later, he called me and told me what to do and who to meet. That was how I got placement. Praise the Lord!

Bro. Komolafe
MFM Headquarters

DIVINE PROTECTION AND HEALING

Last year was a year of frustration and torment for me. The enemy was bent on taking my life both spiritually and physically. But after intensive prayers, the Lord turned it into a year of grace for me. Also, I fell seriously sick towards the end of the year but through prayers from the church, I got healed and was able to attend the cross over night. Praise the Lord!

Sis. Olugbamila
MFM Okokomaiko

GOD DELIVERS ME

A snake bit my hand in a dream and when I woke up, I felt the pain. I prayed seriously concerning this and the strange pain disappeared. Secondly, my child fell ill, I prayed to God and she received her healing. Also, God has been granting my husband, who is a regular traveller journey mercies. Praise the Lord!

Sis. Olamidotun
MFM Ikare

NO MORE SICKNESS

For a long time, I had a very strange sickness which defied medication. Then I decided to go for deliverance. To the glory of God, I received total healing after the deliverance. Praise the Lord!

Sis. Chris
MFM Obadore/Akesan

FRUIT OF THE WOMB AFTER 6 YEARS

I was childless for six years. I attended many church programmes and prayers but nothing happened until I met the General Overseer, who prayed for me and prophesied that I would carry my baby. By the awesome power of God,

I took in and was delivered of a bouncing baby. Praise the Lord.

Sis. Bukola
MFM Headquarters

PROPHETIC UTTERANCE

Recently, the pastor prayed for me and my family and made prophetic utterances concerning us. Very soon after that, I was blessed materially and also received international benefits from Spain. Praise the Lord!

Sis. Ify
MFM Kampala, Uganda

GOD GRANTS US TOTAL DELIVERANCE, BREAKTHROUGH AND HEALING

I went for deliverance in this church and the Lord delivered me from serpentine spirit, long term strange movement in the body and the strongman that has hindered my breakthroughs for a long time. The Lord also healed my mother of a long term illness. Praise the Lord!

Sis. Mary
MFM Abeokuta

HEAT INSIDE THE HEAD DISAPPEARS

I was directed to undergo deliverance in this church. The first day I started the programme, I experienced serious purging. Then I prayed and prophesied to myself that it must stop on its own and it did. Secondly, I used to have terrible heat inside my head. To the glory of God, during the deliverance progromme, I was completely healed. Praise the Lord!

Bro. Emma
MFM Ibusa

DIVINE INTERVENTION

I pursued a job for a long time but could not get it because of some evil competitors. I went for a deliverance programme because of the issue. The last time I travelled to Abuja for the business, I was told that three of those blocking me have been transferred and one was dead. I was given the job. Also, recently, after a Power Must Change Hands programme, one of the telecommunication companies requested for a space on my plot of land for their site. I accepted and was paid a huge sum of money for the space. Praise the Lord!

Bro. Nelson,
MFM Orisumbare

GOD CANCELS EVIL MANIPULATIONS

Recently, as I was driving along Victory Estate road, suddenly my car knocked down a five-year old boy and he died. But to the glory of God, he was revived after series of prayers. Praise the Lord!

Bro. Akinyemi
MFM Iba

NOW ON SALE

At last! The two long awaited books are back on the stand. Ever potent for all your deliverance and prosperity needs. Hurry now for your copies Stock is limited. Price N170 each.

Hello Children!

Your popular Spiritual tonic "Junior Fire in the Word" Is on the stand again. It is still as refreshing as ever. Now you have more opportunities to win Fanstastic prizes every month as you send in your entries Hurry grab your copy from the vendors. The price is still N20.

FIRE IN THE WORD, is a weekly Spiritual Bulletin of the Mountain of Fire and Miracles Ministries, published by Tracts and Publications Group. All Enquiries should be addressed to The Editor, Mountain of Fire Magazine, 13, Olasimbo Street, off Olumo Road, Onike, P.O. Box 2990, Sabo Yaba, Lagos, Nigeria. Telephone 01- 867439, 864631, 868766, 08023180236.E-mail: mfmtractsandpublications@yahoo.com Copyright reserved.

FIRE IN THE WORD

Ye Shall Know the Truth, and the Truth Shall Make You Free (John 8:32)

ISSN 1595 - 7314   Vol. 12   No. 34   Sun. 29th June - Sat. 5th July, 2008

The Principles of
HEARING FROM GOD

My year of unprecedented greatness and unmatchable increase
Deuteronomy 28:13, Psalm 71:21, Ephesians 3:20, Psalm 92:10

This week, we are looking at the message entitled, "The principles of hearing from God.". Revelation 2:7 says, *"He that hath an ear let him hear what the Spirit saith unto the churches..."* God the creator of man knows that man has two ears to hear, and yet He says, "He that hath an ear let him hear." It shows that He is not talking about just physical hearing. It means that somebody can hear but is not listening.

The most important need of any serious child of God is hearing clearly from God. When you begin to hear from God, progress will begin in your life. The reverse is also true. When you begin to hear from the devil, destruction begins. It is a great period in your life the day you learn to hear God's voice clearly, and on daily basis. In fact, when God begins to talk to you, this transient world will lose its hold upon you. What other people run after and want to die for will make no meaning to you. When you begin to hear God, faith will rise in your heart. When you begin to hear God, you will stop doubting. Things will begin to happen; you begin to enjoy prayer because you are communicating with God. Communication with God satisfies the deepest longing of the human heart and God's heart also.

We are created to fellowship and talk with our Creator. Children of God need to be able to hear clearly from the Lord their God. Hearing God's voice does not come automatically. The Adamic nature is born deaf to the voice of God. Therefore, for most people, hearing God's voice has to be learnt. As a matter of fact, the key to all God's blessing is hearing and obeying His voice. One of the greatest diseases among Christians these days is inability to hear clearly what God is saying. Many people roam around the house of prophets because they cannot hear what God is saying by themselves.

God wants all His children to be able to communicate freely with Him. God expected to be communicating with the Israelites but the first time God spoke, they felt His voice was thunderous. So, they told Moses to be talking to God on their behalf. They technically relinquished their privileges unto Moses. Unfortunately, today, we have many Christians who go about from one man of God to another to pray for them. They do not realise that if they would consecrate their lives and be serious with their Maker, He would open their eyes and begin to talk to them. They would discover to their amazement that they are much better than some of the prophets they have been visiting for help. The problem is that they have refused to discover themselves.

God asked Moses to select some people who would be assisting him and Moses did so. However, they

FOR THE NAME OF JESUS TO BE POWERFUL IN A PERSON'S MOUTH, IT MUST BE THROUGH FIRSTHAND KNOWLEDGE

were some people who were not invited to the party but they spiritually gatecrashed into it. Numbers 11:25-29 says, *"And the Lord came down in a cloud, and spake unto him, and took of the spirit that was upon him, and gave it unto the seventy elders; and it came to pass, that, when the spirit rested upon them, they prophesied, and did not cease. But there remained two of the men in the camp, the name of the one was Eldad, and the name of the other Medad: and the spirit rested upon them: and they were of them that were written, but went not out unto the tabernacle; and they prophesied in the camp. And there ran a young man, and told Moses, and said, Eldad and Medad do prophesy in the camp. And Joshua the son of Nun, the servant of Moses, one of his young men, answered and said, My Lord Moses, forbid them. And Moses said unto him, Enviest thou for my sake? Would God that all the Lord's people were prophets and that the Lord would put his spirit upon them!"* Moses was saying that life would have been a lot easier if they could all hear from God.

HOW DOES GOD COMMUNICATE?

God speaks to people in three ways:

1. Through revelation.
2. Through inspiration.
3. Through illumination.

DELIVERANCE CASE (THE STORY OF MY LIFE - PART 21)

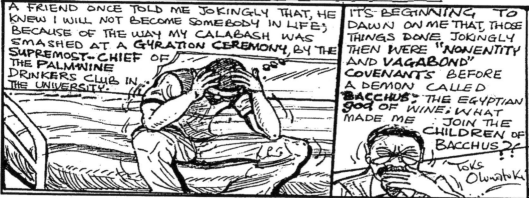

Revelation is when God reveals something to you.

Inspiration is when the anointing of the Holy Spirit falls upon you and things that were not clear to you start to become clear. Illumination is when God opens your understanding beyond your own capacity. Those are the three methods by which God communicates.

DIVINE GUIDANCE

Without the guidance of God in life and service, we would miss our divine target. It is not possible to do God's will when you do not even know what He wants you to do. If God opens the eyes of some people and shows them who they are, and they see a little bit of the glory of their destiny, they will not commit sin again because they will see that all the sins they are committing are dulling the sword of their destiny. Many people struggled to enter into the university but before they even got into the place, the enemy has already finished their destiny perhaps while they were still in the secondary school. So, no

matter what degree they get, they will have problems because they have already played into the hands of the enemy. Anything done outside the will of God is a wasted effort and will lead to a wasted destiny.

Knowing God's will is the root to a straight path in life. The desperate need of today is hearing clearly from God. In those days, it was "Speak Lord for your servant is hearing." But now it is, "Hear Lord for your servant is speaking." It is the reverse. We need to wake up and know what to do. If you want to hear from God clearly and you are serious about it, there are some questions you must answer. Job 42:5 says, *"I have heard of thee by the hearing of the ear: but now mine eye seeth thee."*

QUESTIONS TO ANSWER IF YOU WANT TO HEAR CLEARLY FROM GOD

1. **Do you have an unforgettable encounter with the Lord?** That

is the first question you should ask yourself. Have you been visited by God Almighty? The question is not how many churches you have attended? It is not whether you are a pastor or which important post in church do you hold? The question is not whether you come from a Christian home or not. The question is, have you had an unforgettable encounter with the Lord? Can you honestly say like Job that you have seen the Lord? Have you met the Lord? That is the question. If you meet the Lord, you will know that you had an encounter. You will know that something happened to you. I know the day it happened to me. The question is not whether you have been baptised or gone through deliverance. Many people who go for deliverance are not born again because if they are born again, some of the things they are saying God should remove will not be there. Have you met the Lord? If your answer is yes, the next question is:

2. **How did you meet Him?** Was it in singing, preaching or praying?

What date was it? Do you have a record of it? Can you point to an instance in your life, when you can say, "Yes, I met the Lord?" Unfortunately, many churchgoers are secondhand disciples. When you have an encounter with God, you would want to be with Him always. You do not talk about loneliness because His communication with you satisfies the longing of your heart. You will not be satisfied with a third party telling you about Him. It is one thing to have somebody telling you about the Lord, it is another thing to have a personal encounter with Him. The majority of the present-day believers are secondhand variety of Christians. For you to have effective power in your life, it must be a firsthand matter, one on one with God. A secondhand relationship with God would make you a prey in the hands of demons. The sons of Sceva had only a secondhand knowledge; they went to that demonic person, and said, "In the name of Jesus whom Paul preacheth" not whom they preach, "Come out!" The demons knew more than the sons of Sceva. So, they overpowered them. The lack of power in the church today is due to the fact that most Christians in church do not have a firsthand encounter with God. For the name of Jesus to be powerful in a person's mouth, it must be through firsthand knowledge. The person must be able to hear clearly from the Lord.

Every Christian can and should know how to hear the voice of God.

The spiritual growth of any Christian who does not hear from God will be stunted. Hearing from God is not something for spiritual giants alone. God wants all His people to experience daily communion with Him. As far as God is concerned, it is abnormal for a Christian not to hear His voice. But the good news of the scripture according to Hebrew 13:8 is this: *"Jesus Christ the same yesterday, today and forever"*

God communicates with man through his spirit. God speaks to a man's spirit and not his brain. He communicates with the inner man deep inside. The core of his being that is where he begins to hear God speaking. The Bible says, "The spirit of man is the candle of the Lord…" (Proverbs 20:27). He speaks to the spirit inside man and the spirit talks to him. Unfortunately, there are many people who do not hear from God at all. It is very dangerous for somebody's spiritual monitor to be dead.

There are various ways through which human beings communicate among themselves. Likewise, there are various ways through which God communicates with men.

ANYTIME GOD GIVES YOU INSTRUCTION AND YOU CARRY IT OUT IMMEDIATELY, HE WILL BE WILLING TO TALK TO YOU AGAIN.

VEHICLES OF DIVINE COMMUNICATION

1. Face to Face. He spoke to Adam and Moses this way. You may say it is impossible. But as far as God is concerned nothing is impossible.

2. By voice.

3. By dreams. Unfortunately, this is the area where most people have become experts. But the disadvantage of dreams is that you must sleep before you dream. Sometimes, we find ourselves in situations where we need to hear from God instantly. In that case, dream becomes unhelpful.

4. Open vision. This is when you see what is going on without sleeping or closing your eyes.

5. Close vision. This is when you are praying and you are seeing something.

6. Trance.

7. By angels. Angels are still moving around these days to talk to us.

8. By writing.

9. By miracles.

10. Through the written word.

11. Reference to passages. Sometimes, while praying, a Bible passage could drop into your spirit without your thinking about it before, and when you open it, it will minister to you.

12. Anointed messages and teachings. Sometimes, during services, God ministers to people's needs during the course of the message for that day.

13. Anointed counselling.

14. Walking with holy men and women.

15. Anointed music.

16. Anointed meditation.

17. The conscience. Everybody has a conscience. Anytime you are doing something bad, your conscience will prick you. Whether you are a Christian or not, you have a conscience. Your conscience is the policeman of your soul. The voice of your conscience is the voice of God. And if you allow your conscience to be incubated by the Holy Spirit, it will be talking to you clearly from the Lord.

18. Burden of the heart.

19. Divine ideas.

20. Intuition. This is instinctive knowledge; knowing something without having to discover or perceive it.

21. Internal understanding.

22. Impression of the heart.

23. Inward witness.

24. Inner voice.

25. Outer voice.

26. Closed outer voice. This is when you are the only one hearing the voice like the case of Samuel. Samuel heard the voice of the Lord but Eli who was sleeping a few feet away from him did not hear it.

27. Still small voice.

28. Sudden impulse.

29. Favourable and positive circumstances.

30. Difficult circumstances.

31. Word of wisdom.

32. Word of knowledge.

33. Faith.

34. Healing.

35. Working of miracles.

36. Prophecy.

37. Discerning of spirit.

38. Interpretation of tongues.

39. Remembering the truth.

40. Intercession from within.

41. Conclusive evidence. The Bible says, "By their fruit, ye shall know them" (Matthew 7:16)

42. Divine visitation.

Man is body, soul and spirit. Proverbs 20:27 says, *"The spirit of man is the candle of the LORD, searching all the inward parts of the belly."* 1 Corinthians 2:11 says, *"For what man knoweth the things of a man, save the spirit of man which is in him? Even so the things of God knoweth no man, but the Spirit of God."*

So, God normally speaks to our spirit, He informs our spirit and our spirit passes the information to our mind. The human spirit has a voice. That voice is what people call conscience. The conscience of somebody who is not born again is unregenerated and an unsafe guide. But the conscience of somebody who is born again, and is growing spiritually through the word of God and regular prayer will know how to catch information from God.

Isaiah 30:15 says, *"For thus saith the LORD God, the Holy One of Israel; In returning and rest shall ye be saved; In quietness and in confidence shall be your strength;"* Ecclesiastes 3:7 says, *"A time to rend and a time to sew: a time to keep silence, and a time to speak."* Quietness or stillness is essential to receiving information from God. If your life is too noisy, you will not know when God is speaking.

THE PROPHET | David versus Goliath 21

WHAT TO DO SO THAT YOU CAN HEAR THE VOICE OF GOD

1. Make sure you have a living encounter with God.
2. Cultivate the habit of prompt obedience to the Lord. The longer you delay in obeying God, the harder it becomes. Lot delayed in obedience and that was his undoing. Be prepared to look foolish in the eyes of the people. The Bible says, to become truly wise you have to start by becoming a fool. Noah was building an ark on dry land. It was a very foolish thing but it was the wisdom of God. Therefore, when God says do something, do it very quickly. If you do not do it or delay in doing it, He may not talk to you again. His voice may not come the clear way it used to come to you again. Anytime God gives you instruction and you carry it out immediately, He will be willing to talk to you again. What He may ask you to do may look foolish but once He has spoken, you must obey. Naaman was asked to go to River Jordan. It looked very foolish but it was the wisdom of God.
3. Be careful what you listen to. Do not listen to gossips and slander. Do not keep the kind of friends that will pull down your spiritual life.
4. Take time to meditate deeply. Joshua 1:8 says, *"This book of the law shall not depart out of thy mouth; but thou shalt meditate therein day and night..."* Meditation is very important.
5. Receive the baptism of the Holy Spirit. If you have not received the baptism of the Holy Spirit with the evidence of speaking in tongues, you better do so very quickly. Without the baptism of the Holy Spirit, your prayer life will be low. Every believer should have it. The Bible says, "These signs shall follow them that believe, in my name shall they cast out devils; they shall speak with new tongues"(Mark 16:17).
6. Receive the gifts of the Holy Ghost. These gifts are different from the baptism of the Holy Ghost.
7. Do not judge people by what you see with your physical eyes. If you do that, you will not hear God.
8. Always pray fervently. If it is only two minutes you have to pray, do it fervently. God is satisfied with somebody who wakes up by 12 midnight and prays for 10-15 minutes with full concentration and power than a person, who does three hours sleeping and waking up.

Every believer must have at least one way by which God talks to him or her regularly. It is therefore important for you to take a decisive action that would remove all blockages to hearing God's voice. You need to hear clearly from God so that you will be able to fulfill your divine destiny.

PRAYER POINTS

1. My Father, I want to see you, appear, in the name of Jesus.
2. Spiritual blindness and deafness, die, in the name of Jesus.
3. My Father, I want to experience your power, in the name of Jesus.
4. Every power of my father's house that wants me to die in this condition, die, in the name of Jesus.
5. Every power of my mother's house that wants me to die in this condition, die, in the name of Jesus.

THE PRINCIPLES OF HEARING FROM GOD
is a message delivered at the Mountain of Fire and Miracles Ministries by the General Overseer, Dr. D.K. Olukoya.

A CALL TO SERVE
Are you a member of MFM with a burden to help the needy, are you interested in alleviating the plight of the poor or in the spread of the gospel through the sponsorship of the publication of tracts? Your resources, time and talent can be extended to several groups that are in charge of these areas. These groups include:
o   We care Ministry,
o   Mission Outreach
o   Tracts and Publications
o   Ministry to Drug addicts
o   Campus fellowship
o   Ministry to Schools
o   Ministry to Glorious Children, etc.
Thus says the Lord, "Verily I say unto you, in as much as ye have done it unto one of the least of these my brethren, ye have done it unto me" Matthew 25 : 40.

WONDERFUL JESUS!

GREAT DELIVERANCE

For many years I was having sex with my mother in the dream but since I came here and have been fasting and praying, God has delivered me. I had a vision where I saw her running after four men. Later, I saw her again but this time she had been stabbed to death. Since then the satanic dream has stopped. Praise the Lord!

Bro. Aina
MFM Iju

DELIVERED FROM MYSTERIOUS BODY WEAKNESS

I have been suffering from general weakness of the body for some years before the PMCH of 07/07/07. At that programme, the G.O. prayed on anointing oil and water. Immediately I drank some of the oil, there was a churning in my stomach and I went to the toilet to ease myself. After that I became whole immediately. I have been very strong ever since and the satanic body weakness has disappeared. Praise the Lord!

Sis. Uche
MFM Upper Mission Benin City

DIVINE PROTECTION

I thank God who delivered us from the wicked hands of armed robbers. On our way to Lagos, they jumped out from the bush and tried to stop our driver but he drove off. Other vehicles behind us were trapped and robbed, while we left unhurt and untouched. Glory be to God!

Bro. Mozea
MFM Ibusa

GOD SAVES A LOST MAN

A drunkard entered the church one Sunday morning during service and sat beside me. The stench of alcohol enveloped me and other people around. The Spirit of God led me to ask him if he had a Bible and he said no. I quickly ran home, got some money and bought a Bible for him. I encouraged him to surrender his life to Christ and attend church programmes. To the glory of God, the man is now born again and a full and active member of this ministry. Praise the Lord!

Bro. Edwin
MFM Omiyale, Ejigbo

GREAT DELIVERANCE

For sometime, some animals have been killing my chicken. I started praying seriously about it and about two weeks later, I noticed a dead snake by the side of the poultry area. A close look revealed that the head of the dead snake has been bruised by the chicken that are in the mini poultry cage. This is miraculous. Praise the Lord!

Sis. Barnabas
MFM Ughelli

DIVINE PROVISION

I joined MFM in 2001, jobless. I went into a covenant with God to be faithful in paying tithes. The Lord provided a job for me. Due to my faithfulness, the windows of heaven have remained permanently opened unto me. The Lord also delivered me and my family from a demonic house after aggressive prayers. Praise God!

Sis. Mgbakor
MFM Iju

SEVEN YEARS HEADACHE GONE

The enemy afflicted me with a serious headache for over seven years. I was introduced to this church and after counselling, I went for deliverance. After the deliverance programme, the Lord healed me of the long term affliction. Praise the Lord!

Bro. Matthew
MFM Morogbo

GOD AVERTS DISASTER

Recently, I received an urgent call to return home immediately. On getting home, I discovered that our neighbour's building had collapsed. It affected our own house but nothing happened to my children. Praise the Lord!

Sis. Cecelia
MFM Ogudu/Ojota

GOD IS MARVELLOUS

I thank God for my daughter. She got a super distinction in her examinations. God healed two men whom I prayed for, one with a swollen throat and another with a sick hand. Finally, God saved me from an accident. Praise the Lord!

Bro. Andrew
MFM Kampala, Uganda

NOW ON SALE

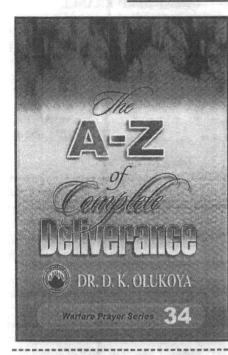

At last! The two long awaited books are back on the stand. Ever potent for all your deliverance and prosperity needs. Hurry now for your copies Stock is limited. Price N170 each.

FIRE IN THE WORD, is a weekly Spiritual Bulletin of the Mountain of Fire and Miracles Ministries, published by Tracts and Publications Group. All Enquiries should be addressed to The Editor, Mountain of Fire Magazine, 13, Olasimbo Street, off Olumo Road, Onike, P.O. Box 2990, Sabo Yaba, Lagos, Nigeria. Telephone 01- 867439, 864631, 868766, 08023180236. E-mail: mfmtractsandpublications@yahoo.com Copyright reserved.

FIRE IN THE WORD

Ye Shall Know the Truth, and the Truth Shall Make You Free (John 8:32)

ISSN 1595 - 7314 Vol. 12 No. 35 Sun. 13th - Sat. 19th July, 2008

WATCHING THE SERPENT OF THE MAGICIAN

My year of unprecedented greatness and unmatchable increase
Deuteronomy 28:13, Psalm 71:21, Ephesians 3:20, Psalm 92:10

This week, we are looking at the message entitled, "Watching the serpent of the magician."

This message is for those who are tired of frustration and those who are tired of watching unbelievers collecting what they are supposed to get. It is also for those who are determined that a transaction must happen in the heavens that would turn things around for good in their lives.

Exodus 7:9-10 says, *"When Pharaoh shall speak unto you, saying Shew a miracle for you: then, thou shalt say unto Aaron, Take thy rod, and cast it before Pharaoh, and it shall become a serpent. And Moses and Aaron went in unto Pharaoh, and they did so as the Lord had commanded: and Aaron cast down his rod before pharaoh, and before his servants, and it became a serpent."* Pharaoh was not afraid; he was not perturbed by the actions of Moses and Aaron, meaning that the conversion of things was not new to Pharaoh.

Exodus 7:11-12 says, *"Then Pharaoh also called the wise men and the sorcerers: now the magicians of Egypt, they also did in like manner with their enchantments.* (That is they duplicated what Moses did but that was not the end) *for they cast down every man his rod, and they became serpents; but Aaron's rod swallowed up their rods,"*

This is one of the most interesting passages in the Old Testament. It opens our eyes to many deep spiritual truths. It exposes certain things to us that may not be very clear to the modern man. My prayer is that God will deliver Christians from ignorance.

In Nigeria, one regular feature of street magic in the past was the public display of serpents. Many people gather and watch this magic. But most of the spectators do not know that this kind of activity is a satanic strategy to collect virtues. However, there are some intercessors and prayer warriors who pray these people out of business. All the places where these magicians normally operate lack development.

I had a friend, a young brother who took up a ministry, which was a ministry to frustrate magicians. So anytime he was passing by and saw any magician performing, he would join the spectators. As the magicians made their incantations, he would say, "I frustrate it, in Jesus' name. I trample upon it and it would not come to pass, in Jesus' name." They would try and nothing would work for them that day. So, when they saw that they were having problems, they would stop the magic and look around the spectators, point out all

IT IS A DANGEROUS THING TO STAND AROUND WATCHING THE SERPENT OF THE MAGICIANS

the grey-headed people and chase them away. They believed it was old people who had sufficient power to stop what they were doing whereas the fellow causing the confusion was just 22 years old. It was the operation of people like that young brother that reduced the number of magicians in our streets.

Thousands of people are initiated into occultism just by watching magic. Unfortunately, many Christians do not know that the display of magic that took place in the parlour of Pharaoh is the same as what goes on in our streets, and many do not know how to counter them.

LESSONS FROM THE SCRIPTURES (Exodus 7:9-12)

1. **There are three kinds of power:** Positive power, negative power and neutral power. The rod of Moses was the positive power. The rod of the magicians was the negative power. And the human beings who were there represent the neutral power, meaning that it is to whom you yield yourself to obey that controls you. So, a man can be negatively or positively powered.

2. **There are only two major sources of spiritual power:** The power of God and the power of darkness.

3. **There is something known as the power of darkness:** Whether you believe it or not, it is not relevant. It is wrong to teach people

DELIVERANCE CASE (THE STORY OF MY LIFE - PART 22)

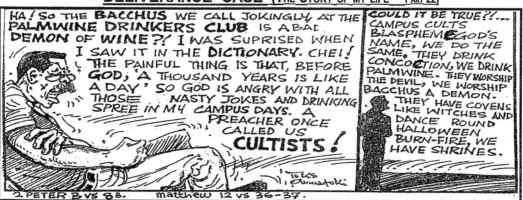

that the enemy has no power. A lot of people are jumping up and proclaiming that some powers are under their feet. But the enemy can only be under your feet if your own head is under the feet of Jesus. If not, you are just wasting your time.

4. There is something known as the hour of darkness: The hour may expire but before that, the magic would have worked. By the time Moses got to a certain level, the hour of darkness expired and their magic could no longer work.

5. There are satanic intermediaries: In that scripture, we see three categories of people; the wise men, the sorcerers, and the magicians. These are human beings and not spirits. There are many of them around us.

6. The power of God can be counterfeited: A person can work signs and wonders that do not originate from God. The devil can cause healing to take place when he is the one responsible for the sickness. So, he can take it from

somebody and give it to another person. Moses threw down his rod and Pharaoh's magicians did the same thing.

7. There is a serpent of darkness and there is also a serpent of God: You can read more about the serpent of God in Amos 9.

8. These two serpents are at war: But one serpent has the power to swallow the other.

9. When a weaker power comes against a stronger power, the weaker power must bow.

10. There is something known as the mystery of serpent against serpent: When serpents were biting the Israelites in the wilderness and Moses cried unto the Lord, the solution was another serpent. That is using the coin of the enemy to pay back the enemy.

11. There is a group of people called the evil wise men: They are the people who follow people's stars. They have evil

intelligence. The Bible recommends that we should pray that such people should be turned backward.

12. There is a group of people called sorcerers and magicians: The recommended Bible prayer against them is to speak madness upon them. The Bible says, "That turneth their wise men backward and maketh their knowledge foolish" (Isaiah 44:25).

13. Spiritual warfare is not entertainment: It is real war.

14. The palace is the centre of satanic operation: That is why people who come from royal families have royal pollution and they need royal deliverance. The palace of Pharaoh was the arena of the battle of the serpents, and he was there watching them. So, the palace is a place of power as well as an axis of evil.

15. The contest of the serpents was a violent one: It ended in tragedy for the dark serpents. The result of the encounter was total destruction for the dark party. Elijah dealt with 850 prophets of Baal with violent prayers.

16. Your former colleagues in the dark kingdom will be your first confronters when you turn to God: The magicians who faced Moses were his former colleagues when he was in the palace. So, when Moses came along, they thought it was still the same kind of power they knew that Moses was still operating. But when Moses got to a higher level, they said to Pharaoh, "This is the finger of God." They owned up that they were facing a higher power.

17. If you stand around to watch the serpent of the magician, you will die: This is a very important point. All those who watched the battle of the serpents eventually had problems. Although Moses was the one that threw down the rod, he did not get to the Promised Land. Aaron, the bearer of the rod did not get there. Pharaoh himself ended up dead in the Red Sea. So, it is a dangerous thing to stand around watching the serpents of the magicians. If you stand around to watch these serpents, you will die.

WHAT IN PRACTICAL SPIRITUAL TERMS DOES IT MEAN TO WATCH THE SERPENT OF THE MAGICIAN?

If you have ever been served food in your dream and you could not resist it, you are watching the serpent of the magician. If you cannot resist spirit spouses when they come to you in the dream; they succeed in messing you up, you are watching the serpent. If in your dream, some people were running after you with all kinds of weapons and when they used them against you, they worked, you are watching the serpent. Inability to resist spiritual arrows indicates that you are watching the serpent of the magician. It is time for you to cry out in anger that the fire of God should burst forth in your life, it is time for you to pray that God should make you hot coals of fire, too hot for the enemy to move close to. It is time to pray to receive the fire that no evil power can resist. Whatsoever affects your spiritual life negatively and leaves you helpless and you just become a spectator, is a killer. You must deal with it.

MARKS OF THOSE WHO ARE WATCHING THE SERPENTS

1. Inability to resist spiritual arrows.
2. Inability to come against dream attackers.
3. Weakness in the face of spiritual attacks.
4. Lack of knowledge of the operation of evil powers.
5. Inability to fight and win. When you are tired of evil attacks and drop your prayers because anytime you pray them, you will be attacked, you are watching the serpent of the magician.
6. Inability to fight back.
7. Lack of knowledge of the identity of the serpent.
8. When the enemy is using your body to test new spiritual weapons, you are watching the serpent of the magician.
9. When you engage in watching dangerous and strange sights, you are watching the serpent of the magician.
10. Anytime the weapons of the enemy prosper in a person's life or the enemy disarms a person, the person is watching the serpent of the magician.
11. When you are completely ignorant of the kind of warfare that you are fighting, you are watching the serpent of the magician.
12. When your words do not carry weight in heaven or on earth, you are watching the serpent of the magician.

That is why you need to cry out and declare that the lion of your life must roar, and fear must enter into the camp of your enemies. And the fear must cause a scattering. Your life should roar and let the enemy scatter.

SPIRITUAL LAZINESS IS A GREAT SIN OF THE MODERN MAN

WHY DO PEOPLE BECOME SPECTATORS AT THE ARENA OF THE SERPENTS OF THE MAGICIANS?

1. Ignorance.

2. **Worldliness:** Many sisters are becoming more and more worldly. They wear transparent clothes even on Sundays. Some wear the kind of blouses that expose their chests. Worldliness makes the serpent to rage. Some threw away their giant earrings and replaced them with tiny ones. It is worldliness. If God wanted you to put on earrings, He would have punched your ears from your mother's womb. If God wanted men and women to be smoking cigarettes, He would have put chimneys on their heads from the womb. So, God knows what He is doing. He is a God of perfection but many Christians do not understand what they are doing. Occultists would design jewelry and believers who are supposed to have knowledge would buy and put it on. And after they have put it on, they begin to sing, "Spirit husband, go back to your sender, go back to your

sender." Who is the sender? The spirit husband will not go because his material is on their body. Wearing of earrings started with slavery. An earring in one ear indicated that the wearer belonged to one slave master. Two meant two slave masters, you served one in the morning; and the other one in the evening. When slavery eased out, the slaves who were ashamed in the market place or wherever they were, began to use something to block those holes. So, Christians who use these things are copying slavery.

3. **Lack of internal peace:** Your peace of mind is your proof of victory. Jesus commanded peace during the storm and there was peace. That was the evidence of His authority. When the powers of darkness did their worst with Jesus at the parlour of Pilate, He was cool, calm and collected. If you do not have peace in your life, you have war

and if you have victory, you have peace. That is why the Bible says, "The God of peace shall bruise satan under your feet (Romans 16:20).

4. **Unbelief:** This prevents a person from resting in God.

5. **Lack of recognition of the authority in Christ.**

6. **Attack by forces of evil renewal:** This is talking about the powers that wake up things that are already dead.

7. **Laziness:** Lazy people do not begin things. Sometimes, they will agree to do a thing only to put it off. Little by little, they surrender until it becomes total defeat. Lazy people never get going. Procrastination is the child of laziness. People who never develop a sense of urgency about life drift from one action to another. Some people are too lazy to pray, read the Bible and witness. They do not face what they are supposed to face. They do not contribute much to other people's lives. That is why it is a disaster in marriage when one partner is lazy. The whole family may lie in poverty because one party is too lazy. The lazy man is always restless. He wants more but does not want to put in more. The lazy man is a useless person because he will not do what he is supposed to do. If you are lazy, God cannot use you in His plan. If you are lazy, you will continue to be a servant to others all your life. A lazy man is an unbeliever. He has no faith. He would say, "Ah, this is

THE PROPHET | David versus Goliath 22

wonderful but I won't be able to do it." A lazy person would be poor. So, spiritual laziness is the number one factor that turns people to spectators in the arena of the battle of the serpent. When a person is spiritually lazy, he would have deep hatred for anything that would make him sit down and read the Bible or pray. He would have deep hatred for anything that would move his spiritual life forward. When a lazy man begins a spiritual exercise, all of a sudden, other things that he has left undone will begin to surface and call for his attention. When a lazy man engages in a spiritual exercise, whether Bible study or prayer, something inside him would ask him to stop. The lazy man turns about on his bed but does not get out of it. And eventually, when he is out of that bed, he would wish to go back there. The lazy man would sleep at 10.00pm and still feel too lazy to get up at 7.00am. He would sleep half the day and waste the major part of the day watching television. He is too lazy to nourish even his own spiritual life. Spiritual laziness is a great sin of the modern man. All forms of dryness in spiritual life can be blamed on laziness. Sometimes, poor attendance to church services is due to laziness. This is why you need to pray that the Lord should deliver you from anything that would sit you down in the arena of the battle of the serpents and make you a mere spectator.

If you keep watching the serpent, a time would come when the serpent would travel to your direction and bite you. Today, come to terms with yourself, confront your laziness and weakness. Pray that your zeal and fire should come to the boiling point. When you are burning hot with the fire of God, no demon can come near you.

If you have not yet surrendered your life to Jesus, then you cannot deal with the serpent of the magician disturbing your destiny. If you want to give your life to Christ, please say the following prayer:

"Father, in the name of Jesus, I come before you now, I acknowledge that I am a sinner. Forgive my sins and cleanse me with your blood. I renounce the devil and all his works. Come into my life Lord Jesus and take control of my life, in Jesus' name. Amen.

PRAYER POINTS

1. My life, explode by fire, in the name of Jesus.
2. My life, burst forth, in the name of Jesus.

3. Thou suppressing power, die, in the name of Jesus.
4. O serpent of God, arise, kill the serpent of my father's house, in the name of Jesus.
5. My life roar like a lion and kill your problems, in the name of Jesus.
6. Every good thing that has passed me by, come back and locate me, in the name of Jesus.
7. Every foundational power sitting on my wealth, die, in the name of Jesus.
8. Every power that has vowed to die instead of allowing me to have my breakthrough, what are you waiting for? Die, in the name of Jesus.
9. Serpent of God, swallow any serpent monitoring my life, in Jesus' name.
10. O God arise, kill every serpent of my father's house, in the name of Jesus.
11. My spirit man, be charged with the fire of God that no enemy can touch, in the name of Jesus.
12. You lion of my life, roar by fire, pursue your pursuers, in the name of Jesus.

WATCHING THE SERPENT OF THE MAGICIAN is a message delivered at the Mountain of Fire and Miracles Ministries by the General Overseer, Dr. D.K. Olukoya.

A CALL TO SERVE

Are you a member of MFM with a burden to help the needy, are you interested in alleviating the plight of the poor or in the spread of the gospel through the sponsorship of the publication of tracts? Your resources, time and talent can be extended to several groups that are in charge of these areas. These groups include:

o   We care Ministry,
o   Mission Outreach
o   Tracts and Publications
o   Ministry to Drug addicts
o   Campus fellowship
o   Ministry to Schools
o   Ministry to Glorious Children, etc.

Thus says the Lord, "Verily I say unto you, in as much as ye have done it unto one of the least of these my brethren, ye have done it unto me" Matthew 25 : 40.

WONDERFUL JESUS!

GOD INTERVENES

I got information that sister and her husband had accommodation problem. I went to them and prayed with them for God's intervention. To the glory of God, our prayers were answered and they now have their own place. Praise the Lord!

Bro. Ignatius
MFM Egan

EVIL POWER OF MY FATHER'S HOUSE DISGRACED

I took my daughter to my village when she was 3 years old and both of us slept in my father's bedroom. That day, she urinated on the bed and since then she started bed-wetting up until she was 21 years old and a student of Delta State University. I did not allow her to stay in the hostel because of her predicament. Rather she was staying with my sister, and the bed-wetting persisted. I appealed to my sister to bear with us. When she came to Lagos, I took her for deliverance and after the deliverance she developed rashes. Though she was disturbed but I knew that she had been fully delivered. Suddenly my step-mother who never talked to me nor called me for years telephoned me and said that the bedsheet that was supposed to be given to me after the death of my father suddenly caught fire and I said glory be to God. Since that day, the bed-wetting stopped. Praise the Lord!

Bro. Charles
MFM Headquarters

DELIVERED FROM TUBERCULOSIS

My sister had chronic tuberculosis which defied all medication. A lot of money was spent on the case but all was to no avail. But to the glory of God, during the "Enough is enough" programme organized here, my sister received her complete deliverance and healing. Praise the Lord!

Sis. Uzoma
MFM Ajangbadi

DIVINE FAVOUR

Recently, after a service, a sister gave me a sealed envelope. When I opened it, I found the sum of ten thousand naira. Praise the Lord!

Sis. Sarah
MFM Upper Mission, Benin city

SAVED FROM ARMED ROBBERS

I thank the Lord because He stood by me when I needed Him. I was on official assignment to the bank to pay some money and suddenly, two armed robbers appeared and held me hostage at gun point. But as they were about to accomplish their evil mission, a police patrol team appeared and the robbers disappeared into thin air. Praise the Lord!

Sis. Adenubi
MFM Alagbole

DREAM INVADERS DESTROYED

I rarely dreamt and when I did at all, I would not remember. So, I was counselled to go for deliverance. Immediately I started the programme, God restored my dream life. I now dream with a lot of revelation from God. My life has moved forward. Praise the Lord!

Bro. Ubuo
MFM Festac

GOD OF DIVINE SOLUTION

Sometime ago, my daughter woke up from sleep and complained of earache and sore throat. I anointed her mouth and throat with my anointing oil which I obtained from the Prayer City, and she was healed. Praise the Lord!

Sis. Ese
MFM Ughelli

GOD RESTORES MY HAND

Few years ago, I went to the mill, where I fell and broke my right hand. I was taken a native doctor to help restore the hand but all the efforts of the native doctor failed and the hand began to stink. I was told the hand would be amputated but I cried to God in fervent prayers. To the glory of God, the hand is now restored and not amputated. Praise the Lord!

Sis. Esther
MFM Ikare

BREAST PAIN DISAPPEARS

I had breast pain for ten years but during a deliverance programme here, the Lord visited me and the pain ceased. Praise the Lord!

Sis Abosede Daniel
MFM Headquarters

NOW ON SALE

At last! The two long awaited books are back on the stand. Ever potent for all your deliverance and prosperity needs. Hurry now for your copies Stock is limited. Price N170 each.

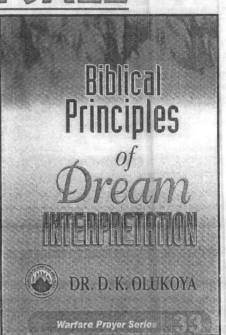

Hello Children!

Your popular spiritual tonic "Junior Fire in the Word" Is on the stand again. It is still as refreshing as ever. Now you have more opportunities to win Fanstastic prizes every month as you send in your entries Hurry grab your copy from the vendors. The price is still N20.

is a weekly Spiritual Bulletin of the Mountain of Fire and Miracles Ministries, published by Tracts and Publications Group. All enquiries should be addressed to The Editor, Mountain of Fire Magazine, 13, Olasimbo Street, off Olumo Road, Onike, P.O. Box 2990, Sabo Yaba, Lagos, Nigeria. Telephone 01- 867439, 864631, 868766, 08023180236.E-mail: mfmtractsandpublications@yahoo.com Copyright reserved.

FIRE IN THE WORD

Ye Shall Know the Truth, and the Truth Shall Make You Free (John 8:32)

ISSN 1595 - 7314 Vol. 12 No. 36 Sun. 20th - Sat. 26th July, 2008

THE BONDAGE OF THE BLACK MAN

My year of unprecedented greatness and unmatchable increase
Deuteronomy 28:13, Psalm 71:21, Ephesians 3:20, Psalm 92:10

Isaiah 14:3 says, *"And it shall come to pass in the day that the Lord shall give thee rest from thy sorrow, and from thy fear, and from the hard bondage wherein thou hast made to serve."*

The Bible did not mince words; it describes the bondage. It calls it hard bondage.

Verses 4-6: *"Thou shalt take up this proverb against the king of Babylon, and say, How hath the oppressor ceased! The golden city ceased! The Lord hath broken the staff of the wicked, and the scepter of the rulers. He who smote the people in wrath with a continual stroke, he that ruled the nations in anger, is persecuted, and none hindereth."*

The black people as a race seem to be hugging and entertaining their bondage.

WHAT IS BONDAGE?

Bondage is inability to begin when you wish to begin and to stop when you wish to stop. Bondage is confinement or imprisonment. It is a type of confinement that does not need to have walls surrounding the captive. A person can be as free as a bird and yet be in serious bondage.

A lot of black men are in bondage consciously or unconsciously. This is not clear to many people. Unfortunately, many people try to reason out the things of God with their brains. But the human brain is not only limited but can only operate in the physical realm. The brain becomes a useless material when it comes to spiritual things because there are realms in the spirit that are beyond the highest level of human reasoning. An honest and right thinking person would admit that something somewhere is wrong with the black man. Unfortunately much of what we call Christianity is absolute rubbish going by Bible standard. A lot of things we call Christianity are ritual ceremonies of ignorance.

A close study of the Bible reveals that many of the things that have been imported to Africa in the name of Christianity are not in the Bible. That is why the Bible is a neutral book, which deals with all races equally. The gospel cannot be polluted or diluted. It is not a Nigerian or African gospel, neither is it a British or American gospel. The gospel is the Bible. The gospel approaches men of all races and calls them to arise from the dust. It calls them to lift up their heads. It calls them to break their fetters. That is why the nations which seem to be doing well now are nations whose foundations were built on the Bible. And because they were built on the gospel, they were

NIGERIA AND INDEED AFRICA OCCUPY A STRATEGIC POSITION IN THE AGENDA OF THE ALMIGHTY.

able to lift up their heads and break their fetters.

The gospel causes men to be set free. It shows them Jesus. It does not show them the pastor. The gospel shows Jesus, the captain of our salvation. It shows us Jesus as the leader who has never lost a battle. Jesus never loses a man unless the man wants to be lost. Jesus begs men to cast forth their prison fetters and chains. He urges them to march towards their sparkling crown of glory.

But what answers do men give to the gospel? Multitudes and multitudes hate the voice that would arouse them for good. Multitudes are kissing and hugging their bondage. If we do not break this bondage, it will soon become our internal scorpion. We must be very careful.

There is a lot of bondage working against the black man. All these are problems of the black man. When I got born again, I began to ask questions such as: Does God use black people? Are black people on God's agenda? Answers to these questions are in the Bible.

In the Bible, we come across names such as Adam, Keturah, Abraham's wife after the death of Sarah, Asenath, the wife of Joseph, Zipporah, the wife of Moses, Jethro, the black man who taught Moses ministerial administration and the ways of God. All these were black people. Anytime God had a major work to do in the history of man,

DELIVERANCE CASE (The Story of My Life - Part 22)

one way or another, a black man would come along. Whenever God has a major step to take, one way or another, He would pick somebody from the continent of Africa to protect and support His move. Whenever the world was in a crisis, God made a black man to appear on the scene. But the position of the black man over time shows that something is basically wrong. In spite of the agenda of the Almighty God for the black man as presented in the Bible, things are not working well.

DISEASES OF
THE BLACK MAN

You hardly find a black nation that is doing very well. There seems to be a diabolical attack against blacks to stop them from fulfilling their destiny. Before this kind of collective bondage came in place, there was already individual bondage. Why should things like poverty, inferiority, accommodation, illiteracy etc be associated with the blacks? It is because something is wrong somewhere. This is why there are

all kinds of funny stories about blacks. We must understand that if Christians do not begin to receive mental freedom and to set themselves free from these things, their future generation would be in danger.

A close look at blacks shows that anyone among them that wants to rise is pulled down. The person that would bring prosperity to others is pulled down. Most times, there is a design to pull down anyone that wants to prosper the black race. The ones that are praised are those who want to destroy them. This is very sad.

THE BREADWINNERS'
CEMETERY

Another disease of the black man is that the battles of the people with colourful destinies start from the cradle, and if they do not have prayerful parents, they die. In Africa, you have the breadwinners' cemetery. Breadwinners are located and

killed. Major firstborns are used as torchlights so they always find it very difficult to prosper.

Polygamy is highly promoted amongst blacks. This has done so much to destroy the destiny of the black man. It is in black nations you find presidents who feed their citizens to lions. In secondary schools, seniors would give their juniors strange punishment. For example, a senior would ask a junior to write a sentence 150,000 times with different colours of pens. When such seniors take over government, the people will be in trouble. These seniors intimidate and extort provisions from their juniors. So, when they become leaders in the society in future, they will begin to steal money and maltreat people. Black nations are the cemetery of good things. We need to get out of these things.

There are some terrible trademarks upon the black people. For example:
- Trademark of sit-tight and confused leadership. It is an African

trouble.

- Trademark of poverty.
- Trademark of starvation.
- Trademark of famine.

If Christians do not rise against these things there will always be problems, even for future generations.

THE EARLY MISSIONARIES

The early missionaries did well. They brought schools but did not understand the black man. They brought a little bit of the Bible, church attendance, communion, schools, western clothes and western culture. So, the people who used to eat with their fingers began to struggle with cutlery. They changed so many things including music. They did not really introduce us to the Saviour. In some cases, it was a change from one idol at the back of the house to another idol called Mary inside the house. They did not introduce us to the new nature in Christ. People were going to church but were still serving their idols at home. We had deacons and deaconesses who belonged to occult groups. They did not see anything wrong in it. They did not teach us the new nature in Christ. A lot of European culture was introduced Christianity, and it was becoming difficult to separate the chaff from the wheat. Pagan festivals were mixed with Christianity. For example, something like Lent is not found in the Bible. It has its origin in idolatry.

Easter too is not found in the Bible. The name Easter is got from the worship of the sun god.

Christmas is not found in the Bible. Jesus was not born in December. December 25 was the date for worshipping the sun god. The missionaries introduced all these to Africans but did not teach them how to acquire a new nature. That was why Christianity made no impact on the black man until God raised local people who understood their foundation. Africans need to be liberated from this mental slavery. They need to recover the image of the black man so that they can be a channel of blessing to other nations of the world.

AFRICA'S BIBLICAL HERITAGE

Africa is the richest continent on earth. The minerals and other resources that God has planted there is enough. The Bible reveals that Africa has a biblical heritage and present-day black Christians need to rediscover this heritage and pray for a reconnection to that which God has for them right from the beginning. For example, Joseph the best administrator the world ever knew was trained in Africa. Moses, the great deliverer was also trained in Africa. All the materials

YOU MUST REFUSE TO IDENTIFY WITH THE NEGATIVE IMAGE THAT HAS BEEN GIVEN TO THE BLACK MAN

used to build the tabernacle and the garments of the Levites were taken from Africa. Also, immediately Jesus was born, the covenant God had with Africa had to be fulfilled; Jesus was taken to Egypt before He came back again. From Abraham to Jesus Christ, Africa's biblical heritage remains very clear. The gospel got to Africa before Europe. When it came here, it was mixed up with idolatry and witchcraft. It had to come a second time through the missionaries.

During the days of Moses, Egypt was the capital of the world; it was the most civilized nation of the world. Egyptians then were all blacks. But the Pharaohs of Egypt spent many years worshipping satan. Today, there are no more Egyptians in Egypt. From the archives and libraries of Egyptians, you will discover that all their Pharaohs and kings were blacks. But due to idolatry, witchcraft etc, the Arabs went into Egypt, killed the blacks and chased some of them to neighbouring countries. The proper Egyptians are wallowing in poverty now.

Nigerians should thank God for their country. God has endowed the country with many beautiful things: some of the best pilots in the world come from Nigeria. I read somewhere that a Nigerian designed the best bus station in London and a Nigerian also did the drawing for the concord plane.

Also, I heard that a Nigerian designed the fastest computer for drilling oil. So Nigerians are endowed with creative productivity. And God has a plan for every Nigerian Christian. Every Nigerian has what is called the extra sense, a rare kind of smartness and intelligence, which makes him different from other black people.

Nigeria and indeed Africa occupy a strategic position in the agenda of the Almighty. We must allow Christianity to flow into our character anywhere we are and reconnect ourselves to our biblical heritage. It is a tragedy that evil powers have made blacks to be using their grace and divine endowment negatively. If we must move forward, we must prepare ourselves to reconnect to our Bible heritage. It is an individual thing that has to start with everyone.

REQUIREMENTS TO RECONNECT WITH GOD

1. **Holy dissatisfaction:** The first thing you need to reconnect with God and break free from the bondage of the black man is holy dissatisfaction with your present level. You must be very angry with your present level and decide not to remain the way you are. You must refuse to identify with the negative image that has been given to the black man. If they say that the black man lacks organization, you must reject it and refuse to align with it. If they say the things of black people do not work, reject it and declare that your own things must work. If we start this individually, very soon, it will become collective. Christianity is meant to liberate our minds and make us what God wants us to become. God has an agenda for us, which we must fulfill. If our

generation refuses to do so, God does not mind to kill it off and look for another generation.

2. **Kill witchcraft:** Decide that every form of witchcraft in or around you must die. Witchcraft does not have to do with just drinking blood. The Bible makes us to understand that rebellion is as iniquity as idolatry and stubbornness as witchcraft. Therefore, rebellion in any form to God is witchcraft. If the witch in you does not die, there is no way you can conquer the external one. It is the witch in us that invites the external one. Adam was the first witch in the Bible. He rebelled against God. Every black person, one way or another, either through family connection or environment, has some witchcraft powers to deal with. Anyone who sleeps with a witch is in trouble. You need to deal with any witchcraft in your ancestry because you cannot move from your bondage if there are still there. That is why God pronounced death on all forms of witchcraft.

3. Pray destiny-changing prayer; the kind of prayer that Jabez prayed. He prayed some prayers, which did wonders in his life. We have to wake up from whatever spiritual sleep the enemy has put us.

4. **Pursue excellence:** Determine to pursue excellence in everything you do. Do not be satisfied with anything lower than excellence or what God expects you to do. Do

THE PROPHET David versus Goliath 22

not be satisfied with lower existence. Decide to be different. Pursue excellence in whatever you do.

5. Live a constant life of holiness: Do not live a life that can be polluted, demoted or destroyed. You must be very watchful. We live in a very unfriendly environment and it is deceitful to think that there are people who cannot see your destiny very well. The enemy has put a lot of things in the way; our forefathers have laid terrible foundations and many generations have been sold even before they were born. And when you begin to get from bondage to bondage, you strengthen the power of your enemy. You must pray to break out of your limitation and step into a new horizon. You must pray desperately so that you can move from sorrow to honour, and soar into your domain of achievement.

It is a strange aspect of life to see that some people will hate you just because you are doing well. Such people are known as envious witches. They are part of the things plaguing the black man. You must rise against the agenda of the enemy for your life and enter into your divine inheritance.

PRAYER POINTS

1. Ask the Lord to forgive you for any sin that will hinder your prayers. Ask Him to forgive you for any sin that will not allow you to make impact in your own generation.

2. I shall arise and shine. Any power saying no to that, die, in the name of Jesus.

3. Every problem that came into my life through the blood of my parents, die, in the name of Jesus.

4. Any problem that came into my life through anything I have eaten or swallowed, die, in the name of Jesus.

5. Any problem that has entered into my life through witchcraft and polygamy, die, in the name of Jesus.

6. Any problem that has entered into my life through anything I have stepped upon, die, in the name of Jesus.

7. Any problem that entered into my life through the first food I ate in my life, die, in the name of Jesus.

8. Any problem that entered into my life through any bad dream, die, in the name of Jesus.

9. Any problem that entered into my life through marriage, die, in the name of Jesus.

10. Any problem that entered into my life through my naming ceremony, die, in the name of Jesus.

11. Any problem that entered into my life through any dead relative, die, in the name of Jesus.

12. Thou power of envious witchcraft, die, in the name of Jesus.

13. Bondage, limitation, stagnation, hear the word of the Lord, my life is not your candidate. Therefore, die, in the name of Jesus.

14. Nigeria, jump out of the cage of witchcraft, in the name of Jesus.

15. As the Lord lives and His Spirit lives, I shall be head and not tail. My God, arise, if you need to sack, sack, if you need to retire, retire, if you need to kill, kill, but I must be the head and not the tail. I repossess everything I have lost sevenfold. This week, I possess my possession, in Jesus' name.

THE BONDAGE OF THE BLACK MAN
is a message delivered at the Mountain of Fire and Miracles Ministries by the General Overseer, Dr. D.K. Olukoya.

A CALL TO SERVE

Are you a member of MFM with a burden to help the needy, are you interested in alleviating the plight of the poor or in the spread of the gospel through the sponsorship of the publication of tracts? Your resources, time and talent can be extended to several groups that are in charge of these areas. These groups include:

o   We care Ministry,
o   Mission Outreach
o   Tracts and Publications
o   Ministry to Drug addicts
o   Campus fellowship
o   Ministry to Schools
o   Ministry to Glorious Children, etc.

Thus says the Lord, "Verily I say unto you, in as much as ye have done it unto one of the least of these my brethren, ye have done it unto me" Matthew 25 : 40.

WONDERFUL JESUS!

DELIVERED FROM HOUSEHOLD WICKEDNESS

After my late father's burial, I was physically attacked with charms attached to a horsewhip because of his properties, which I was not interested in. After the attack, I became sick. So, I went for deliverance and the Lord delivered and healed me. Praise the Lord!

Sis. Modupe
MFM Ijegun 1

SPIRIT OF THE GRAVE DEFEATED

Recently, after a church programme, the man of God asked us to anoint the centre of our rooms which I did. Thereafter, I had a dream where my daughter was missing and I started calling her. She was answering me but I could not see her. I woke up and prayed seriously about it. Secondly, during the burial ceremony of our landlord's mother which was done in the compound, my daughter collapsed and went into coma. After a long prayer session, God revived her. Praise the Lord!

Sis. Afolabi
MFM Abaranje

GOD RESTORES MY VISA

I boarded a commercial bus and when I got off, I discovered that I had lost my passport and visa in the bus. After some hours of frantic search, God intervened and I got back the documents intact. Praise the Lord!

Sis. Toyin
MFM Alagbole

EVIL PERSONALITY DISGRACED OUT OF MY LIFE

As I was preparing to get married at the age of 24, suddenly my fiancé died mysteriously. After that incident I became sickly and could not sleep. I was taken back to the village and while there, a pastor from MFM came and prayed for me. He told me that I was okay and could return to Lagos. He emphasized that when I got back to Lagos I should be attending MFM. When I came to Lagos, I wrote a letter to see the General Overseer and was referred to a pastor who placed me on G.O's deliverance. After the programme, there was a word of knowledge that there was an old woman living inside me. Instantly, the old woman packed her load and left. Seven days after the prophecy, I met my husband and we got married. Praise the Lord!

Sis. Ayo
MFM Headquarters

GOD SAVES MY BROTHER FROM UNTIMELY DEATH

During the 2006 edition of the 70 Days Fasting and Prayer programme, I prayed with my elder brother who travelled to Abuja. On the way, the luxurious bus he boarded was attacked by armed robbers and 44 passengers were killed. But God delivered my brother from their hands. He is alive today. Praise the Lord!

Sis. Rebecca
MFM Ajangbadi

EVIL ATTACKS CEASE

Before I started coming to MFM I was always tormented by evil spirits. Sometime ago, an invisible hand slapped me and I was hearing strange voices around me. But now they have all gone to the glory of God. Secondly, I had a dream in which I went to school and saw that my result was bad. When I woke up, I prayed about it very well. I cancelled the evil dream and declared that my deliverance programme would not be in vain. Later, I had a dream again where I passed and was promoted. And it came to pass physically. Praise the Lord!

Sis. Blessing
MFM Oworo 1

GOD REVIVES MY BUSINESS

I experienced a lot of troubles in my business. As a result of this my wife brought me to this church. I was advised to undergo a deliverance programme but I refused because of pride. Eventually, I agreed and went for it. To the glory of God, my dead business has come alive again just after the programme. Praise the Lord!

Bro. Emma
MFM Igando

GOD HEALS ME MIRACULOUSLY

Since 1996, I have been having a terrible sickness. All my family members and those of my husband were fed up with me. It was so much that sometimes I prayed for death. I refused to attend the house fellowship for a long time for no reason. But recently, I attended the house fellowship and on this particular day, God surprised me. The 8 year old sickness disappeared before the end of the fellowship. I have been totally healed. Praise God.

Sis. Edna
MFM Isheri, Idimu

DIVINE HEALING

For a long time, I had a problem with my eyes, tears used to flow from my eyes. The situation defied medical treatment. So, I put it before the Lord during the first deliverance programme in the new year. To my greatest surprise and thanks to God, the tears ceased mysteriously. Praise God!

Sis. Grace
MFM Lekki

NOW ON SALE

FIRE IN THE WORD, is a weekly Spiritual Bulletin of the Mountain of Fire and Miracles Ministries, published by Tracts and Publications Group. All Enquiries should be addressed to The Editor, Mountain of Fire Magazine, 13, Olasimbo Street, off Olumo Road, Onike, P.O. Box 2990, Sabo Yaba, Lagos, Nigeria. Telephone 01- 867439, 864631, 868766, 08023180236.E-mail: mfmtractsandpublications@yahoo.com Copyright reserved.

FIRE IN THE WORD

Ye Shall Know the Truth, and the Truth Shall Make You Free (John 8:32)

ISSN 1595 - 7314 Vol. 12 No. 37 Sun. 27th July - Sat. 2nd Aug., 2008

THE RESURRECTION VOICE

My year of unprecedented greatness and unmatchable increase
Deuteronomy 28:13, Psalm 71:21, Ephesians 3:20, Psalm 92:10

This message is for those who believe that they serve the God that knows no impossibility. He is the God who does not tolerate contest. He refused to tolerate the contest of Pharaoh. The message is also for those who believe that they serve the God whose power is unchallengeable.

When what is required to move a person forward has been caged, a particular power is needed to revive it.

John 11:25 says, *"Jesus said unto her, I am the resurrection and the life: he that believeth in me, though he were dead, yet shall he live."*

There is a personality called the resurrection and the life. That personality is the Lord Jesus Christ.

Jesus was at the tomb of Lazarus, who had been dead for days. John 11:41-42 says, *"Then they took away the stone from the place where the dead were laid. And Jesus lifted up his eyes, and said,* (He spoke normally) *Father, I thank thee that thou hast heard me. And I knew that thou hearest me always; but because of the people which stand by I said it, that they may believe that thou hast sent me. And when he has thus spoken, he cried with a loud voice, Lazarus, come forth."*

He spoke to His own Father quietly but when He faced another power, which is known as the power of the grave, He cried with a loud voice and mentioned one name; the name of Lazarus. If He had issued the command without mentioning a name, all the dead would have heard His voice and would have come out.

Verse 44: *"And he that was dead came forth, bound hand and foot with grave clothes: and his face was bound about with a napkin. And Jesus said unto them, Loose him, and let him go."*

We have identified a personality that is known as the Resurrection and the life.

THERE IS NO SITUATION THAT CAN RESIST THE VOICE OF RESURRECTION

In Philippians 3:10, Paul said, *"That I may know him and the power of his resurrection..."* There is a power known as the power of resurrection. There is a personality known as Resurrection. In Ezekiel 37, we see this power in display in another way:

Ezekiel 37:1-8 says, *"The hand of the Lord was upon me, and carried me out in the spirit of the Lord, and set me down in the midst of the valley which was full of bones.* (The bones were dead. When somebody has become just bones, the person is very dead. The flesh has been eaten off and only the skeleton is remaining. That was where God sent Ezekiel). *And caused me to pass by them round about: and behold, there were very many in the open valley, and lo, they were very dry. And he said unto me, Son of man, can these bones live? And I answered, O Lord God, thou knowest. Again he said unto me, Prophesy upon these bones and say unto them, O ye dry bones, hear the word of the Lord. Thus*

DELIVERANCE CASE (The Story of My Life - Part 25)

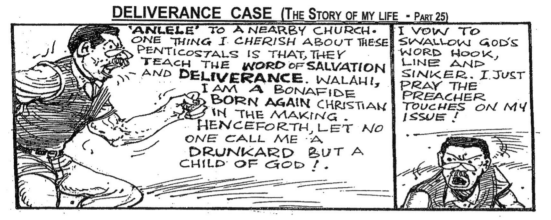

'ANLELE' TO A NEARBY CHURCH. ONE THING I CHERISH ABOUT THESE PENTICOSTALS IS THAT, THEY TEACH THE **WORD OF SALVATION** AND **DELIVERANCE**. WALAHI, I AM A BONAFIDE BORN AGAIN CHRISTIAN IN THE MAKING. HENCEFORTH, LET NO ONE CALL ME A DRUNKARD BUT A CHILD OF GOD!.

I VOW TO SWALLOW GOD'S WORD HOOK, LINE AND SINKER. I JUST PRAY THE PREACHER TOUCHES ON MY ISSUE!

saith the Lord God unto these bones; Behold, I will cause breath to enter into you, and ye shall live (There is something known as "Resurrection prophecy"). *And I will lay sinews upon you, and will bring up flesh upon you, and cover you with skin, and put breath in you, and ye shall live and ye shall know that I am the Lord. So I prophesied as I was commanded; and as I prophesied, there was a noise, and behold a shaking, and the bones came together, bone to his bone."*

Jesus was meek and gentle. That is well understood by all. However, sometimes, He became loud and noisy. He is the resurrection and the life. Things can remain still and quiet until the power of resurrection is manifested. The stillness and quietness of a cemetery would disappear if resurrection takes place. Sometimes, Jesus shouted. The Bible says that when He got to the tomb of Lazarus, He cried with a loud voice.

So far, we have identified the following:

- The personality of resurrection.
- The power of resurrection.
- The resurrection prophecy.

A certain man of God called Smith Wigglesworth was at a funeral where the deceased was laid in state. He was one of the sympathizers who came to pay their last respect to the dead. When it got to his turn in the long queue of people to bow and leave, he did something else. He gripped the suit of the dead man, pulled him out of the coffin and said, "In Jesus' name, I command you to live." And he released him. The corpse fell down on the floor and there was pandemonium. All those who queued behind Smith Wigglesworth quickly disappeared. The bold ones stood by the window to see what would happen. Wigglesworth picked up the deceased again and said again, "I command you, in the name of Jesus, live." He left the man and he fell on the ground a second time. Wigglesworth gripped him again and said, "Look, I have spoken to you twice. I am only going to say it one more time, I command you in the name of Jesus, live," and the man opened his eyes and said, "Who died?" He converted the funeral to a revival. Therefore, resurrection is not a quiet issue. It is very noisy.

In Luke chapter 7, the son of a certain widow was being taken for burial. The boy was the only son. Jesus stopped the funeral procession; He broke it up and spoke to the dead young man. I believe He spoke in a loud voice. He called the man back from the grave. The young man heard and obeyed that voice that can shake the earth. He came and reunited with his body. The resurrection voice called the boy back from the spirit world.

In Matthew 27, when Jesus shouted again with a loud voice, the Bible says there were earthquakes, graves heard the voice and the dead there were released. We need that resurrection voice today to speak to every situation. It is important for you to know that there are powers that can speak life. There are powers that can speak death. There are powers that can speak possibility, breakthroughs, promotion, etc. In the beginning, when the earth was without form and void, and

darkness was upon the face of the deep, the whole world was in a confused state. In that confusion, a voice spoke and said, "Let there be light" and there was light. Then things began to change. It was then the process of creation continued. When Jesus was inside the boat on the sea, there was a satanic revival taking place in the sea, and there was confusion, until He stood up and spoke, rebuking the sea, the storm, and the waves and all of them went silent.

Beloved, all that is required now is for that voice of resurrection to speak to any situation in your life. There is no situation that can resist the voice of resurrection.

When the voice of resurrection speaks backed by the power of resurrection, dead things come alive. Dead things here do not refer to things that are physically dead alone. A marriage may be dead, finances may be dead, career may be

THE TONGUE THAT MUST SPEAK LIFE MUST AVOID SIN

dead, business may be dead, a person's calling may be dead, and many things that people lay their hands upon may be dead. But there is a voice that can speak to them and they will obey, that is the voice of resurrection.

The same voice of resurrection that spoke in the days of old is still available now to speak. And when it speaks, whether it is to the mountains or to the deepest sea, the heavenlies or the trees, they will hear what it is saying and yield to it. The voice of resurrection speaks and when it does, things happen.

WHAT IS THE VOICE OF RESURRECTION?

- It is the voice that maketh alive.

- It is the voice that killeth without hands. I have watched this voice kill cancer, ulcer, failure, tumours and all kinds of infirmity. It is the voice that kills without hands.

- It is the voice that makes things to consist; it holds things together. The voice that holds things together can also command them to come apart and no power can glue them together.

- It is the voice that changes dry bones.

- It is the voice that speaks creative words.

- It is the voice that brings forth living winds, the kind of wind that blew on the bones that Ezekiel saw. Just like there is living winds, we have dead winds. Many people have testified that wind blew on them and they fell sick. When a dead wind blows on a person, the person will have problems immediately.

- It is the voice that destroys stagnation by eliminating decay.

- It is the voice that raises the physically dead.

- It is the voice that raises the spiritually dead. When a life is spiritually dead, the voice of resurrection can call it to arise.

- It is the voice that speaks living words to dead things. You can speak living words to your certificates, career, marriage, interviews, dead situations, etc.

- It is the voice that speaks words that are respected in the grave.

- It is the voice that speaks words that scare away death.

- It is the voice that arrests coffin spirits. Coffin spirits are the spirits that render a thing dead while the thing is still living.

- It is the voice that handles the key of hell and of death.

The implication is that:

- You can speak life into any dead thing in your life.

- You can preserve your own life.

- You can experience heaven on earth.

- You can withdraw power from unfriendly powers.

- You can speak death and decay to every power that is militating against your life.

- You can convert your dry bones to living flesh and bones.

- You can arrest the spirit of death in your dream.

- You can speak life to your finances, business, academics or career.

- You can speak to the wind blowing around and it will carry your word to where you want it to work. You can say, "O wind, carry these words to the camp of the enemy."

- You can bind killer words and dead words.

- You can speak the waters of life into any dead situation.

- You can remove life from any enemy that wants to pull you down.

You need to ask this voice to speak for you today. You need to practically speak the

| THE PROPHET | David versus Goliath 25 |

... DAVID RETURNED FROM THE SLAUGHTER OF GOLLIATH; ABNER [A COMMANDER OF ISREAL'S ARMY] BROUGHT HIM TO SAUL, WITH THE HEAD OF GOLLIATH. 1SAM. 17:57.

OH! THANK YOU SIR, CAPTAIN ABNER, MEETING THE KING IS A GREAT HONOUR

GOOD BOY. KING SAUL IS MORE THAN WILLING TO HONOUR YOU FOR THIS VICTORY

prophecy of resurrection to your situation. For example, your marriage, academics, parental problems, spiritual life, career, constant attack etc with the format of words with which you have never spoken to them before.

THINGS TO DO FOR THIS VOICE TO SPEAK FOR YOU

There are certain things you must do for the voice of resurrection to speak for you.

1. Repent of all known sins.
2. Control and tame your tongue. The tongue that must speak life must avoid sin.
3. You must die to self.
4. You must have the fighting spirit. The Bible says, "Fight the good fight of faith, lay hold on eternal life..." (1 Timothy 6:12).

When you speak to your situations in a way that you have never spoken to them, things will begin to happen very quickly.

PRAYER POINTS

1. Every arrow of darkness shooting down my glory, die, in the name of Jesus.
2. Thou resurrection power, incubate my life, in the name of Jesus.
3. By the power of resurrection, O God arise, and move me forward, in the name of Jesus.
4. By the keys of life, it is my turn to laugh, in the name of Jesus.
5. Every evil power holding me down, your time is up, die, in the name of Jesus.
6. By the power of resurrection, my hands shall not beg, my hands shall bless, in the name of Jesus.

7. Every power mocking the power of God in my life, what are you waiting for? Die, in the name of Jesus.
8. O voice of resurrection, speak life unto my destiny, in the name of Jesus.
9. Every masquerade of death in my family line, die, in the name of Jesus.
10. O voice of resurrection, speak to my dream life, in the name of Jesus.
11. Every dry bone in my life present in the valley of witchcraft, arise by fire, in the name of Jesus.
12. O grave attached to my family line, hear the word of the Lord and release my virtues, in the name of Jesus.
13. Every good thing in my life that the powers of wickedness have killed, come alive, in the name of Jesus.

THE RESSURRECTION VOICE
is a message delivered at the Mountain of Fire and Miracles Ministries by the General Overseer, Dr. D.K. Olukoya.

A CALL TO SERVE
Are you a member of MFM with a burden to help the needy, are you interested in alleviating the plight of the poor or in the spread of the gospel through the sponsorship of the publication of tracts? Your resources, time and talent can be extended to several groups that are in charge of these areas. These groups include:

o   We care Ministry,
o   Mission Outreach
o   Tracts and Publications
o   Ministry to Drug addicts
o   Campus fellowship
o   Ministry to Schools
o   Ministry to Glorious Children, etc.

Thus says the Lord, "Verily I say unto you, in as much as ye have done it unto one of the least of these my brethren, ye have done it unto me" Matthew 25 : 40.

WONDERFUL JESUS!

GOD DELIVERS ME FROM SCORPION BITE

I came back from the farm and hung my pair of trousers in the usual place. Unknown to me a scorpion had crawled into the trousers overnight. The following morning, I wore the trouser to the farm only to discover a live scorpion in my pocket after three hours. The Lord prevented the scorpion from stinging me. Praise the Lord!

Bro. Fedinard
MFM Ibilo

GOD OF ABUNDANT BLESSING

God's goodness in my life is uncountable but I have not testified. God released me from police cell. He paid up my debt to save me from the harassment of my creditors and miraculously provided seven contracts for me in one day. My business has been fully restored. Praise the Lord!

Bro. Kayode
MFM Aguda

GOD RESTORES MY SLEEP

Few weeks ago, I could not sleep due to severe body pain particularly around my abdomen. I came to the church and after series of prayers with the Hospital ministry, I was set free and the abdominal pain disappeared. Since then I have been sleeping very well. Praise the Lord!

Sis. Funke
MFM Ejigbo

PROMOTION AFTER 10 YEARS

Before I came to this church, I was on the same level in my office for 10 years. But when I got to this church and started praying, God answered me and I have been promoted. Praise the Lord!

Sis. Ogedengbe
MFM Agbelekale

GOD SETS ME FREE

I was sent to the prison for some crimes I committed and was on the death row. While in the prison, God manifested Himself to me and I surrendered my life to Jesus. After ten years, God effected my release from the prison. I am now a free and new person. Praise the Lord!

Bro. Fatai
MFM Iyana Ipaja

TOTAL DELIVERANCE FROM BONDAGE

I give glory to God Almighty for His great power that set me free from my family idol bondage. Things were not working for me and everywhere was tight for a very long time. After a deliverance programme, I had a dream where I found myself in my hometown and was flogging some masquerades seriously with boldness and power. Since then new things have started happening in my life and my life has changed for the better. Praise the Lord!

Bro. David
MFM Ado-Ekiti

GOD GIVES ME MULTIPLE BLESSINGS

I applied for a visa at the British High Commission and prayed the prayer points given to me. I was given a 3 year visa. Secondly, my daughter who lives in London was indisposed and at that time, the General Overseer was in London. There came a word of knowledge from him that those afflicted with sicknesses would receive the divine healing of God. My daughter claimed it and to the glory of God, she received her healing totally. Praise the Lord!

Sis. Aganiga
MFM Headquarters

THE YOKE OF SLAVERY BROKEN

I thank the Lord for the salvation of my soul and the great deliverance He granted me. I came to Prayer City for deliverance and saw in my dream that I was being commanded to work as a slave. I also noticed that I was in chains with two people standing beside me. But the Lord delivered me. Secondly the Lord removed me from darkness into His light. He also delivered me from spirit husband. Praise the Lord!

Sis. Omotola
MFM Prayer City

DIVINE HEALING

I am a member of Deeper Life Bible church, Ibadan. I was afflicted with several sicknesses and also, I had appendectomy which made me to bend and I could not walk straight again. But someone encouraged me to go for deliverance which I did at MFM Headquarters, Lagos. The Lord made me whole and I can now stand straight and the sicknesses have vanished. Praise the Lord!

Emmanuel Olabanji
MFM Headquarters

NOW ON SALE

At last! The two long awaited books are back on the stand. Ever potent for all your deliverance and prosperity needs. Hurry now for your copies Stock is limited. Price N170 each.

Hello Children!

Your popular Spiritual tonic "Junior Fire in the Word" is on the stand again. It is still as refreshing as ever. Now you have more opportunities to win Fanstastic prizes every month as you send in your entries Hurry grab your copy from the vendors. The price is still N20.

FIRE IN THE WORD, is a weekly Spiritual Bulletin of the Mountain of Fire and Miracles Ministries, published by Tracts and Publications Group. All Enquiries should be addressed to The Editor, Mountain of Fire Magazine, 13, Olasimbo Street, off Olumo Road, Onike, P.O. Box 2990, Sabo Yaba, Lagos, Nigeria. Telephone 01- 867439, 864631, 868766, 08023180236.E-mail: mfmtractsandpublications@yahoo.com Copyright reserved.

FIRE IN THE WORD

Ye Shall Know the Truth, and the Truth Shall Make You Free (John 8:32)

ISSN 1595 - 7314   Vol. 12   No. 38   Sun. 3rd - Sat. 9th Aug.,   2008

SPEAK WOE UNTO EVERY DARK PATTERN

My year of unprecedented greatness and unmatchable increase
Deuteronomy 28:13, Psalm 71:21, Ephesians 3:20, Psalm 92:10

This week, we are looking at the message entitled, "Speak woe unto every dark pattern."

2 Samuel 3:28-29 says, *"And afterward when David heard it, he said, I and my kingdom are guiltless before the Lord for ever from the blood of Abner the son of Ner: Let it rest on the head of Joab, and on all his father's house; and let there not fail from the house of Joab one that hath an issue, or that is a leper, or that leaneth on a staff, or that falleth on the sword, or that lacketh bread."*

He decreed through a curse that in the family of Joab, there must always be people who would have the issue of blood, people who would be lepers, people who would lean on staff, people who would fall by the sword and people who would lack food.

WHAT IS A PATTERN?

A pattern is an order, arrangement or design. A divine pattern is a divine order. A divine arrangement is a divine pattern. There is a rule in the spiritual world which does not change, and that is the rule which states that all lives must be patterned after something. Jesus Himself was described in 1 Timothy 1:16 as "God's pattern son." God too is a God of pattern. For example, God gave four patterns in the scriptures: The first pattern He gave was for Noah's ark. God gave Noah the entire pattern by which he would build this mighty ship and for that, God went into civil engineering, construction and carpentry. As far as Noah followed that pattern, the ark was in order.

The second pattern found in the scriptures is the pattern of the redemption of the Israelites from the bondage of Egypt. God gave

YOU CAN
DECIDE TO GET
OUT FROM EVERY EVIL
UMBRELLA AND IT
SHALL BE SO

Moses the pattern of the Passover. The Israelites had never heard of the word "Passover" before the Lord gave it to them. He showed them how to kill the animal and how to apply the blood on the doorpost. Refusal to follow that pattern would have spelt destruction.

The third pattern of God in the scriptures was the pattern of the tabernacle, which was delivered to Moses with a severe warning that he should see to it that he did everything according to that pattern.

The fourth pattern in the scriptures was the pattern for taking the city of Jericho. The pattern that brought that city down was directly from the Lord. The pattern did not follow any known military strategy for warfare. All these show us that God Himself is a God of pattern.

QUESTIONS TO CONSIDER

Is your life following a divine pattern? Are you still

DELIVERANCE CASE (THE STORY OF MY LIFE - PART 26)

your divine original self or have you been altered? Upon which pattern is your life being run now? Jesus says, "The Son of man goeth as it is written of him." Are you going as it is written of you? Or are you going as it is not written of you? Are you going as it is written by your enemies? Or are you going as it is written by God?

Failure starts in life when there is no balance between the pattern of God for your life and what you are doing now. Disaster happens when you are following the pattern of the enemy for your life. All deliverance ministers know that in trying to help people they sometimes probe to see whether there is a problem in the person's lineage or family. The occurrence of a similar problem in a person's family line is usually taken as a root of bondage. For example, there are some families, in which the firstborns never live beyond the age of forty. It is an evil pattern. In some families, people find it difficult to get married. If they get married, the marriage will break down. In some families, there is always the case of insanity at one point or another. In some families, there is a pattern of failure at the edge of success. If these evil patterns are not arrested, they can continue from year to year.

The devil was with God where he understood a little bit of the principle and workings of heaven. Therefore, he took the principle of pattern, corrupted and polluted it and is now running men and women through evil patterns.

From the scriptures in 2 Samuel 3:28-29, we understand that anyone from the lineage of Joab is in trouble going by what David said to him. It means that people from the lineage of Joab would be victims of tragedy wherever they are. They would be victims of stray bullets, accidents etc. Little problems would become big in their lives. The daughter of Joab may go for a simple operation such as removal of a tooth and would die due to complications. The children of Joab may be constant victims of armed robbery attacks although they have nothing a thief would desire. They may become victims of cancer and die. If a descendant of Joab was working in a hospital, he would be the person to contact infections because the curse working against him says, "There shall not lack in his family any that hath an issue, or that is a leper or that has a broken leg." So, when a curse is from the root of a person's life, based on an evil pattern, and is not broken, the pattern will go from year to year. These things must be arrested.

WHAT DOES IT MEAN TO ARREST?

1. It means to bring to a stop.
2. To make inactive.
3. To keep in custody.

Beloved, there is a network of powers of satan terminating divine patterns and installing evil ones. Look at your life right now. What is it patterned after? Do you like this pattern that has been going on for years to continue? Do you observe any evil pattern in your family line? Have you observed the pattern of lying, deceit, irresponsibility, marital turbulence, under age single parents, sexual impurity, anger, bad habit, unforgiveness, gossiping, confusion, lack of helpers, evil marks, misfortune, financial failure, bad health, laziness, mental disorder, evil dreams, worry, anxiety, etc in your family line? You need to arrest them now.

Adam had a divine pattern for his life but the enemy disrupted it. So, the second Adam had to come. Eve had

THERE ARE POWERS THAT SPONSOR EVIL PATTERNS FROM GENERATION TO GENERATION

a divine pattern but the enemy disrupted it. Cain had a divine pattern as first son but the enemy dealt with him. Aaron was patterned as first priest but the enemy dealt with him. Samson was patterned as first judge but the enemy dealt with him also. You can decide to get out from every evil umbrella and it shall be so.

At this juncture, I would like you to do some good thinking. Is there any evil pattern in your family line? Is there a pattern of the enemy stealing from you? Are there terrible things happening per year in your family? Is there a pattern of the enemy running after members of your family? Take a close look at your father's side and your mother's side and make up your mind that your case will be different. If others have become candidates of powers that destroy divine patterns, you should make up your mind that your case must be different.

I would like you to ask the Lord to forgive you in every area where you have released your life to powers that want to destroy the pattern of God for your life. Ask the Lord to forgive you where you have deviated from your original plan, where the enemy has replaced the pattern of God for your life with another one. Also, repent on behalf of your parents and ancestors. Do this genuinely from your heart so that no evil pattern will follow you for the rest of year.

POWERS THAT SPONSOR EVIL PATTERNS

There are powers that sponsor evil patterns from generation to generation. There are also powers that scatter the divine pattern for a person's life and replace it with their own evil pattern. They do this by not allowing people to locate their original pattern. Sometimes, they relocate people from the place of blessing to a place of curses.

Sometimes, they plant something inside a person's life to hinder the person from locating the place of blessing. Sometimes, they cause a lack of interest in what would benefit the person. That is, what would make the person to prosper would be completely unattractive to the person. Sometimes, they programme a person into a wrong marriage in order to scatter the divine pattern of the person's life.

HOW TO SPEAK WOE TO THESE POWERS?

1. Surrender your life to Jesus. Do not continue as a rebel unto God. Have a determination to purify your life and to possess your possession.

2. Hate the evil pattern with perfect hatred. May be you come from a polygamous home and the enemy is already programming you into a polygamist, hate that agenda of the enemy with perfect hatred.

3. If you have not yet surrendered your life to Jesus, you cannot speak woe unto every dark pattern in your destiny. If you want to give your life

THE PROPHET | David versus Goliath 26

GREAT KING. I AM GLAD YOU APPRECIATE THIS VICTORY SIR.

THAT WAS EXCELLENT MY BOY. PLEASE. TELL ME. WHO IS YOUR FATHER?

I AM THE SON OF YOUR SERVANT JESSE.

to Christ, please say the following prayer: "Father, in the name of Jesus, I come before you now, I surrender my life to you. I acknowledge that I am a sinner. I know that you died for my sins. Lord Jesus, forgive me all my sins and cleanse me with your blood. Write my name in the book of life. As from today, I renounce the devil and his works. I enter into the kingdom of light. Lord Jesus, come into my life and take control of my life, in Jesus' name. Amen.

4. Begin to identify anything that has formed a dark pattern in your life; deliberate on the pattern you no longer want in your life.

5. Mount prayer warfare to kill the evil patterns so that they will no longer follow your destiny.

PRAYER POINTS

1. Every pattern of darkness in my family line, die, in the name of Jesus.

2. Every pattern of witchcraft power in my family line, die, in the name of Jesus.

3. I fire back every arrow of evil pattern, in the name of Jesus.

4. (Raise your right hand to the heaven) Oh heavens over my prosperity, open by fire, in the name of Jesus.

5. Every power that does not want to let my prosperity go, what are you waiting for? Die, in the name of Jesus.

6. The Sun will not smite me by day nor the moon by night, in the name of Jesus.

7. I remove my name from the quota of disaster this year, in the name of Jesus

8. Oh heavens, declare your glory over my life, in the name of Jesus.

9. I declare that it is well with my soul, in the name of Jesus

10. I shall not be a negative example, in the name of Jesus.

11. Any power delegated to waste my life this year, die, in the name of Jesus

12. Every enemy of the peace of Nigeria, I bury you now, in the name of Jesus.

13. Any power planning war for Nigeria this year, what are you waiting for? Die, in the name of Jesus.

14. Oh glory of Nigeria, arise and shine, in the name of Jesus.

15. Oh Prince of peace, reign in Nigeria, in the name of Jesus.

SPEAK WOE UNTO EVERY DARK PATTERN
is a message delivered at the Mountain of Fire and Miracles Ministries by the General Overseer, Dr. D.K. Olukoya.

A CALL TO SERVE

Are you a member of MFM with a burden to help the needy, are you interested in alleviating the plight of the poor or in the spread of the gospel through the sponsorship of the publication of tracts? Your resources, time and talent can be extended to several groups that are in charge of these areas. These groups include:

o We care Ministry,
o Mission Outreach
o Tracts and Publications
o Ministry to Drug addicts
o Campus fellowship
o Ministry to Schools
o Ministry to Glorious Children, etc.

Thus says the Lord, "Verily I say unto you, in as much as ye have done it unto one of the least of these my brethren, ye have done it unto me" Matthew 25 : 40.

WONDERFUL JESUS!

EVIL DEATH AVERTED

There was a word of prophecy in the course of a vigil that someone would die in my village and I should not go. The following Wednesday, my father telephoned me and said that my uncle who had boasted evil against us had died. Praise the Lord!

Sis. Calister
MFM Iju

VICTORY OVER SATANIC DREAMS

To the glory of God before anything would happen to me at any given time, God would reveal it to me. But all of a sudden, I realized that I was having satanic dreams which made me to go for deliverance. Even as I went for deliverance, I was still oppressed by these dark powers. I cried to God who answers by fire and He answered me. Praise the Lord!

Sis. Funso
MFM Ilado

EVIL GROWTH DISAPPEARS

Five years ago, I noticed a growth on my left hand. I went to the hospital and the doctors said it would require surgery but I should allow the evil growth to develop more. At that point I started applying anointing oil on it. Three months later, the evil growth totally disappeared. Praise the Lord!

Sis. Adeyanju
MFM Ketu

GOD SAVES ME FROM A FATAL ACCIDENT

Recently, the man of God said there was a woman who must not miss the programme scheduled for that week but I chose to travel. As we left Benin for Lagos, no sooner had we crossed a village called Oniparaga than one of the rear tyres of the vehicle pulled off. Suddenly, the bus began to swerve from left to right and started tumbling. At the end, five people died instantly, and one of the deceased had his head and two legs cut off. Sympathisers that came to assist us did not believe I was in the bus. The other survivor was a man of God as he later identified himself. Praise the Lord!

Sis. Tosan
MFM Ekenwan Benin City

SPIRIT OF DEATH AND HELL DESTROYED

I used to see myself walking in the midst of coffins and dead people in the dream. Also, there was a satanic tse-tse fly that always troubled me and chased me about. I thank God Almighty that all these were destroyed during the deliverance programme. Praise the Lord!

Bro. Michael
MFM Oyo

GOD OF DELIVERANCE

Indigenes of my village are usually initiated and dedicated to marine powers. When I came to Lagos, these powers kept troubling me. My landlady brought me to MFM. I went for counseling and gave my life to Christ. Later, I went for deliverance. Today, I thank God, I am totally free. Praise the Lord!

Sis. Charity
MFM Benson Ikorodu

SPIRIT OF INSANITY DESTROYED

I served as a personal assistant to the General Overseer of a popular church in Lagos. They performed lots of miracles which he said were genuine and by the Holy Ghost as well. But I started noticing strange movements all over my body and I became mentally insane. For this reason I was driven away by the General Overseer. Miraculously, I got introduced to MFM and went through the deliverance programme. Now the Lord has delivered me. I am mentally alright. Praise the Lord!

Bro. Ekundayo
MFM Itire/Ijesha

NOW ON SALE

At last! The two long awaited books are back on the stand. Ever potent for all your deliverance and prosperity needs. Hurry now for your copies Stock is limited. Price N170 each.

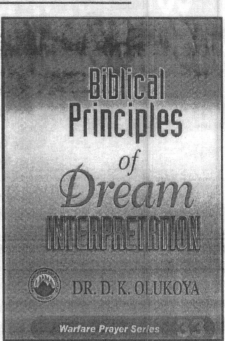

Hello Children!

Your popular Spiritual tonic "Junior Fire in the Word" is on the stand again. It is still as refreshing as ever. Now you have more opportunities to win Fanstastic prizes every month as you send in your entries Hurry grab your copy from the vendors. The price is still N20.

FIRE IN THE WORD, is a weekly Spiritual Bulletin of the Mountain of Fire and Miracles Ministries, published by Tracts and Publications Group. All Enquiries should be addressed to The Editor, Mountain of Fire Magazine, 13, Olasimbo Street, off Olumo Road, Onike, P.O. Box 2990, Sabo Yaba, Lagos, Nigeria. Telephone 01- 867439, 864631, 868766, 08023180236.E-mail: mfmtractsandpublications@yahoo.com Copyright reserved.

FIRE IN THE WORD

Ye Shall Know the Truth, and the Truth Shall Make You Free (John 8:32)

ISSN 1595 - 7314 Vol. 12 No. 39 Sun. 10th - Sat. 16th Aug., 2008

YOUR CONDITION & CONCLUSION

My year of unprecedented greatness and unmatchable increase
Deuteronomy 28:13, Psalm 71:21, Ephesians 3:20, Psalm 92:10

This week, we are looking at the message entitled, "Your condition and your conclusion."

Psalm 34:17 says, *"The righteous cry and the Lord heareth, and delivereth them out of all their troubles."* Verse 19 says, *"Many are the afflictions of the righteous: but the Lord delivereth him out of them all."*

Psalm 9:9 says, *"The Lord also will be a refuge to the oppressed, a refuge in times of trouble."*

Nobody can run away from trouble and problems. There is no place that far that you can run to and trouble will not find you. As a matter of fact, all of life is one trouble or another. So, anyone who is telling you that you can have a problem-free existence is giving you a fraudulent dream. No one including the righteous is immune from trouble. Unfortunately, problem has no respect for anybody. Problems have no regard for anyone. A problem-free life is only available in the cemetery. Problems come any way, whether you invite them or not, and God in His own training school always leaves a challenge in your life for you to conquer. And in a bid to conquer that challenge, you become stronger.

Life itself is a process of solving problems all through. But to the believer who has surrendered his life to Jesus, every problem is a miracle in disguise. God will not deliver you from your problem but will deliver you in the problem. The deliverance of Shadrach Meshach and Abednego did not come outside the fiery furnace but inside the fire. They were delivered inside the fire.

Problems can make you better or bitter. Your problems can build you up or burst you up. But the mystery of the matter is that every problem has an expiry date. But people do not know this secret because God does not reveal everything to us at once. Sometimes, God's process of deliverance may appear as a challenge but many people do not understand so they get very worried. They think it is a problem whereas God knows better. Therefore, problems, one way or another are the springboards to success.

A little bit of the rain of trouble falls into every life. Many

YOU CAN COMPLETELY ALTER THE COURSE OF YOUR LIFE BY YOUR ATTITUDE

people start their battle from the womb. Some start at a young age while some start theirs in their old age. But a little bit of rain will fall, and you cannot be victorious if you are not in the battle. The big truth that I want you to know is this: Your condition is not as important as your conclusion. What matters is what happens in you because of what happened to you. When you have problems and draw the wrong conclusion about your situation, your condition will not change. When a child of God comes to the church, depressed and with his head down, God cannot speak to him. He would leave the same way he came because with that state of mind, he is saying that his problem is above God.

Many people conclude their problems with weeping. But weeping cannot save anyone. The conclusion of some people is sorrow, self-pity, or hysteria, They go into a rage and throw tantrums of anger. It is a wrong conclusion. The conclusion of some people is cursing. They issue all kinds of curses against people because they have a problem, it is a wrong conclusion. Some even go to the extent of abusing God. It is a wrong conclusion. Problems

DELIVERANCE CASE (The Story of My Life - Part 24)

I MUST RUN TO A CHURCH FOR DELIVERANCE. I AM CONVINCED THAT ALL WE DID IN THE **PALMWINE** DRINKERS CLUB ON CAMPUS WAS "OCCULTIC"! AND I DON'T WANT TO TAKE CHANCES, THAT, I HAVE GRADUATED MANY YEARS AGO; BECAUSE, A THOUSAND YEARS BEFORE GOD, IS LIKE A DAY.

2. PETER 3 VS 88.

make some people to harbour suicidal thoughts. There are some who even attempt suicide. It is a wrong conclusion. When some people have problems, they go into sudden holiness and begin to pray that the Lord Jesus should come quickly. They want Jesus to come because they have problems not out of love. It is a wrong conclusion.

Some people become slaves to prophets when they have problems. They submit themselves to anybody for prayers. Witchcraft powers that never had access to their heads would lay their hands on their heads and command the problems to multiply. Such people compound their problems by handing them over to wolves. Every man and woman will fight his or her own battle. Men of God can assist you but if you have the "prophet syndrome," when the prophet dies, you will be in trouble.

When some people have problems, their conclusion is to become downcast, quarrelsome and withdrawn. They will murmur and complain. They will be discouraged. That is a wrong conclusion and the condition will not change. As long as you conclude negatively, the problems will never go away. The way you handle your problem determines how you end up.

Your condition is not as important as your conclusion. Your conclusion is the prophecy about your problem. But with the right conclusion, God will never allow bad news to be the last news. If you conclude correctly and act accordingly, bad news will not be the last news. Your enemies will not laugh last once your conclusion is correct. God Himself will turn

your night to day. He will turn your mess into miracle and your problems to promotion. Only you can decide what your problem can do to you. Worry and anxiety are the wrong conclusions to problems. They give the enemy opportunity to deal with one terribly.

ATTITUDE

Attitude is one character that makes a big difference among people. It is a very powerful force that many people do not pay attention to and it destroys very quickly. It has to do primarily with the way people react to situations. Attitude goes a long way to show the quality of a person. If your attitude is positive, you will always come to the top. If it is negative, you will come down. There are some people who are always happy no matter their condition. It is attitude. Our happiness and success depends not so much on the problems we face, but how we respond to those problems. A positive attitude can turn situations around for a person. A negative attitude will not solve any problem. A positive attitude towards life and towards whatsoever you are facing will remove the dust from your mind and motivate you to accept the challenge ahead.

Beloved, your conclusion decides your condition. The right attitude will allow you to choose action instead of withdrawal. It will make you to choose growth instead of stagnation. It will make you to choose courage instead of fear. The right attitude will allow you to take encouragement instead of despair. Your attitude will help you to find the good in any situation you are so that you can remain optimistic. But if you handle it wrongly, the problem will continue. If you take an attitude of withdrawal, fighting your wife or your husband or if you keep saying "Since the day I married you, everything has been upside down," things will become rougher. If you worry yourself until you are sick, it is a wrong attitude. Resorting to drugs, alcohol, cigarette, etc is wrong attitude. Many people

are yet to realize that alcohol cannot drown any problem. It is a wrong attitude when you get confused, become insulting, cry all day long, drive recklessly or take an overdose of anything because of any situation. It is a wrong attitude when you begin to overeat because there is a problem. It is a wrong attitude to be bitter against anybody. It is a wrong attitude to fall apart, get angry, have hatred towards others, backslide or go about saying that nobody cares about you and your problems. It is a wrong attitude to keep saying, everybody seems to be against me and I don't know why." Some would say, "I wish this life was over so that we can go away." It is a wrong conclusion. Your conclusion decides your condition.

Nothing should push anyone to the level where he or she decides to marry any man or woman that comes along. When you refuse to sleep because of problems, it is a wrong attitude. The Bible says, "It is vain for you to keep awake because of trouble." Making sarcastic statements is a bad attitude.

HAPPINESS IN LIFE IS DETERMINED BY 10 PER CENT OF WHAT HAPPENS TO YOU AND 90 PER CENT OF HOW YOU REACT

Breaking and destroying properties is a wrong attitude. Throwing objects about in the house is a bad attitude. Moodiness, oversensitivity, discontinuity of prayers and Bible reading constitute a bad attitude. So, your attitude has an impact on your happiness. And it has an impact on the success of those around you.

You can completely alter the course of your life by your attitude. Paul and Silas had no reason to sing praises in the prison. They were beaten, dragged on the floor and thrown into jail. They were not doing their work. They suffered because they were doing the work of God but their attitude was different. There were bruises on their body but their attitude was different. One would have thought that they would stay in one corner, cry their eyes out and blame God, but they sang praises and God was happy with them and things began to happen.

It is often said that the same sun that melts the candle hardens the clay. Your attitude is within your control. Make a decision today that your conclusion must be positive because you are responsible for how you react and for what you allow to influence your life. A positive outlook allows you to stand up and take control of your life.

Attitude is more important than money. It is more important than your circumstances. It is more important than your failures. It is more important than what people say. It is more important than what people think. It is more important than your appearance. It is more important than education.

Happiness in life is determined by 10 per cent of what happens to you and 90 per cent of how you react. It is your positive attitude that makes you to persevere and persist. I read the story of a certain man who is an expert at writing

children's books. The first children book he wrote was rejected by twenty three publishers. But he never gave up; he kept writing them. All of a sudden he had a breakthrough; and the book sold six million copies. Your attitude is very important. Your condition will not change it. They key to living a fulfilled life is the right attitude. Our attitude works twenty-four hours a day for our good or for our bad. If you fail to harness the force of your attitude, it will be a tragedy. It is not your position that matters but your disposition to that condition. Excellence is not a skill. It is not a talent, it is an attitude. That is, your attitude to a situation is geared towards excellence in whatever you do.

Therefore, what happens to you is less significant than what happens in you.

HOW TO YOU MAKE A PROPER CONCLUSION ABOUT ANY CONDITION

1. **Repent of any known sin:** Sin is always a destroyer. If you pray while living in any known sin, your conscience will tell you that you are deceiving yourself. You took some bottles of beer and later began to sing "Holy Ghost, do it again," you are deceiving yourself. Or you beat up your spouse and later begin to pray fire prayers, you are deceiving yourself.

2. **Refuse to wallow in self-pity:** Do not engage in self-pity. I read the story of a fellow who wanted to commit suicide. But before he jumped down from a tall building which he had climbed, a man rushed to him and said, Mr. Man, please I know you want to jump down and kill yourself but before you jump, can I have your shoes, belt and wristwatch." He said, "Why are you asking for these things?" The man answered, "I want them because all my life, I have not been able to afford any of these things and I see that you can afford them and you want to

THE PROPHET | David versus Goliath 24

...DAVID BROUGHT THE HEAD OF GOLLIATH TO JERUSALEM;... I SAM 17:54.

... DAVID, A CHAMPION IN ISREAL.

I WILL BE GLAD AND REJOICE IN THEE: I WILL SING PRAISE TO THY NAME, O THOU MOST HIGH. WHEN MY ENEMIES ARE TURNED BACK THEY SHALL FALL...PSM 9:23.

AND THEY THAT I...N THY NAME WILL PUT THEIR TRUST IN THEE... PSM 9:10.

THOU HAS REBUKED THE HEATHEN, THOU HAS DESTROYED THE WICKED PSM

YEESS-OOOOO!

die, so let me have them." When he heard that, he realized that his case was not that bad. He did not commit suicide anymore.

3. Focus on God not on your condition: God is a specialist at turning up when everyone has given up. He is a specialist at coming in through the back door when you are expecting Him at the front door. Focus on God and not on the problem or condition. If you keep saying, "Everybody is asking me, that is why I am worried," any time they ask say, "It is well." If not, the same people who are asking you will kill you and attend your funeral. They will kill you by the questions they are asking you and you do not know how to answer.

4. Face one problem at a time: Prioritize your problem. Do not fight useless battles. It is wrong to face too many things at the same time. For example, you want to launch war against strange women, fight your household enemies, witches and wizards, pray against spirit husband, bind hypertension, pray against household witchcraft and poverty all at the same time. It is wrong. Pick them one at a time. Do not jumble prayers, take it one at a time.

5. Do not think or confess negatively: Never let anybody push you to the level where you will speak against yourself. Negative confessions and thoughts will put you into trouble.

6. Hold firmly to the promise of God.

7. Expect a divine solution.

8. Have the right attitude to your condition: That is begin to see yourself bigger than that problem.

PRAYER POINTS

1. Ask the Lord to forgive you for your wrong and negative attitude.
2. Thou power of affliction, your time is up, die, in the name of Jesus.
3. Every arrow of affliction fired into my career, die, in the name of Jesus.
4. Every power saying no to my joy, what are you waiting for? Die, in the name of Jesus.
5. Every power calling my name in the court of satan, die, in the name of Jesus.
6. (Pray this on your hands) Every power contesting for the prosperity of my hands, die, in the name of Jesus.
7. (Pray this on your hands) Any deposit of poverty in my hands, die, in the name of Jesus.
8. Every strongman of affliction in my father's house, die, in the name of Jesus.
9. Every power that has vowed to destroy me, die, in the name of Jesus.
10. Every attitude of failure, die, in the name of Jesus.
11. I will not die for my enemy to laugh at me, in Jesus' name.

YOUR CONDITION AND YOUR CONCLUSION
is a message delivered at the Mountain of Fire and Miracles Ministries by the General Overseer, Dr. D.K. Olukoya.

A CALL TO SERVE

WONDERFUL JESUS!

YOKE OF BARRENESS BROKEN

God visited me after eleven years of barrenness and I am now a mother. As we were preparing for the Cross-over night of 2006, I filled one flask with drink to break my fast at the Prayer City and I prayed that during the next Cross-over night, I would be there with my baby's flask. I am very happy that God has taken away my reproach and my baby is God's concrete evidence that He answers prayers. Praise the Lord!

Sis Funmi
MFM Benson

GOD RESTORES MY GLORY

I enlisted in the army 21 years ago. After a short time, I was promoted and given a rank. Few years later, I was due for another promotion. But instead of promotion, I was demoted and my rank withdrawn. I thought it was one of those things in life and did not do anything. Later, somebody introduced me to MFM. I started praying violent prayers and was faithful in my tithing. To the glory of God, my rank has been restored. Praise the Lord!

Bro. Muda
MFM Cotonou

WAIST PAIN GONE

I thank God Almighty for healing me of a chronic waist pain. Secondly, God empowered me to see some satanic cockroaches that were attacking me. I thank God that I succeeded in killing all of them. Praise the Lord!

Sis. Felicia
MFM Awka-Etiti

DELIVERED FROM SATANIC DREAMS

I used to have satanic dreams for a long time and I was counselled to go for deliverance. I went for deliverance and God gave me victory over the strongman that was attacking me in my dream. Praise the Lord!

Bro. Ojo
MFM Abule-Anu

GOD CHANGES MY LIFE

My life was caged for a very long time. Nothing was working for me. However, I was introduced to MFM and went into fire prayers. Now everything about me has changed for blessings. Praise the Lord!

Sis. Betty
MFM Uselu Benin

DELIVERED FROM SUDDEN DEATH AND HEALING FOR MY MOTHER

The last time I travelled, God ordered my footsteps such that I did not enter the bus which got involved in a fatal accident. The bus was actually the next to load when I got to the motor park, but God directed me to the one after that. During the same week, I was informed about my mother's illness. Through prayers, the Lord took control and healed her. Praise the Lord!

Bro. Akintunde
MFM Ibafo

DIVINE HEALING

I had a sickness that defied medical solution but the Lord healed me on the fifth day of the deliverance programme. My brother in-law who was afflicted with the spirit of insanity ran away from home. I contacted the pastor who prayed and asked the angel of God to locate him. The Lord answered and brought him back home. Praise the Lord!

Sis. Folashade
MFM Iju

JINX OF DEATH REMOVED

There was a recurring death of landlords where I built my house. We prayed when we wanted to move to the place and God removed the jinx from our family. We have been living in peace and good health. Praise the Lord!

Bro. Olutade
MFM Morogbo

GOD REMEMBERS ME

I personally trained one of my half brothers who is now wealthy. He had been far away from me in spite of the problems facing me. In view of the challenges I was facing, I went for deliverance. After the deliverance programme, God opened the book of remembrance on my behalf and this my half brother bombarded me and my children with uncommon favours. Praise the Lord!

Bro. Raymond
MFM Ijede

GOD MY PROVIDER

To the glory of God, since I gave my life to Christ, I have not lacked anything. Furthermore, my son was looking for a job and I asked him to bring his certificates. The prayer warriors prayed on them and God provided him a befitting job. Praise the Lord!

Sis. Angelina
MFM Ijegun 1

NOW ON SALE

At last! The two long awaited books are back on the stand. Ever potent for all your deliverance and prosperity needs. Hurry now for your copies Stock is limited. Price N170 each.

Hello Children!

Your popular Spiritual tonic "Junior Fire in the Word" is on the stand again. It is still as refreshing as ever. Now you have more opportunities to win Fanstastic prizes every month as you send in your entries Hurry grab your copy from the vendors. The price is still N20.

FIRE IN THE WORD is a weekly Spiritual Bulletin of the Mountain of Fire and Miracles Ministries, published by Tracts and Publications Group. All Enquiries should be addressed to The Editor, Mountain of Fire Magazine, 13, Olasimbo Street, off Olumo Road, Onike, P.O. Box 2990, Sabo Yaba, Lagos, Nigeria. Telephone 01- 867439, 864631, 868766, 08023180236.E-mail: mfmtractsandpublications@yahoo.com Copyright reserved.

FIRE IN THE WORD

Ye Shall Know the Truth, and the Truth Shall Make You Free (John 8:32)

ISSN 1595 - 7314 Vol. 12 No. 40 Sun. 17th - Sat. 23rd Aug., 2008

SPEAK WOE UNTO FAILURE

My year of unprecedented greatness and unmatchable increase
Deuteronomy 28:13, Psalm 71:21, Ephesians 3:20, Psalm 92:10

This week, we are looking at the message entitled, "Speak woe unto failure."

Deuteronomy 28:13 says, *"And the Lord shall make thee the head, and not the tail; and thou shalt be above only, and thou shalt not be beneath: if that thou hearken unto the commandments of the Lord thy God which I command thee this day to observe and to do them."*

Deuteronomy 28:12 says, *"The Lord shall open unto thee his good treasure, the heaven to give the rain unto thy kind in his season, and to bless all the work of thine hand; and thou shalt lend to many nations, and thou shalt not borrow."*

TEN UNCHANGING TRUTHS ABOUT SUCCESS AND FAILURE

1. Success does not happen by accident. It has a root. Failure too does not happen by accident, it has a root. So, success or failure in life has a root. This is why situations such as national poverty, national economic chaos, etc should be considered as a tree. It would be a waste of time cutting the leaves, the stems and the branches in trying to solve the problem. You should go right down to the root.

2. You are not a failure until you accept that you are one. That is you are only a failure if you tolerate failure.

3. God has given us everything we need for success.

4. The only thing that can be achieved in life without any effort is failure. So, the man that does not make any effort is already born a failure.

5. Human beings can only stop you temporarily. You are the only person who can stop yourself permanently. If you decide now to move away from failure and get determined to succeed, it shall be so.

6. If you have no enemies, it is a sure sign that success has passed you by. If you claim not to have enemies, it is a sign that you are already a failure. The Bible says, "Let God arise, and let all His enemies scatter." So, if God has enemies, you would be deceiving yourself to say that you do not have enemies. If the enemy has given up on you, it means he has already carpeted you.

7. Success is when you use what God has given to you to reach His purpose for your life, meaning that a man is a failure when he is not able to really locate what God wants him to do.

8. Money does not determine success. Many wealthy men have failed at what really matters in life.

9. Education does not determine success. It will certainly help but it

> THE WORST THING ABOUT A CLOSED HEAVEN IS THAT IT PROVIDES A COMFORTABLE CONDITION FOR THE SPIRIT OF POVERTY TO OPERATE

does not determine it. Many highly educated people have made fools of themselves and messed up their lives. I know a highly educated man who was injecting himself with all kinds of hard drugs. His wife warned him to stop but he never could stop until the thing killed him.

10. Opportunity does not determine success. Some have been in the right place at the right time and yet they did not make it.

WHAT DETERMINES SUCCESS?

Success is determined by the ability to identify the purpose of God for your life and to pursue it. Success is when you are in the center of God's will. And that means prospering in your body, soul and spirit. The Bible talks about prosperity in three different areas:

- Spiritual prosperity.
- Material prosperity.
- Good health.

So, prosperity is not only material. Prosperity without good health is worthless. Prosperity accompanied by spiritual blindness will lead to nothing as well. In fact, with spiritual blindness, you may even kill yourself untimely. So, you need to pray for spiritual prosperity, material prosperity and health prosperity. This is why it is often said that although money is very good, it will buy you a bed but will not buy you sleep. Money will buy you books but not brain. Money

DELIVERANCE CASE (THE STORY OF MY LIFE - PART 27)

can buy you pew in your church but will not buy you salvation. Money can buy you a house but cannot buy you a home. Money can buy you food but not appetite. Money can buy you medicine but not health. Money can buy you pleasure and amusement but not happiness. So, true prosperity covers your health, soul, body and spirit. The collective poverty of people is what results in national poverty and collective unrighteousness yields national unrighteousness. Individual lives need to be addressed in order to tackle the national life.

I read the story of certain man that was very eager to possess a lot of land. He got information that he could get a lot of land very cheap in a certain village and he began to search for the place. After travelling for miles, he got to this particular village and went to the chief of the village. The chief said, "If you want land, put your money in this my cap here and the amount of land you can cover by walking and you come back here before sunset would be yours."

The man was very happy. He prepared, took his lunch, and started walking. He covered miles and when he saw that the sun was almost setting, he started coming back to the chief's palace. And just as the sun was about to set, he got to the chief and fell down. The chief said, "Congratulations, you have won so many lands." But the man did not answer. By the time they looked at him, he was dead. The chief brought out a spade, threw it at his servants and said, "Bury him." They buried the man in a small plot of land that was just able to take his body. He was searching for prosperity materially but was spiritually poor.

God is the ultimate source of prosperity and every true prosperity begins from the inner man. When God has access to your inner man and is able to change you internally, then the prosperity will radiate externally, and affect your environment

positively. War is being fought in the world today because men and women have internal wars. It is the internal war that is transferred to the outside. When there is peace inside a person, it radiates. When there is poverty inside a person, the poverty will radiate. So, true prosperity begins from the heart. That is why the Bible says, "Son, give me thy heart." That is where God wants to start. So, if you are concerned about what is happening to you or the way the enemy is sitting on your wealth, the first place you should allow the Lord to work upon is your heart. Prosperity starts from within.

THINGS TO CHECK IF YOU WANT TO SPEAK WOE TO FAILURE

1. Your heaven: Deuteronomy 28:23 says, *"And thy heaven that is over thy head shall be brass..."* It says, "Thy heaven," meaning that unto every man has been allocated a spiritual airspace. Unto every nation has been allocated a spiritual airspace. There is something called a "Personal heaven." That is why it says, "Thy heaven." That personal heaven covers and controls your life. Therefore, the first thing to check is whether your heavens are closed or not. If the heavens over the head of a person are closed, all kinds of terrible things will be happening to the person. So, one powerful prayer you need to pray is for the brassy heavens to be shattered and for the heavens to open.

WHAT HAPPENS IF THE HEAVENS OF A PERSON ARE CLOSED?

1. Demons will overcome the person with ease.
2. The person will start projects but will not be able to finish them.
3. The person will start the same business others do and prosper but will not do well.
4. The person will plant much but reap very little.
5. The whole of life would become a struggle.
6. The person may go for deliverance and confess scriptures but the problem will remain the same.
7. The person will labour so much but achieve so little because devourers have been released unto the labour of the person.
8. The person will be living on old or past achievements.
9. There will be no fresh fire in the person's spiritual life. His prayer becomes an ordinary noise. During prayers, the mind will wander away. Bible reading and quiet time will become dry because the heaven is already closed.
10. The person will find it so easy to coexist with darkness. The person will be living with people who are possessed by evil spirits and will not know, even when they are responsible for the person's problems.
11. The person's expectation would be cut off most of the time.
12. The person will have stubborn satanic dominion fighting against him.
13. The person's businesses will be running into debt.
14. There will be scarcity of testimonies.
15. There will be no vision, dreams or revelations to teach the person where he should go.
16. There will be unexplainable hardship.
17. Darkness will be running after the person instead of light.
18. Anywhere the person goes, his presence would seem to ignite hatred.
19. The worst thing about a closed heaven is that it provides a

GOD IS THE ULTIMATE SOURCE OF PROSPERITY AND EVERY TRUE PROSPERITY BEGINS FROM THE INNER MAN

comfortable condition for the spirit of poverty to operate.

THE SPIRIT OF POVERTY BRINGS FORTH THE FOLLOWING:

- Lack of ideas.
- Laziness.
- Pestilence.
- Fear
- Agents of darkness into one's
- business.
- Breach of business promises.
- Mismanagement of funds.
- Direct attack by the enemies against one's wealth.
- Demonic business capital.
- Nakedness in the dream.
- Sicknesses that drain money.
- Constant disappointment.
- Unfulfilled promises.
- Conversion of businesses to dungeons or desert lands.

All thee are children of the spirit of poverty.

THE HEAVENS REMAIN CLOSED FOR THE FOLLOWING REASONS:

- Sin and disobedience.
- Ignorance.
- Trying ugodly methods to get money.
- Being stingy towards God.
- Ignorance about how to get deliverance.
- Not seeking first the kingdom of God and His righteousness.

KEYS TO SPEAKING WOE UNTO FAILURE

1. Surrender your life to Jesus.

2. Repent and humble yourself. The Bible says, "If my people which are called by my name shall humble themselves..." You need to repent and humble yourself before God.

3. If you have been taking financial advantage of other people, stop doing so. It is the blessing of God that makes rich without adding sorrow to it.

4. Hate poverty with perfect hatred. Hate it with all your heart.

5. Commit yourself to living a life that will fulfill the eternal purpose of God.

6. Contribute willingly and generously to the needs of others.

7. Use your possession to further the things of the kingdom of God.

PRAYER POINTS

1. Oh God, arise and empower me to prosper, in the name of Jesus.

2. Every power sitting on my wealth, die, in the name of Jesus.

3. Every satanic agenda for my prosperity, die, in the name of Jesus.

4. Foundational poverty in my life, die, in the name of Jesus.

5. Oh star of my destiny, arise and shine, in the name of Jesus.

6. Every witchcraft altar working against my prosperity, die, in the name of Jesus.

7. Every witchcraft bag holding my breakthrough, roast, in the name of Jesus.

8. Every ancestral debt collector forcing me to pay for what I did not buy, die, in the name of Jesus.

9. (Place one hand on the head and one hand on the stomach) Every wicked plantation in my life, be uprooted by the power of God, in the name of Jesus.

10. Every failure in my family line, die, in the name of Jesus.

11. Every covenant of death with familiar spirit, die, in the name of Jesus.

12. Inherited backwardness, die, in the name of Jesus.

13. Every satanic investigation into my future, die, in the name of Jesus.

14. It is my turn to prosper therefore, every poverty magnet in my life, die, die, die, in the name of Jesus.

15. Every parasite feeding on my finances, I disgrace you by fire, in the name of Jesus.

16. Every hole created in my pocket, blood of Jesus, block it up, in the name of Jesus.

17. (Point your right finger to the ground) Evil powers of my father's house that are disturbing my finances, this is your burial ground, enter, in the name of Jesus.

18. (Point your right finger to the ground) Evil powers of my mother's house swallowing my money, this is your burial ground, enter, in the name of Jesus.

19. My poverty, bye, bye, in the name of Jesus.

20. In the room of abandonment where I have been forgotten, Oh Lord, bring me out, in the name of Jesus.

21. Oh Lord, make a covenant of favour with me, in the name of Jesus.

22. (Grab your head with your two hands) The favour that came with this head that has been stolen away, Oh Lord, locate it and bring it to me, in the name of Jesus.

| THE PROPHET | David versus Goliath 27 |

23. Every spiritual opposition to my moving forward operating in the heavenlies, scatter, in the name of Jesus.

24. Every foundational opposition to my prosperity in the land of the living and in the land of the dead, die, in the name of Jesus.

25. Environmental wickedness saying 'No' to my prosperity, before I sit down now, die, in the name of Jesus.

26. Oh Lord my God, baptize me with your divine favour for profitable employment, in the name of Jesus.

27. I refuse to work like an elephant and eat like an ant, in the name of Jesus.

28. The anointing to make my money work for me, fall upon me now, in the name of Jesus.

29. Whatever must break for me to have a breakthrough, break now, in the name of Jesus.

30. Every power keeping me in the wrong position, what are you waiting for? Die, in the name of Jesus.

31. Oh God of Israel, take me from where I am to where you want me to be, in the name of Jesus.

32. Every power that is terminating my advancement, Oh thunder of God, destroy it now, in the name of Jesus.

33. Every power that is keeping stagnancy in my family line, what are you waiting for? Die, in the name of Jesus.

34. My life, move forward by fire, in the name of Jesus.

35. Every power distributing failure in my family, disappear, in the name of Jesus.

36. Every fire of failure burning mercilessly in my family line, Holy Ghost fire consume it, in the name of Jesus.

37. Every chronic failure violating my success, die, in the name of Jesus.

38. Any power planning to close down the source of my food, run mad, in the name of Jesus.

39. Let every woe in the Bible bombard all enemies of my career, in the name of Jesus.

40. If I am in the wrong job, Oh God my Father, open my eyes to see the right job, in the name of Jesus.

41. Every mountain of business failure, disappear now, in the name of Jesus.

42. Every tree of business failure, what are you waiting for? Die, in the name of Jesus.

43. I receive wisdom to prosper, in the name of Jesus.

44. Every power of my father's house creating scarcity for me in the midst of prosperity, your time is up, therefore, die, in the name of Jesus.

45. You altar of wastage swallowing my money, vomit my money and die, in the name of Jesus.

46. I shall not die before my testimonies, in the name of Jesus.

47. Fire of deliverance and blood of Jesus, purge my foundation from profitless hard work, in the name of Jesus.

48. I cut down every tree of profitless hard work in my life, in the name of Jesus.

49. Oh God, arise and break the confidence of the wicked, in the name of Jesus.

50. Those who despise me shall witness my progress, in the name of Jesus.

51. Every good thing stolen from my destiny in the dream, I repossess you by fire, in the name of Jesus.

52. Every bewitchment of my labour, I cancel you, in the name of Jesus.

SPEAK WOE UNTO FAILURE

is a message delivered at the Mountain of Fire and Miracles Ministries by the General Overseer, Dr. D.K. Olukoya.

A CALL TO SERVE

Are you a member of MFM with a burden to help the needy, are you interested in alleviating the plight of the poor or in the spread of the gospel through the sponsorship of the publication of tracts? Your resources, time and talent can be extended to several groups that are in charge of these areas. These groups include:

o   We care Ministry,
o   Mission Outreach
o   Tracts and Publications
o   Ministry to Drug addicts
o   Campus fellowship
o   Ministry to Schools
o   Ministry to Glorious Children, etc.

Thus says the Lord, "Verily I say unto you, in as much as ye have done it unto one of the least of these my brethren, ye have done it unto me" Matthew 25 : 40.

WONDERFUL JESUS!

GOD TURNS MY PERSECUTIONS INTO BLESSINGS

For a long time, I suffered persecutions in my marriage and place of work particularly when I joined this church. Whenever I asked for permission to close early from work to enable me attend prayer warriors' meeting, my boss would look for a way to delay me. He went further to include my name on the list of those to be retired, though it was not time for my retirement. But to the glory of God, all the benefits following this retirement that were sat upon by the enemy were released unto me after much prayers. I even received more than three times what I was earning while in office. Now I have more time for the Lord and He has also blessed me with a very good business. Praise the Lord!

Sis. Funmi
MFM Alagbole

I AM BLESSED WITH A BOUNCING BABY BOY

To the glory of God, my marriage has been blessed with a bouncing baby boy against the wishes of household witches and wizards. Praise the Lord!

Bro. Ebongwu
MFM Ajilo, Ondo

JESUS SAVES

Recently, on a Sunday while in the church, I received a phone call that one of the children living with me had convulsion. Immediately I prayed and all the children at home prayed as well and the child was revived. Praise the Lord!

Sis. Bola
MFM Ijaiye Ojokoro

EVIL PLANS CANCELLED

Before I came here I used to have severe headache. I decided to visit a native doctor in my village, who prepared a charm for me but the headache still persisted. However, somebody introduced me to this church and I went for deliverance. On the last day of the deliverance programme, the Lord delivered me. Praise the Lord!

Bro. Andrew
MFM Olowora

ABDOMINAL PAIN GONE

Since I had my last set of twins some years ago, I used to have serious pain in my lower abdomen. I usually took pain relievers whenever the pain came. Recently, I went for a holiday at a relation's place who noticed the pain and she advised me to see a doctor. But at a PMCH programme G.O. gave a word of knowledge about someone who had a problem of chronic stomach upset that was being healed. I claimed the miracle and to the glory of God, the pain has ceased completely. Praise the Lord!

Sis. Oluwakemi
MFM Egbe

UNCOMMON FAVOUR

A friend of mine helped me by transferring her rented shop to me without the consent of the landlord. After sometime the landlord threatened to arrest me with the police. But I was advised to come to this ministry for deliverance which I did. After the deliverance programme, the landlord decided to drop the case against me and allowed me to continue to use the shop. God gave me favour before the landlord. Praise the Lord!

Sis. Favour
MFM Asalu

ISSUE OF BLOOD CEASES

Sometime ago, I was urinating blood for almost 12 days. I prayed to God to reveal the source of my problem, which God did and after several prayer sessions and the use of anointing oil, I got healed to God's glory. Praise the Lord!

Sis. Emily
MFM Idimu

FRUIT OF THE WOMB

I stood in the gap for a sister of mine who was married for 15 years but had no child. Recently, she gave her life to Jesus Christ and now, she has a baby boy. Praise the Lord!

Sis. Aderoju
MFM Apara

MISSING SON FOUND

My son left home to an unknown destination. All efforts to find him did not yield any result. During one of our PMCH programmes, I presented the case to God and some days later, he telephoned me. Praise the Lord!

Sis. Osawe
MFM Benin City

The following winners of the Junior Fire in the Word crossword puzzle and quiz should collect their gifts at the Tracts and Publications office, MFM International Headquarters, Lagos.

Name	Age	Branch
1. Esther Ayomide Garba	10	Headquarters
2. Ruth Igbe	10	Ajegunle 3
3. Godwin Akinbule	9	Ajegunle 2
4. Precious Owolabi	8	Oworon 1
5. Babatunde Olufunke	9	Gasline, Sango Ota

FIRE IN THE WORD, is a weekly Spiritual Bulletin of the Mountain of Fire and Miracles Ministries, published by Tracts and Publications Group. All Enquiries should be addressed to The Editor, Mountain of Fire Magazine, 13, Olasimbo Street, off Olumo Road, Onike, P.O. Box 2990, Sabo Yaba, Lagos, Nigeria. Telephone 01- 867439, 864631, 868766, 08023180236.E-mail: mfmtractsandpublications@yahoo.com Copyright reserved.

FIRE IN THE WORD

Ye Shall Know the Truth, and the Truth Shall Make You Free (John 8:32)

ISSN 1595 - 7314 Vol. 12 No. 41 Sun. 24th - Sat. 30 Aug., 2008

THE AGENDA OF THE STRONG MAN

My year of unprecedented greatness and unmatchable increase
Deuteronomy 28:13, Psalm 71:21, Ephesians 3:20, Psalm 92:10

Our message this week is titled, "The agenda of the strongman." We shall consider the message under seven subheadings.

The Bible does not waste words neither does it exaggerate. If it says that something is strong, it means it must be strong. Matthew 12:29 says, *"Or else, how can one enter into a strong man's house,* (there is a spiritual personality known as the strong man and the strong man has a house), *and spoil his goods,* (the strong man has goods, but whether these goods belong to him or not is another matter) *except he first bind the strong man?* (So, if you want to enter into the house of the strong man, the first thing is to bind him) *and then he will spoil his house."*

If Jesus says you will spoil his house, it means that the material the strong man keeps does not belong to him. It means that one way or another, this strong man is a thief.

Mark 3:27 says, *"No man can enter into a strong man's house, and spoil his goods, except he will first bind the strong man; and then he will spoil his house."*

Luke 11:21-22 says, *"When a strong man armed keepeth his palace, his goods are in peace, But when a stronger than he shall come upon him, and*

overcome him, he taketh from him all his amour wherein he trusted, and divideth his spoils." So, the strong man is armed, and keeps his palace. But thank God there is somebody known as the stronger man.

THE REALITY OF THE STRONGMAN

There is a spiritual force known as the strongman. Sometime ago, during one of our Anointing Services at the TBS, Lagos, we opened the meeting with a prayer point that says, "You strongman standing at the gate of my Promised land, fall down and die, in the name of Jesus." And people began to pray. A certain sister in that prayer meeting fell down immediately the prayer began and did not open her eyes or stand up until we were about to share the grace in fellowship. Before then the people beside her tried to wake her up but did not succeed. According to her, in that sleep, she found herself before a big king that had five wives and she could recognize all those five wives as her four sisters and herself. They all dressed alike. For the first time, a battle started

ONE OF THE MOST CLEVER HOOKS OF THE STRONG MAN WHICH HE HAS USED VERY EFFECTIVELY IS IGNORANCE

between her and the king. As at the time she came for the programme, all the four sisters, including herself had lost their marriages. But as the battle went on while we were busy doing other things, she was able to take off the wedding ring of the king and threw it at him. It was then she heard, "Let us share the grace in fellowship." That was all she saw for the seven hours the programme lasted. By the time she got home, her husband was standing in the cold waiting for her and he begged her for reconciliation. This is what happens when you deal with the strong man. The strong man is real.

At that same crusade, when the same prayer point was going on, one brother vomited a live snake, which had to be killed. Later, he told us that he came from a part of the country where snakes are sacred; they are not killed. He did not know that he had swallowed his own strong man that was controlling his life. The brother is the only person prospering in the whole of his family now.

Also, a certain brother noticed that within a few months, after the wedding of his brothers, their wives would become so sick that they would not be able to come out again. It happened to all his four elder brothers. They married and all their wives were confined

DELIVERANCE CASE (THE STORY OF MY LIFE = PART 28)

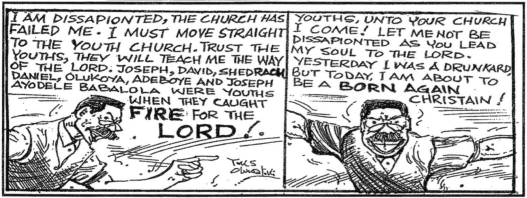

to sickbeds. So, when he joined the Mountain of Fire and Miracles Ministries, he began to pray, and the Lord showed him a revelation of what was going on. At the night of the wedding day, their mother used to pour water on the legs of these women and washed their legs with the water. And the Lord told him that if he wanted to escape, this strong man must not wash the leg of his wife. When the brother wanted to get married, he started praying for divine wisdom on how to escape. The Lord helped him, his wife got to the car before the end of the wedding reception, he joined her and that was how they both escaped. There was an uproar at the reception and the most angry person was his mother because she did not have the opportunity to pour water on the bride's legs like she did with her other sons' wives. By the following morning, she began to swell up and after three days, she confessed that she was the one that dealt with all the wives of her other

sons because she was afraid that once they got married, they would not look after her. By the third day, she was gone. That is the reality of the strong man.

IDENTITY OF THE STRONG MAN

Who is the strongman? The strong man is the controller over a group of bad spirits. It is the ruling spirit over a group of wicked spirits. It is the power source and the dominating influence in a particular situation. The strong man is the principal or leading demon. The strong man is the key to setting a situation free. It is the dominant evil power or the headmaster of demonic powers. It is the prison warder of the devil who stays at the gate and refuses the release of people. The strong man is the main root that energizes problems. It is the commanding general of the evil army. It is the sergeant major

calling the evil command. It is the captain of the stronghold. It is the king in the palace of darkness from whom authority flows down. The senior serpent or senior scorpion is the strong man. It is the stubborn power assigned to a problem or the ancestral power in charge of family bondage. It is the principality in a person's heavens. It is the satanic prince over a particular territory, controlling it.

There are different strong men ruling over particular areas, meaning that a strong man can sit in the heavenlies and rule over the spirits on earth. It is the power that gives order and strength to lower powers. That is, it is from him lesser demons draw strength. It is the Pharaoh amongst a person's pursuers. It is the Goliath among a person's aggressors; the arrow head of a person's attackers and the one that is leading them. It is the commander in chief of the spiritual armed robbery services. It is the manager of the warehouse where people's blessings are caged. It is the satanic angel that challenges God in a person's life. It is that dominating jealous spirit wife or spirit husband, the senior fisherman of satan that fishes for him. It is the power that confronts a person's angels of blessings. It is the kind of prince that confronted the angel bringing the answers to the prayers of Daniel. It is the chief ancestral demon, the first evil power to enter a particular area.

CHARACTERISTICS OF THE STRONG MAN

He is strong. He is armed. He has a palace. He has warehouses. He guards what he has stolen. When the strong man is still inside a person, other wicked spirits will always come back. The strong man has human intermediaries. When there is a battle and the strong man is being challenged, he will first of all send his children to go and fight before the victim encounters him.

Every continent, nation, town, village and family has it own strong man attached to it. A strong man could be attached to a person's career and will not allow the person to move forward. A strong man could be attached to the business life of a person. A strong man could be attached to somebody's marriage, job, house, academics or finance. And until the strong man is identified and dealt with,

problems will continue. Sometimes, there would be a temporary relief and the problems would come back.

It is the strong man that usually considers a person's body as his home. In the military, when the general surrenders, all troops under his command automatically surrenders with him. So, the rule of the game is this: whenever the strong man in a person's life surrenders, all those under him have no option than to surrender. The strong man is the food particle stuck to the bottom of the plate, which you need to scrub off before it goes. It is unlike other ones which you wash off easily, you need to scrub it off.

THE RULE OF THE STRONG MAN

Many people in the world are under a satanic kingdom but they do not know. There is a particular satanic power over all racial groups. Believers need to find out the strong man over their own race, nation, town or village. It is your duty to identify the strong man over your family. For some families, the strongman is a eater of flesh and drinker of blood. That

A SINGLE STRONGMAN IN A FAMILY IS ENOUGH TO DESTROY THE WHOLE FAMILY

is why there are always disputes in such families. Pride, inconsistencies, laziness etc are strong men. We need to discover the strong men over the situation that we have, bind them and set our lives free. The issue of the strong man is more serious when we consider our individual lives.

The strong man is responsible for sudden failure at the edge of breakthroughs. Continuous failure at the edge of success, frustration, continuous disappointment, bad timing, chain problems, etc are signs that a peerson is under the rule of a strong man and needs to identify him and spoil him in order to take what belongs to him or her.

THE HOOKS OF THE STRONG MAN

He has hooks with which he hooks people.

1. Ignorance One of the most clever hooks of the strongman which he has used very effectively is ignorance. When you are ignorant and do not agree that you are ignorant, you are lost. Ignorance is a terrible thing. Ignorance of the word of God and the enemies to fight is a terrible thing. You must know who Jesus is and at the same time, you must know who the enemy is. Physical ignorance is very bad but spiritual ignorance is worse. The Bible says, "My people are destroyed

for lack of knowledge" (Hosea 4:6).

2. **Evil names:** The strong man has used this hook so effectively. Beloved, please check the name you are bearing. There is need also to be careful about some Bible names. Some believers call themselves Job. The meaning of Job is hated, persecuted. By such names people invite curses on themselves everyday. I am yet to see a man bearing Job who does not have serious trouble. Some sisters too call themselves Mary or Miriam, which mean bitterness and rebellion. Be sure you know what name you have given to yourself. Even the biblical ones must be checked out. A certain man of God had to change his name from Paul to David because he discovered that Paul means small.

So Paullina too means small. When people call such a person, they are saying the person will never get big. Do not bear a name because it sounds good. Christians must be careful about the names they bear. Some even bear idolatrons names and claim that they do not need deliverance. The strong man can use your name against you if it is a bad one.

3. **Unconfessed sin:** Proverbs 28:13 says, *"He that covereth his sins shall not prosper: but whoso confesseth and forsaketh them shall have mercy."* Some people think that if they do not confess their sins to God, God will never know about them. When God forgives sins, He blots them off. So, if you have some sins you are keeping and refuse to confess, it is enough hook

for the strong man to come upon you and hold you tight.

4. **Unforgiving spirit:** The Bible says, 'When you pray, forgive.'

5. **Occult involvement:** You cannot bind the strongman when you have demonic materials in your possession. If you come from a family where they are all occult members, you need to pray and set yourself free.

6. **Covenant with idols:** Once a person has been given to an idol, the strong man will use that to pursue the person. Anyone who is born in some cities in Nigeria need to go for deliverance without any argument because of the enshrined idolatory in those places.

7. **The effect of a curse:** If a person is working under a curse, the strong man will take advantage of that to afflict the person. The Bible says, "Why do the heathen rage, and the people imagine a vain thing? The kings of the earth set themselves, and the rulers take counsel together, against the Lord and against his anointed." These are the powers called the strong men.

BINDING THE STRONG MAN

Colossians 2:15 says, *"And having spoiled principalities and powers, he made a show of them openly, triumphing over them in it."* The Bible says, "Whatsoever you bind on earth

THE PROPHET | David versus Goliath 28

I SAMUEL 18:4.
... JONATHAN STRIPED HIMSELF OF HIS GARMENT (ROBE),... AND GAVE IT TO DAVID,... EVEN HIS SWORD, ... BOW AND HIS GIRDLE,...

THIS IS UNBELIEVABLE JONATHAN!

I SAMUEL 18:5
DAVID WENT OUT WITHERSOEVER SAUL SENT HIM, AND BEHAVED HIMSELF WISELY: AND SAUL SET HIM OVER THE MEN OF WAR,...

YES SIR! GREAT KING SAUL!

shall be bound in heaven." The initiative for the binding comes from the earth. Then the heavens will respond. If you bind nothing on earth, the heavens too will bind nothing.

WHAT DOES IT MEAN TO BIND?

To bind means:

1. To stagnate.
2. To polarize.
3. To paralyze.
4. To make it hard for a person to move.
5. To yoke.

SPOILING THE STRONG MAN

To spoil means:

1. To snatch away.
2. To remove things by force.
3. To cease things from him.
4. To carry off the thing as a spoil.

The Bible says all these you can do if you deal with the strong man.

SIGNS THAT A STRONGMAN IS INCHARGE OF A SITUATION

1. Unpardonable mistakes.
2. Messing up with breakthroughs.
3. Inability to unseat the enemy.

A single strong man in a family is enough to destroy the whole family. Gideon eventually relocated his family to poverty. From abundance, they came to zero. He had seventy sons from various wives. He was not satisfied, he had an extra one with a prostitute who became a strong man and killed sixty-nine others

Prayers against the strong man are not gentle ones. They are not prayers to joke with. They must be done aggressively in order to silence the strongman completely.

If you have not yet surrendered your life to Jesus, you cannot bind the strong man and cannot spoil his goods. If you want to give your life to Christ, please say the following prayer:

"Father, in the name of Jesus, I come before you now. I acknowledge that I am a sinner, forgive my sins and cleanse me with your blood. I renounce the devil and all his works. Come into my life Lord Jesus and take control of my life, in Jesus' name. Amen.

PRAYER POINTS

1. Every strong man of my father's house, die, in the name of Jesus.
2. Every strong man of my mother's house, die, in the name of Jesus.
3. Strong man of poverty, your time is up, die, in the name of Jesus.
4. Witchcraft strong man, your time is up, therefore, die, in the name of Jesus.
5. Every strong man attached to my career, die, in the name of Jesus.
6. Every strong man attached to my ministry, die, in the name of Jesus
7. Every strong man attached to my marriage, die, in the name of Jesus
8. Internal strong man, come out with all your roots, in the name of Jesus.

THE AGENDA OF THE STRONG MAN
is a message delivered at the Mountain of Fire and Miracles Ministries by the General Overseer, Dr. D.K. Olukoya.

A CALL TO SERVE

Are you a member of MFM with a burden to help the needy, are you interested in alleviating the plight of the poor or in the spread of the gospel through the sponsorship of the publication of tracts? Your resources, time and talent can be extended to several groups that are in charge of these areas. These groups include:

o   We care Ministry,
o   Mission Outreach
o   Tracts and Publications
o   Ministry to Drug addicts
o   Campus fellowship
o   Ministry to Schools
o   Ministry to Glorious Children, etc.

Thus says the Lord, "Verily I say unto you, in as much as ye have done it unto one of the least of these my brethren, ye have done it unto me" Matthew 25 : 40.

WONDERFUL JESUS!

MIRACULOUS DELIVERY

My daughter was taken to the hospital by her husband for delivery. The doctor told them that he would not be able to handle it and referred them to another hospital. I was called and as we were going to another hospital, the taxi had a problem. The husband went to look for another taxi. Then I remembered the water that was blessed during 07-07-07 programme. I prayed and gave her the water to drink and before the husband came back, she gave birth inside the taxi. God is marvellous.

Sis. Alice
MFM Akute

GOD DELIVERS MY SON FROM CONSEQUENCES OF EVIL ACTION

Last year, one of my sons yielded to evil advice and went for money rituals using my photograph. The ritual was not successful and he consequently became mad. He was taken to an hospital where he confessed to his evil deeds. To the glory of God, he is now hale and hearty and back to his normal sense. I am also alive and healthy. Praise God!

Sis. Elizabeth
MFM Ijegun

GOD MANIFESTS HIS POWER

For about four weeks, I had typhoid fever. My daddy said I should take herbal concoctions which I refused. He took me to the hospital yet the fever did not go. I was sent back to the hospital the second time yet the sickness refused to go. My daddy said I was the only one out of his children who received Christ and refused to take herbs and that he would forsake me. Then I cried to the Lord, and asked brethren to join me in prayers. God healed me and my parents were surprised. To further manifest His power, He gave me another job. Praise God.

Bro. Olatunji
MFM Itire/Ijesha

GOD ANSWERS PRAYERS

My brother was out of the country for some years and failed to communicate with us at home. I kept requesting for prayers concerning him and to the glory of God, I recently got his contact and we have since been communicating. He even supported me financially in getting a place for my business. Praise God!

Bro. Chibuzo
MFM Iba

GOD HEALS MY INFIRMITIES

During the last Power Must Change Hands programme (PMCH), I received healing from a particular illness. Secondly, one of my sons-in-law lost his job but miraculously, God provided another one for him. Lastly, I thank God for saving my daughter from being one of the casualties of the last explosion that occurred in London. Praise the Lord!

Sis. Adejobi
MFM Idimu

GOD SILENCES MY ENEMIES

My enemies were silenced when the Lord delivered me safely of my baby like the Hebrew women. Also, the Lord perfected His provision for me through a shop for business, a motor car for my husband and good health care for my children. Praise the Lord!

Sis. Aderinto
MFM Alagbole

CHEST PAIN DISAPPEARS

I thank the Lord for healing me of a long-term chest pain after I went through a weekend deliverance programme. Now I enjoy a healthy life. Praise the Lord!

Bro. Benjamin
MFM Ogudu/Ojota

GOD VINDICATES ME

There was a quarrel over a missing telephone handset, between my son and his friends. The quarrel turned to an armed robbery and illegal possession of fire arms case against my son. The Landlord Association stepped into the matter and it was found that my son was innocent of the charges. I thank the Lord for coming to my rescue. Praise the Lord!

Sis. Bridget
MFM Abaranje

Junior Fire in the Word

"Ye shall know the truth and the truth shall set you free" John 8:32   Vol 7:9

The following winners of the Junior Fire in the Word crossword puzzle and quiz should collect their gifts at the Tracts and Publications office, MFM International Headquarters, Lagos.

Name	Age	Branch
1. Esther Ayomide Garba	10	Headquarters
2. Ruth Igbe	10	Ajegunle 3
3. Godwin Akinbule	9	Ajegunle 2
4. Precious Owolabi	8	Oworon 1
5. Babatunde Olufunke	9	Gasline, Sango Ota

- -

Hello Children!
Your popular Spiritual tonic "Junior Fire in the Word"
Is on the stand again. It is still as refreshing as ever.
Now you have more opportunities to win Fanstastic prizes every month as you send in your entries
Hurry grab your copy from the vendors.
The price is still N20.

FIRE IN THE WORD, is a weekly Spiritual Bulletin of the Mountain of Fire and Miracles Ministries, published by Tracts and Publications Group. All Enquiries should be addressed to The Editor, Mountain of Fire Magazine, 13, Olasimbo Street, off Olumo Road, Onike, P.O. Box 2990, Sabo Yaba, Lagos, Nigeria. Telephone 01- 867439, 864631, 868766, 08023180236.E-mail: mfmtractsandpublications@yahoo.com
Copyright reserved.

FIRE IN THE WORD

Ye Shall Know the Truth, and the Truth Shall Make You Free (John 8:32)

ISSN 1595 - 7314 Vol. 12 No. 42 Sun. 31st Aug. - Sat. 6th Sept., 2008

When your MARRIAGE Needs DELIVERANCE

My year of unprecedented greatness and unmatchable increase
Deuteronomy 28:13, Psalm 71:21, Ephesians 3:20, Psalm 92:10

Beloved, our message this week titled, "When your marruage needs deliverance" is very important for all married people and those who want to get married.

God completed everything He needed to do in the Garden of Eden, passed it through His spiritual laboratory and declared that the whole thing was good. But all of a sudden in Genesis 2:18 we come across something that was not good. Genesis 2:18: *"And the Lord God said, It is not good that the man should be alone; I will make him an help meet for him."* This is the beginning of marriage. There is no history book that goes further than this. Verse 24: *"Therefore shall a man leave his father and his mother, and shall cleave unto his wife; and they shall be one flesh."* The Bible says: The man shall leave his parents but if he is still tied to their apron strings then deliverance would be needed. It means that it is possible for a man to be married without leaving his parents. The Bible says, "...he shall cleave unto his wife..." wife in the singular, meaning one. It did not say, "his wives." Also it says, "Therefore shall a man" and not a boy. "... And they shall

be one flesh." This is the foundation of marriage.

THE FAMILY

The family is the foundation of civilization. It is a church within a church. It is a world within a world. It is the building block of the society. The family is the root of both the church and the state.

The family is like a book; the children are the pages and the parents are the cover. Nobody has a choice how he is to be born or given birth to. The concept of family originated from God and it is the school of human virtues. If things go right in the family, if marriages go right, everything will go right everywhere.

FORCES OF MARRIAGES DESTRUCTION

There are powers called, "The powers of marriage destruction." Sometimes, their work starts in the womb. It does not only start when somebody gets married. Once they discover that a person's marriage will move God's purpose forward, they will begin to create problems. They

WHEN PEOPLE RUSH INTO MARRIAGE DUE TO PREGNANCY, THERE WOULD BE PROBLEMS

are specific powers delegated to pull marriages down.

Many years ago, I prayed with a sister who wanted to get married but her marriage was considered to be very risky by the devil. It was the kind of marriage the devil did not want to permit. One day as we were praying, I saw her standing before me and twelve men were queuing up in her front. The number twelve at the back was the right man, her husband. The Lord was saying that the devil was going to send eleven men before the right person. And one by one, they were coming; the handsome, rich, educated polished etc seeking to marry her but she was able to turn them down through prayers. Eventually the right person came along and she was able to fulfill the will of God. However, she almost fell for one of them, whom she really liked; it was the enemy trying to confuse her.

There are specific powers delegated to pull marriages down. Some time ago, some witches gathered in South Africa and fasted for two hundred and one days against Christian marriages. Many marriages are bewitched and sometimes affected persons carry the bewitchment to church, and it is

DELIVERANCE CASE (The Story of my life - Part 29)

very obvious. Once you see a couple going to church and the husband is walking fast not wanting the wife to be by his side, you know that bewitchment has set in already. Unfortunately, many people do not attach importance to the issue of marriage. Some rush into any kind of marriage just to appear to be married. It is a tragedy that so many sisters have died untimely due to wrong marriages. They would have remained alive if they had not married. The marriage became graveyards to them. It is sad to know that many people do not really care about the type of marriage they get involved in.

A person's life never remains the same after marriage. Wedding is just for one day while marriage is for life. Many marriages have broken up due to seemingly light issues, but that is the work of bewitchment.

WEDLOCK OR PADLOCK

Many people will help you to organise your wedding but marriage is between two people. The next horrible thing after hell fire is a bad marriage. Marriage is an institution created by God. Marriage can make or mar your life in no small measure. But a good and godly marriage is a bedrock of correct living and success.

There is no difference between wedlock and padlock. Wedlock is padlock – those concerned are padlocked. Marriage is either a holy wedlock or an unholy padlock. The wedding ring that many people desire so much is the smallest handcuff in history. The truth is; it is better to be laughed at that you are not married than for you to be unable to laugh because you are married.

Anyone who enters into a marriage relationship because the woman is beautiful or because the man is handsome is like a man who bought a house because he likes the paint. If a child of God marries a child of the devil, satan his or her father- in-law will trouble his or her life.

When a marriage is wrong, the children from such a marriage are in bondage. If marriages work in our society, a lot of things will start going on very well. A lot of marriages have been caged by the enemy. That is why you find some pastors beating up their wives. The enemy knows that once he causes disunity in a home, that family will not move forward. Also, the devil has a way of bringing problems when couples are at the edge of their breakthroughs and they will start fighting and miss the breakthroughs.

WHAT KIND OF MARRIAGES NEED DELIVERANCE?

1. Marriages where communication has broken down. I have seen couples that write notes to themselves instead of talking and they live in the same flat. The man would bring his girl friend home and the woman too would bring her boy friend home. The boy friend of the woman and the man's girl friend would greet each other but the couple would not talk to each other. When communication breaks down, it is a sign that bewitchment has set in. Deliverance is therefore needed. It means that the enemy has become a third party in the marriage. It is very unfortunate to know that marriages conducted in Pentecostal churches break down now unlike in the olden days when it was unheard of.

2. Marriages where in-laws have taken over, deliverance is needed.

3. Marriages retained by money. The couple stays together as long as there is money. Immediately there is no money, it breaks down.

4. Regretted marriages. These are situations where partners do not have time for one another.

5. Marriages where both parties are actors and actresses. They pretend as if things are alright but within, fighting, cursing and quarrelling dominate the relationship. There are many acting husbands and wives.

6. When the marriage has entered into a third party cage. That is the home is controlled by a third party. It could be the husband's friends or in-laws.

7. Shallow marriages. This is where there is no true love. The people involved just got married for some purposes.

8. Marriages where there is an abusive husband and a stubborn wife.

9. Marriages where both parties are committing adultery. The only way a person can be free from this is to remain on fire always.

10. Troubled marriages. These are situations where you have sicknesses, satanic attacks, surgical operations, children problem, lack of peace etc.

11. Marriages where couples beat and bite one another. Baby husbands beat their wives and baby wives bite their husbands.

12. Polygamous marriages. Anyone who is a product of

FAMILIES THAT DO NOT PRAY TOGETHER ARE LOOKING FOR SERIOUS TROUBLE

polygamy, needs to go for deliverance. All polygamous marriages need restitution and deliverance.

13. Marriages with the foundation of sex before marriage. If a couple had sex with each other before they were joined in marriage, the marriage would suffer attacks from the enemy because they have offended God. The Bible says that marriage is honourable and the bed must remain undefiled but God will judge adulterers and adulteresses. Once you build the foundation of your marriage on sex before marriage, you will certainly have troubles.

14. Marriages to satanic agents.

15. Marriages with the foundation of accidental pregnancy. When people rush into marriage due to pregnancy, there would be problems.

16. Marriages as a result of demonic consultation.

17. Forced marriages. Marriages where couples were forced into the relationship either by parents or others.

18. Child marriages. Situations where children of age eight, twelve, thirteen etc are given out for marriage would create problems.

19. Marriages based on tribal sentiments.

20. Marriages as a result of demonic prophecies.

21. Marriages with the foundation of trial and error. Marriages entered into after some samplings have a bad foundation.

22. Marriages with blood covenant.

23. Marriages in which the bride's legs were washed with water on the wedding day.

24. Marriages in which a goat or any other animal was attached to any of the parties, or the couple was given a small girl to take away.

25. All marriages done in a crude traditional way need deliverance. Deliverance is needed for marriages done with alcohol, alligator pepper, cola nuts etc.

26. Marriage in which the bride was stolen. That is there was no dowry, no engagement and no marriage. The woman just moved into the man's house. For such marriages, correction marriage alone is not the answer, deliverance is needed.

27. Marriages for the purpose of obtaining documents.

28. Couples that have the problem of spirit husband and spirit wife. Such marriages need deliverance.

29. Marriages where the husband sleeps with his in-laws.

30. Marriages where the couples secretly carry out abortions.

31. Marriages where both families never agree and the couples too are not born again.

Beloved, the enemy has really worked hard in this area of human life and is still doing so. The enemy knows that marriage goes beyond the two people involved. It concerns generations and family trees on both sides. The enemy struggles hard to ensure that marriages are built on wrong foundations so that he can do his work of destruction very well. Unfortunately for the ladies, many nice men do not start out very rich and those that are rich treat women like money.

There are demonic influences fighting against marriages that try to work. This is why family prayers are essential for Christians. The family that prays together stays together. God is angry with Christian couples who do not pray together. Families that do not pray together are looking for serious trouble.

Jeremiah 10:25 says, *"Pour out thy fury upon the heathen that know thee not, and upon the families that call not thy name: for they have eaten up Jacob, and devoured him, and consumed him, and have made his habitation desolate."*

Many dangers are done at night. The Bible says, "While men slept the enemy came and sowed tares." Danger comes when husband and wife go to sleep without clearing their disagreement. If you do not settle

THE PROPHET | Saul versus David 3

ISAMUEL.18:5B AND HE (DAVID) WAS ACCEPTED IN THE SIGHT OF ALL THE PEOPLE, AND ALSO IN THE SIGHT OF SAUL'S SERVANTS.

HIGHLY HONOURED SOLDIERS OF THE LORD, THANK YOU FOR ACCEPTING ME!

ISAMUEL 18: 6... WHEN DAVID...RETURNED FROM THE SLAUGHTER OF THE PHILISTINES, THAT THE WOMEN CAME OUT OF ALL CITIES OF ISREAL, SINGING AND **DANCING**... WITH **JOY**...

your disagreement before going to bed every night, there will be a third party on your bed with you. The devil will be the third party. Some husbands are possessed; some wives too, are possessed. There are some people whose natural body would like to preserve the marriage but the spirits within them will be seeking to destroy it; and when there is trouble, they begin to regret. They apologise to one another only to go back to the trouble again.

A sister whose husband is a womanizer, or a drunkard, or a smoker or a grambler or someone that uses charms and believes in it, reads occult books or attends occult meetings or has unbelievers as his friends will only survive in that marriage by carrying out spiritual warfare every night because any time he goes out, he brings in new demons. You need to understand what you are doing so that you do not get involved in that which will pull your life down.

Marriages where couples talk to themselves in a bad language will be destroyed. Nagging and quarrelling in a marriage are signs that there is a bewitching force pursuing that marriage.

HOW TO DELIVER YOUR MARRIAGE

What you should do to avoid these attacks:

1. Get born again. The first thing is new birth. If you got married as unbelievers, or your partner is not born again, you need to pray for new birth.
2. Complete repentance.
3. You must seek God's face for the right partner that is if you are not married yet. If you are, it is too late. You must pray foundational deliverance prayer for your marriage. If you discover that marriages do not work in your family, do not deceive yourself by thinking that those forces will not attack your own.

4. You must cultivate the garden of your heart daily- pray about it daily.
5. Pray consistently for your partner.
6. Your family altar must be on fire.

PRAYERS

1. Every strong man of marriage destruction, die, in the name of Jesus.
2. Every problem introduced into my life by the marriage of my parents, die, in the name of Jesus.
3. Every ancestral spirit husband/wife, your time is up, die, in the name of Jesus.
4. Every witchcraft power of my father's house, release my marriage, in the name of Jesus.
5. Every owner of evil load in my marriage, carry your load, in the name of Jesus.
6. Within seven days, every power pursuing my peace shall be buried, in the name of Jesus.
7. O God, arise and advertise your power in my life, in the name of Jesus.
8. Every evil tree growing in my family line, die, in the name of Jesus.

WHEN YOUR MARRIAGE NEEDS DELIVERANCE is a message delivered at the Mountain of Fire and Miracles Ministries by the General Overseer, Dr. D.K. Olukoya.

WONDERFUL JESUS!

GOD SETS ME FREE

I was sent to the prison for some crimes I committed and was on the death row. While in prison, God manifested Himself to me and I surrendered my life to Jesus. Ten years later, God effected my release from the prison. I am now a free and new person. Praise the Lord!

Bro. Fatai
MFM Iyana Ipaja

I WAS PROMOTED AFTER 10 YEARS

Before I came to this church, I was on the same level in my office for 10 years. But when I got to this church and started praying, God answered me and I have been promoted. Praise the Lord!

Sis. Ogedengbe
MFM Agbelekale

GOD RESTORES MY SLEEP

Some weeks ago, I could not sleep due to severe body pain particularly around my abdomen. I came to the church and after series of prayers with the hospital ministry. I was set free and the abdominal pain has disappeared. Since then I have been sleeping very well. Praise the Lord!

Sis. Funke
MFM Ejigbo

GOD OF ABUNDANT BLESSINGS

Recently, God released me from police detention. He paid up my debt to save me from the harassment of my creditors and miraculously provided seven contracts for me in one day. My business has been fully restored. Praise the Lord!

Bro. Kayode
MFM Aguda

ENEMY OF PROGRESS DISGRACED

I lost my mother some years ago but the enemy of my mother vowed that my younger brother and I will not prosper as long as she was alive. Everything was upside down for us until we joined MFM. God has nullified the evil spell and disgraced the enemy openly. We are now making progress. Praise the Lord!

Sis. Faramabe
MFM Apata

GOD SAVES MY BROTHER FROM STRANGE DEATH

I thank God for saving my elder brother who travelled on official assignment. The vehicle in which they were travelling had an accident on the way and many lives were lost. My brother was the only survivor with no injury on him. Praise God.

Sis. Pat
MFM Aguda

GOD IS INDEED THE GOD OF DELIVERANCE

As I was praying aggressively during the programme titled, "7 Hours with God," I saw a big snake crawling away from me. I also saw a masquerade leaving too. Praise the Lord for the great deliverance. Praise the Lord!

Sis. Agbana
MFM Ado Ekiti

BROKEN MARRIAGE RESTORED

My marriage which was broken down for 14 years has been restored miraculously by God. I was given out in marriage at the age of 15 years. But after sometime, I was sent away from my matrimonial home by my husband with the assistance of my mother in law. During the period of separation, I was introduced to MFM where I gave my like to Christ. I went through series of deliverance and the matter was presented to God. The God that answers by fire answers me last month and restored my marriage after 14 years and peace now reigns in my home. Praise the Lord!

Sis. Juliet
MFM Ajangbadi

GOD AVERTS TRAGEDY

Before I came to this church, nothing I laid my hands on prospered. But since I joined this ministry, things have changed for the better. Also recently, as I was crossing an express road, I lost control suddenly and fell down right at middle of the road. God kept away vehicles for that moment and I was not crushed. Praise the Lord!

Sis. Victoria
MFM Ketu

GREAT DELIVERANCE

I was reluctant to go to Prayer City for 888 Programme because of my children but a friend of my encouraged me to go. She helped me to carry one of the children and my luggage. I used to have severe stomach ache and my stomach was big as if I was pregnant to the extent that people were asking when I would put to bed. But during the ministration, the G.O. gave a word of knowledge concerning my case, immediately the pain disappeared and my stomach became flat. When I got home, the enemy wanted to use my husband to steal my breakthrough but I prayed with my children and God took control. Praise the Lord!

Sis. Chinyere
MFM Olopomeji

SCHOOL OF PRAYER

Presents
OLD STUDENTS' RETREAT

Theme:
"Maintaining the Fire on the Altar"

Date:
Friday 12th December, 2008

Time:
5.00pm-5.00am

Venue:
MFM Prayer City
Km 12, Lagos/Ibadan Expressway, Ibafo.

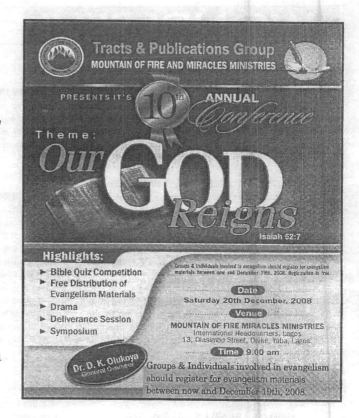

Tracts & Publications Group
MOUNTAIN OF FIRE AND MIRACLES MINISTRIES

PRESENTS IT'S 10th ANNUAL Conference

Theme:
Our GOD Reigns
Isaiah 52:7

Highlights:
▸ Bible Quiz Competition
▸ Free Distribution of Evangelism Materials
▸ Drama
▸ Deliverance Session
▸ Symposium

Dr. D. K. Olukoya
General Overseer

Groups & Individuals involved in evangelism should register for evangelism materials between now and December 19th, 2008. Registration is free

Date
Saturday 20th December, 2008
Venue
MOUNTAIN OF FIRE MIRACLES MINISTRIES
International Headquarters, Lagos
13, Olasimbo Street, Onike, Yaba, Lagos.
Time 9.00 am

Groups & Individuals involved in evangelism should register for evangelism materials between now and December 19th, 2008.

The MFM 2009 Anointed Diary is now on sale. It is a daily devotional guide for Bible Reading and Spiritual Warfare that will make everyday of the year 2009 AD a fulfilling and victorious one for you.

Grab your copy from the vendors.

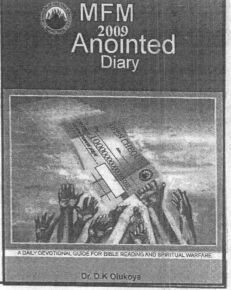

MFM 2009 Anointed Diary

A DAILY DEVOTIONAL GUIDE FOR BIBLE READING AND SPIRITUAL WARFARE

Dr. D.K Olukoya

FIRE IN THE WORD is a weekly Spiritual Bulletin of the Mountain of Fire and Miracles Ministries, published by Tracts and Publications Group. All Enquiries should be addressed to The Editor, Mountain of Fire Magazine, 13, Olasimbo Street, off Olumo Road, Onike, P.O. Box 2990, Sabo Yaba, Lagos, Nigeria. Telephone 01- 867439, 864631, 868766, 08023180236.E-mail: mfmtractsandpublications@yahoo.com Copyright reserved.

FIRE IN THE WORD

Ye Shall Know the Truth, and the Truth Shall Make You Free (John 8:32)

ISSN 1595 - 7314 Vol. 12 No. 43 Sun. 7th - Sat. 13th Sept., 2008

The Negative HARVEST

My year of unprecedented greatness and unmatchable increase
Deuteronomy 28:13, Psalm 71:21, Ephesians 3:20, Psalm 92:10

Our message this week is entitled, "The negative harvest." It is important for a sorrow-free life.

The Bible is a book of truth. Any other opinion or the unbelief of anyone does not change what the Bible says. The Bible says that the scriptures cannot be broken (John 10:35). Hosea 8:7 says, *"For they have sown the wind, and they shall reap the whirlwind; it hath no stalk; The bud shall yield no meal; if so be it yield, the strangers shall swallow it up."* Jeremiah 17:10 says, *"I the Lord search the heart, I try the reins, even to give every man according to his ways, and according to the fruit of his doings."* Ecclesiastes 8:10-11 says, *"And so I saw the wicked buried, who had come and gone from the place of the holy, and they were forgotten in the city where they had so done; this is also vanity. Because sentence against an evil work is not executed speedily, therefore the heart of the sons of men is fully set in them to do evil."* Amos 9:2-4 says, *"Though they dig into hell, thence shall mine hand take them, though they climb up to heaven, thence will I bring them down: And though they hide themselves in the top of Carmel, I will search and take them out thence; and though they be hid from my sight in the bottom of the sea, thence will I command the serpent, and he shall bite them; and though they go into captivity before their enemies, thence will I command the sword, and it shall slay them; and I will set mine eyes upon them for evil, and not for good."* In the New Testament, the book of Matthew 26:52 says, *"Then said Jesus unto him, Put up again thy sword into his place; for all they that take the sword shall perish with the sword."* Galatians 6:7 says, *"Be not deceived; God is not mocked; for whatsoever a man soweth, that shall he also reap."*

THE GRINDING MACHINE OF GOD

God has a grinding machine. The grinding machine of God grinds very slowly yet it grinds exceedingly small. A day of reckoning will certainly come; there must be a pay day some day. Judgment maybe slow but it will certainly come. Anyone who thinks he is very wicked will eventually do to himself what he has done to others. Also, it is important to understand that nothing in this world is determined by empty talk. Anyone that swallows the poison of God must die. As a person's action is so is his reward. Whatsoever a

PEOPLE MAY BURN DOWN BUILDINGS TO HIDE THEIR INIQUITY, BUT GOD'S RECORDS CANNOT BE BURNT

man soweth that he shall also reap. Many people who are struggling under a demonic attack and all kinds of troubles believe they are fighting one powerful witch or wizard somewhere whereas what is happening is that the pay day has arrived, the day of reckoning and retribution has come. That is why it is often said that ashes fly back unto those who throw them. A bad action may not produce its fruit at once but eventually it will cut off the roots of those that committed it.

A certain man hated his neighbour with perfect hatred. When war broke out in their city, both of them ran and the soldiers pursued them. One hid inside a big pot of dye and the other hid behind a tree. This man hated his neighbour so much that he forgot that the soldiers were looking for them. The soldiers looked at the first, second and third pot and did not bother to continue and wanted to leave. But because of hatred, he shouted telling them that his neighbour was in the next pot. So, they first of all got him and later took his neighbour also. If you must throw mud at other people, you will first of all stain your own hands. The net of heaven is cast wide open, although the holes are large, nothing can slip through it. It will catch even the minutest sin.

There is a pay day for every form of immorality. And the cost is very

DELIVERANCE CASE (THE STORY OF MY LIFE • PART 30)

heavy. No one can escape from the consequences of his evil deeds. And as a person is planning evil for someone else, heaven too is planning for him or her. Recompense, judgment and retribution will follow evil or good as the shadow follows the substance (Revelation 22:12).

The Bible says that whatsoever a man soweth that shall he reap also. Everyone is sowing something every minute and hour of the time. You either sow in words, thoughts or deeds. Everyday of your life you are writing a book- there is a reaping coming your way for what you have sown. One of the most powerful hymns in our hymn book talks about the people of harvest coming. If those who dance while singing it take a very close look at it, they will stop dancing because it says God will take all the chaff and put them in the fire. The chaff refers to human beings. Beloved, there is a reaping coming; a day of reckoning is coming.

A certain man mistakenly fell into a river. According to him, as soon as he took some gulps of water and was about to drown because he could not swim, all the evil he ever did was played like a video film before his eyes. Fortunately, someone who could swim rescued him and he was very grateful because he knew that if he had died that day, he was on his way to hell fire. The evil that a person does will surely come back to him or her. Sinners and saints alike will reap whatever they sow. Many people are suffering now because of what they have sown; what they have sown has caught up with them. The law of sowing and reaping cannot change. Whatsoever a man soweth, that he shall reap also.

There is an evil harvest waiting for all evil deeds, whether great or small. If you are cheating people, the man who will cheat

you is on the way. If you are backbiting, the man who will backbite against you is coming behind you. If you are causing confusion, the one who will confuse you is coming behind you. If you are the one responsible for bringing division, the person who will bring confusion into your life is coming behind you. Are you busy stabbing people at the back? The one who will stab you at the back is coming. If you are stealing money, the one that will steal your destiny is coming behind you. If you are digging a pit for your fellow human being, the person who will push you into your own pit is coming behind you. If you are digging a pit for anybody, you might as well dig two because it is a matter of time before you fall into your own pit yourself (Ecclesiastes 10:8). If you are snatching people's husbands, wives, or fiancés, you will pay heavily for all these.

Whatsoever a man soweth that he shall reap also. As a child the way you treat your parents is the same way your children will treat you except you repent. If you continue to insult your parents, be ready for you will be beaten up by your children. If you are a girl and your poor father sweated to put money together to put you in school and you decided to waste his money by getting pregnant for one irresponsible man somewhere, be ready, for your own children will do the same unless you repent and cry to God. If you disrespect your elders now, do not worry, your own result is approaching; someone will certainly duplicate those actions to you. Many young men are suffering now because of some casual sex they had in the secondary school with whoever.

Sometime ago, a certain young man of seventeen was brought to me. At the age of seventeen he had visited over 200 prostitutes. He pulled down his trousers and there were sores all over his male organ. And with all the sores he still visited a prostitute the day before even in his state. And the prostitutes allowed him because of the money he could pay. By the time I would know his father, he was a teacher in a school who had messed up other people's children. The repercussion had caught up with him. Anything you do will be duplicated to you too. We might lose some of our records here on earth; you can even set the

building ablaze to hide what you have done, but God keeps His records, and they cannot be destroyed. People may burn down buildings to hide their iniquity, but God's records cannot be burnt.

When David committed his sin with Bathsheba, he thought his actions were covered but they were not. As far as God is concerned, you might have killed a Goliath and your powerful music might have driven out unclean spirits, but you must reap what you sow. If you caused stress and sadness in a family, you will surely not escape.

The pregnancy you terminated to hide shame you will reap the harvest. That sex before marriage that you did not tell the pastor about before you were joined together, you will pay for it. The woman or man you jilted because you have seen somebody you think is better, of course you will pay for it. The lady whose baby you are denying the fatherhood, you will pay for it. I know a man who denied just one baby and abandoned both baby and mother. He married another woman and they had four children. Now the four children are in the psychiatric

OWING PEOPLE MONEY AND INSTEAD OF PAYING, YOU ARE PRAYING FALL DOWN AND DIE PRAYERS, YOU WILL REAP THE HARVEST

hospital- whatsoever a man soweth, that he shall reap also.

From a single grain of corn that you sow you can reap four hundred grains. This is why evil is bad. The evil you may reap from an evil action will be more devastating than what you sowed. If you are sowing discord, you will face the negative harvest. Every sin has a day of visitation. I want you to understand that deliverance is not solution to every problem. If there are things in your life that you are hiding from God, things in your life that are stinking in God's nostrils, things you will be embarrassed about if shown on a projector, then you should know that you need to repent quick.

Judges 1:5-7 says, *"And they found Adonibezek in Bazek: and they fought against him and they slew the Canaanites and the Perizites. But Adomibezek fled; and they pursued after him, and caught him, and cut off his thumbs and his great toes. And Adonibezek said, Three score and ten kings, having their thumbs and their great toes cut off, gathered their meat under my table; as I have done, so God hath requited me. And they brought him to Jerusalem, and there he died."* Whatsoever a man soweth, that shall he reap also.

Every sin has a day of visitation. The day may come after many years. It may come when you do not expect it. It may come after you have married and had all your children. You may get away from the law because you hired a very good lawyer, but there is still another court at which you must appear and the judge there does not make mistakes. The safest place to be at any time is wherever there is no appearance of evil. Flee from every appearance of evil (1 Thessalonians 5:22). Do not wait for it to become evil before you flee, because once it is evil, the pay day will come.

Perhaps you are saying that you are not that bad, you only take occasional bribe, you will pay. You may say that you commit fornication but not with every girl or every man, you will pay. You may say, "Well I don't sleep with every married woman, I only sleep with those whose husbands do not love; I just care for them," you will pay. Or you

say, "I don't sleep with every woman but only those who need comfort," you will pay. You may say, "I only sleep with divorcees," you will pay. Or you say, "Well I have only three boy friends and I want to marry one, but I need the money of the other two," you will pay. Or you say, "Well I don't drink much, only 5 bottles," you will pay. "Well, I tell lies, but only business lies, commercial lies. You know in this line of business, you need to tell occasional lies," you will pay for every lie that you tell. If your job requires that you have to be telling lies, you better leave it and ask God to provide another one for you. You might say that you are not a fornicator because you do not engage in the proper act but the truth is that if you undress a woman or man in the laboratory of your heart,

the Bible calls you a fornicator and a rapist. If you say, "Well I get angry and after some time, I cool down," you will pay because God does not only judge actions but intensions, motives, reasons, way of life, thought processes and the cravings of the heart. The Bible says that no liar will enter into the kingdom of God; whether he is a professional liar, occasional liar, commercial liar, romantic liar, academic liar, etc.

All that some sisters need to be told before they surrender themselves for fornication is, "I want to marry you." Once they hear that, they are finished. You will reap what you sow.

A sister that has repented of fornication and adultery but still keeps the complimentary card of her former boy friend will pay because she has not burnt the bridges. She will pay for the bridge of iniquity that she refused to burn.

There are four places where I have seen men praying and listening to the word of God with full concentration.

1. Leprosy colonies: They are social outcasts. Nobody wants them and nobody loves them. So when you go there to minister, they listen with rapt attention. When you say pray, they pray like wounded lions.

2. The prison yard.

THE PROPHET Saul versus David 4

I-SAMUEL 18:7... THE WOMEN... PLAYED, AND SAID SAUL HAS SLAIN HIS THOUSANDS, AND DAVID HIS TEN THOUSANDS.

PRAAISE GOD FOR GIVING US DAVID: HE IS OUR HEROE!

YESSS oooo

?!!

I-SAMUEL 18:8 AND SAUL WAS VERY WROTH, ... AND... DISPLEASED...; AND HE SAID, THEY HAVE ASCRIBED UNTO DAVID TEN THOUSANDS AND TO ME... BUT THOUSANDS; AND WHAT CAN HE HAVE MORE BUT THE KINGDOM?

THIS BOY AGAIN?!

WHAAT?! THIS IS ANOTHER OPEN ROYAL DISGRACE!

3. **Men that have been condemned to death.**

4. **The cemetery.** Sometime ago, I called some prayer points at the cemetery and the rate at which some people prayed made some graves to cave in; they had forgotten they were standing on graves.

Why do people pray hard in these places? It is because at that level, the tablet and the laboratory of their heart cannot play games with God anymore. Are you playing games with God? Your sins will find you out, and you will reap a negative harvest.

A woman that ran away from her husband and married another man shall reap a terrible harvest. Maybe you are owing some people money now, and so you keep changing your seat inside the church, the harvest is waiting for you. All these things hinder breakthroughs because the negative harvest will resist you. Maybe you have done some hidden abortion; your evil harvest is awaiting you. Or you are working with a fake certificate, your negative harvest is waiting for you. Or may be you slept with your cousin, or your house help, nephew, niece, etc and nobody saw you, your harvest is waiting for you. Sisters that are extremely clever with their contraceptives should know that their harvest will catch up with them. If you do not deal with all the secret lusts in your heart and the secret children you have outside your matrimonial home, you will reap the harvest. Prayer City cannot help in this case. You need to repent because when you are at the edge of your privilege, blessing, provision or at the gate of moving into the great things God has for you, the negative harvest will come and say, "Excuse me sir/ma you have not settled my case, I am still here. As you are growing, I am growing too." You need to make up your mind because anything you do that is bad will attract a consequence. Deception will attract a consequence. Lying will attract a consequence. Doing the work of God with deception will attract a consequence. Owing people money and instead of paying, you are praying fall down and die prayers, you will reap the harvest. Any Christian that practises oral sex will reap the harvest of iniquity.

Beloved, you need to talk to the Lord to forgive you for anything in your life that is piling evil harvest for you. Tell the Lord to forgive you and have mercy on you. Cry to the Lord to help you with any evil harvest that you are reaping. The greatest spiritual breakthrough a sinner can have is to see himself in the sinner's position. The way God sees you is what matters. You need to cry to the Lord to help you with whatsoever is making you to stink in His nostril, whatsoever is blocking you from seeing the visions of heaven or whatsoever is strengthening the enemy against you. This is the truth Beloved.

PRAYER POINTS

1. Every power pushing me unto negative harvest, die, in the name of Jesus.

2. Iniquity of my father's house, stop pursuing my life, in the name of Jesus.

3. Lord Jesus, I surrender all to you, in the name of Jesus.

4. You spirit of self-destruction, my life is not your candidate. Therefore, die, in Jesus' name.

5. I shall not be a castaway, in the name of Jesus.

THE NEGATIVE HARVEST
is a message delivered at the Mountain of Fire and Miracles Ministries by the General Overseer, Dr. D.K. Olukoya.

A CALL TO SERVE

Are you a member of MFM with a burden to help the needy, are you interested in alleviating the plight of the poor or in the spread of the gospel through the sponsorship of the publication of tracts? Your resources, time and talent can be extended to several groups that are in charge of these areas. These groups include:

o **We care Ministry,**
o **Mission Outreach**
o **Tracts and Publications**
o **Ministry to Drug addicts**
o **Campus fellowship**
o **Ministry to Schools**
o **Ministry to Glorious Children, etc.**

Thus says the Lord, "Verily I say unto you, in as much as ye have done it unto one of the least of these my brethren, ye have done it unto me" Matthew 25 : 40.

WONDERFUL JESUS!

DELIVERANCE FROM SATANIC DREAMS

Before I came to MFM I had dream attacks every night for two years. But since I came to MFM for prayer, I have been delivered completely from satanic dreams and powers of the night. Praise the Lord!

Sis. Alony
MFM Kampala, Uganda

OPEN HEAVENS IN MY MARRIAGE

My marriage was attacked by the powers of darkness and I was facing a lot of difficulties. I lost my dream life completely and life was becoming hell. I went for counselling and deliverance. God answered my prayers and my marriage is now experiencing open heavens to the glory of God. Praise the Lord!

Sis. Josephine
MFM Warri

SATANIC DREAM DIES

Sometime ago, in the church, we were given a prayer point to pray before going to bed. After the prayers I had a dream in which I was eating noddles. I continued with the prayers every night before going to bed for sometime. To the glory of God, in another dream, I vomited all those things I ate in the earlier dream. Praise God!

Sis. Florence
MFM Ilado

DIVINE TOUCH

After a vigil at the church, I discovered that the pain in my abdomen has disappeared. Secondly, God delivered me from satanic walking stick. I can now stand with my two legs without the use of a walking stick. Praise the Lord!

Sis. Ajayi
MFM Abule Anu

GOD RELEASES MY PROMOTION LETTER

When the last promotion result was released in my place of work, my name was among the successful ones but my letter of promotion was not released. However, after some prayers, it was released to me and at that same time, my brother telephoned me to go and clear some gifts at the airport. Praise the Lord!

Sis. Banjo
MFM Ijebu-Ode

THE YOKE OF SLAVERY BROKEN

I thank the Lord for the salvation of my soul and the great deliverance He granted me. I came to Prayer City for deliverance and the chains of slavery upon my life were broken. Secondly, the Lord removed me from darkness into the light and also delivered me from spirit husband. Praise the Lord!

Sis. Omolola
MFM Prayer City

DIVINE INTERVENTION

I thank God for His divine intervention. My husband works as a police man. After a night duty, he was queried for the missing luggage of a man that arrived from abroad. He knew nothing about it but he was locked up. To the glory of God, his boss who knew about the case came in and mentioned the name of the person who was responsible and instructed some people to go and inspect his house. By the time they got there, the kuggage was found intact including his mobile phone. As soon as they recovered those things, my husband was released. Praise the Lord!

Sis. Akinmosu
MFM Olopomeji Oworonshoki

DELIVERANCE FROM BEDWETTING

For about five years I was bedwetting. I came for deliverance in this church and during the deliverance programme, God touched and delivered me from the spirit of bedwetting. Praise the Lord!

Sis. Theresa
MFM International Headquarters

FIRE IN THE WORD

Ye Shall Know the Truth, and the Truth Shall Make You Free (John 8:32)

ISSN 1595 - 7314 Vol. 12 No. 44 Sun. 14th - Sat. 20th Sept., 2008

Defeating
REDESIGNING POWERS

My year of unprecedented greatness and unmatchable increase
Deuteronomy 28:13, Psalm 71:21, Ephesians 3:20, Psalm 92:10

This week, we are looking at the message entitled, "Defeating redesigning powers."

Matthew 19:12 says *"For there are some eunuchs, which were so born from their mother's womb; and there are some eunuchs, which were made eunuchs of men and there be eunuchs, which have made themselves eunuchs for the kingdom of heaven's sake. He that is able to receive it, let him receive it."*

This passage of the Scriptures makes us to understand that there are some eunuchs who did not want to become eunuchs but which were made eunuchs by men. That is, their lives were redesigned by other men.

Ecclesiastes 10:6 says, *"Folly is set in great dignity, and the rich sit in low place."* Here, we see a rearrangement; the rich has been brought down while the foolish is promoted to the top one way or another.

Ecclesiastes 10:7 says, *"I have seen servants upon horses, and princes walking as servants upon the earth."*

There are so many masquerading princes around who have been redesigned to become servants.

God has created everyone uniquely. Everything you need to succeed has been incorporated into your life on the day you were created. God has an original intention for your life; He has something written about you. God has a specific blueprint for all the human beings He has created. But there are some wicked powers that redesign people. They were the powers that captured Saul. He began with prophecy but gradually these evil powers began their evil work, and by the time they

AS A MATTER OF FACT, UNLESS THERE IS A DIVINE INTERVENTION, MOST REDESIGNED PEOPLE DIE IN THAT STATE

finished, Saul began to consult witches. He began with prophecy and ended up with witchcraft. The redesigning powers did not stop until the prophet became a witch. These redesigning powers remove a person from the original divine intention. When these redesigning powers begin their operation, all advices to their victims fall on deaf ears. They no longer listen to sermons. They consider counselling and warnings as foolish. When they hear messages that are supposed to make them break down and cry to the Lord to change them, they will not be moved because the evil designers have started their wicked operation.

These powers move a person from a superior life to an inferior one. It is a disgrace for servants to capture the horses of believers. And it is not right for the enemy to move them from the front to the back. These redesigning powers mar

DELIVERANCE CASE (THE STORY OF MY LIFE - PART 31

WHATY BULL-SHIT OR COW-DUNG IS THIS?! ALL THE CHURCHES I ATTENDED, NONE COULD LEAD ME TO CHRIST. COME TO THINK OF IT, WHAT IS THE PARAMOUNT MISSION OF THE CHURCH AND CHRISTIANS, IS IT NOT EVANGELISM?! WHY IS IT THAT MANY HAVE ABANDONED SOULS FOR OTHER WILD GOOSE CHASE ?!!! WHERE ARE THE OLD TIME CHRISTIANS ?...

IF NO ONE COMES TO MY RESCUE, GOD WILL! BECAUSE GOD LOVES DRUNKARDS BUT HATES DRUNKENESS!

MARK 16 VS 15-18.

the pot in the hands of the potter in order to spoil thee original design. This problem has been affecting many people right from when they were in the womb. Some of the problems that leave deliverance ministers confused are problems from the womb. A person who has been designed as a prophet can be redesigned by these powers to become a witch as we can see in the case of Saul.

A person that has been originally designed to pursue an international career can be redesigned to a local champion. It could be the original design of God to make somebody the owner of a large company but if

care is not taken that person could be redesigned to be managing a small store. Somebody that has been designed by God to be brilliant could be redesigned into a dullard by these powers.

The younger brother of a certain man discovered through occult means that the man would have a son who would be very brilliant so he went to a native doctor who assisted in ensuring that the man did not have a son. However, the man had a son contrary to his expectation. He ran quickly to see the native doctor who apologized and told him that there had been

a mistake somewhere. The man said, "Okay, the mistake has been made, so what do we do now?" The native doctor said he would simply turn the boy's brain into that of a goat. It was a terrible thing. So, this boy was such a dullard that at the age of 17, he could not go beyond nursery school. But suddenly, there was revival in the family, this boy's uncle that turned his brain into that of a goat got born again, his father got born again and the boy too became born again but the problem persisted. Then the uncle confessed what he did to him. They all started to pray including the boy. Through aggressively praying, the boy began to pick up his life at the age of 19. He got to primary two at the age of 19. You can see what these powers can do. His conversion to a zombie was not God's original plan. So, if you allow the enemy to redesign you, you cannot be sure to return to the original state. This is why serious prayers are needed.

Sometime ago, a certain man was brought to me. Right from when he was 21, he started seeing the number 39 in the dream. He did not understand what was happening until somebody gave him a tape from MFM which he listened to and prayed the prayers therein. It was then an angel appeared to him and explained that it meant that he would die at 39. Then he started praying and that evil design was removed.

As a matter of fact, unless there is a divine intervention, most redesigned people die in that state. Some ladies have been redesigned as men. Some stars have been redesigned as

dullards. Sometime ago, in one of our crusades abroad, I talked a little bit about these powers and asked people to bring a list of whatever they did not want to see anymore in their lives. After praying on the papers, I asked them to burn when they get home. There was a certain woman there that had been completely redesigned and these redesigning power were very angry with her. For three hours when she got home, her paper refused to burn. The ones for her daughter and brother got burnt easily but her own just refused to burn until she prayed, prayed, and prayed before it started to burn slowly. And they all tore their papers from the same notebook.

Beloved, at this juncture, I would like you to pray the

IT IS THE REDESIGNING POWERS THAT TURN BREADWINNERS INTO BEGGARS

following prayer points before you read further:

1. Any power assigned to suck me like orange, die, in the name of Jesus.
2. Any power stealing what will announce me to the world, die, in the name of Jesus.

SIGNS THAT A PERSON IS UNDER THE ATTACK OF REDESIGNING POWERS

A person who is under the attack of evil redesigners becomes a spectator in life. Such a person is consigned to the dustbin of life. The person gets leftovers instead of his entitlement. No man cares to know his name or who he is. He has talent but the talent is not recognized. It expires with him. Such a person would be captured by forces of limitation. Anytime he arises and wants to move, a voice will say, "No this is how far you will go. You cannot go further."

There will be persistent attack from satan when a person is

under the attack of the rage of the redesigners, and the person hardly gets anything easily. They will harm the person in all areas, swallow the virtues, bury the person alive and slaughter the person's destiny. They would waste the youth of the person and make the flower of his life to waste away. They waste youth. They waste the flower of people's lives a mostly by making them live a wayward and sexually loose life.

Somebody in the secondary school who has procured abortions is being wasted. Some young people do not realize that the fellow who is saying, "I love you" to them is actually telling them that he or she has been sent to them to redesign their lives and to waste them. That "I love you" is from the bottom of the pit.

It is the redesigning powers that turn breadwinners into beggars. They repackage a person contrary to how God has packaged him.

HOW TO DEAL WITH REDESIGNERS

1. Release the fire and arrows of God at them.

2. Command them to carry their load and go.

3. Feed them with their own bread of sorrow and affliction, which they have been bringing before you so that they can feed on their own food.

4. Command them to be buried in the grave they have dug for you.

5. Command their boasting to become empty.

6. Command the boiling anger of the Lord to fall upon them.

7. Pray for a reconstruction, a replacement of that which they have stolen. That is a return to your original design.

8. Pray barricading prayers so that they do not move close to you again.

However, if you have not yet surrendered your life to Jesus, then you cannot invite God to redesign your life. You cannot even ask for divine intervention. But there is power in the blood of Jesus to set you free. If you want to give your life to Christ,

THE PROPHET Saul versus David 5

please say the following prayer: "Father, in the name of Jesus, I come before you now. I acknowledge that I am a sinner. Forgive my sins and cleanse me with your blood. I renounce the devil and all his works. Come into my life Lord Jesus and take control of my life, in Jesus' name. Amen.

PRAYER POINTS

1. Every secret thing that is oppressing me, scatter, in the name of Jesus.

2. Every power knocking down my life, die, in the name of Jesus.

3. Every spell placed upon my life, backfire, in the name of Jesuss.

4. Good doors that have refused to open, open now, in the name of Jesus.

5. Giants opposing my breakthroughs, your time is up, die, in the name of Jesus.

6. My enemies, hear me well: I refuse to be a permanent defender, I pursue you to death, in the name of Jesus.

7. Waters of marah, pass over me; dry up, in the name of Jesus.

8. Every power that attacked me in the womb, what are you waiting for? Die, in the name of Jesus.

9. My story must change; I must laugh, in the name of Jesus.

10. Reproach, hear the word of the Lord, give way to my honour. Shame, hear the word of the Lord, give way to my glory. Sorrow, hear the word of the Lord, and give way to my joy. Demotion, hear the word of the Lord, give way to my promotion. Bad luck, hear the word of the Lord, give way to my uncommon favour. Stagnation, hear the word of the Lord, give way to my multiplication, in the name of Jesus.

11. Redesigning powers, hear the word of the Lord, die, in the name of Jesus.

12. O God, arise and establish me by force into the place of my destiny, in the name of Jesus.

13. Every power of the idol of my father's house, die, in the name of Jesus.

14. Every power assigned to repackage my destiny, scatter, in the name of Jesus.

DEFEATING REDESIGNING POWERS
is a message delivered at the Mountain of Fire and Miracles Ministries by the General Overseer, Dr. D.K. Olukoya.

A CALL TO SERVE

Are you a member of MFM with a burden to help the needy, are you interested in alleviating the plight of the poor or in the spread of the gospel through the sponsorship of the publication of tracts? Your resources, time and talent can be extended to several groups that are in charge of these areas. These groups include:

o   We care Ministry,
o   Mission Outreach
o   Tracts and Publications
o   Ministry to Drug addicts
o   Campus fellowship
o   Ministry to Schools
o   Ministry to Glorious Children, etc.

Thus says the Lord, "Verily I say unto you, in as much as ye have done it unto one of the least of these my brethren, ye have done it unto me" Matthew 25 : 40.

WONDERFUL JESUS!

DIVINE PROVISION

Sometime ago, I needed some amount of money which was difficult for me to get. To my surprise, a brother visited me, and as he was about to leave he gave me a huge amount of money which he called a token. The gift took care of my needs. Praise the Lord!

Sis. Ogungbe
MFM Ikare

QUARTERLY MISSIONARY YOKE BROKEN

I joined the headquarters expectant family deliverance programme as a result of loosing my pregnancy constantly at 4 months each time I conceived. The Lord delivered me and now I am a glorious mother of a baby girl. Praise the Lord!

Sis. Aderonke
Expectant family Group
MFM Headquarters

DELIVERED FROM THE SPIRIT OF DEATH

During my ministration on Thursday, the Holy Spirit directed a prayer point against sudden death. I did not know that it had to do with me. On my way to the office on Saturday, I encountered a group of armed robbers who had robbed, wounded and killed many people. I give all glory to the most High God whom I serve for making a way of escape for me. Praise the Lord!

Pastor Michael
MFM Iba

THE LORD HEALS

Some months ago, I experienced a serious illness that totally defied medical solution. It was then I was made to understand that my situation was a spiritual one. I joined this church and took part in the deliverance programme and to the glory of God, I received total healing after undergoing the deliverance programme. Praise the Lord!

Bro. Adedebiyi
MFM Obadore/Akesan

DIVINE PROTECTION

I thank God for divine protection over my family. Armed robbers invaded the bank where my daughter is serving as a youth corper. They killed so many people, wounded some and even bound three of the staff and carried them away but my daughter was left unhurt. The robbers did not touch my daughter, and the Lord kept her. Praise the Lord

Evangelist Esther
MFM Olopomeji, Oworonshoki

DELIVERANCE FROM SEASONAL ATTACK

My child was under the attack of a terrible seasonal sickness. This sickness occurred between May-June every year. This sickness defied medication. This year, I made up my mind to give it a fight and make sure the sickness does not come back again. Therefore, I commenced serious prayers and fasting and also held vigils for his deliverance. To the glory of God, barely four months later, the sickness stopped. Praise the Lord!

Bro. Peter
MFM Omiyale Ejigbo

DIVINE CONVERSION

I ministered the word of God to a coworker of mine but he remained adamant. However, after some prayers of intercession I got information that he has bought a Bible and now attends a Bible-believing church. When I saw him, he confessed to me that he has given his life to Christ and has experienced good changes. Praise the Lord!

Bro. Victor
MFM Iju

GOD OF SUDDENLY

I was jobless for some years before a sister introduced me to this church. I was later told to undergo a deliverance session which I obliged. Three weeks later, I was called to take up a job. Praise the Lord!

Bro. Ukpebitere
MFM Ughellli

TRACTS & PUBLICATIONS GROUP

MOUNTAIN OF FIRE AND MIRACLES MINISTRIES
ORGANISES A SEMINAR TITLED

"WRITING TO PROSPER"

TOPICS INCLUDE:
CHRISTIAN WRITING
-EDITING/PROOF READING
-TRANSCRIPTION METHODS
-DESKTOP PUBLISHING

THIS SEMINAR IS OPEN TO ALL MEMBERS OF THE
CHURCH
DATE: SEPTEMBER SATURDAY 20, 2008.
TIME: 9 AM
VENUE: MFM INTERNATIONAL HEADQUARTERS
13 OLASIMBO STREET ONIKE, YABA ,LAGOS.

MOUNTAIN OF FIRE AND MIRACLES MINISTRIES
(International Headquarters)

War Against Marriage Breakers Task Force

invites U to

A Quarterly Marriage Seminar

THEME:

Holy Spirit and your MARRIAGE

Date: Saturday 20th September, 2008
Time: 10:00am prompt
Venue: Main Auditorium, Headquarters @ 13 Olasimbo Street, Onike Yaba Lagos.

DR. D. K. OLUKOYA
General Overseer (MFM Worldwide)

INSTITUTE OF SPIRITUAL WARFARE (INSWAR)

ADMISSION! ADMISSION!! ADMISSION!!!

ELIGIBLE CANDIDATES ARE HEREBY INVITED TO
APPLY FOR ADMISSION
INTO ANY OF THE FOLLOWING PROGRAMME
OF STUDIES IN INSWAR
(PART-TIME PROGRAMME ONLY)
2009 SESSION (FEBRUARY - OCTOBER 2009)

1. DEPARTMENT OF EVANGELISM & CHURCH PLANTING
2. DEPARTMENT OF SPIRITUAL RED CROSS
3. DEPARTMENT OF CHILDREN EDUCATION
4. DEPARTMENT OF PRAISE WORSHIP
5. DEPARTMENT OF CHURCH MUSIC
6. DEPARTMENT OF DELIVERANCE (EVENING)
7. DEPARTMENT OF LANGUAGES & CULTURE
8. YORUBA DEPARTMENT
   A. BIBLICAL STUDIES
   B. DELIVERANCE
   C. PRAYER

ADMISSION REQUIREMENTS
1. YOU MUST BE BORN AGAIN
2. BAPTISM IN THE HOLY SPIRIT
3. MEMBERSHIP IN MFM MINISTRIES

PURCHASE APPLICATION FORMS FROM INSWAR STORES AT MFM
INT'L HEADQUARTERS, 13 OLASIMBO STREET ONIKE-YABA. DATE OF
ENTRANCE EXAM: DEC. 13, 2008
VENUE: MFM INT'L HEADQUARTERS TIME 7.00AM

FROM TAPES MINISTRY

SPECIAL RELEASE OF DR. D.K OLUKOYA'S MESSAGES AVAILABLE ON BOTH AUDIO TAPES AND CDS

1. THE HOLY SPIRIT AND PROBLEMS We120397
2. THE BATTLE AT THE EDGE OF BREAKTHROUGH Su261299
3. THE MIDNIGHT BATTLE We161099
4. OVERCOMING WITCHCRAFT SPONSORED DISEASES Su230599
5. PRIVATE BATTLES, PRIVATE DEVILS Su190498
6. DESTROYING SATANIC MASKS We270396
7. THE GOD OF DELIVERANCE We271196
8. THE ENEMY ON RAMPAGE Su291198
9. MY ENEMY SHALL DIE IN MY PLACE We 031297
10. WHEN YOU ARE KNOCKED DOWN Su101099
11. RECOVERING YOUR LOST YEAR Su121195
12. POWER AGAINST EVIL CONSUMPTION M0091095
13. POWER AGAINST SPIRITUAL SPIDERS We300797
14. THE SPIRIT OF THE CRAB We230497
15. BREAKING FREE FROM FAMILY BONDAGE Su191299

Available in MFM International Bookshop and Vendors' stands.

FIRE IN THE WORD

Ye Shall Know the Truth, and the Truth Shall Make You Free (John 8:32)

ISSN 1595 - 7314 Vol. 12 No.45 Sun. 21st - Sat. 27th Sept., 2008

Holy Spirit & ADVERSITY

My year of unprecedented greatness and unmatchable increase
Deuteronomy 28:13, Psalm 71:21, Ephesians 3:20, Psalm 92:10

Hosea 7:8-9 says, *"Epharaim, he hath mixed himself among the people; Ephraim is a cake not turned. Strangers have devoured his strength, and he knoweth it not; yea, gray hairs are here and there upon him, yet he knoweth not."*

There are many people who have mixed themselves up with spiritual nonentities, and many too have become unturned bread. It is quite obvious that something is wrong with the churches of our days. Many people come to church but there is no specific change in their lifestyles. Many come and their old behaviour and operations are still in place. Many people come to church and they are still scared of voodoo, juju, magic, wizards and witches. Many lack very simple faith in the Almighty God. Many come to church everyday but fail to conquer sin in their lives. A lot of people are married to sin and they refuse to let them go. A lot of people cannot pray when they get home. Many Christians who come to church do not know the voice of God neither do they understand it. To many Christians, God looks unreal, they believe He is one old man somewhere with gray hairs whom they do not even know what He is doing.

Many Christians have unjustifiable and unnecessary attacks from the enemy. And more than any other time the enemy is killing Christians on a regular basis now. Many people do not even have independent faith in the Lord. Many who come to church are becoming spiritually static. We have many believers who mix concoctions, drugs and holy water together. Unfortunately, many are gambling with their lives everyday with satan. Indeed something is wrong somewhere. A lot of pastors are getting heart attack; a lot of men of God are suffering from high blood pressure because of the kind of babies that are gathered in the churches. Many have been coming to church for a while and still cannot explain what justification or sanctification means. Some bring strange women as wives to the church. Many pastors are getting confused and losing their focus. It is because something is missing somewhere.

THE BANE OF TODAY'S CHURCH

One serious sickness of the present-day church is the absence of two kinds of baptism. When these two types of baptism are absent in a life, such a person behaves like a baby in the house of God. John the Baptist said of Jesus; "Behold someone is coming after me, the latchet of whose shoes I am unfit to untie. He shall baptize you with the

ABSENCE OF LIGHT IN A PERSON'S LIFE MAKES IGNORANCE TO REIGN

Holy Ghost and with fire!" (Luke 3:16). The absence of these two baptisms have killed many believers unexpectedly. And there are many people who come to the house of God but they have no power. If you rely on somebody else to pray and fight your battles for you all the time, what happens when the person is sick?

THREE CLASSES OF CHRISTIANS

All the Christians that come to church can be divided into three categories:
1. Those who have not received the baptism of the Holy Spirit.
2. Those who have received the baptism of the Holy Spirit but have not received the baptism of fire.
3. Those who have received the baptism of the Holy Spirit and fire.

It is the power of the Holy Spirit that differentiates Christians from people of other religions. The Bible says, "As many as received Him, to them gave He power to become the sons of God" (John 1:12). The Bible tells us categorically that anyone who does not have the Spirit of Christ is none of His although he may be going to church. The Bible says that it is the spirit that quickeneth, the flesh profiteth nothing. When that quickening spirit is not in you, you become prey in the mouth of eaters of flesh and drinkers of blood. The Bible says, "You shall receive power after the Holy Ghost has come upon you"

DELIVERANCE CASE (THE STORY OF MY LIFE - PART 31)

MARK 16 VS 15-18.

(Acts 1:8). If you do not have this baptism, you cannot have this power. Although the apostles moved with Jesus for three years or more, yet immediately Jesus left, they were still afraid and went back fishing. It is only a dead fish that floats. But when a fish is alive, no matter what current blows against it, it will swim against the current. The reason the storms of life carry so many people away is that they are like a dead fish floating in the river. Reading of Psalms without this power will amount to nothing. It is like going to the battlefront without weapons. To pray some acid prayer points without the baptism of the Holy Spirit is to look for trouble because immediately you start praying those prayers, powers of darkness will check to find out whether you have the fire. If not, they will send out demons to attack you. Many people are speaking in powerless tongues because there is no fire and power in them.

FRESH FIRE

Many Christains need to cry to God for fresh heavenly fire. Many people need to understand that the only thing the enemy respects and runs away from is the fire of the Holy Ghost burning in their lives. There is nothing that can kill or suppress a person that is filled with the Holy Ghost and fire. People need to understand that the day they get filled with the baptism of the Holy Spirit and fire marks the end of poverty in their lives. Unfortunately, many do not understand that even if they have received the baptism of the Holy Ghost a long time ago, there is possibility of getting fresh fire, power and anointing all the time. The initial baptism of the Holy Spirit a person got 5 or 10 years ago may not be able to help the person in some situations now. There is need for a fresh infilling always. Zechariah 4:6 says, *"Then he answered and spake unto me, saying, This is the word of the Lord unto Zerubbabel, saying, Not by might nor by power, but by my Spirit, saith the Lord of hosts. "*

Unfortunately, many believers do not even understand the Holy Spirit. Many think of the Holy Spirit as a wind, cloud or force somewhere. Many do not know that the Holy Spirit is a complete personality. And that when the power falls on a life and moves into a life, there will be a complete change. The apostles who became cowards and ran away when Jesus died became different human beings immediately they received the baptism of the Holy Spirit.

The Holy Spirit is God's executive agent in the world today. The Holy Spirit is confirming the work that Jesus began. The Holy Spirit is just not an experience, He is a personality. He is not a feeling or emotion but a personality, the most valuable asset of Christian living now. He is the chief executive agent of God on earth. Coming to the house of God without the filling of the Holy Spirit is a waste of time. And if you are still speaking the kind of tongue you learned in a dead church, you had better start doing something about it. Or if you are speaking the tongues you heard from somebody somewhere; and anytime there is a serious prayer and people are praying in the spirit, you become dizzy and develop headache, it means there is something within you that is resisting the power.

Indeed, the present-day believer needs to cry to the Lord for fresh fire. Yesterday's fire may not be enough for the problem of tomorrow. The anointing that you were priding yourself in 10 years ago may not be alright now. Ephraim had mixed himself among the people, he had become a cake not turned. Many have remained as they were. Merely repeating what you have memorized before you got born again will make you to become an unturned cake. And when you are an unturned cake, strangers will move in and devour your strength. Sometimes when some people are praying, the enemy will organize the demons around for attack because they already know what the person is going to say. Until a person cries desperately from his heart for this power, the person is in serious trouble. When you are co-existing with witches and wizards, and they find you very comfortable and convenient, it is because there is no fire.

WHAT IS ADVERSITY?

Proverbs 24:10 says, *"If thou faint in the day of adversity, thy strength is small."* What is adversity? Adversity is the state of

hardship or a state of affliction. Adversity is a state contrary to well being; a condition contrary to well-being. It means misfortune, distress; tragedy, poverty, and circumstances that cause sorrow, suffering, trial and opposition. But the Bible says if it is in the day of adversity that you faint, your strength is small. Therefore, the day of adversity is the wrong day to become weak because the enemy out of desperation to stop a captive from going free, may look for reinforcement. If at the time of the enemy's regrouping and reinforcement you relax then problems will accumulate.

Perhaps you have been speaking the language of adversity: "Nobody cares about me, everybody seems to be against me, nothing I touch works right, life is not fair to me, nobody really cares whether I live or die, whatever I do with my life is not the business of anyone. I want to cut my life short. Why can't there be breakthrough for me like every other person." And you are terribly discouraged. These are signs of weakness in the days of adversity. The reason most people are weak in the days of adversity is that they lack the baptism of fire and the Holy

BY THE POWER OF THE HOLY SPIRIT YOU CAN SEE INTO THE FUTURE AND CAN RESTRAIN THE POWER OF SATAN

Spirit. When you become an unturned cake, strangers will devour your strength.

We see the first appearance of the Holy Spirit in the Bible and what it was associated with in Genesis 1:1-3: *"In the beginning, God created the heaven and the earth. And the earth was without form, and void;* (meaning there was trouble) *and darkness was upon the face of the deep.* (Then something happened). *And the Spirit of God moved upon the face of the waters. And God said, Let there be light; and there was light."*

So right from the beginning, the Holy Spirit has always been attached to adversity. The Holy Spirit was hovering above the waters waiting for the Word. The situation was chaotic at that time, but immediately the Word went out- "Let there be light," there was light. The Spirit of the Lord was incubating the waters, sitting on the water like a hen sitting on eggs. The Holy Spirit was sitting on the waters, and the Word came forth: "Let there be light," and there was light.

The same light is important in our lives. If we walk in the light, we shall be able to separate between good and evil. If we walk in the light, our ways will be illuminated, and the light will guide our path. Then we will be able to shine as the light too. When the Holy Spirit incubates your life, light comes in. If you do not have that spiritual light, many things will go wrong. When you pray asking the Holy Spirit to incubate your life; incubation takes place and you begin to experience His light. Absence of light in a person's life makes ignorance to reign and falling will be very easy, problems will hide and the person will not know who are his friends or enemies. He may even fight his friend and think he is the enemy. When there is no light, a person may have evil success, that is he will be successful in the wrong things. Also, progress could be very slow or there would be no progress at all. That is why you should pray that the Holy Spirit should incubate your life. And the reason the word "Holy" is used to qualify this Spirit is that there are many unholy spirits around that people can receive. So when the Holy Spirit faces adversity, something must happen. He reveals what exactly is wrong. A lot of people are suffering now because they really do not know what is

wrong; they have information but no revelation, but you need revelation to fight. The Holy Spirit will reveal to you what exactly is wrong, the evil participants in the matter, and the way out of the problem. Also, the Holy Spirit will reveal to you the preventive measures for the problem.

It is the Holy Spirit that tells us what to pray and how to pray it well. He will design the prayers that will be acceptable. Only the Holy Spirit can correctly apply wisdom. You may be very wise but not be able to apply wisdom without the Holy Spirit. The Holy Spirit is the source of wisdom. He can create and give life. He can help our infirmities and correct our prayers. The Bible says the Holy Spirit searches all things. By the power of the Holy Spirit you can see into the future and can restrain the power of satan. The Bible says, "When the enemy comes

against you like a flood, the Spirit of God shall raise a standard against him" (Isaiah 59:19). The Holy Spirit does all these things.

Many years ago, a certain woman had very serious problems. She visited all available doctors both at home and abroad. At the hospitals, they told her to forget about childbearing because she had no womb. So, she started going for prayer meetings. She attended a department of the prayer meeting called miscellaneous problems and nothing happened. Then she went for counselling, and the man of God advised her to go to where they pray for the baptism of the Holy Ghost. She went and prayed from her heart. This woman prayed so hard that her blouse was soaked in sweat. All of a sudden, she started having stomachache as if she was in labour. She ran to the toilet thinking she was going to pass out faeces but she passed out a snail. And beginning from that day, the doctors could see the womb they said was not in place. That was how she received her breakthrough simply by praying for the baptism of the Holy Ghost and fire.

Sometimes when people start praying that the power and fire of the Holy Ghost should fall upon their lives, it is a very difficult prayer because so many powers do not want that power to come into their lives. There are many people moving about with things inside them that are resisting the power of God.

THE PROPHET | Saul versus David 6

There are people who have foundational and ancestral demons inside their bodies resisting the power of God. So when you begin to pray for that power to fall upon you, the first thing God does is to chase out the traders in the temple of your life. That is why many people fall down when aggressive prayers are going on. There are certain things resisting the power of God that are wiped out of position. But if you are resisting the power of God, or there is no connection between your heart and what you are saying, there is no way the power of God will come upon your life.

When the power of God and the anointing falls upon your life, the first thing it will do is to break your personal yokes. There are many who have been locked up by the enemies for years, and they do not even know who they are. Many of such people do not dream because their spirits have been rendered deaf and dumb. They have become spiritual dunces. But the Holy Spirit can open the door. Many people do not know that it was the Holy Spirit that provided the Saviour His earthly body. Many people have taken the vessels of their lives to evil mechanics who have polluted their bodies and caused all kinds of trouble for them. But the Holy Spirit is able to wipe away those problems. When the fire of God comes upon your life, you will know and those who know you too, will know.

When adversity confronts the Holy Spirit, and when the Holy Spirit confronts adversity, something must happen. The Holy Spirit will reveal to you the root of the problem, whether it is sin, curses, satanic attacks, carelessness, demonic attacks, unfriendly friends, and household wickedness. That is why sometimes what you see physically may not be what you pray against. But the Holy Spirit will help you to pray the right prayers. Sometimes, people pray for blessings that are already available, whereas they should be standing against the binding power. The fact that God is raining down showers of blessings from above does not mean that everyone will get it. God may be pouring rain of blessings from above, but if your hands are tied, you will not get it. If your spiritual pockets are leaking, the blessing will just

go in and come out. It is the Holy Spirit that will help you to fight the right warfare. The Holy Spirit will guide you aright to what you should do, and help you to address whatever needs to be addressed. Samson confronted a lion; something happened to Samson which the lion was not aware of. The Bible says, "And the Spirit of God came upon him." The lion could not understand that. The lion only saw Samson, but when the Spirit of God came upon Samson, then came the obituary of the lion.

Beloved, the greatest thing a man can have is the baptism of the Holy Ghost and fire. A person who is filled with the Holy Ghost and fire has the fullness of God and is fearless. You need to pray for this power and fire to come into your life for a victorious living.

PRAYER POINTS

1. Holy Ghost fire, incubate my life, in the name of Jesus.
2. Holy Ghost fire, break my yoke, in the name of Jesus.
3. Holy Ghost fire, disgrace my adversity, in the name of Jesus.
4. My Father, I want fresh fire, in the name of Jesus.
5. Holy Spirit, dispel my darkness, in Jesus' name.

HOLY SPIRIT AND ADVERSITY
is a message delivered at the Mountain of Fire and Miracles Ministries by the General Overseer, Dr. D.K. Olukoya.

A CALL TO SERVE

Are you a member of MFM with a burden to help the needy, are you interested in alleviating the plight of the poor or in the spread of the gospel through the sponsorship of the publication of tracts? Your resources, time and talent can be extended to several groups that are in charge of these areas. These groups include:

o We care Ministry,
o Mission Outreach
o Tracts and Publications
o Ministry to Drug addicts
o Campus fellowship
o Ministry to Schools
o Ministry to Glorious Children, etc.

Thus says the Lord, "Verily I say unto you, in as much as ye have done it unto one of the least of these my brethren, ye have done it unto me" Matthew 25 : 40.

WONDERFUL JESUS!

JOB BREAKTHROUGH

Sometime ago, an evil personality prophesied that I would soon lose my job. I rejected it and fervently prayed against it. I came to this church because the man's prophecy eventually came to pass and I lost my job. I came for deliverance and to the glory of God, a few weeks later, God provided a better job for me with a higher responsibility and position. The Lord used my setback to move me forward. Praise the Lord!

Bro. Femi
MFM Ejigbo

GOD INTERVENES AND PROVIDES FOR ME

I thank God because the devil attacked me when I was on my way to Ayetoro to serve. I lost my food stuffs and other valuable things. I became stranded but the great God saw me through. Praise the Lord!

Bro. Festus
MFM Ayetoro

GOD OF RESTORATION

Sometime ago, my younger sister in the USA telephoned to tell me that she lost her job. This according to her happened immediately the day after she sent money to our mother to pay house rents. I took the matter to God in prayers. Not quite long she called again to tell me she has gotten a better job with mouth watering salary. Praise the Lord!

Sis. Blessed
MFM Upper Mission, Benin City

DELIVERANCE FROM KOLANUT ADDICTION

For a very long time I was a kolanut addict. It got to an extent that I use to eat it even in the dream. This made me to know that it was a bad signal. Then I went for deliverance and the Lord intervened. I have since stopped eating it physically and in the dream. Praise the Lord!

Bro. Francis
MFM Lekki

THE LORD INDEED IS THE GREAT PHYSICIAN

I got pregnant contrary to an evil pronouncement. However, there were series of attacks during the pregnancy but God delivered me from them all. At the time of delivery, God again intervened as I was delivered safely and normally at exactly 7.50pm. The Lord truly did it all as prophesied by my house fellowship leader who had earlier prayed with me and the doctors were all amazed. Two weeks later, I suffered a stroke but during the General Overseer's ministration at MFM Ikeja on a Thursday, I was permanently made whole. Finally, the Lord provided a shop for me before the end of July which was my prayer request during a programme in June titled; "7 hours with God." Praise the Lord!

Sis. Bukola
MFM Abule Egba

GOD REVIVES MY PRAYER PARTNER'S SON

The son of my prayer partner travelled to Zaria and was expected back the following Monday. But on that day, he was nowhere to be found. The following day, my prayer partner telephoned him but it was another person who answered the telephone. The person explained that the owner of the telephone was involved in a ghastly motor accident that claimed the lives of thirteen people. The person said the accident was so bad that some of the victims had their heads broken. My prayer partner left for Zaria. Her son was even certified dead and buried in the morning of the following Friday. But by 11.00pm on the same day, he arose and people started running away taking him for a ghost. He told them not to run away from him that he was real and not a ghost. Some even threw sand at him. It was when the people were convinced that he was real that they stopped running away from him. Praise God!

Sis. Olu
MFM Headquarters

GOD OVERCOMES THE SPIRIT OF FAILURE IN MY LIFE

I thank God for His mercy and protection over me and my family. I overcame the spirit of failure that I experienced in the dream during my teaching practice programme. My supervisor came to my centre and commended me positively on my effort. Praise God!

Sis. Afolabi
MFM Prayer City

MOUNTAIN OF FIRE AND MIRACLES MINISTRIES
OGIJO
H. M. C. CRUSADE
Presents
2-days Crusade

Theme: OGIJO FOR CHRIST

Come and meet with God and have solution to your Time problem
Venue: St. John Ang. Pry School, Ogijo
Date: 27th – 28th September 2008.
Time: 5:30pm.

PRAISE NIGHT
@: The Church auditorium,
58, Oluye Street, by Action Base
Date: 26th September 2008
Time: 10p.m Till Dawn

Ministering
ANOINTED MEN OF GOD
DR. D.K.OLUKOYA
General Overseer.

JESUS IS LORD

INSTITUTE OF SPIRITUAL WARFARE (INSWAR)

ADMISSION! ADMISSION!! ADMISSION!!!
ELIGIBLE CANDIDATES ARE HEREBY INVITED TO APPLY FOR ADMISSION
INTO ANY OF THE FOLLOWING PROGRAMME OF STUDIES IN INSWAR
(PART-TIME PROGRAMME ONLY)
2009 SESSION (FEBRUARY - OCTOBER 2009)

1. DEPARTMENT OF EVANGELISM & CHURCH PLANTING
2. DEPARTMENT OF SPIRITUAL RED CROSS
3. DEPARTMENT OF CHILDREN EDUCATION
4. DEPARTMENT OF PRAISE WORSHIP
5. DEPARTMENT OF CHURCH MUSIC
6. DEPARTMENT OF DELIVERANCE (EVENING)
7. DEPARTMENT OF LANGUAGES & CULTURE
8. YORUBA DEPARTMENT
  A. BIBLICAL STUDIES
  B. DELIVERANCE
  C. PRAYER
ADMISSION REQUIREMENTS
1. YOU MUST BE BORN AGAIN
2. BAPTISM IN THE HOLY SPIRIT
3. MEMBERSHIP IN MFM MINISTRIES
PURCHASE APPLICATION FORMS FROM INSWAR STORES AT MFM INT'L HEADQUARTERS, 13 OLASIMBO STREET ONIKE-YABA. DATE OF ENTRANCE EXAM: DEC. 13, 2008
VENUE: MFM INT'L HEADQUARTERS TIME 7.00AM

FROM TAPES MINISTRY
SPECIAL RELEASE OF DR. D.K OLUKOYA'S MESSAGES AVAILABLE ON BOTH AUDIO TAPES AND CDS

1. THE HOLY SPIRIT AND PROBLEMS We120397
2. THE BATTLE AT THE EDGE OF BREAKTHROUGH Su261299
3. THE MIDNIGHT BATTLE We161099
4. OVERCOMING WITCHCRAFT SPONSORED DISEASES Su230599
5. PRIVATE BATTLES, PRIVATE DEVILS Su190498
6. DESTROYING SATANIC MASKS We270396
7. THE GOD OF DELIVERANCE We271196
8. THE ENEMY ON RAMPAGE Su291198
9. MY ENEMY SHALL DIE IN MY PLACE We 031297
10. WHEN YOU ARE KNOCKED DOWN Su101099
11. RECOVERING YOUR LOST YEAR Su121195
12. POWER AGAINST EVIL CONSUMPTION M0091095
13. POWER AGAINST SPIRITUAL SPIDERS We300797
14. THE SPIRIT OF THE CRAB We230497
15. BREAKING FREE FROM FAMILY BONDAGE Su191299

Available in MFM International Bookshop and Vendors' stands.

FIRE IN THE WORD, is a weekly Spiritual Bulletin of the Mountain of Fire and Miracles Ministries, published by Tracts and Publications Group. All Enquiries should be addressed to The Editor, Mountain of Fire Magazine, 13, Olasimbo Street, off Olumo Road, Onike, P.O. Box 2990, Sabo Yaba, Lagos, Nigeria. Telephone 01- 867439, 864631, 868766, 08023180236.E-mail: mfmtractsandpublications@yahoo.com Copyright reserved.

FIRE IN THE WORD

Ye Shall Know the Truth, and the Truth Shall Make You Free (John 8:32)

ISSN 1595 - 7314   Vol. 12   No. 46   Sun. 28th Sept. - Sat. 4th Oct., 2008

FROM STRENGTH
TO STRENGHT

My year of unprecedented greatness and unmatchable increase
Deuteronomy 28:13, Psalm 71:21, Ephesians 3:20, Psalm 92:10

The title of our message this week is taken from Psalm 84:7 which says, *"They go from strength to strength, every one of them in Zion appeareth before God."*

Anyone that must survive in the present wicked world need to move to a higher ground of power. For anyone to survive in his life, career, business, calling, etc he needs to move to a higher ground of power. There is a satanic revival of strange powers now. Men are acquiring strange powers in order to fulfill their own personal and selfish desires. And what they sometimes do is unimaginable.

A long time ago, somebody came to me and said he needed prayers because he wanted to win a political office but I told him that people like him do not usually come to me. He said he had tried everything they asked him to do including driving a new car into the sea. But when they asked him to bring the head of an albino, he stopped. That is the extent to which people can go. No wonder the Bible says in Ephesians 6:10: *"Finally, my brethren, be strong in the Lord,* (not in quarrelling, fighting, bitterness, gossiping, fornication, adultery) *and in the power of His might."*

God wants us to be strong in the power of His might. And when we are talking about the power of God, the shape and size of a person is irrelevant; degrees or the loudness of a voice does not even matter. What really matters is whether the power is resident in your inner man. The power content of the inner man is what really matters to God. That is what God looks at, even the devil too. That is why people with evil satanic eyes can look at a person and know whether the person is very strong or not because they can see the power deposit in the person's life. You may call yourself a champion but the enemy sees you as a weakling. By the time the enemy attacks you, the truth will be revealed. If you have never had the consciousness to rebuke evil spirits with the word of God when they attack you in the dream, it means that your inner man is weak. Many people complain about spirit spouses but when they come to them in the dream, they cannot resist

> THERE IS
> NO GENTLE
> METHOD
> OF ARRESTING
> ANYTHING EVIL

them. They only wake up with anger and pray hard, but they should have stopped them at the dream level. The simple truth is that the power content of their inner man is weak. If the enemy pursues you in the dream and you wake up sweating, it means your inner man is weak. Some people died in their sleep because they could not resist the attacks in their dreams.

Your power content determines how far you go with God. When your power level is low, you become a spiritual dwarf and cannot resist spiritual pressure, you will not be able to resist the enemy. You cannot resist the weakness that the enemy brings upon people when your power level is low.

TWO KINDS OF PASTORS

There are two kinds of pastors in the house of God; there are pastors who are working as professional ministers, career pastors or textbook pastors. And there are those who are pastors by calling. It is easy to differentiate between the two groups. For example, a certain pastor was sent to a church where he took control of the church. But there was a big tree at the back of the church which nobody dared to

DELIVERANCE CASE (THE STORY OF MY LIFE - PART 32)

WHAT IF GOD DECIDES NOT TO SAVE MY SOUL ?. I DON'T THINK HE CAN! IS GOD NOT THE ONE THAT PROMISED TO SAVE SINNERS REGARDLESS oTHE MAGNITUDE OF OUR CRIMES. DID HE NOT SAY HE WILL SAVE ANY ONE THAT COMES TO HIM ?!

GOD, I AM JUST A DRUNKARD, MY SIN CANNOT BE COMPARED WITH THE LIKES OF WITCHES, PROSTITUTES, ARMED-ROBBERS, CRIMINAL POLITICIANS, CULTISTS E.T.C. BUT WAIT A MINUTE, THERE IS NO SIN THAT IS LESSER OR WEIGHTIER BEFORE GOD. IF THE ROBBER REPENTS FIRST HE WILL BE EMBRACED BY GOD.

cut. And sometimes when services were on, idol worshippers would gather by the tree performing sacrifices. The pastor found it quite embarrassing. He got annoyed and cut the tree but instead of the tree to emit normal fluid, blood was coming out with screams. This pastor went into the church and by the time he came back, the tree was up again. By the next day, the pastor was dead. Another pastor was sent there. After hearing what happened to the former pastor, he left the tree until he was transferred. A third pastor came and started speaking destruction to the tree right from the first day. One day, he cut the tree down, and as blood was oozing from the tree, he confronted the blood with his anointing oil, and there was a loud scream. The chief priest died that day. The pastor worked there and expanded the work of God.

The spiritual content of your inner man is very important. The power within you determines your spiritual success. If there is no power in your inner man, you will be very weak on the altar of prayer. When your power content is low, your prayer power will be low. You will not be happy to go for prayer meetings and long prayer sessions will bore you. It is very dangerous to have a weak inner man in this present age. You cannot allow your level to remain the same every month because it is very dangerous. Immediately you are seen as a threat, or your destiny is seen as a threat, you qualify for attack. Immediately your marriage is a threat and the enemy sees that it is dangerous to him, and you do not do anything about it, there will be trouble.

Nowadays, we see open confrontation by satanic powers. But when your power content rises, the enemy would be running away from you. They would be afraid, terrified and scared whenever they see you. But unfortunately this is very rare nowadays.

WHAT IS SPIRITUAL POWER?

Spiritual power is ability to overcome any negative power working against you. It is the ability to exercise control.

When I got born-again and received the baptism in the Holy Spirit, we were encouraged to pray for two hours everyday. Due to my prayer life then, things were easy for me. When I got to my lecturers and made any request, they would be running helter skelter to please me. Favour followed me everywhere I went. This is what happens when your power content goes up. Anyone who can pray for 30 minutes everyday for one month will be a different person before that month runs to an end.

Many people do not know what they are missing by living powerless lives. Many people do not know yet that ice cream Christianity and kindergarten prayers will not get them anywhere again. Many people do not recognize that there is no gentle method of arresting anything evil. Unfortunately, due to the powerlessness of believers nowadays, the judge is becoming the accused. Any believer that is fully endued with power is a terror to the kingdom of darkness. And when he speaks, his words carry power.

Unfortunately, the powerlessness in this generation has become legendary. The concentration of the believers of this age is on attachments, wearing tight dresses, etc. This present generation of believers is concentrating its attention on the wrong things, and that is what the enemy wants. Due to lack of focus, so many terrible things are happening in so many lives. Many people cannot even tell what is going on. Sisters who are supposed to be prophetesses unto the Lord cannot hear from God because they have punched extra holes in their ears. If you are powerless, you will become a chewing stick to the power of darkness. Sometimes, people who are possessed with witchcraft powers surrender their lives to Jesus after they might have destroyed other people's lives and the Lord would accept them. That is the mystery of the Christian faith.

Beloved, if you do not want to be wasted then you must be concerned with the power-content of your inner man. It is an insult on your salvation for Pentecostal witchcraft, hypnotism, magic and voodoo to work on you - it is an insult to God. The most important thing in life is the inner man. No matter how you polish the outer man, it will go back to dust one day. It is compulsory for us to have adequate power in our inner man. We are supposed to move from strength to strength, and not from strength to weakness. Therefore the supreme need of this hour is the

> ANY CHRISTIAN THAT CANNOT PRAY IN TONGUES WILL BE OVERPOWERED BY THE ENEMY

power from above as opposed to the power from beneath which is troubling the whole world now. When it is power against power, the weaker power must bow. Something has to give way. The Bible says evil men and seducers are waxing stronger and stronger. In the book of Acts of Apostles, we see that the people of Ephesus were intensely interested in witchcraft, demonic possession and astrology, which is very much like our nation today. Young men are using demonic powers to attract ladies. Men go to the cemetery to do sacrifices for power and money. People are kidnapping and cutting off body parts because they want money. There are people, who do blood-bathing everyday, and there are people who walk into crowded places just to try their charms on people; and all kinds of things are happening. That was what was happening in Ephesus until the power of God took control.

FOUR POWER LEVELS IN THE SPIRITUAL REALM

There are four power levels in the spiritual realm and everyone belongs to one level or another.

1. Delegated spiritual authority: This level of power is not resident in the operator. It is only delegated to him but it belongs to another person. It is usually given because of the relationship with the owner of the power and the delegate. As soon as a person gets born-again, certain amount of spiritual power is deposited into his spirit. He begins to tread upon serpents and scorpions and take harmful things without any harm. Every believer has that delegated authority. No price is paid for it, it is given freely at salvation. But delegated spiritual authority is the lowest energy level in the Christian life because authority is different from power. Luke 4:36 says, *"And they were all amazed, and spake among themselves, saying, What a word is this! For with authority and power he commandeth the unclean spirits, and they come out."* There is a difference between authority and power. So, the first level of power is delegated authority. The day you backslide or turn back on God, the authority will be taken away from you. A vast majority of believers operate at this level alone. There is a need to move higher.

2. Holy Ghost power: Acts 1:8: *"But ye shall receive power, after that the Holy Ghost is come upon you: and ye shall be witness unto me both in Jerusalem and in all Judea, and in Samaria, and unto the uttermost part of the earth."* When you get baptized in the Holy Ghost, you get something higher than the delegated spiritual authority. Any Christian that is not filled with the Holy Ghost is missing a lot. Any Christian that cannot pray in tongues will be overpowered by the enemy. You must receive the baptism in the Holy Ghost with the evidence of speaking in tongues. The Bible says, "These signs shall follow them that believe, in my name they shall cast out devils and shall speak with new tongues." These signs are for all believers. If you have not received the baptism of the Holy Ghost, your power remains at the first level. And the first energy level is not enough to handle African household witchcraft let alone ancestral powers. That is why you must be filled with power.

When you pray in tongues, you charge your battery. 1 Corinthians 14:2 says, *"For he that speaketh in an unknown tongue speaketh not unto men, but unto God; for no man understandeth him; howbeit in the spirit he speaketh mysteries."* 1 Corinthians 14:18: *"I thank my God, I speak with tongues more than ye all."* You get resident fire in your spirit by constantly and consistently

THE PROPHET Saul versus David 7

I SAMUEL 18:13.
THEREFORE SAUL REMOVED HIM FROM HIS PRESENCE. AND MADE HIM HIS CAPTAIN OVER A THOUSAND;---

A LETTER FROM KING SAUL, YOU ARE NOW A CAPTAIN!

CAPTAIN OVER A 1,000

I SAMUEL 18:14.
AND DAVID BEHAVED HIMSELF WISELY IN ALL HIS WAYS, AND THE LORD WAS WITH HIM.

...I'LL REST IN THE LORD, AND WAIT PATIENTLY FOR HIM. I'LL NOT FRET.... OF THE... WICKED SCHEMES.

PSALM 37:7.

praying in tongues. This is the second level of power.

3. Accumulated spiritual energy: This comes from consistent or prolonged period of prayer and fasting. Many people are at the second level and they stop there; and that is how they actually die.

God is happy with a fasted life. God prefers you fasting and breaking in the afternoon three times a week than not fasting at all for a whole month. Without a fasted life, there can be no power. What you get would be disappointment, frustration, and the enemy pursuing you. So if you want to be someone special for God, and be involved in the ministry, you must go beyond the second level of spiritual power. When mountains refuse to move, sickness are not going, and demons refuse to go, you need to go to this next level. You have a price to pay. Once you pay the price, nothing will be impossible. Elijah and Moses fasted for 40 days each. Daniel fasted and our Lord Jesus Christ also fasted for 40 days. They had the accumulated spiritual energy.

4. Dominion: This is the topmost power level. This is the kind of power that God gave to man originally in the garden of Eden. Joshua exercised this power by asking the sun to stand still. He did not get there in one day, he moved through different levels. Moses talked to the earth and the Bible says that the earth obeyed instantly. When you are a man of dominion, you will operate in great signs and wonders.

WHAT TO DO

1. **Desire:** You must desire to be strong.
2. **Decision:** You must decide that you will be strong.

3. **Determination:** You must be determined that at whatever cost you must move from strength to strength and from glory to glory.
4. **Discipline:** There can be no power without discipline.

PRAYER POINTS

1. Thou power of God, incubate my life, in the name of Jesus.
2. Power that cannot be insulted by the forces of darkness, fall upon my life, in the name of Jesus.
3. My words are charged with power, in the name of Jesus.
4. Holy Ghost fire, come upon my life, in the name of Jesus.
5. Dominion power, come upon my life, in the name of Jesus.
6. Fire of God, come upon my life, in Jesus' name.
7. Thou satanic prayer against the power of God in my life, die, in the name of Jesus.

FROM STRENGTH TO STRENGTH
is a message delivered at the Mountain of Fire and Miracles Ministries by the General Overseer, Dr. D.K. Olukoya.

A CALL TO SERVE

Are you a member of MFM with a burden to help the needy, are you interested in alleviating the plight of the poor or in the spread of the gospel through the sponsorship of the publication of tracts? Your resources, time and talent can be extended to several groups that are in charge of these areas. These groups include:

o   We care Ministry,
o   Mission Outreach
o   Tracts and Publications
o   Ministry to Drug addicts
o   Campus fellowship
o   Ministry to Schools
o   Ministry to Glorious Children, etc.

Thus says the Lord, "Verily I say unto you, in as much as ye have done it unto one of the least of these my brethren, ye have done it unto me" Matthew 25 : 40.

WONDERFUL JESUS!

DIVINE INTERVENTION

I got a visa to visit my husband overseas. Three days to my departure, my husband called to tell me that I was no longer his wife. I decided to go through the deliverance programme. After the programme, my husband suddenly called again to tell me that instead of the three months visa, he would send a one year visa to me. Praise the Lord!

Sis. Pricilla

MFM Olowora

GOD HEALS MY GRANDSON

Sometime ago, my grandson was sick and hospitalized. I prayed to God for healing and declared that he would not die but live. To the glory of God, he recovered quickly and has since been discharged from the hospital. Praise the Lord!

Sis. Elizabeth

MFM Abaranje

GOD RESTORES ME TO MY GENDER

I am a lady physically but I had masculine spirits controlling my life. These wicked spirits made me to cherish only the things that pertain to men. I always dressed like a man. In fact, my wardrobe was full of men's dresses even from my youth. Also, these spirits even made me incompetent in all domestic chores. I found it difficult to cook. Going to the market, washing clothes, and cooking were big tasks to me. Whenever I was forced to do any of them, I always lost direction. But when I got to MFM and went for deliverance, God restored my original gender and by the grace of Jesus Christ, I have started to love and perform things that have to do with women. Praise the Lord!

Sis. Favour

MFM Onitsha

GLORIOUS FRUIT OF THE WOMB

I have been a member of this ministry since 2004 immediately I got married and was believing God for the fruit of the womb. I quickly joined the expectant family programme and since then I have become a regular member. Each time I came for service, I would sit anywhere believing that God sees everywhere. Last year, the G.O. organized a programme tagged, "Joy cometh in the morning." That day, when I arrived, I decided to change my position and sat in the front believing God would see me from all corners. The

G.O. gave a word of knowledge concerning my case. He said there was a woman who had been crying that she had her menses again that month but that she should not worry. Even though she had her menses, God would still visit her. Instantly I claimed the word of God and God visited me. The following month, I took in and I am now carrying my baby to the glory of God. Praise the Lord!

Sis. Nwamaka

MFM Headquarters

GOD HEALS MY MARRIAGE

I was having serious problems in my marriage. This situation brought me to MFM. After series of prayers, God intervened and healed my marriage. All the problems ceased. Also, God saved my son from untimely death. Praise the Lord!

Sis. Olorundamisi

MFM Ijegun

DELIVERANCE FROM SUDDEN
AND UNTIMELY DEATH

I was driving on a very busy road with heavy human and vehicular traffic. Suddenly, the entire front part of my car pulled off. I shouted the name and blood of Jesus and the car stopped immediately. The miracle was beyond my imagination and everybody was surprised at what God did for me. Praise the Lord!

Bro. Joseph

Omiyale-Ejigbo

SPIRIT OF DEATH AND HELL DISGRACED

I thank God Almighty for defeating the spirit of death and hell in my life. My sister had a dream in which I was knocked down by a moving vehicle. The dream actually manifested shortly after. I was hospitalized but I bless God today that I am still alive to praise His name. Praise the Lord!

Sis. Lauvina

MFM Iju

MOUNTAIN OF FIRE AND MIRACLES MINISTRIES
OGIJO
H. M. C. CRUSADE
Presents
2-days Crusade

Theme:
OGIJO FOR CHRIST

Come and meet with God and have solution to your Time problem
Venue: St. John Ang. Pry School, Ogijo
Date: 27th – 28th September 2008.
Time: 5:30pm.

PRAISE NIGHT
@: The Church auditorium, 58, Oluye Street, by Action Base
Date: 26th September 2008
Time: 10p.m Till Dawn

Ministering
ANOINTED MEN OF GOD
DR. D.K.OLUKOYA
General Overseer.

JESUS IS LORD

INSTITUTE OF SPIRITUAL WARFARE (INSWAR)

ADMISSION! ADMISSION!! ADMISSION!!!
ELIGIBLE CANDIDATES ARE HEREBY INVITED TO APPLY FOR ADMISSION INTO ANY OF THE FOLLOWING PROGRAMME OF STUDIES IN INSWAR
(PART-TIME PROGRAMME ONLY)
2009 SESSION (FEBRUARY - OCTOBER 2009)

1. DEPARTMENT OF EVANGELISM & CHURCH PLANTING
2. DEPARTMENT OF SPIRITUAL RED CROSS
3. DEPARTMENT OF CHILDREN EDUCATION
4. DEPARTMENT OF PRAISE WORSHIP
5. DEPARTMENT OF CHURCH MUSIC
6. DEPARTMENT OF DELIVERANCE (EVENING)
7. DEPARTMENT OF LANGUAGES & CULTURE
8. YORUBA DEPARTMENT
   , A. BIBLICAL STUDIES
   B. DELIVERANCE
   C. PRAYER

ADMISSION REQUIREMENTS
1. YOU MUST BE BORN AGAIN
2. BAPTISM IN THE HOLY SPIRIT
3. MEMBERSHIP IN MFM MINISTRIES
PURCHASE APPLICATION FORMS FROM INSWAR STORES AT MFM INT'L HEADQUARTERS, 13 OLASIMBO STREET ONIKE-YABA. DATE OF ENTRANCE EXAM: DEC. 13, 2008
VENUE: MFM INT'L HEADQUARTERS TIME 7.00AM

FROM TAPES MINISTRY
SPECIAL RELEASE OF DR. D.K OLUKOYA'S MESSAGES AVAILABLE ON BOTH AUDIO TAPES AND CDS

1. THE HOLY SPIRIT AND PROBLEMS We120397
2. THE BATTLE AT THE EDGE OF BREAKTHROUGH Su261299
3. THE MIDNIGHT BATTLE We161099
4. OVERCOMING WITCHCRAFT SPONSORED DISEASES Su230599
5. PRIVATE BATTLES, PRIVATE DEVILS Su190498
6. DESTROYING SATANIC MASKS We270396
7. THE GOD OF DELIVERANCE We271196
8. THE ENEMY ON RAMPAGE Su291198
9. MY ENEMY SHALL DIE IN MY PLACE We 031297
10. WHEN YOU ARE KNOCKED DOWN Su101099
11. RECOVERING YOUR LOST YEAR Su121195
12. POWER AGAINST EVIL CONSUMPTION M0091095
13. POWER AGAINST SPIRITUAL SPIDERS We300797
14. THE SPIRIT OF THE CRAB We230497
15. BREAKING FREE FROM FAMILY BONDAGE Su191299

Available in MFM International Bookshop and Vendors' stands.

FIRE IN THE WORD, is a weekly Spiritual Bulletin of the Mountain of Fire and Miracles Ministries, published by Tracts and Publications Group. All Enquiries should be addressed to The Editor, Mountain of Fire Magazine, 13, Olasimbo Street, off Olumo Road, Onike, P.O. Box 2990, Sabo Yaba, Lagos, Nigeria. Telephone 01- 867439, 864631, 868766, 08023180236.E-mail: mfmtractsandpublications@yahoo.com Copyright reserved.

FIRE IN THE WORD

Ye Shall Know the Truth, and the Truth Shall Make You Free (John 8:32)

ISSN 1595 - 7314 Vol. 12 No. 47 Sun. 5th - Sat. 11th Oct., 2008

THE WICKED
FERTILIZER

My year of unprecedented greatness and unmatchable increase
Deuteronomy 28:13, Psalm 71:21, Ephesians 3:20, Psalm 92:10

Our message this week, entitled, "The Wicked Fertilizer" is a warfare message. In it, we would be looking at one of the wicked operations of the enemy. Therefore, I would like you to read it carefully.

THINGS TO UNDERSTAND ABOUT THE WICKED

1. If God opens your eyes to see the wicked operations of the enemy and you are able to see a little bit of what they do, you will understand what Jesus meant when He says, "Pray without ceasing." They work like automatic machines. They do not rest. They do not go on holiday. They work hard at what they are doing to populate hell fire.

2. A lot of wicked operations are so strange that some people think it is superstition.

WHAT DOES IT MEAN TO FERTILIZE A THING?

It means to enrich a thing. A fertilizer is something that is used to enrich something. When you supply a thing with nourishment, you are fertilizing it. When you do something that will make another thing to germinate quickly, you are fertilizing the thing. Fertilization is also real in the spiritual realm. You can fertilize for good or for evil.

SOME QUESTIONS TO CONSIDER ON WICKED FERTILIZATION

1. Can life be used for life? Yes, it is possible. Can a person's life be used for another? The Bible says it is possible. Isaiah 42:4 says, *"Since thou wast precious in my sight, thou hast been honourable, and I have loved thee; therefore will I give men for thee, and people for thy life."* Life can be used for life. Somebody may be killed so that another person can live. Somebody can be made poor so that another person can be rich. Somebody can be rendered a vagabond so that another person can have direction. Can life be used for

THE DEVIL HAS NO POWER TO CREATE ANYTHING BUT HE IS THE MOST SUCCESSFUL ROBBER IN THE UNIVERSE

life? Yes it is possible and is being done day by day. Proverbs 11:8 says, *"The righteous is delivered out of trouble and the wicked cometh in his stead."*

2. Can virtue be transferred from person to person? Is it possible to steal the intelligence and wisdom of somebody and transfer them to another person? Yes, it is possible. They are tangible items that can be moved from place to place. Genesis 48:13 says, *"And Joseph took them both, Ephraim in his right hand toward Israel's left hand, and Manasseh in his left hand towards Israel's right hand, and brought him near unto him."* Normally, the firstborn should have the right hand laid on his head and the second born should have the left hand laid on his head. But in this case, there was an exchange. Verse 14 says, *"And Israel stretched out his right hand, and laid it upon Ephraim's head, which was the younger, and his left hand upon Manasseh's head, guiding his hands wittingly;*

HE SLEPT OFF AS HIS THOUGHTS LINGER ON ....
GOD IS NOT A RESPECTER OF ANYONE, HE CAN DECIDE TO SAVE A HARDENED CRIMINAL AND PUNISH A DECENT LOOKING PERSON WHO REFUSES TO GET **INTIMATE** WITH **HIM**; THINKING THAT MERE GIVING ALMS AND GOING TO CHURCH ON SUNDAYS IS TOTAL CHRISTIANITY.

for Manasseh was the firstborn." The virtue of Manasseh was transferred to his younger brother. This is the trouble of many firstborns. Their lives have been used for lives and their virtues have been transferred.

3. Can blessing be exchanged or taken away? Yes, it has happened before. Genesis 25:30-34 says, *"And Esau said to Jacob, Feed me, I pray thee with that same red pottage; for I am faint; therefore was his name called Edom. And Jacob said; Sell me this day thy birthright. And Esau said, Behold, I am at the point to die; and what profit shall this birthright do to me? And Jacob said, Swear to me this day, and he swore unto him; and he sold his birthright unto Jacob. Then Jacob gave Esau bread and pottage of lentils; and he did eat and drink, and rose up, and went his way; thus Esau despised his birthright."* This man exchanged his own blessing.

4. Can promotion be stolen? Yes, it is possible. It has happened before. The story of Jacob and Esau is also a case in point.

5. Can a man become an animal and still remain a man physically? Yes, it is possible. The life of a man can be reduced to that of an animal? The Lord did it to Nebuchadnezzar. Daniel 4:16 says, *"Let his heart be changed from man's and let a beast's heart be given unto him; and let seven times pass over him."* This is the reason behind the unreasonable behaviour of some people. Their real personalities have been transferred and an animal spirit has been given to them. When the real heart of a person is taken out and a dog's spirit is projected inside the person, the person will become an established prostitute, male or female.

6. Can problems be transferred? Yes, somebody's problem can be transferred to another person. You can lay your hands on the sick and the sickness will be transferred to you. It has happened before. 2 Kings 5:27 says, *"The leprosy therefore of Naaman shall cleave unto thee ..."* Look at the choice of words very well; the leprosy of the person to be transferred was specified. It was once the

problem of Naaman before it was pushed to Gehazi. So, problems can be transferred.

7. Can peace, joy and love be withdrawn? Yes. The Bible says it is possible. The power of darkness can turn somebody's love for a person to hatred. Luke 10:5-6 says *"And into whatsoever house ye enter, first say, Peace be to this house. And if the son of peace be there, your peace shall rest upon it; if not, it shall turn to you again."* Peace can move up and down.

8. Can God make a promise to a person and later withdraw it? Yes, He can. The enemy can manipulate a person to a position where the earlier promise made by the Lord is withdrawn. I Samuel 13:13 says, *"And Samuel said to Saul, Thou hast done foolishly: thou hast not kept the commandment of the Lord thy God which he commanded thee: for now would the Lord have established thy kingdom upon Israel for ever."*

The family of Saul would have been reigning in Israel forever.

There would have been nothing like the house of David reigning there. Verse 14 says, *"But now thy kingdom shall not continue; the Lord hath sought him a man after his own heart, and the Lord hath commanded him to be captain over his people, because thou hast not kept that which the Lord commanded thee."* God withdrew the promise, He transferred the destiny of Saul to David. It is possible too in the negative way.

9. Is it possible for somebody to work and somebody else who did not work reap the fruit? Yes, it is possible. Isaiah 65:21-22 says, *"And they shall build houses, and inhabit them: and they shall plant vineyards, and eat the fruit of them. They shall not build, and another inhabit; they shall not plant, and another eat..."* So, it is possible to work and not reap the benefits.

BELIEVERS SHOULD NOT SIT DOWN AND ALLOW THE ENEMY TO BE OPERATING WHAT THEY KNOW IS NOT THE ORDINANCE OF GOD

10. Can one life be demoted and wasted in order to fertilize another life? The answer is yes. In Ezekiel 13, we can see how the souls of people can be hunted down and transferred. We see how the soul of a person can be made to fly out so that another person might live.

Many years ago, a certain man rushed his daughter to me. The name of the girl was Uswa. She ran mad suddenly. As I wanted to start praying for her, the Lord said, "Don't pray. Ask this man to go to his father's house and tell the father to break open the centre of his sitting room. There, he will find a small coffin. Destroy that coffin and Uswa would be well." The man broke down and cried thinking I did not want to pray for his daughter. I encouraged him to believe the word of the Lord. So, he went to his father's house and told him what the Lord said. To his amazement, his father confirmed it. The place was broken and the small coffin was brought out. Inside the coffin was a script on which the name of Uswa was written. The idea was to terminate and waste Uswa so that her grandfather would continue to live. Immediately the coffin was destroyed there, Uswa became well. By the time her father came back, she was already taking a drink and was laughing and playing with others. An evil exchange was programmed to take place.

The devil has no power to create anything but he is the most successful robber in the universe. He can steal, transfer and exchange virtues. He can exchange a person's spirit with a terrible spirit. He can do body exchange and the affected person would look older than his or her age. The presence of the person will be inviting irritation also. He can do brain exchange, where he replaces the brain of a person with that of a goat. He can do child exchange in the womb. He can do wealth exchange. He can withdraw money from one place to another. He can do hair manipulation, virtue exchange, talents exchange, partner exchange, promotion exchange, etc. He uses people's lives to do terrible things.

SIGNS TO SHOW THAT A PERSON IS BEING USED AS A WICKED FERTILIZER

1. The person will experience what is called "firstborn demotion."
2. There would be constant failure at the edge of serious breakthroughs.
3. Unexplainable health failure.
4. Brain failure.
5. The person's children would become his enemies.
6. All kinds of terrible spiritual problems will come in. The person may find it very difficult to grow in the things of God because certain things have been taken out. His virtues have been removed.
7. The person may have a low self-image.
8. The person would have terrible nightmares especially nightmares in which he sees himself serving others all the time.
9. The person will experience a life of struggle and battle always.

WAY OUT

1. Surrender your life to the Lord. There is no other way.
2. Pull down the altars of the wicked fertilization.
3. Command a reverse of what the enemy has done wrong to you.

THE PROPHET | Saul versus David 7

1 SAMUEL 18:13. THEREFORE SAUL REMOVED HIM FROM HIS PRESENCE, AND MADE HIM HIS CAPTAIN OVER A THOUSAND...

A LETTER FROM KING SAUL. YOU ARE NOW A CAPTAIN!

CAPTAIN OVER A 1,000

1 SAMUEL 18:14. AND DAVID BEHAVED HIMSELF WISELY IN ALL HIS WAYS, AND THE LORD WAS WITH HIM.

...I'LL REST IN THE LORD, AND WAIT PATIENTLY FOR HIM. I'LL NOT FRET.... OF THE... WICKED SCHEMES.

PSALM 37:7.

Believers should not sit down and allow the enemy to be operating what they know is not the ordinance of God.

PRAYER POINTS

1. Every satanic obituary written against my destiny, die, in the name of Jesus.

2. Every witchcraft agent in my place of work, receive the stripes of fire, in the name of Jesus.

3. I will not go to my enemies for help, in the name of Jesus.

4. Pharaoh of my life, rush and perish in the Red sea, in the name of Jesus.

5. My Father, contend with those who contend with my destiny, in the name of Jesus.

6. Every satanic surveillance over my life, I bind you, in the name of Jesus.

7. Every witchcraft prayer targeted against my destiny, die, in the name of Jesus.

8. Every evil power of my father's house, vomit my virtues, in the name of Jesus.

9. Every power nominating me for demotion, your time is up, die, in the name of Jesus.

10. My life, refuse the handwriting of the wicked fertilizer, in the name of Jesus.

11. The timetable of my favour shall not be frustrated, in the name of Jesus.

12. The sons of strangers shall build up my wall and kings shall minister unto me, in the name of Jesus.

13. My Father, I recover by fire my birthright that I have unconsciously sold out, in the name of Jesus.

14. Every power caging my greatness, die, in the name of Jesus.

15. Every power that wants to waste my life, your time is up, die, in the name of Jesus.

16. Every dry bone of my virtues, come alive, in the name of Jesus.

17. I withdraw my virtues from the waters, in the name of Jesus.

18. Every power planning to use me as a wicked fertilizer, die, in the name of Jesus.

19. Every power planning to use my life as a wicked fertilizer, die, in the name of Jesus.

20. Every wicked replacement of my destiny, scatter, in the name of Jesus.

21. Satanic exchange of my destiny, die, in the name of Jesus.

THE WICKED FERTILIZER
is a message delivered at the Mountain of Fire and Miracles Ministries by the General Overseer, Dr. D.K. Olukoya.

A CALL TO SERVE

Are you a member of MFM with a burden to help the needy, are you interested in alleviating the plight of the poor or in the spread of the gospel through the sponsorship of the publication of tracts? Your resources, time and talent can be extended to several groups that are in charge of these areas. These groups include:

o   We care Ministry,
o   Mission Outreach
o   Tracts and Publications
o   Ministry to Drug addicts
o   Campus fellowship
o   Ministry to Schools
o   Ministry to Glorious Children, etc.

Thus says the Lord, "Verily I say unto you, in as much as ye have done it unto one of the least of these my brethren, ye have done it unto me" Matthew 25 : 40.

WONDERFUL JESUS!

DIVINE INTERVENTION

MFM Ughelli

My son was in detention at Kirikiri prison before I came for deliverance in this church. I gave his picture and name to the deliverance ministers. To the glory of God, he was miraculously released even before my completion of the deliverance programme. Praise the Lord!

Bro. Sunday

MFM Idimu

DELIVERANCE FROM

ARMED ROBBERY ATTACK

As I got home after a forty-day vigil programme held in our church, six gun men pointed torchlights and guns at me through the window and ordered me to open the door for them to come in. Immediately, I heard the Holy Spirit telling me to rebuke them and plead the blood of Jesus. This I started doing immediately and before I knew it, they all ran away through different directions. There is certainly power in the blood of Jesus. Praise God.

Sis. Helen

MFM Asoro, Benin City

TOTAL DELIVERANCE

Things were not working for me so I went for deliverance, during which I had a dream where I found myself in my hometown flogging some masquerades seriously with boldness and power. Since then new things have started happening in my life and my life has changed for the better. Praise the Lord!

Bro. David

MFM Ado-Ekiti

EMPLOYMENT BREAKTHROUGH

God has done great and wonderful things in my life. There was a programme where we were asked to write 21 prayer requests and part of my own prayer requests was for a job. Now God has provided a job for me. Praise the Lord!

Sis. Joy

GOD GRANTS MY REQUEST

For a very long time, I sought transfer from my place of work but my request was always turned down without any reason. Then I decided to take it to the Lord in prayer. I went for deliverance and thereafter I was given some prayer points to pray. Surprisingly one day, I got to the office and my letter of transfer was waiting for me. Praise the Lord!

Sis. Jesudiran

MFM Agodo

GOD REVIVES MY LIFE AND BUSINESS

I attended this church one Sunday and decided to go for deliverance thereafter. After the deliverance, God revived my business and spiritual life. Praise the Lord!

Sis. Mary

MFM Isheri/Idimu

DIVINE FAVOUR FROM THE LORD

I was living in a room apartment, where I had problems with my landlord. I moved in with a friend who later rejected me. But later to the glory of God, God provided a 2 bedroom flat for me where I did not have to pay agency and agreement fees. The place is also close to the church. Praise God!

Bro. Emmanuel

MFM Morogbo

GOD TURNS MY MOURNING
INTO LAUGHTER

I had a dream in which I found myself in a pool of blood after beating up a small girl who stole my money. Later on, I put to bed through a ceasarien session on a Saturday and the baby died on Sunday, the following day. I started attending the headquarters Expectant Family programme. God heard my cry and I conceived but doctors said that I had hepatitis B and the baby was wrongly positioned. I came to the church, and ministers of God prayed for me. To the glory of God, I put to bed a bouncing baby boy. Praise God!

Sis. Nwanokwu

MFM Headquarters (Expectant Family Group)

RESULT OF 1ST SURU-LERE ZONAL YOUTH BIBLE QUIZ HELD ON SATURDAY 23RD OF AUGUST, 2008

A. YOUTH CATEGORY – WINNERS

NAME	BRANCH	POSITION	PRIZES
Bro. Oladele Oladimeji	Masha	1st	LG Flatron 15" Tv Set
Bro. Omojuwa Joseph	Owode-Ajegunle	2nd	Generator (Tiger TG950DC)
Sis. Olagoke Sola	Haastrup	3rd	DVD Player
Sis. Tochukwu Charles	Irepodun	4th	Sandwich Toaster
Bro. Tope Williams	Akinyele - Aguda	5th	Consolation
Bro. Odinaka Chukwudolu	Akinyele - Aguda	6th	Consolation

B. TEENAGE CATEGORY – WINNERS

NAME	BRANCH	POSITION	PRIZES
Bro. Tolulope Shafau	Owode Ajegunle	1st	Bicycle (Eastman Model)
Sis. Moyin Abiola	Headquarters	2nd	Sandwich Toaster
Bro. Aderemi Oluwapelumi	Masha	3rd	Nokia Mobile Handset (1200)
Bro. Ayonike Ayomide	Haastrup	4th	Electric Iron (Dry)
Sis. Pelumi Abiola	Headquarters	5th	Consolation (Food Flask)
Sis. Olafunio Adedokun	Akinyele - Aguda	6th	Consolation (Jug)
Bro. Nlendic Alinu	Ajao	7th	Consolation (Food Flask)

INSTITUTE OF SPIRITUAL WARFARE (INSWAR)

ADMISSION! ADMISSION!! ADMISSION!!!
**ELIGIBLE CANDIDATES ARE HEREBY INVITED TO APPLY FOR ADMISSION
INTO ANY OF THE FOLLOWING PROGRAMME OF STUDIES IN INSWAR**
(PART-TIME PROGRAMME ONLY)
2009 SESSION (FEBRUARY - OCTOBER 2009)

1. DEPARTMENT OF EVANGELISM & CHURCH PLANTING
2. DEPARTMENT OF SPIRITUAL RED CROSS
3. DEPARTMENT OF CHILDREN EDUCATION
4. DEPARTMENT OF PRAISE WORSHIP
5. DEPARTMENT OF CHURCH MUSIC
6. DEPARTMENT OF DELIVERANCE (EVENING)
7. DEPARTMENT OF LANGUAGES & CULTURE
8. YORUBA DEPARTMENT
   , A. BIBLICAL STUDIES
      B. DELIVERANCE
      C. PRAYER

ADMISSION REQUIREMENTS
1. YOU MUST BE BORN AGAIN
2. BAPTISM IN THE HOLY SPIRIT
3. MEMBERSHIP IN MFM MINISTRIES

PURCHASE APPLICATION FORMS FROM INSWAR STORES AT MFM INT'L HEADQUARTERS, 13 OLASIMBO STREET ONIKE-YABA. DATE OF ENTRANCE EXAM: DEC. 13, 2008

VENUE: MFM INT'L HEADQUARTERS TIME 7.00AM

FROM TAPES MINISTRY
SPECIAL RELEASE OF DR. D.K OLUKOYA'S MESSAGES AVAILABLE ON BOTH AUDIO TAPES AND CDS

1. THE HOLY SPIRIT AND PROBLEMS We120397
2. THE BATTLE AT THE EDGE OF BREAKTHROUGH Su261299
3. THE MIDNIGHT BATTLE We161099
4. OVERCOMING WITCHCRAFT SPONSORED DISEASES Su230599
5. PRIVATE BATTLES, PRIVATE DEVILS Su190498
6. DESTROYING SATANIC MASKS We270396
7. THE GOD OF DELIVERANCE We271196
8. THE ENEMY ON RAMPAGE Su291198
9. MY ENEMY SHALL DIE IN MY PLACE We031297
10. WHEN YOU ARE KNOCKED DOWN Su101099
11. RECOVERING YOUR LOST YEAR Su121195
12. POWER AGAINST EVIL CONSUMPTION M0091095
13. POWER AGAINST SPIRITUAL SPIDERS We300797
14. THE SPIRIT OF THE CRAB We230497
15. BREAKING FREE FROM FAMILY BONDAGE Su191299

Available in MFM International Bookshop and Vendors' stands.

FIRE IN THE WORD, is a weekly Spiritual Bulletin of the Mountain of Fire and Miracles Ministries, published by Tracts and Publications Group. All Enquiries should be addressed to The Editor, Mountain of Fire Magazine, 13, Olasimbo Street, off Olumo Road, Onike. P.O. Box 2990, Sabo Yaba, Lagos, Nigeria. Telephone 01- 867439, 864631, 868766, 08023180236.E-mail: mfmtractsandpublications@yahoo.com Copyright reserved.

FIRE IN THE WORD

Ye Shall Know the Truth, and the Truth Shall Make You Free (John 8:32)

ISSN 1595 - 7314 Vol. 12 No. 48 Sun. 12th - Sat. 18th Oct., 2008

The Internal
MAGNET OF DARKNESS

My year of unprecedented greatness and unmatchable increase
Deuteronomy 28:13, Psalm 71:21, Ephesians 3:20, Psalm 92:10

This week, we are looking at the message entitled, "The internal magnet of darkness."

Every human being has a measure of positive and negative charges inside his or her life, especially when the person has not fully surrendered to the Lord. But the ratio of one charge to the other may differ from person to person. You could find a sister who is jovial and a fantastic cook but she might have a bad temper which would nullify all the goodness she has.

Sometime ago, in England, I read about a certain professor in a newspaper and I almost wept. This professor was dragged to court for getting drunk and fighting in a bar. He was supposed to be jailed but the judge could not send him to jail because he was practically the best professor on heart disease in the whole of the UK. The largest grant on heart research was given to him. But here was this brilliant man, well respected all over the world in international scientific circles getting drunk and fighting. He had a measure of both negative and positive charges.

Many years ago, we had a wonderful doctor on our street, who was very kind. Whenever he was not in the hospital, many patients would rather go home because they preferred to see him. But as good as he was in his medical field, he was hooked on hard drugs and eventually died of an overdose of hard drugs. Although he was a wonderful doctor there was this negative aspect of him.

Many years ago, I had a brilliant classmate, who slept a lot in class. He was very bright only when he remained awake.

Also, I know a woman of God who was so good that when she arrived in the service and started praise worship, miracles would be happening before her

SIN IS EASILY INTRODUCED TO SOME PEOPLE BECAUSE OF THE NEGATIVE CHARGE IN THEM

husband who was the pastor came to the pulpit. But the last I heard about her was that their landlord had impregnated her and to worsen the case, he had taken her to Mecca.

So, in the lives of people, you find positive and negative charge. A person whose negative charge is higher than the positive would rarely see anything bright no matter how hard he prays. He would rarely see the visions of heaven because he is loaded with the negative. In some people, there is 50% positive charge and 50% negative charge. Some have 90% positive and 10% negative. It varies with individuals. But the big truth which many people do not understand is that a person attracts the kind of charge he emits to others. If a person emits or releases positive charges towards people, for example, love joy, respect etc, people will respond positively too to him.

Proverbs 16:7 says, *"When a man's way please the Lord,*

DELIVERANCE CASE (THE STORY OF MY LIFE - PART 34)

STILL DREAMING.
WHAT IS THIS?! I ASKED FOR GOD, SEE WHAT IS EMERGING FROM THE GROUND, CAN THIS BE GOD?! MAYBE THIS IS GOD'S STAFF OF OFFICE; HERALDING HIS PRESENCE. BUT THROUGH THE BIBLE, GOD NEVER EMERGED FROM THE GROUND; WHAT TRICK IS THIS?!

he maketh even his enemies to be at peace with him."

This is not normal peace, it is compulsory peace. Each time the enemy brings a battle against such a person, they encounter total and solid defeat. So they just learn to be at peace with the person. They will be afraid to attack the person because they know that if they give the person a blow, they will receive seven. So, they are at peace with the person compulsorily. That is if the person's way pleases the Lord. But if on the contrary, a person is emitting a negative charge, he will attract a negative charge to himself.

No matter how negligible a negative charge inside a person may appear, it has the capacity to attract the negative charge in

another person. For example, if a person who has anger is dealing with another person who has anger in him or her, that negative charge of anger in him will arouse the anger in the other person too. It is the same thing with lust. Unfortunately, this is what some people call love. Sometimes when it leads to marriage, the marriage ends up in chaos.

The 5% negative charge that a person has can attract 90% negative charge against that person. Luke 6:38 says, *"Give, and it shall be given unto you good measure, pressed down, and shaken together, and running over, shall men give unto your bosom. For with the same*

measure that ye mete withal it shall be measured to you again."

If you emit the positive charge of generosity, generosity too will locate you. That is you attract to yourself what you give or emit to others. When somebody wears seductive dresses; dresses of fornication, they will be emitting a negative charge. And a man that is already walking about with a negative charge of sexual problem in his life will get attracted to the person. This is what is responsible for most cases of rape in the campuses and even in the cities. That is, the dragon inside one person arousing the dragon in another person.

If you discover that you find it easy to make enemies instead of friends, there is a negative charge in you. If people find it difficult to get along with you, it means you are emitting a negative charge. If you are the kind of person who attracts controversy and antagonism against your person everywhere you go, you are emitting a negative charge. If you really want to marry but find that only the wrong men or women are coming your way, it means there is something in you attracting them.

A businessman who is always meeting the wrong people or investing his money in the wrong things all the time should pray against negative charge. It takes somebody with a good charge to spread goodness. And if you decide that you want your life to emit positive charges, it shall be so.

A brother had a motor accident three times, and on each occasion he just had slight bruises but other people in the vehicles either died or sustained serious injuries. One day as he was about to take some people

to a crusade, the pastor, who was a wise man quickly asked him to come down and asked another brother to take over. There was something in that brother that attracted accidents.

One indication of the kind of charge you carry is the kind of discussion people have with you, what they talk to you about. When people come to you, do they talk about God, Christianity, the sermons they heard, holiness, the power of God etc? Or when they come to you although, they know you are a Christian, even a pastor, all they talk about is business. That is your charge. These things like forces, will attract themselves. This is why a particular lady would be the only one every man in her place of work wants to touch. There was a certain sister whose name was submitted by ten brothers to the marriage committee as the will

A SIMPLE NEGATIVE CHARGE IN A PERSON IS ALL THE ENEMY NEEDS TO GET INSIDE

of God for them in marriage. And all of them claimed it was God leading them. The marriage committee became confused. It was obvious that God did not tell them anything. There was something attracting them, pulling them towards her.

Why is it that in your place of work you are the only one everyone is quarrelling with? You hardly find somebody who agrees with you. Why is it that the day you do not come to work, they are very happy and rejoicing not because you are very strict but because you are very violent. There are people who are known to always have the latest gossips in town. It is a negative charge.

A certain sister came for counselling with three different divorce letters and another one came with three abandoned children. The men who fathered them abandoned them and refused to support them.

Sin is easily introduced to some people because of the negative charge in them. This is not the case with people who are living a life of holiness. There are terrible things planted within some people which are called, "Traders in the temple." The horsewhip of the Lord Jesus Christ is needed to get them out.

Sometime ago, a woman brought her husband to me, the man had impregnated three house helps. And when I asked him what was wrong, he could not explain. It was due to the kind of charge in him.

There is something known as a spiritual magnet. The enemy can put a tangible object, visible or invisible inside the body. This deposit could be in any part of the body. A person can have a plantation of darkness in his soul, spirit and flesh. This is not a demon. When there is a satanic magnet inside a life, several things would begin to happen.

THINGS THAT HAPPEN WHEN A SATANIC MAGNET IS IN PLACE

1. You may notice irregular attacks.
2. You may notice blockages.
3. You may notice that you are being pushed here and there.
4. You may notice that things that ought not to come close to you are getting close to you.

A negative magnet inside the body can cause the following:
1. Bad luck.
2. A bad aura around a person.
3. Attraction to other negative charges around.

There are some people who make terrible mistakes. When such people discover through prayers that somebody very close to them is a witch, they would go and challenge the person physically. It is foolishness. Even if you know that somebody is a witch, it is better to keep quiet and watch the person carefully. By so doing, you will be able to know all the friends that the person has because the negative charge of that person will attract other witches around. So very soon you will be able to know all of them. But when you scream, they will cover their tracks and before you see them again, they would have transferred your case file far away.

There is need to understand that there are mysteries about our world that are not clear to many people. It is very sad that

THE PROPHET | Saul versus David 8

even now, there are people that have been completely swallowed by household wickedness but on Sundays they are present in one church or another dancing away. And they are wasting time. Sometimes by the time they come to a place like MFM, their situation would have gone beyond repairs. There is need to pray really hard because the simple negative charge in a person is all the enemy needs to get inside.

You must deal with the evil magnet now because no matter how terrible a serpent is if you break it when it is at the egg level, there would be no dragon to attack you.

PRAYER POINTS

1. O God, arise and destroy any power delegated to waste my life, in the name of Jesus.

2. Every property of the enemy in my life, catch fire, die, in the name of Jesus.

3. Every assignment of the enemy for my head, backfire, in the name of Jesus.

4. Every magnet of darkness in my body, die, in the name of Jesus.

5. Every magnet of darkness in my body, die, in the name of Jesus.

6. Every magnet of darkness in my family line, die, in the name of Jesus.

7. Every ladder of darkness in my body, die, in the name of Jesus.

8. Every negative charge in my spirit, scatter, in the name of Jesus.

9. Every anti-prosperity magnet in my life, die, in the name of Jesus.

10. Every power circulating my name in witchcraft covens, die, in the name of Jesus.

11. Every ladder of darkness of my father's house, die, in the name of Jesus.

12. Goodness and mercy, follow me by fire, in the name of Jesus.

13. Every testimony allocated to my destiny, I possess it by fire, in the name of Jesus.

14. Every good thing that I touch shall prosper, in the name of Jesus.

15. Stretch forth your two hands and begin to bless yourself with all kinds of blessings in the name of Jesus.

16. Ask the Lord to reveal to you where you need to change, so that you will change and rise, in the name of Jesus.

THE INTERNAL MAGNET OF DARKNESS
is a message delivered at the Mountain of Fire and Miracles Ministries by the General Overseer, Dr. D.K. Olukoya.

A CALL TO SERVE

Are you a member of MFM with a burden to help the needy, are you interested in alleviating the plight of the poor or in the spread of the gospel through the sponsorship of the publication of tracts? Your resources, time and talent can be extended to several groups that are in charge of these areas. These groups include:

o　　　We care Ministry,
o　　　Mission Outreach
o　　　Tracts and Publications
o　　　Ministry to Drug addicts
o　　　Campus fellowship
o　　　Ministry to Schools
o　　　Ministry to Glorious Children, etc.

Thus says the Lord, "Verily I say unto you, in as much as ye have done it unto one of the least of these my brethren, ye have done it unto me" Matthew 25 : 40.

WONDERFUL JESUS!

ULCER GONE

Before I came for deliverance, I had ulcer for seven years. But during the deliverance programme, the Lord healed me. Praise the Lord!

Sis. Adetomi
MFM Headquarters

DIVINE APPOINTMENT

I thank God for divine victory in my place of work. There was a vacant post and two of us contested for it. My opponent spent a lot of money to canvass for votes but I resorted to prayers. At the end of the election, I won by a wide margin. I now use my new position to evangelise. Praise the Lord!

Bro. Osinaike
MFM Ijebu-Ode

GOD HEALS US

I was down with a terrible sickness for some days and my son too experienced a similar sickness at the same time. Everybody around us panicked but after prayers, we were made whole. Praise the Lord!

Sis. Tayo
MFM Shibiri

GOD GRANTS MY HEART'S DESIRE

I was posted to Zamfara State for NYSC. I thank God for journey mercies. Also, I prayed to be posted to where I could put my profession into practice and God granted my request and I was posted to an hospital. Praise the Lord!

Sis. Nike
MFM Dopemu

DIVINE INTERVENTION

Recently, after the house fellowship, I unknowingly boarded a taxi with the men of the underworld. There was nothing I could do but to pray. After sometime, they suddenly stopped and pushed me out of the cab. Secondly, God granted me and my family journey mercy to Port-Harcourt. Praise the Lord!

Bro. Adeleke
MFM Apata

GOD GIVES ME A GOOD JOB

God gave me a job in East African Development Bank. Also, God healed my friend of heart failure. God protected me from being knocked down by a car when I fell down while crossing the road. Praise the Lord!

Bro. Emmanuel
MFM Kampala, Uganda

DELIVERANCE FROM UNTIMELY DEATH

I thank God for His blessings upon my family since I joined this ministry. Secondly, I took a motorbike and before I got to my destination, we had an accident, but the good Lord delivered us from untimely death. Praise the Lord!

Bro. Jofoba
MFM Egan

GOD HEALS ME

Sometime ago at Abuja, I had an accident and got injured on my left shoulder. Since then I had been praying that the injury would be completely healed but all to no avail. Thereafter I made a vow to the Lord that if I received my healing, I would come to testify to His goodness upon my life. Glory be to His name that today, I am healed. Praise God!

Bro. Amobi
MFM Alabi

THE HEALING POWER OF GOD

My daughter was sick and rushed to the hospital. The doctor examined her and discovered that she had ruptured appendicitis. I brought her to the man of God who prayed with us. She also drank anointing oil. To the glory of God, the situation disappeared totally. Praise the Lord!

Sis. Ofongbai
MFM Uromi

Junior Fire in the Word *Vol. 76*

The following winners of the Junior Fire in the Word crossword puzzle and quiz should collect their gifts at the Tracts and Publications office, MFM International Headquarters, Lagos.

Name	Age	Branch
1. Oyebode O. John	10	Igbo-Elerin
2. Godwin Topman	12	Headquarters
3. Stephen Ekulide	10	Itire/Ijesha
4. Isioma Okobi	6½	Fadeyi
5. Tolu John	11	Ori-Okuta

MOUNTAIN-TOP INTERNATIONAL BIBLE COLLEGE
MOUNTAIN OF FIRE AND MIRACLES MINISTRIES
INTERNATIONAL HEADQUARTERS
13 Olasimbo Street, Off Olumo Road, Onike, P.O. Box 2990, Sabo, Yaba, Lagos, Nigeria

FULL-TIME / PART-TIME PROGRAM OF STUDIES

1. Certificate in Christian Ministry (CCM: One Year)
2. Diploma in Theology (Dip. Th: Two Years)
3. Bachelor of Theology (B. Th: Three Years)

ADMISSION REQUIREMENTS

A. Certificate in Christian Ministry / Diploma in Theology
1. Three credits and other passes (including English Language) in WASC or
2. Three credits and other passes in NECO or
3. The Teachers Certificate Grade 2 with Merit in three subjects Including English Language.
4. Qualification equivalent to the aforementioned with proficiency in English Language.

B. Bachelor of Theology
1. Five credits passes (including English Language) in the General Certificate of Education (GCE) or Senior School Certificate Examinations (SSCE) or
2. Five credits passes (including English Language) in National Examination Council (NECO) or
3. Five credit passes (including English Language) in the General Certificate Education (GCE) or Senior School Certificate Examinations (SSCE) or
4. The Teachers Certificate Grade 2 with merit in three subjects including English Language or
5. Qualification equivalent to the aforementioned with proficiency in English Language.

Date of Entrance Exam: DEC 13, 2008
Venue: MFM Int'l headquarters
Time: 7:00am

APPLICATION FORMS NOW ON SALE

INSTITUTE OF SPIRITUAL WARFARE (INSWAR)
ADMISSION! ADMISSION!! ADMISSION!!!

ELIGIBLE CANDIDATES ARE HEREBY INVITED TO APPLY FOR ADMISSION INTO ANY OF THE FOLLOWING PROGRAMME OF STUDIES IN INSWAR (PART-TIME PROGRAMME ONLY) 2009 SESSION (FEBRUARY - OCTOBER 2009)

1. DEPARTMENT OF EVANGELISM & CHURCH PLANTING
2. DEPARTMENT OF SPIRITUAL RED CROSS
3. DEPARTMENT OF CHILDREN EDUCATION
4. DEPARTMENT OF PRAISE WORSHIP
5. DEPARTMENT OF CHURCH MUSIC
6. DEPARTMENT OF DELIVERANCE (EVENING)
7. DEPARTMENT OF LANGUAGES & CULTURE
8. DEPARTMENT OF DISCIPLESHIP & MISSIONS

ADMISSION REQUIREMENTS
1. YOU MUST BE BORN AGAIN
2. BAPTISM IN THE HOLY SPIRIT
3. MEMBERSHIP IN MFM MINISTRIES

PURCHASE APPLICATION FORMS FROM INSWAR STORES AT MFM INT'L HEADQUARTERS, 13 OLASIMBO STREET ONIKE-YABA. DATE OF ENTRANCE EXAM: DEC. 13, 2008

VENUE: MFM INT'L HEADQUARTERS TIME 7.00AM

APOLOGY

We wish to apologise to our numerous beloved readers for the error on the page 2 of our last week's edition of Fire in the Word. We regret any inconvenience caused.
MANAGEMENT

FIRE IN THE WORD, is a weekly Spiritual Bulletin of the Mountain of Fire and Miracles Ministries, published by Tracts and Publications Group. All Enquiries should be addressed to The Editor, Mountain of Fire Magazine, 13, Olasimbo Street, off Olumo Road, Onike, P.O. Box 2990, Sabo Yaba, Lagos, Nigeria. Telephone 01- 867439, 864631, 868766, 08023180236. E-mail: mfmtractsandpublications@yahoo.com Copyright reserved.

FIRE IN THE WORD

Ye Shall Know the Truth, and the Truth Shall Make You Free (John 8:32)

ISSN 1595 - 7314   Vol. 12   No. 49   Sun. 19th - Sat. 25th Oct., 2008

Becoming a Spiritual
SCAPEGOAT

My year of unprecedented greatness and unmatchable increase
Deuteronomy 28:13, Psalm 71:21, Ephesians 3:20, Psalm 92:10

This week, we are looking at the message entitled, "Becoming a spiritual scapegoat."

1 Timothy 5:22 says, *"Lay hands suddenly on no man, neither be partaker of other men's sins: keep thyself pure."*

If laying on of hands generally imparted only blessings, there would not have been any need for this passage in the Bible. It is clearly written there that you should be careful so that you will not be a partaker of other men's sins, and that you have to keep yourself pure.

The implication of the passage in a nutshell is this: a hand laid on a person can bring blessings and can also bring trouble. It can bring breakthrough and can also bring demotion depending on the kind of hands that were laid upon a person. A hand laid upon your life can make you to be a partaker of other people's sins. This is made clearer when you consider the significance of the scapegoat in the Old Testament. It was from this metaphor that 1Timothy 5:22 was derived.

Leviticus 16:7-10 says, *"And he shall take the two goats, and present them before the Lord at the door of the tabernacle of the congregation. And Aaron shall cast lots upon the two goats; one lot for the Lord, and the other lot for the scapegoat. And Aaron shall bring the goat upon which the Lord's lot fell, and offer him for a sin offering. But the goat, on which the lot fell to be the scapegoat, shall be presented alive before the Lord, to make an atonement with him, and to let him go for a scapegoat into the wilderness."*

We understand that on the day of atonement, two goats would be presented before the Lord. Lots would be cast to select the one to be sacrificed to the Lord, which would be killed at the altar. But the scapegoat would remain alive. The high priest would lay both hands on the head of the scapegoat and would confess the sins of the whole nation in the previous year upon the head of that innocent goat. The goat would be led to an uninhabited wilderness and would be left to wander about. Since this ritual was very critical, the high priest would usually cleanse himself and his household thoroughly before going to officiate over the sins of the nation. But today, we have situations where believers

THE SCAPEGOAT SPIRIT NEVER ALLOWS A PERSON TO GET ESTABLISHED

submit themselves; their heads and bodies to be touched by just anybody. Now, there are situations where a fornicating priest lays hands upon the head of a young lady and thereby transfers an unclean spirit of fornication into her life. And the lady who becomes an innocent scapegoat starts doing things she normally does not do. When hands are laid on you by vessels that are not of God, there could be a transfer of iniquities and all kinds of things into your life. And this is why many people are becoming spiritual scapegoats. And all kinds of terrible things are happening to them.

It is possible for somebody to be a spiritual scapegoat unconsciously. Leviticus 16:7-10 makes it clear that it is possible for somebody to be punished for a crime he did not commit.

WHO IS A SCAPEGOAT?

A scapegoat is a kind of sacrifice. A scapegoat is a substitute, a victim, a target, somebody that was set up or an easy mark. A scapegoat is someone who is punished for the errors of others. He is a person that is made to bear the blame for others. And there are many people around today, who have been made spiritual

DELIVERANCE CASE (THE STORY OF MY LIFE - PART 35)

scapegoats. This is actually the major trouble that many firstborns are facing. They were used as a touchlight for other people to come into the world. They become spiritual scapegoats, roaming about in the wilderness of life.

The scapegoat spirit is very terrible, it forces people to roam around all the time aimlessly. If you notice that you are always highly victimized or you are always more adversely affected than others around you then you are a scapegoat. When something happens somewhere, and you are the person that gets injured most, you are a scapegoat. When something happens somewhere and you are the one that is subjected to the most serious oppression, you are a scapegoat. Somebody who is subjected to a loss more than any other person around could be a scapegoat. If you are subjected to suffering more than

any other person around, it means that there is a spirit following you; it is the scapegoat spirit.

When somebody is a scapegoat, he becomes an easy casualty; a prey for all kinds powers of darkness. The person becomes like a sitting target; a play thing in the hand of the enemy. No matter how intelligent this kind of a person is, the scapegoat spirit will make nonsense of his intelligence. It will envelope the true destiny of the person and doors of goodness and mercy would be closed just like the goat in the book of Leviticus that was released into the wilderness after it had been made to bear the iniquities and sins that it did not commit.

If you got married before you got born again and went through all the traditional wedding rites and all kinds of people laid hands on you in

the name of praying, you may need to pray seriously. If it was an occult person that was asked to pray for you, and he laid his dirty hands on your body, know for sure that something would have been transferred into your body which might not have manifested immediately. This is the cause of the wilderness life which many people are living now. The scapegoat is always hit by stray bullets.

The scapegoat spirit is like an evil spell or an evil influence. It can bewitch a person. It brings a negative aura around a person and the person invites hatred wherever he or she goes. He or she makes enemies very quickly and has difficulty making friends. Unfortunately, there are many people both young and old, who are suffering under this situation. Some of these people do not have any focus in life. They wander from city to city. The men go from one woman to another while the women go from one man to another. They go from one job to another.

The scapegoat spirit never allows a person to get established. There are many young men and women roaming about in the wilderness of life without direction. There are many men of God who are completely lost, they do not have direction. They do not really know where to throw their nets in the ocean of life. Victims of the scapegoat powers keep failing in all their endeavours, including marriage. And they live in a constant state of discontentment and restlessness. They get sacked from their jobs. They never seem to be able to keep any job in a stable manner. If the scapegoat forces are after you, no matter how many times you go for deliverance, they will remain in place until you address them.

SIGNS THAT A SCAPEGOAT SPIRIT IS IN OPERATION IN A PERSON'S LIFE:

1. The person will find it very difficult to have favour with people.
2. There will be financial bondage and debt.
3. When the scapegoat syndrome is upon a person, the labour of the person will be bewitched. If the person opens a restaurant, there will be no customers. If he starts selling meat pie, one day, all those who eat the meat pie will begin to complain of stomach trouble. All of a sudden they will start avoiding the person's shop. If he starts selling kerosene, one day, a careless person will set the whole place ablaze and there will be trouble again and the person cannot sell kerosene anymore. Beloved, if this is your own experience, you need to sit down and examine your life. And one of the easiest ways the enemy can introduce this is when an evil man or woman lays hands on you. If a native doctor has performed a satanic surgery on you, for example, incisions, your blood would be polluted and that might be affecting you negatively now. Perhaps your father and grandfather were drunkards, and they laid hands on you and prayed for you, that spirit of drunkenness might have been transferred to you. If they were polygamists and prayed for you, laying hands on you, that anointing may be what is working against you now.

IF YOU DO NOT KNOW WHO YOU ARE, THE ENEMY WILL TELL YOU, WHO HE WANTS YOU TO BE

4. When somebody is being harassed by scapegoat powers, he or she will find it very difficult to establish a good and lasting relationship. If it is a sister, her husband will fight her always. He would smile at everybody else but as soon as he sees the sister, his countenance will change. Such a person needs to pray and cancel the consequences of the evil hand that were laid on her in the name of Jesus.

For any person that is pursued by the scapegoat powers, deliverance takes a long time because in the course of going from one place to another, he picks up different spirits. This is part of the reasons why pasting money on people's forehead during ceremonies is dangerous. Those who normally do not have access to a person's head will seize that opportunity to programme what they want into that head.

Beloved, at this juncture, I would like you to take the following prayer points:

1. Every power laying evil hands upon my life, your time is up, die, in the name of Jesus.
2. Every evil power that has gained access to my blood, your time is up, die, in the name of Jesus.
3. Every negative spiritual mother and every negative

spiritual father, your time is up, die, in the name of Jesus.

SYMPTONS OF THE SCAPEGOAT POWERS

The following are the symptoms that you notice when someone is under the control of the scapegoat powers:

1. Wandering.
2. Aimlessness.
3. Homelessness.
4. Floating life.
5. Abandonment.
6. Lack of direction.
7. Confusion.
8. Rejection.
9. Unfair displacement.
10. Restlessness.
11. Idleness.
12. Great poverty.
13. Alcoholism.
14. Sexual perversion. The person cannot rest until he or

she has committed fornication.
15. Debt.
16. Drugs.
17. Constant failure.
18. Depression.
19. Weariness.
20. Nervousness.
21. Suicidal tendency.
22. Hopelessness.
23. Bitterness.
24. Closed doors.
25. Great disappointment.
26. Financial frustration.
27. False friends.
28. Hardship.
29. Drifting.
30. Hard luck.
31. Meaningless dreams.
32. Imprisonment.
33. Seeking endlessly.
34. Daydreaming.
35. Lack of result for effort expended.

36. Door mat: That is others just walk on the person any how.
37. Business failures.
38. Unsatisfied thirst for spiritual filling.
39. Moving from one lover to another.
40. Prone to besetting sin.
41. Inability to stay in one church.
42. Guilt.
43. Calamity.

This why it is easy for anybody who is controlled by the scapegoat powers to walk into the snare of the fowler. The person will always be exploring and trying new things, new styles, new concepts, new religion but will not be settled. The person will be experimenting with life itself.

We need to cry out with everything within us to reject the scapegoat spirit. This is important to avoid being affected by other people's iniquities.

In our local setting here, a lot of people who claim to be enjoying life are just enjoying death because the enemy has already finished their account and is waiting to feed on them like the Christmas goat.

THE WAY OUT OF THE SITUATION

1. Depart from all known sins. Do not be a habitual sinner.

THE PROPHET | Saul versus David 9

ISAMUEL 18: 17... SAUL SAID TO DAVID,... MY DAUGHTER MERAB, I WILL GIVE THEE TO WIFE: ONLY BE VALLIANT FOR ME, AND FIGHT THE LORD'S BATTLES. FOR SAUL SAID,... LET... THE HAND OF THE PHILISTINES BE UPON HIM.

ISAMUEL 18: 18. AND DAVID SAID UNTO SAUL, WHO AM I?...OR MY FATHER'S FAMILY IN ISREAL... BE SON-IN-LAW TO THE KING?

HHHMMM... DAVID, MUST FALL THIS TIME. MERAB, MY... DAUGHTER. YESSSS!... I BET, THIS WILL SURELY WORK!

... DAVID-DAVID! FIGHT THIS BATTLE FOR ISREAL, AND I'LL GIVE YOU MERAB, MY DAUGHTER.

...KKKKING,... THAT'S IMPOSSIBLE! ME DDAVID... KINGS INLAW?!

2. Pray enquiry prayer. Find out from the Lord if you are receiving blame for something that another person has done. Find out whether you are a scapegoat.

3. Pray to know the secret of your own life. This is a very important prayer. If you do not know who you are, the enemy will tell you, who he wants you to be.

4. Make a spiritual atonement for any iniquity that has been passed to you. Repent before the Lord, hide under the cross of Jesus and apply the blood to make an atonement for any iniquity that was transferred into your life by any instrument of darkness.

5. Deliver yourself from the scapegoat powers. The Lord will shake many people to the root because if the root is holy then the branch will be holy. But if the root is dirty and diseased, it will show on the tree.

However, if you have not yet surrendered your life to Jesus, then you cannot invite God to deal with the spiritual scapegoat power in your life. If you want to give your life to Christ, please say the following prayer: "Father, in the name of Jesus, I come before you now. I acknowledge that I am a sinner. Forgive my sins and cleanse me with your blood. I renounce the devil and all his works. Come into my life Lord Jesus and take control of my life, in Jesus' name. Amen."

PRAYER POINTS

1. My Father, send your axe of fire to the foundation of my life and destroy every witchcraft plantation, in the name of Jesus.

2. Every dark cloud blocking the sunlight of my glory, die, in the name of Jesus.

3. Thou power of spiritual slumber, die, in the name of Jesus.

4. Every mirror of darkness that is beholding my face, break, in the name of Jesus.

5. Every scapegoat power of my father's house, die, in the name of Jesus.

6. Every word empowered by the devil against me, fall down and die, in the name of Jesus.

7. Every negative power that follows me to my arena of breakthrough, your time is up, die, in the name of Jesus.

8. Evil hands, hear the word of the Lord, my life is not your candidate. Therefore, die, in the name of Jesus.

9. Magnet of prosperity, come upon my hands now, in the name of Jesus.

10. Every habitation of wickedness gathered against my breakthrough, scatter, in the name of Jesus.

11. Thou power of evil conversion, die, in the name of Jesus.

12. Every power rejoicing against me, your time is up, die, in the name of Jesus.

BECOMING A SPIRITUAL SCAPEGOAT

is a message delivered at the Mountain of Fire and Miracles Ministries by the General Overseer, Dr. D.K. Olukoya.

A CALL TO SERVE

Are you a member of MFM with a burden to help the needy, are you interested in alleviating the plight of the poor or in the spread of the gospel through the sponsorship of the publication of tracts? Your resources, time and talent can be extended to several groups that are in charge of these areas. These groups include:

o   We care Ministry,
o   Mission Outreach
o   Tracts and Publications
o   Ministry to Drug addicts
o   Campus fellowship
o   Ministry to Schools
o   Ministry to Glorious Children, etc.

Thus says the Lord, "Verily I say unto you, in as much as ye have done it unto one of the least of these my brethren, ye have done it unto me" Matthew 25 : 40.

WONDERFUL JESUS!

GOD ANSWERS PRAYERS

Last year, I prayed to God for certain things and He granted me most of them. Also, late last year, the good Lord gave me a very good job with lots of benefits attached. Also, my sister met her would be husband and their wedding is slated for this year. God is indeed a prayer answering God. To Him be the glory forever. Amen

Bro. Christopher
MFM Abaranje

GOD PROMOTES ME

I was an ordinary worker in an oil company. Miraculously, God promoted me to the position of a Station Manager. Praise the Lord!

Bro. Okon
MFM Igbo-Elerin

DELIVERANCE FROM UNTIMELY DEATH

I am very grateful to God for deliverance from untimely death. In my dream, my mother-law took me to the grave of my dead children and commanded me to enter their graves. I refused and suddenly a strong wind appeared and took me away from the place. The next day, I fell sick and was rushed to the hospital. But God took absolute control and healed me. Secondly, armed robbers invaded our compound, though my door was wide open during their operation, they did not enter my apartment. Praise the Lord!

Sis. Victoria
MFM Ijaiye Ojokoro

ANOINTING BREAKS THE YOKE

My wife had prolonged labour and the doctor recommended ceaserian operation. But I called on my pastor and together, we prayed for God's intervention. After the prayers, I applied anointing oil on her. Suddenly God performed a spiritual operation and she had a safe and normal delivery. Praise the Lord!

Bro. Adeyemi
MFM Alagbole

MARITAL BREAKTHROUGH

I thank the Lord for giving me marriage breakthrough after a long wait for His will. God has also attached so many blessings to the marriage. All the people involved in our wedding have been blessed one way or another. Praise the Lord!

Sis. Adeolu
MFM Ajilo

ANOINTING SECURES MY LIFE

Armed robbers invaded our compound and as they were operating in other apartments, I quickly anointed my doorpost. Then I decreed that they will not go away with any of my property. They actually entered my house but didn't touch a pin or attacked me. They came in and left on their own accord. Praise the Lord!

Sis. Blessing
MFM Owo

GOD GUIDES AND PROTECTS

I thank God Almighty for saving me and my home. I plugged my electric kettle and went to Ketu. Four hours later, I remembered that I left the electric kettle on. So, I rushed back home. I thank God that at the time I got home, the water was still boiling. Secondly, I thank God for deliverance from the spirit of death and hell after undergoing a deliverance programme. Praise the Lord!

Sis. Bebe
MFM Ojodu

GOD OF MIRACLES VISITS ME

Firstly, I thank God for His protection over me and my family. Secondly, God did not allow evil to happen in my compound. The four children playing in my compound were asked to leave the portion of the compound where they were. Not quite long they left, a parked vehicle without anybody in it, moved towards the direction where they were, hit the gutters and destroyed some things. Thank God no life was lost. Praise God.

Sis. Rachael
MFM Aboru

INSTANT HEALING

During last November Power Must Change Hands Programme, I was instantly and perfectly healed of mild paralysis which rendered my left arm useless after my case was mentioned by the man of God. Praise the Lord!

Sis. Nnena
MFM Ewutuntun

DELIVERANCE FROM EVIL GRIP

For a long time I used to see my late father sleeping beside me in the dream. I was always afraid to sleep at night. I came for deliverance and on the third day of the programme, after the vigil, as I was lying on my bed, God opened my eyes to see a strange shadow rose beside me and went out of the door. Immediately this shadow departed, my bad sight and ear problem disappeared instantly. I can now see and hear well. Praise the Lord!

Sis. Patience
MFM Ojo

HELP AT LAST!

Are you passing through stress, trials and tribulations. Are you thinking of giving up or taking your life because you are tired of everything that is happening around you? I want you to know that you have a stronger warrior behind you, and that is the Lord Jesus Christ.
Through the messages in this magazine by Dr. D.K Olukoya, you will come out a champion no matter the challenges facing you.
You will move from adversity to testimonies!
Hurry now for your copies.
Price N100 only

is a weekly Spiritual Bulletin of the Mountain of Fire and Miracles Ministries, published by Tracts and Publications Group. All Enquiries should be addressed to The Editor, Mountain of Fire Magazine, 13, Olasimbo Street, off Olumo Road, Onike, P.O. Box 2990, Sabo Yaba, Lagos, Nigeria. Telephone 01- 867439, 864631, 868766, 08023180236.E-mail: mfmtractsandpublications@yahoo.com Copyright reserved.

FIRE IN THE WORD

Ye Shall Know the Truth, and the Truth Shall Make You Free (John 8:32)

ISSN 1595 - 7314   Vol. 12   No. 50   Sun. 26th Oct. - Sat. 1st Nov., 2008

When Your MARRIAGE IS SICK

My year of unprecedented greatness and unmatchable increase
Deuteronomy 28:13, Psalm 71:21, Ephesians 3:20, Psalm 92:10

This week, in our message titled, "When your marriage is sick," we would be looking at reasons why marriages become sick, signs of a sick marriage and the ways of dealing sucessfully with a sick marriage.

Genesis 2:18 says, *"And the Lord God said, It is not good that the man should be alone; I will make him a help meet for him."*

Verses 21-25: *"And the Lord God caused a deep sleep to fall upon Adam, and he slept; and he took one of his ribs, and closed up the flesh instead thereof; And the rib, which the Lord God had taken from the man, made he a woman, and brought her unto the man. And Adam said, This is now bone of my bones, and flesh of my flesh. She shall be called Woman, because she was taken out of man. Therefore shall a man leave his father and his mother, and shall cleave unto his wife; and they shall be one flesh. And they were both naked; the man and his wife, and were not ashamed."*

The marriage institution was created by God. It is a very senior serious divine institution. It is even senior to the church. It is something from the heart of God and because of that, God was the first officiating minister of a wedding. Therefore, marriage is the first human institution ordained by God.

There are five cardinal factors to be followed for this institution to be successful. Failure to follow them will result in sickness.

Nowadays, many marriages are sick. Many marriages are marriages of convenience. There are Christian homes where the couples fight day and night. Marriage counsellors are amazed by the way many husbands and wives fight themselves. Many children have come to me saying that if this is how husbands beat their wives and wives beat their husbands, they will not marry. The situation is actually becoming worse than before. Unfortunately, half of the children born today are born to unwedded mothers. So, the evil circle continues again.

If believers sit down and do nothing, the enemy will only do more havoc. All through the ages, the family has been the most assaulted institution by satan, even witches and

THE HEADSHIP OF THE HOME BELONGS TO THE HUSBAND

DELIVERANCE CASE (The Story of My Life - Part 36)

wizards hate marriage with perfect hatred.

FIVE CARDINAL RULES TO BE FOLLOWED FOR A SUCCESSFUL MARRIAGE

If any of these rules are contravened, the marriage will become sick.

1. Genesis 2:24: *"Therefore shall a man leave his father and his mother..."* The first rule is for the man to leave his father and mother. If this first key is not followed, a marriage will be sick.

God demands that after a wedding ceremony, when the marriage contract is in force, the man should be separated from his parents and should go and live with his wife. I know many men and women who are tied to the strings of the mothers or fathers' aprons. The marriage of anybody like that will be sick. The Bible does not give you permission to remain in your family house after marriage. If you remain there, that marriage will be sick. No matter how friendly the people are in that house, the marriage will be sick because it is in contrast with the word of God. It is better for a man and his wife to go for one room somewhere else than to stay in a mansion family house. The only way a married couple can remain in a family house and the marriage will not be sick is when the man is the only child of his parents, who are dead and the house was willed to him.

2. *"...and shall cleave unto his wife: and they shall be one flesh."*

The second rule is that there must be a cleaving. That is, the couple must stay together under one roof. In some marriages, the husband would travel abroad for five, ten etc years, leaving the wife behind. Such an arrangement makes a marriage sick. People in such situations need to pray. It is either the woman joins him or he comes back to the woman. Any type of job that takes a husband away for years without seeing his wife should not be encouraged.

3. Genesis 2:24 *"Therefore shall a man leave his father and his mother, and shall cleave unto his wife..."*

It did not say "his wives." The original blueprint from God for marriage is monogamy – one man one wife. If a man would need more than one wife, God would have taken two or more ribs out of his side and created more women for him. Polygamy is not permitted.

4. Genesis 2:25: *"And they were both naked, the man and his wife, and were not ashamed."*

There must be unity and intimacy. This scripture makes it clear that a couple has no privacy between each other. There should be

MARRIED COUPLES WHO DO NOT PRAY TOGETHER ARE INVITING SERIOUS TROUBLE

nothing to hide and nothing to be ashamed of. The only thing they cannot share is clothing.

5. Ephesians 5:23: *"For the husband is the head of the wife, even as Christ is the head of the church: and he is the Saviour of the body."*

The headship of the home belongs to the husband. The husband is the head just as Christ is the head of the church. That is how God ordained it. The wife is a help meet for the man. The wife is not just one female person somewhere. She is not a house girl or a harlot, or a concubine or a slave but help meet for him and should not be treated like a slave.

There was the case of a certain brother. Two months before his wedding, he stopped washing his clothes. When he was asked why, he said it was because his wife was coming. To him a wife means a slave.

SIGNS OF A SICK MARRIAGE

- If a marriage is sick, there will be lack of togetherness.
- There will be accusation and counter-accusation.

- There will be faultfinding and blame-shifting.
- When day-to-day quarrel in a family has to be reported to a third party, the marriage is sick already. It is a tragic day for a marriage, when the in-laws come to settle quarrels between the husband and wife.
- When a couple cannot settle a quarrel by themselves, it means that sickness has set in.

themselves, it means that sickness has set in.
- When a couple no longer talk to each other, the marriage is sick.
- When a couple maintains separate rooms, avoiding each other, the marriage is sick.
- Sexual pervasion is another sign of a sick marriage. When a couple engage in oral

| THE PROPHET | Saul versus David 10 |

sex, anal sex etc the marriage will be sick.

WAY OUT

1. The couple should surrender their lives to Jesus.
2. Make God their senior partner in the family.
3. Intensify the fire on their family altar. Married couples who do not pray together are inviting serious trouble. There must be daily family altar, where they share the word of God, sing praises and pray. The family that prays together stays together. The family that does not pray now will eventually pray under harsh conditions. There must be family altar in the home.
4. Do not allow a family dispute to go beyond a day. Settle it before you go to bed. If you go to bed with dispute, the devil will be your bedfellow.
5. Accept your fault when you are wrong and apologize. Many problems in the world can be solved with "I am sorry."

Any man or woman who is looking for someone without any fault or blemish for marriage can only find such a person in a mortuary or cemetery. Sometimes, God brings two opposite people together in marriage so that there will be a balance in the equilibrium. The man may be stingy while the wife would be generous etc. Tolerance is very important for a successful marriage. Be determined that your marriage will succeed according to the will of God and it shall be so.

PRAYER POINTS

1. Every evil marital pattern working against my life, scatter, in the name of Jesus.
2. Thou power of God that divided the Red sea, visit my family, in the name of Jesus.
3. Arrow of deliverance, enter into my marriage now, in the name of Jesus.
4. Every poison of marital failure in my life, come out now, in Jesus' name.

WHEN YOUR MARRIAGE IS SICK
is a message delivered at the Mountain of Fire and Miracles Ministries by the General Overseer, Dr. D.K. Olukoya.

A CALL TO SERVE

Are you a member of MFM with a burden to help the needy, are you interested in alleviating the plight of the poor or in the spread of the gospel through the sponsorship of the publication of tracts? Your resources, time and talent can be extended to several groups that are in charge of these areas. These groups include:

o   We care Ministry,
o   Mission Outreach
o   Tracts and Publications
o   Ministry to Drug addicts
o   Campus fellowship
o   Ministry to Schools
o   Ministry to Glorious Children, etc.

Thus says the Lord, "Verily I say unto you, in as much as ye have done it unto one of the least of these my brethren, ye have done it unto me" Matthew 25 : 40.

WONDERFUL JESUS!

SPIRIT OF BACKWARDNESS DISGRACED

In my dream, I was always seeing myself in a vehicle on the reverse without a visible driver. At a service, a word of knowledge concerning my case came from the man of God and a prayer point was raised, I prayed it aggressively and felt the touch of God. The following morning, somebody called me on phone and informed me that I had just won a huge contract. Praise the Lord!

Bro. Augustus
MFM Ojo

THE PRAYER ANSWERING GOD

I thank God for seeing me through my deliverance programme. Secondly during the Power Must Change Hands programme, the G.O told us to write what we needed. I wrote what I needed according to the order of their importance. To my surprise the Lord has answered my entire request. In addition, the Lord gave me a job and a shop. Praise the Lord!

Bro. Patrick
MFM Olowora

DIVINE FRUIT OF THE WOMB
AFTER 12 YEARS

For over 12 years, I was married but had no child. It was a turbulent time. The devil tormented me in many ways but the Lord saw me through. After listening to my case, the G.O placed me on corridor prayers, After sometime, the Lord answered me and I now have a baby boy after 12 years. Praise the Lord!

Sis. Remi
MFM Headquarters

LONG-TERM DISEASE DISAPPEARS

I had a neck problem for a long time. I went through a lot of deliverance programmes concerning the problem but all to no avail. However, when I informed the pastor about the problem, he referred me to the headquarters for deliverance. To the glory of God, after the deliverance programme at the headquarters, the problem disappeared completely. Praise the Lord!

Sis. Lawal
MFM Ijegun

DELIVERANCE FROM UNTIMELY DEATH

Sometime ago, I boarded a commercial bus which caught fire in motion. God took control and all the commuters disembarked without any injury. Praise the Lord!

Sis. Elizabeth
MFM Olowora

DELIVERANCE FROM EVIL LOAD

Before I joined this ministry, as I was just passing by the church one day, I overheard a prayer point which touched me. Later, I came back for counseling after which I went through a deliverance programme and before I knew it, the loads of problem in my life were lifted away. Praise the Lord!

Sis. Ugochi
MFM Alaba

GOD IS FAITHFUL

Last year, things were rough for my family. However, I saw the problems as forerunners of my blessings. My husband and I travelled and came back safely. Also, my mother was sick, we prayed for her and she became well. In all these, I give glory to God. Praise the Lord!

Sis. Victoria
MFM Idimu

MARITAL BREAKTHROUGH AND HEALING

I thank God for giving my younger sister a husband after a long time of praying and waiting on the Lord. The Lord proved Himself mightily and the wedding ceremony was successful. I also thank God for healing my brother's baby who had a fracture in the ankle from birth. They were going to hospitals for treatment but God healed her. Praise the Lord!

Bro. Stephen
MFM Ijede

GOD HEALS ME

I was always eating in the dream and physically I became very sick. The situation was becoming terrible when I was brought to MFM. I was told to go for deliverance and I did. To the glory of God, since I completed the programme, my constant eating in the dream has stopped and I am now strong and healthy. Praise the Lord!

Sis. Osagie
MFM Ekenwan Road Benin City

HELP AT LAST!

Are you passing through stress, trials and tribulations. Are you thinking of giving up or taking your life because you are tired of everything that is happening around you? I want you to know that you have a stronger warrior behind you, and that is the Lord Jesus Christ.

Through the messages in this magazine by Dr. D.K Olukoya, you will come out a champion no matter the challenges facing you.

You will move from adversity to testimonies!

Hurry now for your copies.

Price N100 only

is a weekly Spiritual Bulletin of the Mountain of Fire and Miracles Ministries, published by Tracts and Publications Group. All Enquiries should be addressed to The Editor, Mountain of Fire Magazine, 13, Olasimbo Street, off Olumo Road, Onike, P.O. Box 2990, Sabo Yaba, Lagos, Nigeria. Telephone 01- 867439, 864631, 868766, 08023180236.E-mail: mfmtractsandpublications@yahoo.com Copyright reserved.

FIRE IN THE WORD

Ye Shall Know the Truth, and the Truth Shall Make You Free (John 8:32)

ISSN 1595 - 7314 Vol. 12 No. 51 Sun. 2nd - Sat. 8th Nov., 2008

As it was in the
DAYS OF NOAH

My year of unprecedented greatness and unmatchable increase
Deuteronomy 28:13, Psalm 71:21, Ephesians 3:20, Psalm 92:10

This week, we are looking at a message entitled, "As it was in the days of Noah."

Matthew says, 24:37-39 says, *"But as the days of Noah were, so shall the coming of the Son of man be. For as in the days that were before the flood they were eating and drinking, marrying and giving in marriage, until the day that Noah entered into the Ark, And knew not until the flood came and took them all away: so shall also the coming of the Son of man be."*

Beloved, these are sober scriptures telling us that we do not have much time. It is making us to understand that this is not the time to play church but to become true children of God. The days of Noah that Jesus prophesied are already with us.

Luke 17:22-30: *"And he said unto the disciples, The days will come, when ye shall desire to see one of the days of the Son of man, and ye shall not see it. And they shall say to you, See here; or, see there; go not after them, nor follow them. For as the lightning, that lighteneth out of the one part under heaven, shineth unto the other part under heaven; so shall also the Son of man be in his day. But first must he suffer many things, and be rejected of this generation. And as it was in the days of Noah, so shall it be also in the days of the Son of man. They did eat, they drank, they married wives, they were given in marriage, until the day that Noah entered into the ark, and the flood came, and destroyed them all. Likewise also as it was in the days of Lot; they did eat, they drank, they bought, they sold, they planted, they builded, But the same day that Lot went out of Sodom it rained fire and brimstone from heaven, and destroyed them all. Even thus shall it be in the day when the Son of man is revealed."*

The days of Noah were days that came before something happened. Those days came until the ark was ready to float and Noah entered into it and closed the door. Immediately Noah entered into the ark and closed the door, God poured out His undiluted fury upon man. The departure of Lot from Sodom and Gomorrah was all the siren that God needed to pour His fury upon those cities. Many people are in the world now not knowing that God is just looking for one little thing which they will not know when it will come to pass for an uproar to take place. Then the words of the scriptures will come alive to those who did not believe and many will understand the meaning of rapture. Many will know that the rapture can meet them where it should not meet them; many will realise that they have wasted their lives. Many will realise that all the time they have spent in church was a bloody waste of time because when the day of reckoning came, they were nowhere to be found, the trumpet met them in the wrong place.

It is true that the Romans introduced many of the structures we see in the military today. In those days, the Roman soldiers were taught to listen to three kinds of trumpets.

UNFORTUNATELY SIN HAS GOT MAN INTO SO MUCH TROUBLE THAT NO TECHNOLOGY CAN GET HIM OUT

The sound of trumpet number one signalled the dismantling of their camp very quickly. When trumpet number two sounded, they went into their army formation. But with the sound of the third trumpet, the Roman army was on the move. Whatever enemy they wanted to fight, when they hear the first, second and third sound of the trumpet, they knew that there was trouble. They could recognise the sound. Unfortunately, the trumpet of the Lord will soon sound and many churchgoers will not hear it. The Bible says in a moment, in a twinkling of an eye, everything will be over. That split second that it takes to blink is all that is necessary.

Theologians have extricated the days of Noah to be about 2000 years. In the book of Genesis 5, the first 10 names summarise the story and history of man. Genesis 5:1-29: "*This is the book of the generations of Adam. In the day that God created man, in the likeness of God made he him; Male and female created he them; and blessed them, and called their name Adam, in the day when they were created. And Adam lived an hundred and thirty years, and begat a son in his own likeness, after his image; and called his name Seth: And the days of Adam after he had begotten Seth were eight hundred years: and he begat sons and daughters: And all the days that Adam lived were nine hundred and thirty years: and he died. And Seth lived an hundred and five years, and begat Enos: And Seth lived after he begat Enos eight hundred and seven years, and begat sons and daughters: And all the days of Seth were nine hundred and twelve years: and he*

DELIVERANCE CASE (The Story Of My Life - Part 37)

died. And Enos lived ninety years, and begat Cainan: And Enos lived after he begat Cainan eight hundred and fifteen years, and begat sons and daughters: And all the days of Enos were nine hundred and five years: and he died. And Cainan lived seventy years, and begat Mahalaleel: And Cainan lived after he begat Mahalaleel eight hundred and forty years, and begat sons and daughters: And all the days of Cainan were nine hundred and ten years: and he died. And Mahalaleel lived sixty and five years, and begat Jared: And Mahalaleel lived after he begat Jared eight hundred and thirty years, and begat sons and daughters: And all the days of Mahalaleel were eight hundred ninety and five years: and he died. And Jared lived an hundred sixty and two years, and he begat Enoch: And Jared lived after he begat Enoch eight hundred years, and begat sons and daughters: And all the days of Jared were nine hundred sixty and two years: and he died. And Enoch lived sixty and five years, and begat Methuselah: And Enoch walked with God after he begat Methuselah three hundred years, and begat sons and daughters: And all the days of Enoch were three hundred sixty and five years: And Enoch walked with God: and he was not; for God took him.

And Methuselah lived an hundred eighty and seven years, and begat Lamech: And Methuselah lived after he begat Lamech seven hundred eighty and two years, and begat sons and daughters: And all the days of Methuselah were nine hundred sixty and nine years: and he died. And Lamech lived an hundred eighty and two years, and begat a son: And he called his name Noah, saying, This same shall comfort us concerning our work and toil of our hands, because of the ground which the LORD hath cursed." So, we have Adam, Seth, Enos, Cainan, Mahalaleel, Jared, Enoch, Methuselah, Lamech and Noah.

The meaning of these names are:
*   Adam – man
*   Seth – appointed
*   Enos – Subject to death
*   Cainan – Sorrowful and lamenting
*   Mahalaleel – From the praise of God
*   Jared – One comes down
*   Enoch – Learning obedience
*   Methuselah – He shall be sent out (Javelin)
*   Lamech – To the poor, brought very low
*   Noah – Rest

We have man appointed, subject to death, sorrowful and lamenting, from the praise of God, one comes down, learning obedience, he shall be sent, to the poor brought very low, then rest. All that summaries God's programme and story of man.

There was a man who was appointed from the praise of God, who died to bring rest to the poor and through Him rest was going to be sent to humanity. From the beginning of the time of Adam to the time of Noah, we have one generation.

Let us look at what began to happen in Noah's days because the Bible says as it was in the days of Noah so shall it be in the day of the Son of man. I thank God for the life of any member of the church. But if a church does not succeed in getting its members to heaven, it has failed in its duty. If the prayers and the message do not make its members better candidates of heaven, it is a failure. The progress of a church is not measured by how large it is but by the number of changed lives. There is no point going to church and your life does not undergo a revival. There is no point going to church when the enemy rejoices anytime you are in your room because he knows that you cannot touch him. I want you to understand that the last days have come upon us, and anything can happen at anytime. What we have nowadays is everything that was happening in the days of Noah multiplied by ten.

SIGNS OF NOAH'S DAYS

Genesis 4:17 says, *"And Cain knew his wife; and she conceived, and bare Enoch; and he builded a city..."* So, the first sign of Noah's days was city-building. Cities are being built every time. A look around our country now and all over the world shows that buildings are rising up overnight. The craze of building one that will be greater than the other is swallowing men and women, and people are either building this or building that. It is the sign of Noah's days and the sign of our days too.

Verse 19: *"And Lamech took unto him two wives; the name of the one was Adah, and the name of the other Zillah."* Polygamy existed in the days of Noah, Lamech had the singular honour of shattering the foundation of marriage. The first Adam of the Bible did not have multiple wives but here Lamech shattered that foundation. There are many men who are taking pride in marrying extra wives. So, there is the epidemic of multiple wives all over the place. Nowadays, we find a man who would put both mother and daughter in the family way – as it was in the days of

Noah, so shall it be in the days of the Son of man.

Verses 20-21: *"And Adah bare Jabel; he was the father of such as dwell in tents, and of such as have cattle. And his brother's name was Jubal; he was the father of all such as handle the harp and organ."* There was then an epidemic of music entertainment. All kinds of music have filled the earth now as it was in the days of Noah. It is a pity that the best selling types of music are the ones that corrupt the mind. The enemy has captured the music industry and is using it to confuse men.

Verse 22: *"And Zillah, she also bare Tubal-cain an instructor of every artificer in brass and iron; and the sister of Tubal-cain was Naamah."* In the days of Noah, there were traces of technology, technology is rising now in our days. For example, we have gone from typewriters to computers. Many things can be used practically with the remote control. Through science and technology, man has achieved quite a lot. Unfortunately sin has got man into so much trouble that no technology can get him out. The book of Daniel says that knowledge shall increase and people shall run to and fro; that is happening now and a lot of strange discoveries are being made. As it was in the days of Noah, so it is now. Technology will continue to increase. This is telling

COWARDS
GO TO HELL,
WISE MEN SEEK
JESUS

us is that we do not have much time any longer.

Genesis 6:5 says, *"And God saw that the wickedness of man was great in the earth, and that every imagination of the thoughts of his heart was only evil continually."* The earth also was corrupt and filled with violence. Violence and wickedness have become epidemic now. People are killing fellow human beings and trading in human body parts because of money. The other time I shook my head in disbelief when somebody told me that he killed and buried his own mother in his sitting room. Ritual kidnapping and killing are signs that there is no time. God will not accept excuses. Many people are reading about hired assassins in the newspapers but they have internal hired assassins. All these things were happening in the days of Noah. Unfortunately, it is not everyone that comes to church wants to make heaven, and also, it is not every pastor that wants to make heaven, and many are just not interested in eternity, which is a very sad development. All that many people are after is how to prosper and do anything to get money – it is a sign of the days of Noah. If you go to church and do not have the baptism of the Holy Spirit and you are not bothered, you are looking for trouble by being nonchalant. I want you to understand that violence and wickedness characterised Noah's days as it is now.

Corruption was also prevalent then as it is now. Genesis 6:11 says, *"The earth also was corrupt before God."* There is a lot of official corruption now and also corruption in the high places. Anything is allowed as long as there is money. That is part of the reason we must be praying for our nation. As far as the nation is corrupt, there will be problem because it is righteousness that exalts a nation.

Sometime ago, the only car of a certain brother was snatched by armed robbers so the brother had to be taking a commuter bus to work. One day, he decided to take a taxi. While in the cab, he could recognise that the car was his though painted in yellow. As they were going, he stopped the taxi in front of a police station and alerted the police men on duty, who promptly arrested the driver. The driver called the owner, who was a very fat wealthy man. On arrival, the owner asked for the DPO. The brother almost fainted when the fat man came out from the DPO's office with the car key in his hand

and abused him as he drove the car away. God will not sit down and allow that kind of system to continue for ever.

In the universities now, you find that girls who are ready to submit their bodies get more marks than those who work hard. Also, nowadays, the spirit of Jezebel has entered into so many women while the spirit of Absalom has entered into so many men. We have old men messing up with ladies their daughters' age, and young girls who agree that members of the wasted generation should be sleeping with them. So, we see the world going in a terrible circle. There is nothing new under the sun, as it was in the days of Noah so it is now.

God asked Noah to build the ark in the shape of a coffin. The people did know what was happening, they

called Noah names and had a lot of technical reasons not to believe his message. During the days of Noah, rain was not necessary; they had a good climate, only dewdrops fell, which aided agriculture. Men were big and strong and lived longer, which is really a principle of nature. The rat lived longer than the ant; the cat lived longer than the rat; man lived longer than dogs etc. So for somebody to be talking about rain then looked mad and unusual. Many years ago, a man was driven from his church because he prophesied that in two years time, men would be walking on the moon. They looked at him disdainfully and chased him out of the church because what he was saying was strange until men began to walk there. What Noah was saying sounded strange until something began to happen. Fire and brimstone had never fallen before until it fell on Sodom and Gomorrah. So, beloved, as it was in the days of Noah, when the people were not prepared: they were busy drinking, smoking, going to church and playing church, going to the house of God without any impact on their lives, going to the house of God to play church politics – just as it was in those days; all of a sudden the trumpet will sound, some will hear and unfortunately, some will not hear. Many will rush to church crying that they were not told, but it would have been over. They would ask for people they thought were mad and foolish and would be told that they are gone because the Bible says two shall be together that day, one shall be taken and the other left. A man and woman will be on

THE PROPHET | Saul versus David 11

the bed, one will be taken, the other would be left behind. There will be chaos, and people will then begin to struggle. Cowards go to hell, wise men seek Jesus.

The Bible says the imaginations of the hearts of men were evil continually in the days of Noah. There was a lot of falsehood. Likewise now, we have a lot of fighting, diseases, satanic doctrines, satanic revival etc. As it was in those days, so shall it be. Many are falling day and night that is why in MFM, we point people's attention to Jesus, the Author and Finisher of our faith. We do not tie people to the apron strings of any pastor. The MFM is a do-it yourself ministry. The post of a pastor is a privilege. The pastoral calling does not make anybody Jesus. Whatever the title does not make anybody Jesus. Focus your attention on Jesus and once that is done, there will be no problem. Follow Him and you will not miss your way. But immediately you take your eyes off Him, there will be trouble.

1 Corinthians 3:1: *"And I, brethren could not speak unto you as unto spiritual, but as unto carnal, even as unto babes in Christ."* Here, Apostle Paul spoke about three levels of Christianity:
- Baby Christians.
- Carnal Christians.
- Spiritual Christians.

You are either a carnal Christian, a baby Christian, or a spiritually matured Christian. To be childlike and baby-like at the proper age can be wonderful, but what a shame and disappointment when at 30, 40, 50 somebody is still a baby. If after two years of getting born again somebody is still sitting you down to say, "Don't fight, don't quarrel, don't keep malice, don't harbour bitterness and unforgiving spirit," you are not growing because these are the marks of a baby Christian. God does not deal much with babies. Babies end up causing more confusion than good in the body of Christ. A carnal Christian has been saved but is still being ruled by his flesh and motivated by the old nature. Comparing yourself with others, concern about what others are thinking about you, the desire to be recognised, feeling important, desire for church post and elevation are signs of carnality. When you are carnal, you will not live like a child of God. You will be living as a servant to the control of Mr. Flesh. Many people are quick to forget that the flesh is not going to give up easily,

in fact, it is determined to defeat anyone.

This issue concerns everybody. The Bible says when you see abomination of desolation entering into the high places, then know that the time is near. The flesh will not give up easily because it has decided to stay on the throne of everybody's life. But when you are a spiritual person, you lose your desire for worldly pleasures, and will not allow anybody to destroy the call of God for your life with five minutes of enjoyment. When you are a spiritual person and Christ is at the centre of your life, you become somebody who could see God face to face. Beloved, no liar will enter into the kingdom of God. If you are a professional liar, you are planning for hell fire. It is the same for occasional, commercial, romantic and academic liars.

All the signs that would precede the second coming of Jesus have come to pass. It is time to cry to the Lord for mercy because anything can happen at any time. Death can come knocking any time. Talk to the Lord now.

PRAYER POINTS

1. My Father, have mercy on me, in the name of Jesus.
2. My Father, wherever I have missed my way, correct me by the blood of Jesus, in the name of Jesus.
3. Every yoke of death and hell in my life, be destroyed by the blood of Jesus now, in the name of Jesus.

AS IT WAS IN THE DAYS OF NOAH
is a message delivered at the Mountain of Fire and Miracles Ministries by the General Overseer, Dr. D.K. Olukoya.

A CALL TO SERVE

Are you a member of MFM with a burden to help the needy, are you interested in alleviating the plight of the poor or in the spread of the gospel through the sponsorship of the publication of tracts? Your resources, time and talent can be extended to several groups that are in charge of these areas. These groups include:

o   We care Ministry,
o   Mission Outreach
o   Tracts and Publications
o   Ministry to Drug addicts
o   Campus fellowship
o   Ministry to Schools
o   Ministry to Glorious Children, etc.

Thus says the Lord, "Verily I say unto you, in as much as ye have done it unto one of the least of these my brethren, ye have done it unto me" Matthew 25 : 40.

WONDERFUL JESUS!

DIVINE PROTECTION

I thank God for saving me from a motor accident when I travelled to buy goods at the market. The tyre of the car burst and the car somersaulted. Some passengers were injured but nothing happened to me. Praise the Lord!

Sis. Esther
MFM Orioke Ogudu

GOD GIVES ME A NEW LIFE

When I joined this ministry with my husband, we were advised to make necessary corrections concerning our marriage. And just after we did that, God blessed us with a parcel of land and consequently a house of our own. Secondly, God saw my daughter through in her academics. Lastly, God gave my husband the courage to burn all the occult materials in his possession. Praise the Lord!

Sis. Maria
MFM Abule-Egba

DIVINE PROVISION

The Lord provided admission for my younger brother into one of the higher institutions despite every household wickedness agenda to frustrate him. Praise the Lord!

Bro. Olufemi
MFM Iba New site

GOD SHOWERS HIS FAVOUR ON ME

After the death of my father, I lost my job. I went through deliverance and God gave me another job. I also got admission into a higher institution and my new employer is sponsoring me. Praise Jesus!

Bro. Chinonso
MFM Owerri

SUDDEN DEATH AVERTED

A car on top speed ran into my kiosk while I was inside it. To God be the glory, I climbed the car and came out unhurt. Praise the Lord!

Sis. Okuobo
MFM Dumez, Benin City

GOD GRANTS MY SON ADMISSION

Last year, my son wanted to write the GCE examination and asked for money to register in a special centre. I refused and told him to rely on Jesus and to pray with the "Seventy

Day's Prayer Book and he did." He wrote the exams and passed. When it was time to write JAMB exams, I also encouraged him in the same manner. He prayed and wrote the exams and to the glory of God, his name came out on the merit list of admission into the university. Praise the Lord!

Sis. Mary
MFM Adaloko

DIVINE INTERVENTION

God delivered me from the hands of my unfriendly friend who came to my house, when I was not at home. She collected my picture, wrote R.I.P on it and took it to an evil altar and placed it there. In one of our revival services, the pastor raised a prayer point concerning evil altars and the place where the picture was caught fire and they started looking for me with the picture. Praise the Lord!

Sis. Mary
MFM Uromi

MOVING OBJECT IN THE HEAD GONE

When I was in the Secondary School, I used to be one of the brilliant students. Suddenly something started moving in my head. As a result of this moving object, my studies got affected and I couldn't continue. I dropped out of school was being taken to different hospitals and white garment churches. The problem did not stop. Somebody introduced me to this church and ever since I started worshiping here with prayers, the moving object in my head has disappeared and now I have secured admission into a higher institution. Praise the Lord!

Bro. Chinedu
MFM Headquarters

FINANCIAL FAVOUR

I was in dire need of money to give to my son who was posted to the Northern part of the country for National Youth Service programme. I decided to stay at home and pray without going out to borrow. God in His infinite goodness sent somebody who came and gave me the sum of N10,000. Secondly, one of my sister's sons that has been living with me for more than ten years got married recently and God took control. Praise the Lord!

Sis. Oyekomi
MFM Dopemu

HELP AT LAST!

Are you passing through stress, trials and tribulations. Are you thinking of giving up or taking your life because you are tired of everything that is happening around you? I want you to know that you have a stronger warrior behind you, and that is the Lord Jesus Christ.

Through the messages in this magazine by Dr. D.K Olukoya, you will come out a champion no matter the challenges facing you.

You will move from adversity to testimonies!

Hurry now for your copies.

Price N100 only

FIRE IN THE WORD, is a weekly Spiritual Bulletin of the Mountain of Fire and Miracles Ministries, published by Tracts and Publications Group. All Enquiries should be addressed to The Editor, Mountain of Fire Magazine, 13, Olasimbo Street, off Olumo Road, Onike, P.O. Box 2990, Sabo Yaba, Lagos, Nigeria. Telephone 01- 867439, 864631, 868766, 08023180236.E-mail: mfmtractsandpublications@yahoo.com Copyright reserved.

FIRE IN THE WORD

Ye Shall Know the Truth, and the Truth Shall Make You Free (John 8:32)

ISSN 1595 - 7314 Vol. 12 No. 52 Sun. 9th - Sat. 15th Nov., 2008

SODOM

The Analysis of
ACCUSATION

My year of unprecedented greatness and unmatchable increase
Deuteronomy 28:13, Psalm 71:21, Ephesians 3:20, Psalm 92:10

This week, we are looking at the message entitled,"The analysis of accusation."

Genesis 18:20-21 says, *"And the Lord said, Because the cry of Sodom and Gomorrah is great, and because their sin is very grievous: I will go down now, and see whether they have done altogether according to the cry of it, which is come unto me; and if not, I will know."*

Another version of the above scripture says, "Then the Lord said to Abraham, There are terrible accusations against Sodom and Gomorrah and their sin is very great, I must go down to find out whether or not the accusations which I have heard are true." (Genesis 18:20-21 Simple Good News Bible).

WHAT DOES IT MEAN TO ACCUSE?

It means to charge a person formally with a wrongdoing. It means to charge somebody with an offence. It means to charge somebody with a fault or to blame somebody. It means to make a claim of wrongdoing or misbehaviour on the part of somebody.

The text above indicates that there were terrible reports of accusations against Sodom and Gomorrah. The question is, who was reporting Sodom and Gomorrah to God? Who was the one urging God to bring justice to Sodom and Gomorrah? Who was the one insisting that God must do something and God had to say, "Okay, I will go down and see with my eyes?" Who was it that reported them so much to God that God had to make Abraham to understand and to be able to serve as an advocate and intercessor between them. Unfortunately, Abraham did not fully understand what God wanted. Instead of pleading for the whole city, he decided to pick some few righteous people. When the ten men agenda collapsed, the whole city was gone. God was looking for Abraham to stand in the middle so that He will not destroy them. But

unfortunately, that agenda failed and there was disaster.

Ezekiel 22-30 says, *"And I sought for a man among them, that should make up the hedge, and stand in the gap before me for the land, that I should not destroy it; but I found none."*

A single man can prevent a whole land or a whole family from being destroyed. God does not derive pleasure from the destruction of a sinner. When He looks for somebody to stand in the gap and cannot find, what is written in Ezekiel 22:31 will follow. It says, *"Therefore have I poured out mine indignation upon them; I have consumed them with the fire of my wrath: their own way have I recompensed upon their heads, saith the Lord God."*

I feel sorry for you if you are supposed to be the prevailer and intercessor for your family line, place of work or location, but you have failed. What is written in Ezekiel 22:31 will happen because God cannot find a man. It means that there are many men but God recognises only one man. When He is looking for men and women to pick, He cannot find some people because He does not see the character of what heaven calls men and women in their lives.

It is clear that somebody was making accusations against Sodom and Gomorrah. But who was it? Who took the case of Sodom and Gomorrah to the supreme court of the Most High? Who complained so bitterly that God had to descend in the company of two angels on a fact-finding mission? The answer is in the scriptures.

WHO IS THE ACCUSER?

Revelation 12:9 -10 says, *"And the great dragon was cast out, that old*

FIGHTING WITH YOUR SPOUSE WOULD BRING STAINS ON YOUR SPIRITUAL GARMENTS

serpent, called the devil, and satan, which deceived the whole world; he was cast out into the earth, and his angels were cast out with him. And I heard a loud voice saying in heaven, Now is come salvation, and strength, and the kingdom of our God, and the power of his Christ: for the accuser of our brethren is cast down, which accused them before our God day and night."

The old serpent, the dragon is the one that accuses people. He is the accuser. He is the one who brings cases unto God. He is the one who quotes the scriptures to say what is written. He would say to God, "O God, You wrote this word and now this person is disobeying what you have written and is praying for breakthrough. You must not answer because it is written..."

The same Bible that believers use to claim God's promises is also the weapon of the accuser. Devil is a legal expert. Much of what is called satanic power is the legal expertise of the devil in the spiritual realm. Having been with God from the beginning, he understands the workings of heaven and the organization thereof. He knows the law and the ordinances and what you should not do if you want God to be your supporter. Immediately somebody does something which he is not supposed to do, and continues in that track, it means that he has been manipulated into trouble. The enemy knows that he is doing the wrong thing, therefore, his authority against the enemy will fail and the enemy will begin to torment his life.

THE MODUS OPERANDI OF THE ACCUSER

You must understand how the accuser operates. He is a wicked personality. He would push a person into iniquity, encourage the person in the iniquity, give the person all the facilities to commit the iniquity and provide a suitable and comfortable

DELIVERANCE CASE (THE STORY OF MY LIFE - PART 38)

I SAY GET LOST! I DON'T WANT YOU IN MY LIFE AGAIN. WHY NOT GO TO THE BLOODY GRAVES OF THOSE PEOPLE YOU CALLED MY FORE-FATHERS, WHOM YOU SAID INVITED YOU MANY CENTURIES AGO?!

YOU ARE GETTING ME WRONG. LISTEN, ALL HUMAN-BEINGS WHO DO NOT HAVE CHRIST, HAVE US! CAN'T YOU JUST WAIT FOR A MOMENT, SO THAT WE CAN TRASH THINGS OUT AMICABLY? HONESTLY, IT'S NOT THAT WE CAN NOT ALLOW YOU TO BE A CHRISTIAN; IF ONLY YOU WILL PROMISE NOT TO BE TOO DEEP WITH CHRIST AND ABANDON US.

Toks Olunatoli.

LUKE 11 vs 23 - 24

environment for the person to stay in the iniquity. He inspires the iniquity and at the same time goes to report the person to God. When God could not find a successful intercessor for Sodom and Gomorrah, what He did was to destroy them. Beloved, do you know what accusations are being levelled against you? Unfortunately, some of these accusations are correct because the devil cannot tell lies to God. If you are a fornicator or a backbiter, you are making the devil happy. If you still have a hot temper; you are making the devil happy. Every habitual sinner makes the devil happy.

Job 1:8-11 says, *"And the Lord said unto satan, Hast thou considered my servant Job, that there is none like him in the earth, a perfect and an upright man, one that feareth God, and escheweth evil? Then satan answered the Lord, and said, Doth Job fear God for nought? Hast not thou made an hedge about him, and about his house, and about all that he hath on every side? Thou hast blessed the work of his hands, and his substance is increased in the land. But put forth thine hand now, and touch all that he hath, and he will curse thee to thy face."*

Job 2:4-5 says, *"And satan answered the Lord, and said, Skin for skin, yea all that a man hath will he give for his life. But put forth thine hand now, and touch his bone and his flesh, and he will curse thee to thy face."*

In the above scriptures, we see the accuser at work against Job. God himself testified of Job that he was a perfect and upright man, a man that feared God and eschewed evil yet the accuser spoke very terribly against him. The devil told God that Job was serving Him because of what he could get out of Him. He told God to remove his wealth and he would curse Him to His face. When satan started, Job lost everything he had but did not deny God. Then satan came back again and told God to touch his body, he wanted to ruin Job. He was inciting God against him to destroy him the same way he was moving God to go and destroy Sodom and Gomorrah. But these were two different issues. Job had committed no offence. He was being accused innocently by the accuser but Sodom and Gomorrah had a case because they were terrible men. If satan could so terribly accuse Job, a man for whom God had great respect, how much more would he speak against Sodom and Gomorrah or against any person who gives him a reason to talk.

Satan is the accuser of the brethren, and is moving the judgement of God against personalities, places, cities and nations. He would keep patients away from a clinic and push girls to that clinic for abortion. And because the clinic is not getting enough

patients, they would be forced to procure abortions for them in order to make money. Then he would be the same person to accuse that clinic and the doctor before God. He would tell God that these ones are killing His prophets, priests and evangelists and God will move against them. That is why clinics and hospitals which are involved in massive abortion never do well. He pushes people into sin, supervises the sin and also reports to God. And the whole system begins to collapse.

JOSHUA VERSUS SATAN

Zechariah 3:1-2 says, *"And he showed me Joshua the high priest standing before the angel of the Lord, and satan standing at his right hand to resist him. And the Lord said unto satan, The Lord rebuke thee, O satan; even the Lord that hath chosen Jerusalem rebuke thee; is not this a brand plucked out of the fire?"* Joshua was in an honourable position. He was standing before the angel of the Lord but something else was happening on the side. Verse 3 gives an answer to why Joshua was suffering from the devil's resistance. It says, *"Now Joshua was clothed with filthy garments, and stood before the angel."*

Joshua was committing a secret sin which nobody could see but satan saw it and waited for him until the right moment when he would appear before the angel of God and said, "No! This one cannot minister here. Look at his garments, they are dirty." Joshua the high priest was performing his routine duty but as he was ministering, he found that he was not making progress; satan was accusing him.

If sometimes when you start to pray, you find it difficult to move or when you are fasting, you are fed at night in your dream or your mind wanders and you know that you are not getting anywhere, or you find it difficult to concentrate on your Bible study, know that you are being resisted by the devil. Although, Joshua was a high priest and got to the level of standing before the angel, satan had a multiple count charge against him. Perhaps there was somebody interceding for Joshua and here he was able to receive mercy. The trouble with mercy is that it is not always available. It depends on God who gives mercy. Satan accused Joshua of many things because of the garment of evil that he was wearing.

Beloved, there is the need for self-examination. Perhaps there are certain things you are doing which others cannot see or there is some money that you are getting now which you really should not be getting. For example, if you are the kind of a person who would spend the night in your friend's place and go to your place of work and claim that you slept in a hotel with fake receipt to cover it up and then pay the tithe and believe that God will forgive you, you are deceiving yourself. Immediately you do that, the dirtiness will appear on your spiritual garments. And the more of those sins you commit the more stains appear on your spiritual garments. Fighting with your spouse would bring stains on your spiritual garments. When you stain your garments thoroughly with abuses and curses, immediately you go to bed, you will have a third bed fellow, which is satan himself because you are already wearing a dirty garment.

Many young men are completely lost because the enemy has destroyed them using masturbation, lust and all kinds of terrible things in the heart. But sometimes they make a lot of noise to cover up what God is saying but the enemy sees that they are dirty and are just pretending.

If God did not come to Joshua's rescue, he would have been finished. God had to order that those filthy garments be removed. I pray that you too will utter the kind of cry that will make God to turn to your enemy and ask them to shut up. And then you will remove the filthy garment that is making the enemy to accuse you day and night. If your spiritual eyes are opened, you will see what you look like in the spiritual realm. You will understand the importance of prayer. This is why one of the greatest prayer points a man can pray is "My Father, show me myself. I want to know who I am, in the name of Jesus." And by the time you see yourself, you will be able to cry like Isaiah who said, "Woe is me: for I am undone because I am a man of unclean lips and I dwell in the midst of people with unclean lips..." (Isaiah 6:5). God showed him himself. I pray that God will show you your true picture. When that happens, you will know where you are going and what you are really doing. You will know whether your feet are on the path of life or death. You will know what God really thinks about you. I know a woman who cried bitterly to the Lord with a loud voice in one of our meetings and said, "O Lord, show me myself, I want to know who I am. I want to know why life is like this." And that night, she had a dream in which an angel of God came to her and showed her a piece of paper on which her score was written. It was 17% and the pass mark was 100%. She told the angel that she

WE CANNOT SIT DOWN AND DO NOTHING ABOUT THE ACCUSER THAT IS PRESSING SO MANY CHARGES AGAINST US

was supposed to have a higher mark since she has a Masters degree in Theology, and a chairlady in her church. She enumerated all her achievements but the angel told her that those things do not carry any mark and do not count before God. Then she said to the angel of God, "Is it because in our church we were told to stop wearing make-up and attachments and I am still wearing them? If I stop using them will it increase my mark? The angel told her that the chain in her heart was not broken, if not she would have stopped wearing those things a long time ago and told her to pray that the chain in her heart would be broken so that she would know what she was supposed to do. She did that and saw another vision where they were many men, women and children tied with ropes crying: "Sister, save us! save us! save us!" She stood before them and could not do anything. The angel told her that she was supposed to set those people free but she herself was not free. The angel told her that their blood was on her. Then she woke up. That sister is now a pastor. What she saw shook her to her root. I pray that the Lord will show you the revelations and visions that will make you to move. Then you will shun laziness and lukewarmness.

Jude1:9 says, *"Yet Michael the archangel, when contending with the devil he disputed about the body of Moses, durst not bring against him a railing accusation, but said, The Lord rebuke thee."*

Angel Michael had a dispute with satan over the corpse of Moses. The devil wanted the body but the body belonged to God. So, God's angel was there for it. It means that as a believer, even your corpse means something to God and He will not abandon it to the devil or to vultures. If God cares so much about the dead body of His servants, how much more the living body of His servants. Michael had to be sent to go and retrieve the body for burial. If angel Michael had to be dispatched to retrieve the body, only imagination can tell us how many angels were guiding Moses while he was still alive. Moses himself may not have realised it but immediately he died, satan the accuser came to contest for his body. What was the reason for the contest? When Moses was by the rock, he spoke harsh words and also smote the rock that he was supposed to speak to. As result of these, Moses could not enter the Promised Land and the enemy wanted to use that against him. Moses was drawn from the waters in Egypt and the name given to him was not from God, it was given by the daughter of Pharaoh. Moses was in the palace of the Egyptians where he learnt all their curious acts. The magicians that contested with Moses were his former colleagues in the palace. So, satan came to contest for the body of Moses because of all these terrible things in his background. But God intervened and saved his body.

Satan may give you every support to commit a sin but will be the first to abandon you, turn around and report to God. He will make you do the wrong thing, help you to do it and turn around and accuse you before God for doing it. This is why we have to know what we are doing. We ought to know that we are in the end time. The devil will push somebody into witchcraft, make the person to confess that she is a witch and engineer people around to stone her to death, and her blood will be on them.

THE CASE OF NINEVEH

The Bible says that the wickedness of Nineveh came up before God. That happened because the accuser reported Nineveh to God and was moving God to go and destroy it. God sent Jonah there to preach to them. The same accuser started to move Jonah not to go there because he just wanted them destroyed. But God forced Jonah to go there and that was their saving grace. Perhaps somebody was interceding for Nineveh at that time and when Jonah preached to them they hearkened to those words and quickly repented. The accuser had put their name on the danger list and was presenting his case against them but there was nobody in the court of God to defend Nineveh. However, Nineveh repented but as soon as Jonah left, they went back to their sin and today, Nineveh is a heap of submerged ruin. The agenda of the accuser for Nineveh eventually came to pass just like his agenda for Sodom and Gomorrah.

This teaches us very serious lessons. Satan does not give up. You may succeed to counter his accusation today and save yourself by fasting, prayers and repentance but your present salvation should not be the cause for slumber later for the enemy can come up against you again and the judgement that you had escaped will now fall on you. If you fall into slumber, the enemy will still raise the accusation again and then this time it will be more terrible. You need to cry to the Lord so that you will not have affliction coming up the second time in your life.

HOW THE ACCUSER CARRIES OUT HIS ACCUSATION

The accuser does his job in four principal ways:

1. He can accuse you before yourself. The accuser can use your dreams to achieve his purpose or voices which you alone hear. The accuser may bring back to you something you have done in the past for which the Lord has forgiven you and say, "Well, this is why you are in trouble." That is why the Bible says, *"Happy is he that condemneth not himself"* (Romans 14:22).

2. He can accuse you before others. When he accuses you before others, some of them will be having strange dreams and strange revelations about you, and they will be calling you the kind of names that do not belong to you. They may even call you a witch, wizard, etc which you are not.

3. He can accuse you before God. We have dealt with this in the message.

4. He can accuse you through others, and people will gather and begin to accuse you.

THE PROPHET Saul versus David 12

I SAMUEL 18:25 ...SAUL SAID, ...SAY TO DAVID, THE KING DESIRETH NOT ANY DOWRY, BUT AN 100. FORESKINS OF THE PHILISTINES,...BUT SAUL THOUGHT TO MAKE DAVID FALL BY THE HANDS OF THE PHILISTINES.

YESSSSS! I KNOW!... DAVID'S DAD: JESSE + HIS LAND + SHEEP + PROPERTIES ALL PUT TOGETHER CAN'T PAY THE KING'S DOWRY!

...TELL DAVID, THE ONLY DOWRY I REQUIRE FROM HIM IS TO FIGHT AND KILL 100 PHILISTINES...

I SAMUEL 18:26 WHEN (SAUL'S) SERVANTS TOLD DAVID,...IT PLEASED DAVID WELL TO BE THE KING'S SON-IN-LAW...

THIS IS NOTHING BUT GREAT... ASSUREDLY I CAN DO IT. BECAUSE THE LORD IS WITH ME!

I SAMUEL 18:27. ...DAVID AROSE AND WENT,... AND SLEW THE PHILISTINES 200 MEN:...DAVID BROUGHT THEIR FORESKINS, AND... GAVE THEM IN FULL TALE TO THE KING, THAT HE MIGHT BE THE KING'S SON-IN-LAW...

...THIS IS A DISASTER! YOU MEAN DAVID CAME BACK VICTORIOUS?!... I FEEL LIKE MELTING.. I FEEL LIKE DYING! HAAAAAA!!!

WHY DOES SATAN ACCUSE PEOPLE?

1. He accuses people because he wants them to be destroyed.
2. He accuses people because he wants to populate hell fire.
3. He accuses people because he wants them to tow his line.

Sometimes, satan accuses the land. He can accuse a city, a nation, a family, an establishment or a church. And he does his research well before accusing anyone before God.

Now, the devil is accusing our nation with so many things such as idolatry, bribery, murder, injustice, oppression, local and international prostitution, armed robbery, etc. That is why the Bible says, *"Pray for the peace of Jerusalem: they shall prosper that love thee."* (Psalm 122:6). If we do not solve this accusation problem, the next thing that would follow is judgement. When you do not deal with your accusation and do not raise intercessors, the judgement of God will be unleashed. And once the judgement comes, it does not recognise those who did not really take too much or a deep part in the matter. It will deal with everyone uniformly. That is why the Bible says in Isaiah 41:21 that you should form a practice of going to the court of God yourself; every believer is a lawyer, an advocate before God. You are qualified to argue your case in the court of the Almighty. We cannot sit down and do nothing about the accuser that is pressing so many charges against us. We should go into our prayer chambers to defend our lands, ourselves, families, and nations.

WAY OUT

Isaiah 41:21 says, *"Produce your cause, saith the Lord; bring forth your strong reasons, saith the King of Jacob."* You are a qualified lawyer, recognized in the court of God.

1. The first thing to do is to cure your spiritual malaria before you begin to move. No matter how intelligent and highly qualified a soldier may be, ordinary malaria will render him useless before his enemies. Ordinary malaria can turn an able-bodied man to jelly. So, if you do not cure a soldier of his malaria before pushing him to the warfront, you will kill him. We need to cure our spiritual malaria before we begin to move.

2. Examine your life, find out who you are.

3. Go into your prayer chamber. Confess all your sins, keep a short account with God, and do not accumulate sins. Do not allow your mistake to last for 24 hours before you quickly sort out yourself before God. You should not be a habitual sinner. The major thing to understand is that the accuser has a long list against people. If the accusations are false, the Lord will set you free without any trouble. But the trouble is that most of the time what the enemy is raising

up to heaven against people is true. Most of the time, people's garments are dirty before the Lord and so He cannot use them. The stain on their garment is sufficient for the enemy to move in.

God is looking for sincere people. Those who sincerely serve God never miss their way for God is a Spirit and they that worship Him must worship Him in spirit and in truth. Is there truth in your heart? Or are you enveloped in falsehood? Any form of falsehood in your life will keep your garment dirty and drive heaven far away from you.

PRAYER POINTS

1. Every satanic desire for my life, die, in the name of Jesus.
2. O heavens, reject the voice of my oppressors, in the name of Jesus.
3. Thou voice of darkness accusing me day and night, be silenced by the blood of Jesus, in the name of Jesus.
4. Every ancestral power accusing me in the heavenlies, die, in the name of Jesus.
5. Every power planning to use my life as a fertilizer, die, in the name of Jesus. (3times).
6. Anything in my life that is making my enemies to rejoice, come out, in the name of Jesus.
7. Every accusation of darkness against my destiny, die, in the name of Jesus.
8. Every danger list containing my name, be torn into pieces, in the name of Jesus.

THE ANALYSIS OF ACCUSATION

is a message delivered at the Mountain of Fire and Miracles Ministries by the General Overseer, Dr. D.K. Olukoya.

A CALL TO SERVE

Are you a member of MFM with a burden to help the needy, are you interested in alleviating the plight of the poor or in the spread of the gospel through the sponsorship of the publication of tracts? Your resources, time and talent can be extended to several groups that are in charge of these areas. These groups include:

o   We care Ministry,
o   Mission Outreach
o   Tracts and Publications
o   Ministry to Drug addicts
o   Campus fellowship
o   Ministry to Schools
o   Ministry to Glorious Children, etc.

Thus says the Lord, "Verily I say unto you, in as much as ye have done it unto one of the least of these my brethren, ye have done it unto me" Matthew 25 : 40.

WONDERFUL JESUS!

DIVINE PROTECTION

A lorry's brake failed and it ran over many of us and hit a house. I lost many valuables but I thank God that neither me nor any of my family members died. Praise the Lord!

Sis. Ifeoluwa
MFM Ibafo

GOD GRANTS ME TWO YEAR MULTIPLE VISA

I was denied visa twice at one of the most difficult embassies in the country. Before my third attempt, I requested to see the General Overseer. During my appointment with him, he asked me to bring my passport and he prayed on it. On the day I visited the embassy, all other applicants were denied visas. But when it got to my turn, God showed me favour and my request was granted. I was given a two year multiple visa. Praise God!

Sis. Oluwakemi
MFM Headquarters

DIVINE SURGICAL OPERATION

I had a protruding stomach for sometime and many people thought I was pregnant. I went to the altar and cried unto God to intervene in my situation and God answered me. During my menstruation that month, I passed out substances like pieces of meat for five days. Since then my stomach has become normal. Secondly, my sister that was taking care of my children fell sick. I prayed to God and God healed her. Praise the Lord!

Sis. Brigget
MFM Olopomeji

GOD SAVES ME FROM DEATH

Recently, I was at Mile 12 market Lagos to buy some foodstuff. Suddenly, some armed robbers struck and started shooting into the air. One of the bullets passed beside me and hit a bowl that a woman was using to sell her goods. I thank God for saving me. Praise the Lord!

Sis. Adebola
MFM Ogudu Ojota

GOD DELIVERS ME FROM LONG-TERM BRAIN DISORDER

Since 1995 after my final exams in the Secondary school, I had been having brain problems. This led me to visiting native doctors through some of my friends. Incisions were made on my head with a view to curing me but instead they aggravated my problem. I was able to secure admission into an higher institution and managed to complete the course with a fair grade. But during the programme tagged, "Night of Solution" there was a word of knowledge from the General Overseer that somebody was being healed from a brain disorder. That was how God healed me. Now, my brain is in order. Praise God!

Bro. Tayo
MFM Headquarters

STOMACH ACHE DISAPPEARS

I used to have persistent stomach pain. But when I went for deliverance in this church, the stomach ache disappeared. Praise the Lord!

Sis. Funmi
MFM Jos

GOD RESTORES MY SIGHT

I used to be blind. But after undergoing a deliverance programme in this church, I regained my sight. Praise the Lord!

Bro. Sunday
MFM Aboru

I THANK GOD FOR HIS MERCIES

Before I went for an operation, I was filled with fear but the message that was preached in the church dwelt on my problem. So, I was encouraged. Also, I applied the anointing oil and to the glory of God, the operation was successful and I am well now. Praise the Lord!

Sis. Chikwe
MFM Ibusa

DIVINE PROVISION

Sometime ago, I was asked to allow my house to be used as a centre for house fellowship. I objected because of the inconveniences I felt it would cause me. However, I gave it further consideration and later offered my house for the Lord's use. To my utmost amazement, within a short period, a lot of things that were not in place were miraculously provided. Praise the Lord!

Bro. Akinola
MFM Iju

GOD OF PROVISION

For about two years, I was living together with my family in the shop which I use as a business centre. I thank God for providing a two bedroom flat for me and my family. My business is also progressing. Praise God!

Sis. Elizabeth
MFM Oworonshoki

GOD OF PERFECTION GRANTS MY DAUGHTER SAFE DELIVERY

I want to thank God Almighty for the manifestation of His power on the 7th July 2007 (7-7-7). I went to the Prayer City on that day with my daughter who was pregnant. Immediately the General Overseer mounted the pulpit, she went into labour and was delivered of her baby at the Prayer City. Praise the Lord!

Sis. Amoke
MFM Prayer City

THESE BOOKS ARE AVAILABLE FOR SALE
ASK YOUR VENDOR

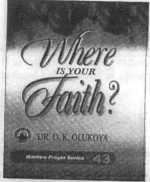

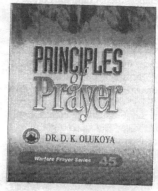

FIRE IN THE WORD is a weekly Spiritual Bulletin of the Mountain of Fire and Miracles Ministries, published by Tracts and Publications Group. All Enquiries should be addressed to The Editor, Mountain of Fire Magazine, 13, Olasimbo Street, off Olumo Road, Onike, P.O. Box 2990, Sabo Yaba, Lagos, Nigeria. Telephone 01-867439, 864631, 868766, 08023180236. Copyright reserved.

21936706R00237

Made in the USA
Middletown, DE
15 July 2015